D1414290

The Business
of Higher Education

The Business of Higher Education

Volume 2: Management and Fiscal Strategies

JOHN C. KNAPP AND DAVID J. SIEGEL, EDITORS

PRAEGER PERSPECTIVES

PRAEGER
An Imprint of ABC-CLIO, LLC

A B C ⬛ C L I O

Santa Barbara, California • Denver, Colorado • Oxford, England

Copyright 2009 by John C. Knapp and David J. Siegel

All rights reserved. No part of this publication may be reproduced, stored in a
retrieval system, or transmitted, in any form or by any means, electronic, mechanical,
photocopying, recording, or otherwise, except for the inclusion of brief quotations in
a review, without prior permission in writing from the publisher.

Library of Congress Cataloging-in-Publication Data

The business of higher education / John C. Knapp and David J. Siegel, editors.
    v. cm. — (Praeger perspectives)
    Includes bibliographical references and index.
    ISBN 978-0-313-35350-5 (set: alk. paper) ISBN 978-0-313-35351-2 (set
ebook) v. 1. Leadership and culture ISBN 978-0-313-35352-9 (v. 1: alk.
paper) ISBN 978-0-313-35353-6 (v. 1 ebook) — v. 2. Management and fiscal
strategies ISBN 978-0-313-35354-3 (v. 2: alk. paper) ISBN 978-0-313-35355-0
(v. 2 ebook) — v. 3. Marketing and consumer interests. ISBN 978-0-313-35356-7
(v. 3 alk. paper) ISBN 978-0-313-35357-4 (v. 3 ebook)
    1. Education, Higher—United States—Finance.   2. Universities and
colleges—United States—Finance.   I. Knapp, John C.   II. Siegel, David J., 1966–
    LB2342.B88   2009
    378.1'060973—dc22   2009027997

13 12 11 10 09   1 2 3 4 5

This book is also available on the World Wide Web as an eBook.
Visit www.abc-clio.com for details.

ABC-CLIO, LLC
130 Cremona Drive, P.O. Box 1911
Santa Barbara, California 93116-1911

This book is printed on acid-free paper ∞
Manufactured in the United States of America

Volume 2, chapter 12. Adapted from Marc Bousquet, *How the University Works: Higher
Education and the Low-Wage Nation* (New York: New York University Press, 2008).

Contents

Foreword

Today, higher education faces a simple choice: reinvention or extinction. I write this with a mixture of caution and optimism. The economic meltdown that has swept the globe has brought colleges and universities to the edge of chaos. Budgets are up. Endowments are down. Too many students and too many families are stranded in debt. These are, by any calculation, difficult times. But they are also times of tremendous opportunity. Financial pressures are bringing to the surface issues that we have kept under the carpet for far too long. Our communities are counting on the promise of post-secondary education more than ever. By abandoning bunker mentality and pushing forward, this can be the moment where we transform our institutions and re-imagine higher education in America.

Change, of course, will not come easy. In fact, it would be hard to imagine a more formidable challenge. The modern university is a juggernaut, with little material resemblance to our ancient roots or nineteenth-century pedigree. At my own institution—The Ohio State University—the sheer complexity of a campus with 60,000 students and 40,000 faculty and staff is mind-boggling, and that is before factoring in development officers, athletics departments, and research facilities that generate more revenue than most small businesses. In their wildest dreams, neither Aristotle nor James Morrill could have imagined schools the size of cities, complete with multi-billion dollar budgets, high-rises, and medical centers.

How do we manage, let alone revolutionize, these vast and sprawling institutions? How do we make them intellectually agile, responsive to the needs of students, and free from Kafkaesque bureaucracies? How do we help the university achieve its pride of place in the American project, as both our economic engine and the center of our civic life?

These are the core questions taken up in *The Business of Higher Education*. And, I am pleased to report, the contributors' answers are both honest and robust. Drawing from a multiplicity of perspectives within the academy, the scholars and administrators in these volumes have carved out the critical debates facing higher education today. Even more importantly, they have framed the debates without taking refuge in that famous false binary: the Ivory Tower versus the corporate university. After nearly 30 years of leading universities, I have yet to meet the oft-demonized bureaucrat who wants to turn the classroom into an assembly line, nor the faculty member whose *raison d'être* is to indoctrinate students and then secede from society. Simplification is a natural response to an overwhelming challenge, but the stakes are simply too high for us to continue invoking scarecrows and boogeymen.

Our metaphors do matter, however, which is why the intellectual haggling that occurs in the chapters that follow is so important. And with all due respect to the editors, I have to take sides on one issue: "business" is too clumsy a word to capture our character or our sublime purpose. Teaching that profoundly changes lives, and research that expands the boundaries of the knowable universe, cannot be reduced to dollars and cents. Further, in order to allow science to flourish, and allow our students to cultivate an appreciation for reason, we must preserve the sanctity of a sphere beyond the influence of commerce and beyond the vicissitudes of politics. How we choose to discuss higher education will indelibly shape it, and equating knowledge with a product, and students with consumers, is neither the best way to envision ourselves, nor an effective way to articulate our unique mission to others.

But just because higher education is not a business does not mean that we should not thrive and compete, or that we should not cultivate and hire the best leadership available. The ideal of the university—whether expressed by Newman or Dewey—is precisely that: an ideal. Historians will never find a university that was not reliant on some measure of business, governmental, or philanthropic support, and the twenty-first century university must forge productive relationships with all three. Competing for federal research dollars, encouraging innovative partnerships with industry, and building the community coalitions that can make a difference in people's lives requires that we maintain state-of-the-art facilities, invest wisely, and manage with superhuman efficiency. It also means that we must harness the tools of marketing, branding, and public relations to champion our achievements. Just as we respect and trust our astrophysicists' ability to chart new planets, or our English professors' knowledge of narrative, so we must rely on the expertise of those who can best steer our course in the economic arena.

Achieving our economic potential while maintaining academic integrity is a monumental task. But it is Herculean, not Sisyphean. Accountability does not mean servility to accountants. Nor does academic freedom mean willful irrelevance. Success will be the tightrope balance between ideals and expediency. We must move swiftly to achieve lasting partnerships with industry, but we must never sacrifice our higher calling to the bottom line. Likewise, we must learn to teach beyond the classroom walls, but we must never forget that departments and disciplines, not politicians and legislators, are the true judges of academic merit.

These challenges will never be resolved in the abstract; they will only take root in the realm of practice. To realign our institutions, we need a mission that demands a re-focusing of our strength. Sustainability—the demand for new thinking about the environment and energy—presents one prime opportunity. At Ohio State, we are already beginning to use sustainability to re-imagine our academic structures, bringing together departments and faculty that for too long have been connected only by a heating plant. Moving beyond "interdisciplinarity" and toward true transinstitutional partnership, these new connections between fields of study, between students, between industries, and even between universities are the first step toward realizing a renewed purpose for higher education, one that shares the fruits of our expertise, assures our relevancy, and gives external partners reasons to invest in us.

Change is a chain reaction, and by casting out old dogmas, we necessarily must reinvent our practices, including our centuries old promotion and tenure model. This is not an argument for eliminating academic freedom; it is an effort to save it. If we wish to encourage innovative faculty collaboration and new forms of scholarship, academic publishing cannot remain our only metric of merit. Contrary to Marx's axiom, it may finally be time to acknowledge that not all of us are cut out to be teachers by day, department leaders in the afternoon, and world-class researchers at night. Let us stop punishing those who excel in *merely* one of these areas, and begin thinking creatively about how to reward everyone for their vital contributions to the university community. And let us use this as an opportunity to fully appreciate the contributions of teachers throughout higher education, especially our embattled and undervalued community college colleagues, who are at the front-lines of higher education.

This will certainly be the most contentious of our conversations. And, as the chapters in these volumes indicate, consensus will not come easy.

But employment is the most critical question facing us, and where faculty, administration, and staff will find agreement is this: true inequity lies in opacity. We must acknowledge a long-overdue moral imperative to be transparent with our teachers, particularly the graduate students who work in the trenches of undergraduate education. Because of the tightening of the job market and changes in the faculty-mentor role, graduate assistantships—most notably in the humanities—have not been true apprenticeships for a generation. As many contributors to this book have noted, we have an obligation to cease such nostalgic talk and be straight with our students and adjuncts about the opportunities and realities of University employment. Only then can we make the adjustments necessary to recruit and retain the best and brightest teachers and thinkers and scientists, too many of whom we are currently losing to the private sector.

The challenges ahead of us are daunting. But the resources at our disposal are unparalleled. Higher education in America is the envy of the world, and at its heart is our thoroughly democratic *ethos,* which says that debate is always more valuable than consensus, and that from furious disagreement eventually comes wisdom and resolve. On campuses across this country, some of the most brilliant minds on the planet walk among us, and the time is now to apply their intellect to saving the institutions that we all hold so dear. We cannot wait for eureka moments, nor can we wait for gradual evolution. In our faculty meetings, hiring committees, conferences, and edited collections, we must begin in earnest to implement the changes we know are necessary for the Academy to emerge from this financial crisis as the rightful centerpiece of American intellectual, cultural, and economic life. The contributors to this volume have made a noble start; it is time for the rest of us to follow through.

E. Gordon Gee
Columbus, Ohio, March 2009

General Introduction

Anyone in and around higher education in recent years cannot have failed to notice the steadily rising hue and cry for academic institutions to operate more like business organizations. Perhaps it is unsurprising that an enterprise as massive, complex, and resource intensive as higher education should find itself the subject of public demands to make it behave like other massive, complex, and resource intensive enterprises, namely, large corporations. After all, like corporations, colleges and universities are increasingly viewed as engines of economic growth and prosperity, as key actors in a sprawling global economy. We in higher education may have differentiated ourselves from business in the past, but societal forces and even our own ambitions have thrust us into a closer relationship and resemblance, prompting one exasperated college president to ask, "Are we in the business of *higher education* or are we in the higher education *business?*"

Of course, this development has not gone uncontested. Many still view the academy as a distinctive institution, one endowed with a special purpose that is simply not subject to the dictates of economic rationalism. In a pluralistic society, as Edward Shils noted, various institutions and occupations must reflect legitimately different societal aims. It would be a mistake to judge any one of them by the standards of the others. Academic institutions, according to this logic, should operate like academic institutions.

There is arguably no issue on the horizon that forces us to explain ourselves—to ourselves, to our stakeholders, and to the general public—more than the push to be like business, because on one level, the "corporatization" of the academy stands as a threat to our very nature. By engaging the issue, then, we seize an opportunity to narrate ourselves to the world and make a compelling case for our survival as a valuable and relevant institutional form—a form that has proven resilient and vital since the middle ages. The matter of whether business models and business thinking help to advance our cause in the 21st century is an open question, one that animates *The Business of Higher Education*.

This three-volume set explores mounting pressures for colleges and universities to change, and it considers the costs and benefits to our institutions and to society when academe embraces business models of cost-efficiency, marketing, employment, or customer service. Thought leaders from various quarters of higher education and business have contributed original essays on a range of topics related to this central theme. Indeed, one of the unique features of *The Business of Higher Education* is that it offers contrasting perspectives—by those within the academy and outside of it—on whether and how higher education and the public interest are ultimately helped or harmed by the application of business methods to essential academic functions. The multiplicity of voices and styles, we believe, fairly captures the complexity of this topic. In these pages, our objective is to model and advance a critical dialogue on the future of higher education in an era of increased public accountability and engagement with all sectors.

Readers may wonder straightaway what is meant by the particular phrasing of *the business of higher education*. We think it best to let the contributors speak to that question, open as the phrasing is to multiple interpretations. Briefly, though, we note that the title—the central organizing principle, as it were—can be read as pertaining simultaneously to the role or *mission* of higher education and the *manner* in which it goes about fulfilling that role or mission. The fact that the phrasing also (and perhaps primarily) suggests an interaction between two arenas that are commonly held to be in opposition—higher education and business—is very much to the point of the dialogue that follows.

As far as this project is concerned, we do not start with a philosophical or ideological orientation with regard to the subject matter it addresses. Our hope is to illuminate key tensions the academy is experiencing as a citadel of learning, a publicly engaged institution, and an increasingly bureaucratic structure. The wide berth we gave to authors is commensurate with our own thinking on the matter, which can be described as ambivalent, conflicted, and (perhaps more positively) open to the merits of strong arguments.

These volumes do not aim to settle an argument. In fact, we observe that the argument has yet to specify its terms. What *is* the business model, for example, that higher education is being asked to emulate or adopt? Should we pattern our culture, strategy, and operations after those of AIG, Apple, or American Airlines? The injunction to become more businesslike does not by itself offer much guidance. It often seems a more convenient than helpful way to talk about how to solve whatever is perceived to be wrong with higher education.

ORGANIZATION OF THE SET

If we wanted to see or experience the business of higher education, where might we look for it? The organization of the book set points to (1) leadership and culture (the subject of volume 1), (2) management and fiscal strategies (the subject of volume 2), and (3) marketing and consumer interests (the subject of volume 3). These three themes may be visualized as concentric circles, with leadership and culture occupying the innermost core (to represent the character, values, and principles that define the academy), surrounded most immediately by management and fiscal strategies (that enable colleges and universities to better serve their purposes), followed by marketing and consumer interests (indicating the stakeholders for whom value is created and delivered, as well as the ways in which we interact with them). We suggest that the circles have dotted lines to indicate permeability; each of these areas constitutes and is constituted by the others. The general progression of the three volumes, then, goes from core values to enabling strategies to external constituencies.

AUDIENCE

Given the broad nature of the topic, the intended readership is wide-ranging. It includes academic leaders, business leaders, those charged with spanning the boundaries between the two sectors, parents, policymakers, scholars, and students.

From the beginning, our idea was to contribute new ideas and perspectives to the ongoing conversation. We invite readers to join the dialogue, by arguing back to the contributors, by writing up their own thoughts, or by engaging colleagues in conversation about the contents of this set. The chapters themselves are a testament to the virtues of unhurried contemplation and disciplined thinking about complex issues, exemplary of how the difficult and contentious dialogue about higher education's future must be conducted. Readers will find little in the way of the rash accusations that are so often hurled by critics of—or apologists for—higher education, who often appear to be more concerned with winning points for their arguments than with illuminating blind spots. In short, we hope readers will use the model provided by our contributors to extend and enrich public dialogue.

ACKNOWLEDGMENTS

For the editors, this project has been a rare opportunity to collaborate with an extraordinary group of thinkers, each of whom brings deep expertise and experience to this important conversation. We extend to them our gratitude for their superb contributions to these volumes. They have added much to our own appreciation and understanding of the multifaceted business of higher education. We also appreciate the guidance provided by Jeff Olson, our able editor and advisor at Praeger Publishers.

On a more personal note, we are mindful that projects such as this, which invariably consume time beyond the normal work day, are not without a cost to our families. David would like to thank Jeanie, Jacob, and Nicholas, whose entreaties to "take a little break" or "speed things up" are always perfectly timed. John is grateful, as always, to Kelly, Amanda, Tracy, Charlie, Mary and Ronnie for their encouragement and remarkable patience. We both are very fortunate indeed.

John C. Knapp
Birmingham, Alabama

David J. Siegel
Greenville, North Carolina

Introduction to Volume 2: Management and Fiscal Strategies

John C. Knapp and David J. Siegel

With Volume 2 of *The Business of Higher Education*, we move the discussion to a consideration of some of the management and fiscal strategies that allow colleges and universities to better fulfill their purposes. One of the subthemes addressed in this volume has to do with higher education's struggle to reconcile academic traditions and the spirit of innovation, including innovations in forms of organization, delivery mechanisms for higher education's products, and economic models.

State appropriations make up a dwindling proportion of the total funding mix supporting public colleges and universities at a time when societal pressures for improved service, access, and quality are expanding. One of the effects of lower state subsidies, notes James Palmer in chapter 1, is that the situation has forced postsecondary institutions to become more entrepreneurial in their cultivation of alternative sources of revenue. "But charting an entrepreneurial course in ways that secure additional financial independence without compromising academic values," advises Palmer, "may require a rethinking of the collegiate organization itself rather than the adoption of specific fund-raising mechanisms." Palmer cites evidence from analyses of entrepreneurial universities to illustrate his point.

Entrepreneurship has indeed emerged as a significant opportunity within American higher education, write Raymond Farrow and Jack Kasarda in chapter 2. This has been due in large part to the vision and financial backing of the Ewing Marion Kauffman Foundation, the leading promoter and funder of entrepreneurship in the United States and the architect of a major $44.5 million initiative begun in 2003 to develop cross-disciplinary approaches to entrepreneurship education at eight competitively selected colleges and universities. The University of North Carolina at Chapel Hill was one of these, and Farrow and Kasarda richly detail how the institution organized the task of crafting a winning proposal and its subsequent efforts to make entrepreneurship "part of the weave and fabric of Carolina." This "grand experiment" offers important lessons and a replicable framework for readers interested in the dynamics of campus transformation.

Universities are increasingly expected to stimulate the local economies and develop the community capacities of their host regions, however such regions are delineated. In chapter 3, Henry Etzkowitz provides a framework for understanding the role of the entrepreneurial university in high-tech regional development. Drawing on examples from the Boston area, Northern Virginia, and Silicon Valley, Etzkowitz explains how regional coalitions of universities, government agencies, and business enterprises (a triple helix of actors) seek to improve the conditions for knowledge-based innovation in particular locales. These political, industrial, and academic institutions form a "regional innovation environment," in which "universities, traditionally producers and transmitters of knowledge, also become factors of production."

Society has long recognized that a core asset of colleges and universities is the intellectual capacity of its faculty. In chapter 4, Joshua Powers observes that whereas innovation and its by-products were historically considered an intellectual commons (owned by none and to be shared freely), in recent years they have been increasingly considered an intellectual property (owned by an institution and its inventors and shared or distributed for a fee). His chapter explores this paradigm change in thinking and practice as it relates to the treatment of academic science output, including how it has served to transform the ways in which scientific research is conducted and the culture and value sets upon which it rests.

Research on behalf of industrial sponsors continues to make many in the academy uneasy, acknowledges Ronald Bohlander in chapter 5, but the question is no longer *whether* to conduct research for private-sector clients but rather *how* to manage the process in a way that is consistent with public and academic values. Bohlander's chapter explores how universities and their industrial partners organize and manage the research process as part of open innovation. He suggests that "both cultures need to invest in programs to build understanding in their people about the other culture" and that these understandings must go beyond the technical details of licensing, contracting, and technology transfer policies.

In chapter 6, Albert Johnson supplies an industrial perspective on the commercialization of university technologies, drawing as he does on his experiences as a negotiator and manager of research contracts for Corning

Incorporated. Commercial technology development may not be the university's primary job or function, but societal and market demands for useful products and services based on advanced science have thrust universities into a much more active role in transforming knowledge. As a consequence, industrial partners are now "dealing with a type of organization that is obviously an academic enterprise but that also is increasingly playing by competitive rather than collaborative business rules" to negotiate favorable intellectual property terms for itself. Johnson offers advice for building trust and strengthening collaborative bonds between universities and industry.

In chapter 7, Cynthia DeLuca and David Siegel document the explosive growth of academic-corporate partnerships and review prominent criticisms of partnership arrangements involving academic institutions. They posit that at least some of the controversy surrounding these relationships is built on unchallenged assumptions about what academic and industrial parties want or expect out of their relationships with each other. The fundamental question of what academic and corporate leaders view as the keys to developing and sustaining productive alliances between the sectors was the subject of a study whose results DeLuca and Siegel share for the first time. The authors use these research findings to talk back to the literature on partnerships and then discuss several relevant implications for partnership formation and development.

Tom McMail considers the different cultural orientations of academic, business, and government organizations from his vantage point as manager of external research programs at Microsoft. Effective multi-sector collaboration depends largely on the capacity to see things through each other's eyes and speak each other's language, writes McMail in chapter 8. Different needs, motivations, and world views must be understood, monitored, and ultimately negotiated by the parties in their common search for innovation. McMail offers some practical recommendations for managing academic-corporate-government relationships in ways that will create greater value for the organizations themselves and for society in general.

Perhaps nowhere is the clash of cultures between the for-profit and the nonprofit worlds more evident than in the for-profit college and university (FPCU) sector, which embodies aspects of both traditions. In chapter 9, Vicente Lechuga takes a close look at this rapidly growing sector and at some of the institutions that comprise it, and he suggests that its rise to prominence has fundamentally altered the landscape of postsecondary education by introducing a new business model that factors in revenue generation, organizational efficiency, employer preferences, and the job market. Despite some notable differences in how for-profit colleges and universities and traditional institutions are organized and managed, Lechuga observes that FPCUs raise familiar public policy issues—of access, selectivity, and completion, for example—common to all of higher education.

In chapter 10, Brent Rubin, Katherine Immordino, and Sherrie Tromp make the case that higher education *is* a business. Moreover, conceiving of colleges and universities as businesses—as healthcare and public sector organizations are now seeing themselves—may offer certain advantages that come with a broader view of our institutions and units "as organizations with stakeholders operating within a complex and dynamic marketplace of ideas and resources." The authors present several business themes, insights, and strategies and describe their relevance to the higher education context. They conclude with a discussion of the *Excellence in Higher Education* (EHE) framework, an adaptation of the Malcolm Baldrige National Quality Award program developed at Rutgers for use specifically with colleges and universities.

In chapter 11, Dan Hurley and Eric Gilbertson examine college costs, public pressures for institutions to manage their costs, and the role cost containment plays in maintaining postsecondary access and affordability. Public calls for greater efficiency, note the authors, tend to hew to a strict business definition of the term, whereas many of the practices—such as intellectual freedom and time for contemplation—that produce the university's greatest value simply "do not always conform to the imperatives of tidy management and steely cost-cutting techniques." Hurley and Gilbertson suggest that the objectives of lower costs, higher productivity, and greater efficiency must always be balanced against the academy's unique values and mission.

Some of the business strategies employed by higher education have human costs. In chapter 12, Marc Bousquet critiques higher education's shift to precarious work arrangements that take the form of contingent employment, permatemping, outsourcing, and the substitution of undergraduate workers for positions formerly filled by full-time personnel. Bousquet's chapter is principally concerned with the situation of the undergraduate worker, who represents the single largest sector of the workforce on many campuses. The demand for cheap student labor, argues Bousquet, must be balanced against mounting evidence that undergraduate work programs often have deleterious consequences for student academic performance. Bousquet illustrates the problem with an extended case example and ultimately calls higher education to account for exploitative practices that are at odds with its mission to serve the public good.

CHAPTER 1

Trends in State Tax Support for Higher Education: Prospects for an Entrepreneurial Response

James C. Palmer

The unprecedented growth of public colleges and universities during the three decades following World War II greatly expanded the role of the states as fiscal guarantors of American higher education. In 1945–46, the nation's 624 public postsecondary institutions accounted for only 35 percent of all colleges and universities in the United States; barely 50 percent of the country's 1.53 million college students attended these institutions.[1] By 1975–76, the number of public colleges and universities had risen to 1,214 (44% of all colleges and universities), and they served 79 percent of the 11.1 million postsecondary students nationwide.[2] Much of this growth was fueled by state fiscal investments in the burgeoning community college systems and in the transformation of small teachers colleges into comprehensive regional universities. State subsidies for higher education increased from $225.2 million in 1945–46[3] to $12.3 billion in 1975–76.[4]

This heady growth did little to prepare higher education leaders for the sustained period of fiscal consolidation that would characterize postsecondary education from 1975 to the present. As the postwar growth spurt predictably wound down, commentators in the 1970s warned of rough fiscal times ahead. For example, Earl Cheit's 1971 Carnegie Commission report on *The New Depression in Higher Education* highlighted a "new fiscal phenomenon—a declining rate of income growth, and in some cases an absolute decline in income." The result, he noted, was an imbalance between anemic income streams on the one hand and rising costs fueled by "inflation and growing demands on the schools for more service, for broader access, for academic innovation, and for higher quality."[5] This fiscal imbalance remains today and, as William Zumeta argues, has become especially intractable in light of structural constraints on state budgets in which "mandatory or near mandatory" claims on state funds from K-12 education, corrections, and Medicaid limit the capacity of states to increase funding for higher education, which remains a discretionary state function.[6] Noting the ever-growing link between higher education and economic outcomes, both for the student and for society at large, Zumeta points out that

> higher education faces the odd paradox of being simultaneously highly sought after by key societal elements, and sharply constrained in its ability to gain effective political support and thereby adequate financial sustenance—at least from its traditional sources—to realize its own aspirations and those society holds for it.[7]

The limitless character of these aspirations and our enduring tendency to link collegiate quality with the reputation that comes with rich endowments, high-priced and competitive faculty members, and appealing campuses make it difficult if not impossible to determine what level of funding is adequate or fair. As Paul Lingenfelter observes, "'More' is unfailingly the request, and a 'fair' allocation is imperative; but more is never enough, and fair varies in the eyes of the beholder."[8] However, trend data since 1980 offer at least three indicators of an attenuated role in state appropriations to help the higher education system meet societal demands. First, although state appropriations remain a large part of the revenue mix supporting public higher education, the proportion of total funding that is provided by the states has declined. Second, the buying power of the state funds that *are* appropriated has increased only marginally, at least in terms of the personnel-heavy costs that are associated with college operations and that are accounted for in the Higher Education Price Index. Finally, the capacity of states to increase funding each year has become less certain in the wake of economic downturns. All have left higher education leaders with the substantial entrepreneurial challenge of adapting their institutions in ways that reduce their dependence on state subsidies while at the same time strengthening the capacity of their institutions to address the perennial imbalance between the demands they face and the resources they have.[9]

STATE APPROPRIATIONS AS A PROPORTION OF TOTAL FUNDING FOR HIGHER EDUCATION

One of the salient trends in higher education since 1980 has been the shrinking proportion of total revenues accounted for by state appropriations. This can be seen in Table 1.1, which draws on published data from

Table 1.1: Percent Distribution of Current-Fund Revenues for Public Institutions of Higher Education, Fiscal Years 1979–80, 1984–85, 1989–90, 1994–95, and 2000–01

Funding Source	Current-Fund Revenues					Change from 1979–80 through 2000–01
	1979–80	1984–85	1989–90	1994–95	2000–01	
From the federal government						
Appropriations	2.6%	2.3%	1.8%	1.5%	1.0%	–1.7%
Grants and contracts, unrestricted	1.2%	1.2%	1.4%	1.5%	0.0%	–1.2%
Grants and contracts, restricted	9.1%	6.9%	6.9%	7.9%	9.7%	0.6%
Other federal	0.2%	0.2%	0.2%	0.2%	0.5%	0.4%
Total federal	13.1%	10.6%	10.3%	11.1%	11.2%	–1.9%
From local governments						
Appropriations	3.4%	3.3%	3.3%	3.6%	3.2%	–0.2%
Grants and contracts, unrestricted[a]	0.0%	0.1%	0.1%	0.1%	0.0%	0.0%
Grants and contracts, restricted	0.3%	0.3%	0.3%	0.4%	0.8%	0.6%
Total local	3.7%	3.6%	3.7%	4.0%	4.0%	0.3%
From state governments						
Appropriations	44.8%	43.6%	39.2%	33.0%	31.9%	–12.9%
Grants & contracts unrestricted[a]	0.1%	0.1%	0.3%	0.3%	0.0%	–0.1%
Grants and contracts, restricted	1.4%	1.4%	2.1%	2.6%	3.8%	2.4%
Total state	46.3%	45.1%	41.7%	35.9%	35.6%	–10.7%
Tuition and fees (IPEDS)	12.5%	14.5%	15.5%	18.4%	18.1%	5.6%

(Continued)

Table 1.1: Percent Distribution of Current-Fund Revenues for
Public Institutions of Higher Education, Fiscal Years 1979–80,
1984–85, 1989–90, 1994–95, and 2000–01 (*Continued*)

Funding Source	Current-Fund Revenues					Change from 1979–80 through 2000–01
	1979–80	1984–85	1989–90	1994–95	2000–01	
Private gifts, grants, and contracts	2.5%	3.1%	3.8%	4.0%	5.1%	2.5%
Endowment income	0.5%	0.6%	0.5%	0.6%	0.8%	0.3%
Sales and services	19.2%	20.0%	21.7%	23.1%	21.7%	2.5%
Other	2.2%	2.6%	2.7%	3.1%	3.7%	1.4%
Total[b]	100.0%	100.0%	100.0%	100.0%	100.0%	

[a]In 2000-01, these data were included under "Contracts and Grants, restricted."

[b]Because of rounding, totals may not add to 100 percent exactly.

Sources: Thomas D. Snyder and Charlene M. Hoffman, *Digest of Education Statistics, 1991,*
NCES 91697, (Washington, DC: National Center for Education Statistics, 1991), 307;
Thomas D. Snyder, *Digest of Education statistics, 1994,* NCES 94115
(Washington, DC: National Center for Education Statistics, 1994), 325;
Thomas D. Snyder and Charlene M. Hoffman, *Digest of Education Statistics, 1999,*
NCES 2000031 (Washington, DC: National Center for Education Statistics, 2000), 359;
Thomas D. Snyder, Sally A. Dillow, and Charlene M. Hoffman,
Digest of Education Statistics, 2007, NCES 2008022 (Washington, DC:
National Center for Education Statistics, 2008), 487.

the U.S. Department of Education's Integrated Postsecondary Education
Data System (IPEDS) to show how revenue sources for public institutions
have shifted from 1979–80 through 2000–01. The overall picture is one of
stability; the change in the proportion of total revenues accounted for by
most of the sources listed in the table fell within plus or minus 2.5 percent
over the 21-year period examined in the table. But state funding on the
one hand and tuition and fees on the other were the notable exceptions.
Between 1979–80 and 2000–01, the proportion of revenues accounted
for by state appropriations fell by almost 13 percentage points—from 44.8
percent to 31.9 percent—and the proportion of revenues accounted for
by all state sources (including grants and contracts as well as appropriations) fell by almost 11 percentage points, from 46.3 percent to 35.6 percent. In contrast, the proportion of total revenues accounted for by tuition

and fees increased by 5.6 percent, rising from 12.5 percent in 1979–80 to 18.1 percent in 2000–01.

Changes in the way revenue data are reported by the National Center for Education Statistics after 2000–01 make it difficult to extend this analysis into subsequent years. But available IPEDS data beyond 2000–01 show that in 2003–04 and 2004–05, state appropriations accounted for 24.3 percent and 23.6 percent (respectively) of revenues at public colleges and universities nationwide.[10] Tuition and fees accounted for 15.8 percent and 16.4 percent, suggesting a slight downturn from the 18.1 percent figure registered in 2000–01.[11] Overall, however, the IPEDS revenue data since 1980 suggest a long-term trend in which a significant portion of the burden of funding higher education has shifted from the states to the students themselves, a trend that has been ameliorated to at least some extent by growth in federal grants, subsidized loans, and tax credits.[12]

This shift has undoubtedly varied in intensity across the states, and it has many root causes. In addition to the structural constraints highlighted by Zumeta,[13] the trends detailed in Table 1.1 may reflect the impact of tax limitation measures on the capacity of states to fund higher education,[14] a growing acceptance of the view that the private benefits of higher education outweigh the public benefits,[15] and economic downturns (discussed below). Whatever unique set of circumstances may have influenced fiscal developments in each of the 50 states, the combined national effect is a reduction in state tax effort on behalf of higher education. This can be seen in Table 1.2, which draws on the *Grapevine*[16] data set maintained by the Center for the Study of Education Policy at Illinois State University to show that even as state appropriations per capita and per full-time equivalent (FTE) enrollment nationwide have increased since 1979–80, appropriations per $1,000 in personal income have declined. Despite the fact that full-time equivalent (FTE) enrollment at public colleges and universities increased by 46.9 percent from the fall of 1979 to the fall of 2005,[17] we are now devoting less of our combined wealth to state tax appropriations for higher education than we did over two decades ago.[18] As Lingenfelter notes, "Without question . . . state investments in higher education have not grown as rapidly as state spending for other purposes."[19]

DIMINISHED BUYING POWER

Another way of examining trends in state funding is to calculate the impact of inflation on the value of state support over time. As Figure 1.1 shows, current-dollar increases in state tax appropriations for higher education since fiscal year 1979–1980 are substantially attenuated when

Table 1.2: State Tax Appropriations for Higher Education, 1979–80 through 2007–08, Per $1,000 in Personal Income, Per Capita, and Per Full-Time-Equivalent (FTE) Student in Public Colleges and Universities

| | State Tax Appropriations for Higher Education | | | |
Fiscal Year	Total (in $1,000s)[a]	Per $1,000 in Personal Income	Per Capita	Per FTE Student[b]
1979–80	19,143,057	9.54	85.49	2,994.56
1980–81	20,857,189	9.35	92.33	3,140.06
1981–82	22,954,495	9.09	100.31	3,384.97
1982–83	24,212,904	8.84	104.80	3,534.43
1983–84	25,823,956	8.89	110.76	3,752.68
1984–85	28,409,534	8.79	120.79	4,249.96
1985–86	30,671,335	8.82	129.26	4,599.93
1986–87	32,212,492	8.77	134.50	4,752.48
1987–88	34,408,082	8.88	142.39	4,959.59
1988–89	36,634,987	8.77	150.22	5,162.11
1989–90	39,109,108	8.64	158.85	5,305.38
1990–91	40,138,905	8.31	161.19	5,310.80
1991–92	39,748,026	7.97	157.49	5,055.17
1992–93	39,483,265	7.46	154.28	4,990.49
1993–94	41,134,822	7.46	158.62	5,265.33
1994–95	42,973,194	7.43	163.68	5,520.43
1995–96	44,364,391	7.28	166.97	5,723.10
1996–97	46,612,151	7.21	173.39	5,979.83
1997–98	49,613,816	7.28	182.35	6,304.36
1998–99	52,920,782	7.20	192.24	6,715.72
1999–00	56,591,115	7.35	203.22	7,056.18
2000–01	60,835,388	7.29	216.03	7,358.88
2001–02	62,905,059	7.24	221.14	7,281.39
2002–03	61,605,774	6.96	214.54	6,798.70
2003–04	60,694,185	6.69	209.56	6,568.12
2004–05	62,895,361	6.57	215.16	6,728.16
2005–06	67,420,857	6.65	228.56	7,179.90

(Continued)

Table 1.2: State Tax Appropriations for Higher Education, 1979–80 through 2007–08, Per $1,000 in Personal Income, Per Capita, and Per Full-Time-Equivalent (FTE) Student in Public Colleges and Universities (*Continued*)

| | State Tax Appropriations for Higher Education | | | |
Fiscal Year	Total (in $1,000s)[a]	Per $1,000 in Personal Income	Per Capita	Per FTE Student[b]
2006–07	72,103,037	6.64	242.14	
2007–08	77,800,730	6.76	258.73	
2008–09	78,527,989	6.50	258.77	

[a]Appropriations data are from *Grapevine* annual reports available at http://www.grapevine.ilstu. edu/historical/index.htm. Because appropriations figures change as states balance their budgets, the *Grapevine* survey asks states to provide appropriations data for the new fiscal year and to provide revised data (if needed) for the appropriations figures reported in previous surveys. The data for 1979–80 through 1989–90 are two-year revised figures. (For example, the data for 1983–84 were drawn from the 1985–86 Grapevine report and represent revised figures sent to *Grapevine* two years after initial appropriations were made.) The data for 1990–91 through 2007–08 are one-year revised figures. (For example, the 2006–07 data were drawn from the 2007–08 *Grapevine* report and represent revised figures sent to *Grapevine* one year after initial appropriations were made.) Data for 2008–09 are initial figures subject to revision in subsequent surveys.
[b]These data represent fall FTE enrollment in public institutions. FTE data are not available after 2005–06.
Sources: Center for the Study of Education Policy, "Grapevine Historical Data," http://www. grapevine.ilstu.edu/historical/index.htm,; Bureau of Economic Analysis, "Regional Economic Accounts," http://www.bea.gov/regional/spi/default.cfm?satable=summary; U.S. Census Bureau, "National and State Population Estimates, Annual Population Estimates 2000 to 2008," http://www.census.gov/popest/states/NST-ann-est.html; U.S. Census Bureau, "Time Series of Intercensal State Population Estimates: April 1, 1990 to April 1, 2000," http://www. census.gov/popest/archives/2000s/vintage_2001/CO-EST2001-12/CO-EST2001-12-00.pdf; U.S. Census Bureau, "Intercensal Estimates of the Total Resident Population of States: 1980 to 1990," http://www.census.gov/popest/archives/1980s/st8090ts.txt; U.S. Census Bureau, Intercensal Estimates of the Total Resident Population of States: 1970 to 1980," http://www. census.gov/popest/archives/1980s/st7080ts.txt; Thomas D. Snyder, Sally A. Dillow, and Charlene M. Hoffman, Digest of Education Statistics, 2007, NCES 2008022 (Washington, DC: National Center for Education Statistics, 2008), 303.

constant dollars are employed, though the rate of attenuation varies considerably depending on the index used to account for inflation.[20] Adjusted against the Consumer Price Index (CPI), which is based on "changes in the prices paid by urban consumers for a representative basket of goods and services,"[21] appropriations increased in constant 2007 dollars by 43.2 percent from 1979–80 to 2006–07, keeping pace with growth in FTE enrollment. But a different picture emerges when the appropriations figures are adjusted against two inflation indexes that attempt a more precise

Figure 1.1 Trends in State Tax Appropriations for Higher Education, 1979–80 through 2006–07, in Current Dollars and in Constant 2007 Dollars

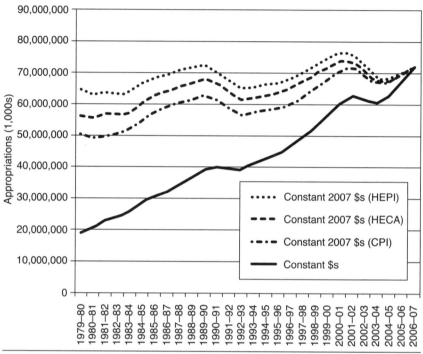

Sources: Center for the Study of Education Policy, "Grapevine Historical Data," http://www. grapevine.ilstu.edu/historical/index.htm; Commonfund, *2008 HEPI Report* (Wilton, CT: Commonfund, 2008), 3, http://www.commonfund.org/Commonfund/CF + Institute/ CI_About_HEPI.htm; State Higher Education Executive Officers, "Supplemental SHEF Data Tables & Figures," http://www.sheeo.org/finance/shef/shef_data.htm.

Note: Appropriations data are from *Grapevine* annual reports available at http://www.grapevine. ilstu.edu/historical/index.htm. See note in Table 2 for information on these data. HEPI = Higher Education Price Index. HECA = Higher Education Cost Adjustment. CPI = Consumer Price Index.

accounting of the costs borne by colleges and universities specifically: the Higher Education Price Index (HEPI), which "measures the average relative level of prices in a fixed basket of goods and services purchased by colleges and universities each year"[22] and the Higher Education Cost Adjustment (HECA) index, which is weighted heavily toward changes in costs associated with white-collar workers.[23] Examined from the more focused perspectives offered by these indexes, state tax appropriations for higher education (in constant 2007 dollars) rose by only 12.1 percent between 1979–80 and 2006–07 according to HEPI and by 28.8 percent according to the HECA index.

Thus, interpretation of the fiscal problems faced by higher educa-tion depends very much "on one's perspective."[24] From the perspective of higher education leaders who must meet the costs of running col-leges or universities, state funding has hardly kept pace with the de-mands made on their institutions. But making the case for additional funding can be difficult, because the picture looks quite different from the perspective of everyday citizens for whom taxes represent foregone consumption. From the taxpayer's perspective, state support for higher education since 1980 may appear quite adequate, even generous. In the political debate about how much states should appropriate to their col-leges and universities, the public (consumer) perspective of adequacy offsets the institutional (provider) perception of inadequacy.[25] This certainly contributes to the paradoxical disjuncture, noted above, be-tween the unabated demand for higher education and the limited ability of higher education leaders to garner the political support needed to increase appropriations.

VULNERABILITY TO ECONOMIC DOWNTURNS

Periodic downturns in the economy add to the difficulties college advocates have in securing additional state funding. Because higher education is a discretionary item in state budgets, and because tuition increases are a potential fallback when state funding levels off, it is rela-tively easy for legislatures to scale back appropriations for higher education following economic recessions.[26] The trend line in Figure 1.2 shows that annual changes in state appropriations tapered off or decreased after the recessions experienced in 1980, 1981–82, 1990–91, 2001, and 2008. These periodic economic downturns have diminished the predictability of state funding, triggering cycles of "recession, retrenchment, and recovery" in many state higher education systems.[27] This cyclical pattern is reflected in Lingenfelter's analysis of state support for higher education over time. He observes that

[d]uring recessions, higher education enrollments generally grow (apparently because a weak labor market reduces the opportunity costs of enrolling) and the economic downturn causes state revenues to decline or lag behind inflation. The average amount of state sup-port per student . . . has declined during every economic recession since 1970, but has rebounded to even higher levels during each subsequent recovery.[28]

Figure 1.2 Year-to-Year Percent Changes in State Tax Appropriations For Higher Education, 1980–81 through 2007–08

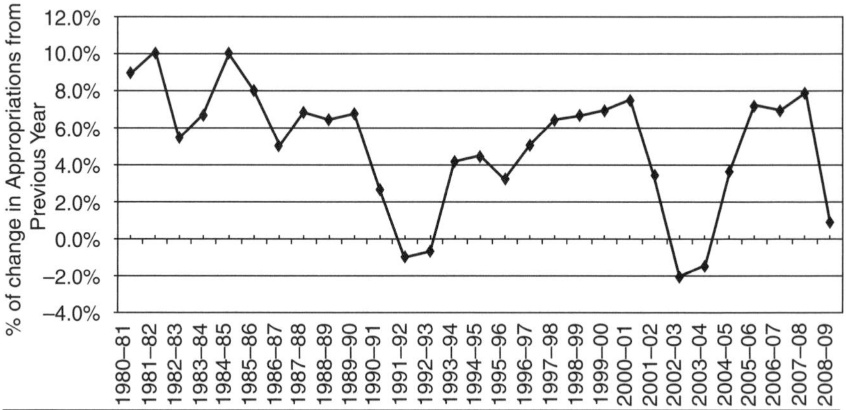

Source: Center for the Study of Education Policy, "Grapevine Historical Data," http://www. grapevine.ilstu.edu/historical/index.htm.

Note: Appropriations data are from *Grapevine* annual reports available at http://www.grapevine. ilstu.edu/historical/index.htm. See note in Table 1 for information on these data.

The retrenchment-and-recovery pattern was particularly turbulent following the 2001 recession. The decline in state appropriations registered in 2002–03 and 2003–04 (see Figure 1.2) were the largest one-year drops registered since the *Grapevine* project began in 1960. Over half (29) of the states began the 2003–04 fiscal year with state appropriations that were lower than those received two years previously, and five states operated with higher education appropriations that were lower than those received five years previously.[29] Increases in subsequent fiscal years, including a 7.9 percent jump between 2006–07 and 2007–08, helped make up for the reductions in 2003–04, but in many states these increases simply compensated for earlier losses and did not represent significant fiscal gains.

Higher education now faces yet another downturn in the wake of the 2008 recession. As of this writing, preliminary findings of the *Grapevine* survey for fiscal year 2008–09[30] indicate that state tax appropriations for higher education nationwide increased by only 0.9 percent between 2007–2008 and 2008–2009. Fourteen states registered declines ranging from –0.4 percent to –17.7 percent, and 10 states reported increases of only 2 percent or less. In addition, many states indicated that 2007–08 appropriations reported in the previous year had been reduced. For example, Florida's 8.8 percent reduction between 2007–2008 and 2008–2009 came on top of a 2.6 percent rescission of initial 2007–2008 appropriations. Similarly, Rhode Island's 7.2 percent reduction between 2007–2008 and 2008–2009 came on the heels of 2.9 percent reduction in funds initially appropriated for 2007–2008. These rescissions illustrate the vulnerability of higher education as states balance their budgets in tough economic times.

Data reported by the Center on Budget and Policy Priorities[31] suggest that the downward trend will most likely continue as states prepare 2009–10 budgets in the most precarious economy since the Great Depression. The Center's data show that as of January 2009, fully 45 states faced midyear revenue shortfalls in their 2008–09 budgets or anticipated revenue shortfalls in 2009–10. The gaps between available resources and budgetary commitments in 2008–09 ranged across the states from 0.5 percent to 13.9 percent of total general fund revenues; anticipated gaps for 2009–10 (based as a percentage on 2008–09 general fund revenues) ranged from 1.7 percent to 25.6 percent. Clearly, the gains achieved after the retrenchment caused by the 2001 recession may be erased as states once again tackle the question of funding higher education with diminished revenues.

THE ENTREPRENEURIAL RESPONSE

This grim picture notwithstanding, states remain significant patrons of higher education. As Lingenfelter correctly argues, the up-and-down nature of state tax support reflects "a struggle to balance state priorities during the ebb and flow of state revenues more than an abandoning of the public commitment to higher education."[32] Yet the precarious and unpredictable flow of state tax appropriations over time suggests that our mechanisms for funding public higher education have not kept pace with the sustained growth of mass higher education and the attendant demands society places on colleges and universities. "Under these circumstances," Lingenfelter notes, "the central question for the U.S. is no longer how should we subsidize higher education for a privileged fraction of the population, but what financing strategies are most conducive to widespread, successful participation?"[33] The answer will not lie simply in politicking for additional state subsidies; rather, it will lie in actions at both the governmental and institutional levels that refine and coordinate multiple approaches to securing funding for colleges and universities, subsidizing student financial aid, and enhancing efficiencies:

> Educators and policymakers will need to become increasingly thoughtful and intentional about balancing appropriations to public institutions, tuition policies, and need-based financial assistance in order to achieve the desired level of access and student success. And institutions will face unremitting pressure to restrain price increases

and increase productivity by focusing relentlessly on priorities and exploiting technology to improve instructional quality and reduce costs.[34]

A key part of this financial restructuring will also lie in entrepreneurial efforts at the institutional level to secure additional funding sources that will reduce the dependence of colleges and universities on state subsidies and allow them greater freedom in planning services for students and other constituencies. Many specific approaches might be employed, such as an enhanced fund-raising campaign, the use of noncredit courses as a cash supplement for the academic program, the contracted sale of services to area businesses, or the strategic marketing of intellectual property developed by faculty members. But charting an entrepreneurial course in ways that secure additional financial independence without compromising academic values may require a rethinking of the collegiate organization itself rather than the adoption of specific fund-raising mechanisms.

This is born out in Burton R. Clark's pioneering analyses of five European universities that successfully reduced their dependence on government subsidies, lowering the proportion of total revenues that derive from these subsidies by 12 percent to 32 percent from 1980 to 1995.[35] All developed—in their own ways—what Clark called a *diversified funding base,* resting on such efforts as a technology transfer program for area businesses, research and development assistance for local industries, and (in the case of one university) a student-led initiative to develop and market a multimedia presentation on local folklore. But the diversified funding base was itself only one of several interrelated features of an institutional transformation that included a *strengthened steering core* consisting of "groups who work diligently to find diverse streams of income for the entire institution . . . and then make hard choices on internal allocation from pooled resources,"[36] an *enhanced developmental periphery* consisting of a "set of units operating on the periphery of the traditional [organizational] structure, reaching across old boundaries and linking up with outside interests,"[37] a *stimulated academic heartland* in which traditional academic disciplines in the humanities and social sciences "eventually . . . [find] educational and economic value in becoming more enterprising" (as the example of the student's multimedia presentation demonstrates),[38] and the emergence of an *embracing entrepreneurial culture,* in which experience along the road to lessened dependency on government funding thoroughly ties entrepreneurialism to beliefs and "sagas" that reflect the organization's identity and aspirations.[39]

In short, the entrepreneurial transformations unveiled in Clark's case studies entailed the cultivation of new fiscal patrons through renewed leadership (the steering core), enhanced boundary-spanning units (the developmental periphery) that tie the institution to outside constituents, and—ultimately—a new organizational culture. This highlights both the difficulties and the promise of entrepreneurial action in the face of uncertain state appropriations. On the one hand, his analysis puts to rest any notion that entrepreneurialism is simply a matter of fund-raising. In fact, it is a more complex, multiyear transformation of the organization itself. But on the other hand, Clark points out that this difficult path provides a more promising and hopeful prospect for collegiate life than does the dour and all-too-common alternative of the fiscally beleaguered institution in which raising money becomes an overriding institutional goal, alienating faculty members (especially in the arts and humanities) and displacing traditional collegiate values of academic inquiry and student development.[40] At the institutions observed by Clark, academic purpose was at the heart of the entrepreneurial effort:

> To build a diversified funding base in a university is to construct a portfolio of patrons to share rising costs. As new patrons contribute, their expectations of what they should get in return readily intrude to become new constraints. Universities then need greater self-consciousness on where they draw the line between what they are willing to do and not do to meet those demands. The collective will, located in the steering core, then comes to play to define new limits around greatly expanded boundaries.[41]

POINTING INWARD AS WELL AS OUTWARD

Trends in state tax support for higher education after the post-World War II growth era point to the continuing challenge states face in advancing educational opportunities and attainment while at the same time expanding access to health care, maintaining transportation infrastructures, encouraging alternative energy sources, and attending to the many other needs of a growing population. Pinning the academy's fiscal hopes solely on appropriations increases without cultivating other sources of fiscal support may be self-defeating in the face of other equally compelling demands made on state budgets. Even worse, it may divert attention from internal, institutional actions that help colleges and universities adapt to a changing fiscal environment. Canvassing prospects for "new directions" in community college funding during the fiscally turbulent 1970s, John Lombardi, a long-time community college educator and leader, presciently noted that

> New directions in finance are predicated on the belief that there is a way out of the financial distress now affecting community colleges. But the new directions point inward as well as outward. It

is, of course, easier to seek relief from taxpayers or students than from increased productivity, better management, and less imposing edifices. But the taxpayers have become reluctant, and increasing fees and tuition may be counterproductive. Moreover, excessive dependence on augmented funds to relieve each crisis may become a ritual of self-absolution which inhibits us from seeking other, perhaps more basic causes for our troubles. We do need more money, but we are deceiving ourselves if we believe more money by itself will be a panacea or create a distinguished institution.[42]

How institutions tend to this internal work will have a great bearing on what future generations of students experience in college. Although they are no panacea, entrepreneurial efforts undertaken as a means toward academic ends and planned alongside a continued rethinking of what constitutes a quality education—and what resources are needed to ensure that quality— may be an essential component of the fiscal restructuring needed to advance societal goals for universal higher education. Additional research along the lines conducted by Clark will help us understand how institutions might find their way to new and academically sound entrepreneurial cultures.

NOTES

1. H. G. Badger, M. J. S. Carr, and M. Farr, *Biennial Survey of Education in the United States 1944–46: Statistics of Higher Education 1945–46* (Washington, DC: United States Office of Education, 1949), 2, 11.

2. Thomas D. Snyder, Sally A. Dillow, and Charlene M. Hoffman, *Digest of Education Statistics, 2007,* NCES 2008022 (Washington, DC: National Center for Education Statistics, 2008), 179, 385.

3. Badger, Carr, and Farr, *Biennial Survey.*

4. Snyder, Dillow, and Hoffman, 486.

5. Earl F. Cheit, *The New Depression in Higher Education: A Study of Financial Conditions at 41 Colleges and Universities* (New York: McGraw-Hill, 1971), 1.

6. William Zumeta, "State Higher Education Financing: Demand Imperatives Meet Structural, Cyclical, and Political Constraints," in *Public Funding for Higher Education: Changing Contexts and New Rationales,* ed. Edward P. St. John and Michael D. Parsons (Baltimore, MD: Johns Hopkins University Press, 2004), 85.

7. Ibid, 79.

8. Paul Lingenfelter, "The Financing of Public Colleges and Universities in the United States," in *Handbook of Research in Education Finance and Policy,* ed. Helen F. Ladd and Edward B. Fiske (New York: Routledge, 2008), 659.

9. Burton R. Clark, "Collegial Entrepreneurialism in Proactive Universities: Lessons from Europe," *Change* 32, no. 1 (2000): 10–19.

10. Snyder, Dillow, and Hoffman, *Digest of Education Statistics,* 488.

11. Ibid.

12. Lingenfelter, "Financing of Public Colleges and Universities," 654.

13. Zumeta, "State Higher Education Financing," 85.

14. Robert B. Archibald and David H. Feldman, "State Higher Education Spending and the Tax Revolt," *The Journal of Higher Education* 77 (2006): 618–44.

15. Ross Hodel, Maureen Laffey, and Paul Lingenfelter, *Recession, Retrenchment, and Recovery: State Higher Education Funding and Student Financial Aid* (Boulder, CO: State Higher Education Executive Officers, 2006), Educational Resources Information Center #ED502180.

16. The *Grapevine* project entails an annual compilation of state tax appropriations for the support of higher education. *Grapevine* data exclude tax appropriations for capital projects and debt service. In addition, states are asked to exclude non-tax monies such as interest income, tobacco settlement subsidies, and lottery funds. Annual *Grapevine* reports going back to Fiscal year 1960–61 can be found at http://www.grapevine.ilstu.edu/.

17. Snyder, Dillow, and Hoffman, *Digest of Education Statistics, 2007,* 303.

18. Zumeta, "State Higher Education Financing," 83.

19. Lingenfelter, "Financing of Public Colleges and Universities," 658.

20. Ibid., 656.

21. Bureau of Labor Statistics, "Consumer Price Index," http://www.bls.gov/CPI/.

22. Commonfund, "About HEPI," http://www.commonfund.org/Commonfund/CF+Institute/CI_About_HEPI.htm.

23. State Higher Education Executive Officers, *State Higher Education Finance, FY 2007* (Boulder, CO: State Higher Education Executive Officers, 2008), http://www.sheeo.org/finance/shef_fy07.pdf, 48.

24. Lingenfelter, "Financing of Public Colleges and Universities," 656.

25. For a discussion of the consumer and provider perspectives reflected in varying indexes used to factor out inflation in analyses of state funding trends, see State Higher Education Executive Officers, *State Higher Education Finance, FY 2007* (Boulder, CO: State Higher Education Executive Officers, 2008), 47–9.

26. Zumeta, "State Higher Education Financing," 85.

27. Hodel, Laffey, and Lingenfelter, *Recession, Retrenchment, and Recovery.*

28. Lingenfelter, "Financing of Public Colleges and Universities," 654.

29. James C. Palmer, *Grapevine Survey of State Higher Education Tax Appropriations for Fiscal Year 2004* (Normal, IL: Center for the Study of

Education Policy, 2005), http://www.grapevine.ilstu.edu//historical/Appropriations%202003-04.pdf.

30. Center for the Study of Education Policy, "Grapevine: An Annual Compilation of Data on State Tax Appropriations for the General Operation of Higher Education," http://www.grapevine.ilstu.edu/.

31. Elizabeth McNichol and Iris J. Lav, *State Budget Troubles Worsen* (Washington, DC: Center on Budget and Policy Priorities, January 14, 2009), http://www.cbpp.org/9-8-08sfp.htm.

32. Lingenfelter, "Financing of Public Colleges and Universities," 658.

33. Ibid., 663.

34. Ibid., 664.

35. Burton R. Clark, *Creating Entrepreneurial Universities: Organizational Pathways of Transformation* (Oxford, England: Permagon, 1998); Clark, "Collegial Entrepreneurialism"; Clark, *Sustaining Change in Universities: Continuities and Concepts* (Maidenhead, England: Society for Research into Higher Education and the Open University Press, 2004).

36. Clark, "Collegial Entrepreneurialism," 14.

37. Ibid., 15.

38. Ibid., 17.

39. Ibid., 17–18.

40. See for example, John S. Levin, "Faculty Work: Tensions between Educational and Economic Values," *The Journal of Higher Education* 77 (2006): 62–88. See also Sheila Slaughter, "Professional Values and the Allure of the Market," Academe 87, no. 5 (2001): 22–6.

41. Clark, *Creating Entrepreneurial Universities,* 140.

42. John Lombardi, "Critical Decade for Community College Financing," in *Perspectives on the Community College: Essays by John Lombardi,* ed. Arthur M. Cohen (Washington, DC: American Association of Community Colleges and the American Council on Education, 1992), 38 (original work published in 1973).

CHAPTER 2

Developing a Culture of Entrepreneurship in the Academy

Raymond B. Farrow III and John D. Kasarda

Much has been written in recent years of the increasing corporatization of American higher education, and most of it is unflattering.[1] Critics perceive undue influence of the private sector in our educational institutions—sullying, they argue, the last bastion of objectivity and truth, the strongest purveyor of humanitarian, liberal, and scientific values, and the bulwark of our civil society. Research agendas, especially in health affairs and the sciences, are increasingly seen as dictated by corporate interests.[2] There is no longer knowledge for knowledge's sake, critics argue, but knowledge sold to the highest bidder. Conversely, conservative watchdog groups scrutinize course offerings and university administrators for ideological balance and work to ensure private enterprise and their own individual views are fully represented and defended.[3]

While these contrasting positions may seem overstated, they do highlight a longstanding and vigorous debate about the proper role of the private sector in American colleges and universities, especially in our public universities, which educate the vast majority of today's students and are supported by taxpayers.[4] The reality is that there is a large and growing dependence on private sources of funding for higher education. This has forced institutions to place a premium on those with wealth or access to wealth, mainly well-to-do alumni and their network of business contacts, a trend that will only increase with the severe 2008–09 economic downturn and the slashing of university budgets.[5] U.S. colleges and universities must now remain in a perpetual state of fund-raising, either in an active campaign or in preparation for launching a new one, often for staggering sums of money.[6]

What is less discussed but increasingly clear is that our universities and the private sector need each other now more than ever. In spite of protests, an isolated academic community disconnected from the realities of the marketplace is no longer feasible or desirable, nor is a curriculum that eschews practical applications and does not prepare graduates for lifetime employment, or provide basic financial literacy, or offer critical skills for functioning successfully in a global economy and a multicultural society.[7] Likewise, increasing pressures from globalization and the rapid advances in technology have U.S. businesses and industries struggling to remain competitive and in some cases relevant. The training of the future American workforce is a serious and growing issue, placing intense demands on our educational institutions to produce graduates who can survive (and thrive) in Thomas Friedman's flattened world as well as Samuel Huntington's "clash of civilizations."[8]

Unfortunately, the privileged position the United States has enjoyed for the last half-century as the premier destination for undergraduate and professional training is eroding as foreign universities increasingly adapt to and dominate the changing landscape. Many offer learning opportunities comparable to even the best American universities. Like everything else, educational institutions now serve a global market and are subject to increasing competitive demands and expectations. American colleges and universities realize that fundamental change is imminent; the days of the cloistered academy are over. It is in this fraught context that entrepreneurship has emerged in the past decade as a new and important opportunity within American higher education.[9]

ENTREPRENEURSHIP AS A CORE MISSION OF HIGHER EDUCATION

As both a discipline and a mindset, entrepreneurship offers a lively alternative to how academia and the private sector might and should work together toward common and mutually rewarding ends. The introduction of entrepreneurship as part of the core mission of higher education is due largely to the efforts of the Ewing Marion Kauffman Foundation.[10] Kauffman, the leading funder and promoter of entrepreneurship in the United States, accelerated an already growing trend with its $44.5 million Kauffman Campuses Initiative (KCI), launched in December 2003. KCI's goal was to seed cross-campus entrepreneurship programs at several major American universities in hopes of embedding in them entrepreneurial concepts, opportunities, and practices, and sparking a larger movement among all universities to act and think more entrepreneurially.

Through its ongoing research, Kauffman understood that the entrepreneurial sector accounts for significant innovations moving into the marketplace and is responsible for generating the majority of net new jobs in the economy. Equally clear was the fact that U.S. higher education was mostly unaware of these phenomena and that little was being done to prepare students to move into entrepreneurship as a potential career choice.[11]

While some university entrepreneurship courses and programs had existed before, they tended to serve a narrow audience, primarily business-school students, and were not mainstream offerings or included in the general core curriculum. Moreover, they were not in fact or perception engines of change on campus, and their broader influence was negligible. Indeed, many entrepreneurs, including some of the country's most important business innovators and industry leaders, have educational backgrounds not in business but in the liberal arts and social sciences. Until recently, entrepreneurship education has remained on the periphery of American higher education and in many instances was simply invisible.

Kauffman understood that in order to be successful, nascent entrepreneurs, especially young entrepreneurs, needed a nurturing environment. Societal attitudes, legal regulations, and access to resources and markets could either facilitate or stifle innovation. In addition, a complete understanding of this broader framework in which entrepreneurship operates required insight from a variety of different disciplines; it also implied that exposure to entrepreneurship in college, where this broader perspective might be introduced and studied, could prove transforming.

From the narrow idea of promoting entrepreneurship as a career choice, Kauffman developed a more comprehensive strategy for making entrepreneurship part of the core mission of higher education. Kauffman proposed that universities should adapt entrepreneurial approaches and concepts to their own administration and management practices. Entrepreneurship principles could also be applied, Kauffman argued, to the way that faculty members approach their research and teaching, to show how different disciplines could include the study of entrepreneurship in society, and to demonstrate how students could bridge theory and practical application in their own education. Kauffman believed successful cross-campus entrepreneurship programs might offer significant contributions to the intellectual life of American universities and make them more creative and productive contributors to society.

As institutions, though, universities tend to be overly bureaucratic, tradition bound, risk and free-market averse, and slow to identify and pursue opportunities to translate research and teaching innovations to the marketplace. Such missed opportunities include not only commercializing faculty discoveries and supporting fledgling student and faculty ventures, but also forging global partnerships and maximizing university relationships with the private sector to impact local communities. Kauffman, therefore, aimed to change the very way universities behave, to help them adopt an entrepreneurial mindset that would unleash more of their creative and venture-creating potential. To do this, it was necessary to free the practice and study of entrepreneurship from the exclusive domain of business schools where it often languished.[12] Kauffman wanted to make entrepreneurship a transformative idea that flourished throughout the university, reaching students and faculty in all disciplines and creating a robust environment for innovation of all kinds.

KAUFFMAN CAMPUSES INITIATIVE

In its first iteration, Kauffman funded cross-campus entrepreneurship programs as part of its Kauffman Campuses Initiative (KCI) at eight universities selected by the foundation and an external review board after a rigorous proposal and selection process.[13] Each university had a different approach to reflect individual institutional cultures and needs, but all were committed to making entrepreneurship education more accessible and visible at their institutions and were prepared to embed entrepreneurship within their universities' core educational mission.

The University of North Carolina at Chapel Hill (UNC) was one of the institutions selected. The Carolina Entrepreneurial Initiative (CEI) is now completing its fifth and final year of seed funding from the Kauffman Foundation.[14] We believe CEI provides an interesting case study of this grand experiment first outlined by Kauffman and argue that cross-campus entrepreneurship programs such as CEI point to some dynamic possibilities between the private sector and academia that may prove valuable for other institutions. During this era of tremendous change in U.S. higher education, it is a model of university engagement and transformation worthy of larger consideration and examination.

BEGINNINGS

The call for applications from the Kauffman Foundation arrived at UNC in April 2003. After several attempts by university administrators and interdisciplinary committees to craft a proposal and rally support among different academic units, the effort stalled. With less than three weeks to go before the final deadline, the university approached the Frank Hawkins Kenan Institute of Private Enterprise (Kenan Institute), an outreach arm of UNC's Kenan-Flagler Business School, to salvage the faltering effort and produce a competitive proposal.

In many ways, the Kenan Institute was an ideal host for the effort from an organizational, philosophical, and reputational perspective. Frank Hawkins Kenan, for whom the institute is named, was an inveterate entrepreneur who had become increasingly convinced during his lifetime that academia was an unwelcoming and even dismissive environment for private-sector concerns and perspectives. In 1985, he and the trustees of the William R. Kenan, Jr. Charitable Trust established the Institute for Private Enterprise at UNC to promote private-sector ideals and solutions within the university, to act as a bridge between the business school and other parts of the university, and, more generally, to leverage the private sector for the public good. Funded by annual gifts from the William R. Kenan, Jr. Fund, the institute works at the crossroads of academia, government, and the private sector in three programmatic areas: entrepreneurship, economic development, and global competitiveness. During the 1990s, the institute dedicated much of its energy and resources to help globalize UNC's Business School, culminating in the establishment of Kenan Institute Asia, a Thai nonprofit institution dedicated to economic development headquartered in Bangkok that now employs 60 people. The opportunity to craft the university's proposal to the Kauffman Foundation marked a welcome return to the institute's roots in entrepreneurship.

CEI brought together two like-minded entities for a common cause. Like Frank Kenan, Ewing Marion Kauffman was a self-made man who believed deeply in the private sector and its power not only to create wealth, generate jobs, and provide livelihoods, but also to do service to humanity. They were both dogged promoters of free enterprise, sensitive to the fact that the American capitalist system, for all its strengths, was frequently misunderstood, misrepresented, and underappreciated. (It is an interesting historical footnote that Ewing Kauffman traveled to Chapel Hill to meet Frank Kenan when he was establishing the Kauffman Foundation to learn from the institute's experiences.) Both men—and the institutions they founded—have remained true to these instincts and committed to a more prominent and integral role for the private sector in higher education.

After agreeing to develop UNC's proposal to Kauffman, the Kenan Institute commenced a two-week, all-hands-on-deck effort, which was consuming but ultimately invigorating. Kenan Institute director John D. Kasarda, who had served as chair of the Department of Sociology in the College of Arts and Sciences for 10 years before his faculty appointment at the business school, assumed leadership of the process. His network among College faculty proved invaluable in convincing skeptics that entrepreneurship was not anathema to their teaching or research interests or to the liberal arts curriculum at the heart of the Carolina undergraduate experience. Conceptually, Kasarda offered a broad definition of entrepreneurship to position the effort as not simply about commercial, profit-making enterprises—a non-starter for many departments and faculty. To traditional business venturing, the proposal added social and civic entrepreneurship (developing self-sustaining nonprofits and government organizations) and academic entrepreneurship (addressing the challenges of educational delivery and university administration in entrepreneurial ways) as new areas of exploration, interest, and emphasis. In this way, the institute hoped to ignite the creative energy and entrepreneurial spirit of students, faculty, and staff whose passions and interests are primarily social, civic, or academic in nature. The broader definition proved to be critical in engaging key faculty and suggesting to a broader university audience that entrepreneurship principles could in fact be widely applied to generate value and produce significant educational outcomes.

The key elements of UNC's proposal can be briefly described by a Venn diagram (Figure 2.1) that identifies four critical components of CEI's programmatic approach: inspire, teach, connect, and create. Activity in one area supports activity in the others and forms a continuous stream of programs to support UNC entrepreneurs and entrepreneurship education at Carolina. First, CEI is committed to *inspiring* students to become entrepreneurs. Second, CEI *teaches* them to be entrepreneurs. Third, CEI *connects* them with alumni mentors, academic experts, and private industry executives to help them be successful. Finally, CEI *creates* new ventures, new knowledge, and new attitudes that will change lives, create jobs, and ultimately transform the culture and operations of the university.

A critical strategy outlined in the proposal was the decision not to invest all the Kauffman resources in designing new, built-from-the-ground-up programs, which at first pass might have been appealing. While several new programs were proposed, including a new undergraduate minor in entrepreneurship, many CEI efforts depended on incorporating entrepreneurial elements into existing faculty and student programs. This approach gave incentives to established efforts (and their faculty leadership) to become involved with CEI without feeling threatened by a new large-scale, cross-campus initiative. Instead of positioning entrepreneurship as something imposed from the outside, the approach was to suggest that entrepreneurship in fact was inherent (or could be inherent) in much of what was already working well on campus. The idea was to have CEI liberate, not dictate—to be a true catalyst for innovation.

The proposal team also engaged the considerable talents of a select group of alumni entrepreneur advisors who counseled the institute and the

Figure 2.1 Inspire-Teach-Connect-Create

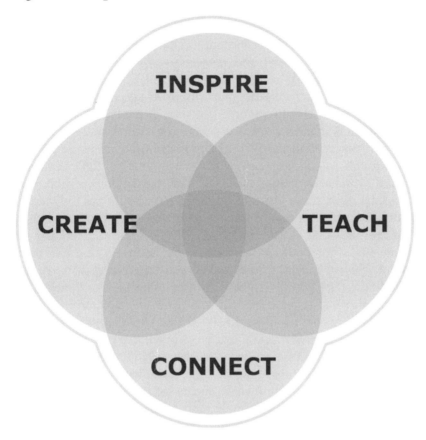

university on its approach and helped to shape program content. Among other suggestions, this kitchen cabinet insisted that we apply entrepreneurial principles to the management of the initiative itself. Failure, they argued, is fundamental to entrepreneurs. Every entrepreneur has a history, often a long one, of ventures that failed or almost failed, and we should anticipate (even welcome) failure of some CEI programs as an indicator that we were assuming sufficient risk to truly effect cultural change. Entrepreneurs, at least the better ones, welcome failure as an opportunity to learn and take corrective action; it feeds their motivation to succeed in the next venture and accelerates their learning.

The same should be true for CEI, they reasoned, and for universities in general. Broken departments, poor instructors, and failed leadership are tolerated in the academy to a degree that would be unacceptable in the private sector. As institutions, universities have their fair share of failures (all institutions do), but they are rarely acknowledged. Failure is not used, as it should be, as the best possible opportunity for universities to change and grow. Risk-taking is not rewarded, and eventually an atmosphere of complacency develops, stifling innovation. To create, one must be willing beyond everything else to fail, and, if necessary, start over and risk failing again. Innovation cannot be planned or predicted, but an atmosphere on campus that encourages creativity must prioritize a process that embraces failure as a necessary step to success.

Accountability, therefore, was a paramount theme in the proposal. Extensive plans were outlined to develop metrics and evaluate CEI programs through an ongoing engagement with the UNC Office of Institutional Research and Assessment.[15] Through surveys, focus groups, and longitudinal studies, the institute proposed to measure not only inputs and outputs, but, more important, impact. A zero-based annual budgeting process provided the flexibility to reduce or zero-out funding for programs that were not meeting expectations and invest more heavily in programs that had gained traction and demonstrated success.

In addition, the institute proposed the establishment of an Innovations Fund, which would provide seed funding for new programmatic efforts that would emerge after CEI launched. Instead of assuming that UNC's proposal was perfect from conception, we believed that better ideas might emerge in future years from students, faculty, or staff about how a cross-campus entrepreneurship program could generate more value to the university. The Innovations Fund would encourage and fund those changes. If we were truly entrepreneurial in our approach and management, CEI in year one would probably look different, we predicted, from CEI in year five. Some programs would succeed, some would fail; some new ideas might be launched, some initial ones discarded. The point was to keep the overall goal in mind: to make "entrepreneurship part of the weave and fabric of Carolina."[16]

Once it was properly positioned, the possibility of a cross-campus entrepreneurship initiative attracted generous support. What we soon realized was that UNC had a strong undercurrent of entrepreneurship already; it just had not been marshaled for optimal impact or described in such a manner to constituents. As a large, mostly decentralized institution, there have always been opportunities at Carolina for students and faculty to pursue new ideas and transform them into enterprises. Moreover, the tradition of public service, which has deep roots at UNC, generated its own brand of entrepreneurial and civic spirit over the years. In fact, there were many examples of students and faculty organizing and launching commercial ventures and nonprofits to respond to needs, either in the local community or, increasingly, abroad. CEI provided a new language to describe and understand much of this activity and offered faculty and students a different conceptual frame within which to think of future endeavors as well as to understand past history.

The state of North Carolina offered an inviting environment for a large-scale push in entrepreneurship by UNC. The nearby Research Triangle Park (RTP) stands as a visible testament to the power of entrepreneurial and visionary thinking. Begun in the 1950s with nothing more than a large tract of deserted farm land, RTP emerged by the 1980s as one of the first and best-known planned corporate destinations. Today, it is the world's largest research park. Building on the intellectual firepower of three major universities (UNC, Duke, and North Carolina State), RTP became a nexus for technology, life science, and pharmaceutical firms. The concentration of company headquarters and a highly educated workforce have spawned a thriving second- and even third-generation of companies, many of them home-grown entrepreneurial ventures. RTP is also headquarters to the Council for Entrepreneurial Development, the largest entrepreneurial support organization in the United States with a current membership of over 5,000 people, representing over 1,100 companies.[17]

While no process anticipates all the dynamics, opportunities, or challenges to be faced, the planning for CEI established a conceptual approach and sensitivity to Carolina's unique culture, environment, and needs that have served the initiative well. The proposal did not mince words, though, about the difficulty of achieving success.

> We are under no illusions about the difficulty and complexity of this undertaking. Historically, institutions of higher education—and particularly large research universities—have been marked by attributes that tend to work against internal cultural change. The compartmentalization and increasing specialization of academic disciplines, a decentralized organizational structure, and an entrenched 'ivory-tower' mentality in which the pursuit of truth is typically conducted at a far remove from business and societal needs present major challenges in this regard. Moreover, the sheer number and variety of fields of study on a campus like ours contribute to enormous vitality but also complicate any attempt to unite these areas under the banner of a common enterprise.[18]

The proposal concluded by admitting that the university had little choice but to forge ahead, for its own best interests were at stake: "We accept it as an article of faith that our institutional capacity to think and behave entrepreneurially, engaging the broadest numbers of students and faculty in this manner, will be a pivotal determinant of our success and relevance in the 21st century." With the announcement in December 2003 that UNC had won the Kauffman award, this understanding—of both the challenges ahead and the necessity of the scope of work—proved prescient.

IMPLEMENTATION

With the award in hand, the Kenan Institute, which had offered its intellectual leadership and administrative infrastructure to house the effort, was charged to move forward. Initially, 14 CEI programs had been proposed, a large undertaking under any circumstance, but for an effort that was interdisciplinary and cross-campus, it was a daunting prospect. Although CEI was centrally administered through the institute, each program had its own faculty (or in one instance student) leaders, or champions, that were responsible for actual implementation and day-to-day management of individual programs. The Kenan Institute saw its role not as a micromanager but as a facilitator, providing a set of resources (e.g., administrative, communications and marketing, financial) that would buttress the champions' efforts. Success depended on: (1) engaging across campus highly regarded faculty who would lead individual programs; (2) effectively coordinating and managing a large, complex enterprise (keeping all the parts moving together); and (3) inspiring and motivating members of the Carolina community to take risks in turning their ideas into enterprises.

Of the three identified determinants of success, the last is, arguably, the most important. The best organization and leadership, we knew, would go nowhere unless we could persuade an increasing number of colleagues and students to start identifying themselves as entrepreneurs and assuming the inherent risks of entrepreneurship. The proposal anticipated this critical issue, what we described as the "last-mile problem."

> What prevents people from taking risks and going the extra mile to put their ideas into ventures? Is it a lack of skills? Lack of interest? Lack of networks or information? Lack of resources? Lack of energy? Whatever it is, perhaps the 'last-mile problem' in human creativity is the inability or unwillingness to convert an idea into a worthwhile and financially rewarding solution. Our challenge then becomes to get the chemists, historians, and artists to take the next big step and put their ideas into tangible ventures so that they and the greatest possible number of people benefit.

While we do not claim to have found a universal solution to this problem, several things have proven important in our own attempts to find a satisfactory response. They are: (1) creating and promoting a risk-taking culture; (2) launching and sustaining an extensive and ongoing communications and marketing strategy; and (3) offering multiple points of entry into an integrated entrepreneurship program.

Creating and Promoting a Risk-Taking Culture

Risk-taking is not an easy behavior to adopt if you are in an environment that is unwelcoming, or if your training or background has predisposed you to avoid it. Academics achieve success (and gain tenure) by specialization and a track record of publications and teaching performance that are extensively reviewed and evaluated by peers in the same discipline. This demanding focus is wonderful training for scholarship, but it does little to provide the training or encourage the behaviors needed by entrepreneurs. Faculty, then, tend to be among the most resistant members in the university community to becoming entrepreneurs. Of even greater concern, they tend to dismiss entrepreneurship as an illegitimate discipline and are weak advocates for entrepreneurship with other faculty and students.

These attitudes, we observed, vary somewhat by discipline. Faculty members in the sciences who are more often exposed to colleagues who have transferred lab research into commercial ventures tend in our experience to be more receptive and enthusiastic about entrepreneurship. Many have friends who have launched a company, or maybe even several. Most have considerable experience winning research grants from corporations, foundations, or government agencies that often involve millions of dollars. These experiences provide important opportunities to develop financial and resource-management skills that make them more likely to launch a venture if they believe they have a marketable innovation. At minimum, they have a greater appreciation for those who do become entrepreneurs.

We discovered UNC faculty from other disciplines, like the fine arts, more difficult to persuade, at least initially. This may be due in part to different experiences within the arts about money—unfortunately, little exposure to large grants or diversified sources of funding—and the free market, which tends to undervalue the arts significantly. For those in the arts, there is a strong conviction that their pursuits often have a greater intrinsic value than what is captured or rewarded by the marketplace. Obviously, there are examples of highly paid performers in the arts, but they are relatively few; as a whole, the arts remain a notoriously difficult profession in which to earn a living wage.

In a field where there is high dependence on philanthropy, the self-actualizing demands of entrepreneurship may seem off-putting. In fact, the role of a benefactor in the arts is still strong—the belief that some person (a patron) or institution (like a university) will support individuals creating art or developing artistic venues without regard to the harsher realities of the marketplace. Entrepreneurship turns that model on its head since it asks artists not to simply pursue their creative impulse simply for art's sake, but to build and grow ventures (commercial or nonprofit) to deliver broader value to society. It is a different expectation altogether and in some ways more demanding.

These descriptions of faculty by discipline, while generalized, remind us that everyone brings different expectations, prejudices, and personal experiences to any discussion of entrepreneurship. In disciplines that are rarely on the winning side of the free market, faculty will be considerably less eager, we discovered, to trust market forces and may voice considerable resistance to entrepreneurship's perceived bottom-line orientation. Over time, we grew to honor and respect those experiences; it may be that even the language we use should reflect the variety of impressions many disciplines have of entrepreneurship and, more broadly, the free-market system. In short, we discovered that conversations with different groups of faculty had their own rhythms and timing. Instead of being discouraged, we eventually understood it was part of an organic process that would ultimately dictate its own resolution.

While we had science faculty clamoring to launch a scientific entrepreneurship track in the undergraduate minor, for instance, a similar track in the arts took twice as long to emerge. While the sciences adhered almost exclusively to a commercial focus in their course offerings, the arts took a much more open (even free-wheeling) and less commercial direction, allowing a range of activities and interests to be incorporated. In short, we believed the Kenan Institute's role to be to introduce entrepreneurship in as many different disciplines and schools as possible. To do so, we decided not to be overly invested in one rigid definition or approach. Risk-taking needs air to breathe, we concluded, and we provided lots of air for entrepreneurship to find traction across campus.

That being said, we were not blind to the difficulties raised by such a motley approach. As the initiative gained traction and developed momentum, we felt increasingly obliged to provide focus and definitional rigor. In providing a big tent where almost anyone could feel comfortable, we recognized that we had to be careful not to accept just any applied effort as entrepreneurial. This was especially true in social entrepreneurship, a term with increasing appeal in popular culture that often runs the danger of losing its true meaning. For instance, we felt it was important to distinguish public service from social entrepreneurship. In public service, a person is contributing to the common welfare but is not expecting any financial or other resource returns for her effort. There is no expectation or desire for a return. True entrepreneurial ventures, even if their aims are social instead of commercial, require some kind of return on investment and, over time, resources that enable the venture to survive and grow.

Such definitional rigor was communicated in several fashions. Most important, there was the power of the annual budgeting process: programs that were not consistently meeting CEI's mission either in implementation or focus were cancelled. For instance, a series of faculty fellowships at UNC's Institute for the Arts and Humanities (IAH) that provided one-semester sabbaticals to faculty who were engaged in research or projects that had an entrepreneurial focus seemed to lose its way as time went on. Some faculty fellows who were selected had projects that, on reflection, were minimally related to entrepreneurship, and the program did little to inculcate a stronger sense of true entrepreneurship. Eventually, we determined IAH was probably not philosophically well equipped to host the effort and it was cancelled.

Likewise, a series of undergraduate summer research fellowships housed at Carolina's Office of Undergraduate Research (OUR) also labored under vague definitions of entrepreneurship. While some funded student projects each year were exemplary, there were a number of students whose understanding of entrepreneurship seemed minimal. In all, the program was successful in that it formally introduced entrepreneurship as a focus where it never existed before. Undergraduate research is a bragging point for Carolina, and it is widely believed to be an important part of our undergraduate education. OUR's mission—providing students the opportunity to conduct primary research, learn firsthand the scientific process of discovery, and to communicate research results through scholarship or public presentations—had significant overlap with core principles of entrepreneurial activity, we believed. The fit proved less perfect in practice, though, than originally thought.

One explanation for this and other relative failures of CEI programs to catch on as planned may be that the operating culture and the mission of some standing programs were so firmly established that the tenets of entrepreneurship, in spite of everyone's best efforts, remained peripheral. In our view, it is unrealistic to think that every university department or unit will adopt entrepreneurship as a core principle. The quest to transform UNC into an entrepreneurial university does not demand perfection; several well positioned and successful efforts will win the day.

The programs we did target, though, were worthwhile experiments. They allowed us to discover where on campus entrepreneurship could flourish and generate the most impact. Over the past five years, some environments worked better than others, sometimes due to philosophical differences, sometimes due to leadership, sometimes due to timing. If expectations were proven incorrect, that was just as valuable an outcome as a rousing success. Under the guise of a cross-campus initiative, we could test our instincts and feel free to explore all options. The risk brought its own rewards. The freedom to experiment programmatically without recrimination established a freer, more creative atmosphere for CEI, which in fact replicated the very entrepreneurial attitudes we were trying to inculcate elsewhere on campus.

An Extensive and Ongoing Communications and Marketing Strategy

Critical to our success was an early and unwavering commitment to a comprehensive, integrated communications and marketing campaign. The complexity of launching a large number of programs at once dictated nothing less. An extensive Web site was launched almost immediately.[19] Advertisements in the *Daily Tar Heel,* the popular daily campus newspaper, were used to announce the initiative and publicize the wave of activities and events sponsored by the Kauffman grant. High-profile speakers such as Bill Drayton, the founder of the Ashoka Foundation and the person who first popularized the concept of social entrepreneurship, were brought to campus early on to attract large audiences. Much of the marketing and publicity for CEI was handled by a communications consultant hired by the Kenan Institute. The dedicated resource paid off many times over, allowing us to populate the CEI Web site and other print and radio venues with entrepreneur profiles and stories about CEI. While some publicity would have occurred naturally, communication resources and staff at the university are sorely limited. A dedicated communications consultant allowed us to augment normal campus coverage with much more extensive and in-depth stories, photographs, and interviews. We coordinated our work closely with the communications staffs of various schools to ensure that CEI was provided significant visibility in individual school publications and Web sites.

The Kenan Institute also produced a number of original printed materials for CEI. An important by-product of CEI was the enhanced ability to project a university-wide brand for entrepreneurship. Early on, for instance, the Kenan Institute produced a campus-wide brochure highlighting the entrepreneurship activities and resources available at UNC. In effect, this brought together all the campus's entrepreneurship efforts, even those that were not formal CEI programs, in one comprehensive and integrated publication. The consistency of message generated outside attention and greater visibility, resulting in a long list of important accolades and awards for UNC. In 2004, for instance, UNC was named the most entrepreneurial campus in the United States by the *Princeton Review* and Forbes.com.[20]

In order to fulfill reporting requirements for the Kauffman Foundation, the institute also began collecting data on entrepreneurial activity, classes, extracurricular opportunities, research, and venture-creation efforts. While enormously difficult to collect, especially in the initial years of the program, this information proved to be a treasure mine. The data bolstered our responses to national surveys and helped us demonstrate real impact and progress.

The Kauffman Campuses Initiative required a strong upfront commitment from top university leaders. Each university chancellor or president, for instance, was required to travel to Kansas City to participate personally in his or her institution's final presentation to the foundation. This meant of course that university leaders were more invested in the effort and felt a stronger sense of ownership in its success. For UNC, then-chancellor James Moeser proved to be an enormous asset. His involvement, especially in the early days of the program, was important in providing CEI immediate credibility and visibility on campus. Our communications strategy included using the chancellor as much as possible to help sell entrepreneurship and its benefit to the university. Moeser had prominent mention in all of our printed materials, and we often included pictures of him at CEI events, which he routinely attended. An annual celebration dinner tied to the final round of our business-plan competition, for example, proved to be a special opportunity to have Moeser recognize CEI's successes from the past year and to articulate the evolving vision of how entrepreneurship was transforming Carolina. The popular and large-scale event offered an appealing platform to announce special achievements, such as faculty members who had received patents during the previous year. The increased attention on innovation and venture creation at high-profile events proved useful in generating more interest in CEI from faculty, staff, students, and alumni. The university celebrates what it values, and the clear message was that entrepreneurship was valued at Carolina.

Risk-taking behaviors associated with entrepreneurship are more prevalent when individuals see their peers participating. At UNC, there is no shortage of examples of campus entrepreneurs whose stories are inspirational and worth sharing. With a coordinated communications and marketing effort geared to both external and internal constituents, CEI brought the stories of these campus entrepreneurs to a much larger audience. For instance, a CEI e-newsletter, which is sent to over 3,000 subscribers 10 times a year, highlights an entrepreneur each month with an extensive profile and description of his or her venture. More recently, CEI ventures have been highlighted in full-page, four-color advertisements in the *Carolina Alumni Review,* the UNC alumni magazine, which is sent to over 200,000 alumni six times a year. The constant stream of profiles and press stories has elevated the entrepreneurial activities of our students, faculty, and staff. They have been encouragements to others on campus to begin pursuing their own entrepreneurial ventures and to enroll in one or more of our CEI programs. These peer role models are critical to establishing and promoting an environment where entrepreneurship is encouraged.

We have been fortunate to have several of our more prominent faculty members receive extended accolades for their entrepreneurial efforts. Holden Thorp, who was viewed as one of the most entrepreneurial of our younger faculty and who served as CEI's first champion for scientific entrepreneurship, was selected chancellor, for instance, at the age of 43. His background as a distinguished scientist, lab researcher, entrepreneur, and businessman were all emphasized at the announcement of his selection.[21] His meteoric rise at the university underscored how an entrepreneurial mindset could pay big dividends not only in the marketplace but also at a major research university. Likewise, Joseph DeSimone, the Chancellor's Eminent Professor of Chemistry, has received national acclaim for his commercial ventures and entrepreneurial acumen. In 2008, he added the $500,000 Lemelson-MIT Prize, the largest and most distinguished prize for inventors in the United States, to a long list of other prominent national awards and recognitions. DeSimone was named the 2008 Tar Heel of the Year by the Raleigh *News and Observer,* generating an extensive front-page profile that detailed how this entrepreneur/scientist was helping to reshape the way that the university is bringing academic discoveries to market.[22] With faculty celebrities like these, CEI has been able to point to home-grown UNC entrepreneurs who have achieved remarkable success. It is a potent argument for how entrepreneurship is assuming a central role in the life—and future—of the university.

Offering Multiple Points of Entry into Entrepreneurship Programs

We have outlined how creating a culture where risk-taking is encouraged and how an aggressive communications and marketing strategy enabled a new, more entrepreneurial environment to take root at Carolina. In addition to these, another critical learning from our experience—and one which we are just now fully realizing—is the need for CEI to provide UNC students, faculty, and staff multiple points of entry into our programs. In the early years when our attention was focused on launching programs, we did not fully consider how the different CEI programs might interrelate and how students or faculty or staff members might move among the multiple CEI offerings. For the most part, we evaluated each program as a discrete effort. Over time, though, we have seen the value of building upon one CEI experience that then leads to another. In short, a program network ladder has developed where participants increasingly learn from one another and forge different paths among CEI offerings to meet their individual needs. For example, a series of first-year seminars in entrepreneurship rooted in different disciplines has proven to be a wonderful feeder for the minor in entrepreneurship.[23]

Likewise, the Carolina Challenge, our business-plan competition, is often used as a class assignment for students in the minor and for teams in our Launching the Venture (LTV) program. For students in the minor, the Challenge offers an opportunity to create a business plan, a considerable undertaking that many have never attempted before, with the rewards and the excitement of the competition as a key motivator. For these students, it is an educational exercise more than a venture-creation strategy. On the other hand, Launching the Venture, a CEI program that helps projected ventures, both commercial and social, move to actual implementation, typically generates a different kind of participant for the Challenge. While all LTV students have already written a business plan through the program, the opportunity to refine the document, present their value proposition and business plan to external judges, and possibly win part of the $50,000 in prizes to help support their venture makes the Challenge an exciting and valuable venture-creation opportunity.

While these two groups of participants have different motivations for entering the competition, the experience transforms their thinking and sometimes their decisions about how to move forward. The Challenge motivates many undergraduate students to apply for Launching the Venture: the business plan that started as an educational exercise has taken hold of their imagination and they want to make it a reality. The Challenge also inspires some LTV participants to seek a deeper grounding in entrepreneurship principles. As undergraduates, they can apply to the minor, or if they are a graduate student, staff or faculty member, they have the option of completing a Graduate Certificate in Entrepreneurship, another CEI program that provides these constituents access to entrepreneurship classes and training. This cross-fertilization of programs has become more pronounced over time and underscores the continuing need for a university-wide brand that helps to bring together all the different offerings. This one-stop-shopping model has provided Carolina students, faculty, and staff an easy, clear-cut way to find a program that suits their specific needs.

Many CEI programs, though, are academically structured, that is, credit-bearing and requiring a significant time commitment, both of which can pose significant barriers to participation. Recognizing that some people who want to learn more about entrepreneurship may not be able to participate in such traditional offerings, CEI has experimented with different types of learning models. For instance, each year we have sponsored a Financial Literacy Workshop. The workshop is a three-hour, intensive program that is offered free to anyone in the university community. Taught by an award-winning professor of accounting from the Kenan-Flagler Business School, the program covers fundamental accounting and financial knowledge, such as how to read a balance sheet and how to manage a budget. Each time the workshop is offered it attracts over 200 people. The popularity of the program has led us to consider launching a series of cross-campus workshops to include other important entrepreneurship topics, such as opportunity recognition, sales training (often an overlooked element in entrepreneurship training), communications and marketing, business modeling, and human resources. By providing more of these educational offerings, we believe we can help release some of the potential for innovation hiding in different parts of campus. In short, multiple points of entry into CEI programs mean more participants; more participants mean more entrepreneurial knowledge more widely distributed and a campus closer to fashioning a true entrepreneurial culture.

WORKING WITH FACULTY

Program leadership has been critical to CEI's success. From the start, we recruited some of UNC's most distinguished faculty as champions of individual CEI programs and were blessed that almost all volunteered to help. A series of university seminars, for example, on rotating topics about entrepreneurship in the academy has been led by several prominent members of our faculty. As mentioned earlier, the first champion for scientific entrepreneurship was Holden Thorp, at the time chair of the Department of Chemistry. In almost every instance, CEI programs benefited from the commitment of some of our most visible campus leaders whose reputation carried enormous weight with their colleagues. This kind of demonstration of support and engagement for CEI from star faculty has made the introduction of entrepreneurship across campus much easier.

That said, these faculty members tend to be easy sells; they are already committed entrepreneurs or are quickly persuaded of the value of entrepreneurship in the university environment. As critical as it is to have faculty leaders promoting entrepreneurship, real change only happens when such positive attitudes filter through to as many faculty as possible in as many departments as possible. For several of our programs, we have adopted a one-plus-one teaching strategy, where we pair a faculty member with a practicing entrepreneur for each course. This has been a successful pedagogical strategy, providing faculty members, some of whom have never had direct experience with starting or running a venture, with a teaching partner with specific knowledge of venture creation and business or nonprofit management. Likewise, for the entrepreneur, the addition of the faculty member helps to strengthen the disciplinary rigor of the course.

Early on, we secured an energetic university entrepreneur-in-residence, Burton "Buck" Goldstein, a UNC alumnus, who worked diligently with faculty and students to promote CEI and helped to teach some of the new classes. A full-time entrepreneur-in-residence offered interested students—of which we had many, even from the start—a regular resource to help them discuss entrepreneurship issues, professional opportunities, and venture-creation strategies. Such a constant presence also provided faculty, especially in the College of Arts and Sciences, the opportunity to interact with an entrepreneur day-in and day-out, an experience many had not had before. Familiarity, we learned, breeds comfort, interest, and trust.

One important way we have nurtured this growing interest by College faculty is to provide as many entrepreneurship-related teaching and research opportunities as possible. One of our more successful programs has been a series of CEI first-year seminars. Like many other institutions, UNC established a first-year seminar program in the 1990s to allow students to experience an intimate setting with a leading faculty member on a specially designed, and often interdisciplinary, topic. The program has been exceptionally popular with students and faculty and was an obvious target for CEI funding. CEI course-development grants allow interested faculty to develop seminar offerings in their own discipline that incorporate entrepreneurial elements. It proved to be a winning strategy to encourage a range of faculty members to explore entrepreneurship and its meaning within their own lives and research.

One of our favorite examples is a seminar developed and taught by Ritchie Kendall, professor of English and associate dean for honors. The seminar, "Economic Saints and Villains: The Entrepreneurial Spirit in Early English Literature," explores how entrepreneurial activity has been described and characterized by authors like Chaucer, Defoe, Dickens, Marlowe, and Shakespeare. The course ends by analyzing three films, Oliver Stone's "Wall Street," Mike Nichols's "Working Girl," and Jon Landis's "Trading Places." According to the course description, "the objective throughout is to analyze how literary art, itself a form of economic activity, simultaneously demonizes and celebrates the 'miracle of the marketplace' and those financial pioneers that perform its magic." While this is far removed from the daily requirements of managing a commercial venture, the class offers a perspective on entrepreneurship that is utterly valid. Kendall was so taken with the subject matter he is considering a book about the topic, an outcome he (or we) never anticipated.

Another effort to broaden the intellectual foundation and dialogue for entrepreneurship studies on campus was an annual series of faculty research seminars. Organized by Howard Aldrich, a world-renowned scholar in entrepreneurial studies and a distinguished professor of sociology, the seminars brought to campus 8 to 10 scholars every year to discuss their research in entrepreneurial studies. Aldrich specifically invited scholars from different disciplines to demonstrate how entrepreneurship has become a legitimate field of study in a variety of disciplines and can represent the highest quality research and scholarship. Disciplines represented have included business, economics, philosophy, political science, and sociology, among others. While this program did not attract large numbers of participants (usually 20 individuals for each session), in its own quiet way it helped to establish a broader intellectual foundation for the cross-campus initiative.

It will be interesting to track whether the seminar's other goal—to inspire faculty and graduate students to pursue research in entrepreneurship who otherwise might not have—will be met. Early indications suggest not, but such outcomes may not be apparent for several more years, since research agendas are slow to evolve. The major difficulty in expanding the range of scholars engaged in entrepreneurial studies is the lack of incentives within many departments to explore such issues and the still begrudging respect entrepreneurship has within the academy as a legitimate field of study. The CEI research seminars did make significant headway, though, in softening faculty attitudes by highlighting the high quality research in entrepreneurship that is being published in top journals.

Finally, CEI has offered funding for interested teaching faculty to attend training programs to learn more about venture creation and effective pedagogical strategies for incorporating entrepreneurship into the classroom. The Price-Babson teaching seminars, for example, have been attended by almost a dozen faculty members to date. In the summer of 2009, the College of Arts and Sciences hosted its own version of the seminar for a selected group of faculty. Additional training opportunities will be critical as we move forward.

MANAGING THE ENTERPRISE

We have described some of the administrative and management functions assumed by the Kenan Institute as the university administrator for CEI. Two important issues are worth elaborating: the governance and operations of the initiative and the central role of evaluation in managing outcomes.

Governance and Operations

Critical to the ongoing administration of CEI was the commitment by senior staff to meet weekly as part of the Operations Committee. The one-hour morning meetings set the tone for the rest of the week, helping to highlight action items and to keep everyone accountable for the work that needed to be done. In addition to senior Kenan Institute staff, key representatives from some of the core CEI programs are regular attendants in the meetings as well.[24] Meetings are not simply about the mundane administrative details of executing events or activities; they have also become a forum for discussions, sometimes heated, about program content and direction. Obviously, the ongoing dialogue helps to improve communication among different groups, which is a high priority when there are so many different CEI programs operating at one time. In addition, the meetings often discuss strategy about publicity and marketing; identify leadership or management issues that need to be resolved; and serve as a useful forum for the exchange of new ideas. After each session, a set of notes is distributed that includes highlights, agreed-upon action items, and a list of upcoming events and important deadlines. In this manner, we have a record of our commitments and ensure that details are captured in a comprehensive manner that helps to prevent problems from occurring.

The work of the Operations Committee, we believe, is one of the primary reasons for CEI's success. Without the weekly discipline of the meetings, the cross-campus initiative would be difficult to sustain. Likewise, leveraging the permanent infrastructure of the Kenan Institute has been critical. Without the institute, CEI would have needed to spend considerably more time on staffing up and on the mechanics of program implementation. As it was, the ready-made infrastructure and program expertise of the institute permitted UNC to focus more of its energy on program content and service delivery, enabling us to move quickly on numerous fronts.

While the CEI director and the Operations Committee oversaw the day-to-day needs of the initiative, the ultimate authority for the program rested with the CEI Management Committee. This committee comprised the dean of the College of Arts and Sciences, who served as chair; the dean of the Kenan-Flagler Business School; and the vice chancellor for research and economic development. This trio formed an impressive leadership body and ensured that the effort as it was being launched and implemented maintained the character of the proposal and was balanced among different schools and constituents. The committee also chose the recipients of awards from the Innovations Fund, described earlier, that provided seed funding for new programmatic initiatives. Finally, the Management Committee provided ongoing guidance and policy oversight of the CEI director and his staff.

The selection of the dean of the College as chair of the committee was symbolically important since it signaled the effort was not being driven from the business school, but was emanating from the heart of the university, the College. It also was appropriate in the sense that the majority of new CEI programs were targeted for the College and undergraduate students. As the initiative matured, however, CEI began to work more closely with the professional schools, especially in health affairs where there is significant unmet demand for entrepreneurship training. These increasing forays into the professional schools did not detract from activity in or resources from the College; rather, it took full advantage of the deep competencies of the business school and broadened them to the full university. Even after five years, there is a surprising amount of new activity developing.[25] Recently, the dean of the School of Pharmacy has joined the CEI Management Committee to reflect the growing involvement of health affairs in CEI programming.

This operational and management system proved to be durable and reasonably responsive to the needs of CEI over the course of its five-year run. While CEI benefited from a decentralized approach for managing individual programs, issues arose from time to time about the allocation of resources or the burdens of keeping within the financial or management restrictions imposed by the grant. Whenever possible, we tried to resolve such issues through increased communications among different units. For any issues that resulted in an impasse, the CEI Management Committee served as the final arbiter.

Evaluation

Much was made in the proposal of our commitment to evaluation and the accountability it imposed on our efforts. This actually proved to be true: we jokingly refer to CEI as the most evaluated program in UNC history. The combination of our own internal efforts and the external reviews sponsored by Kauffman has consumed a fair amount of our energy and time. Fortunately, the UNC Office of Institutional Research and Assessment (OIRA) has made this burden manageable. It has assumed leadership for all evaluation efforts, coordinating with the Kauffman Foundation; Mathematica, the external firm hired by Kauffman to evaluate its cross-campus programs; and other affiliated researchers and scholars who have approached UNC about conducting surveys about our entrepreneurship efforts. UNC has volunteered to participate in every evaluation opportunity that has been presented for our consideration.

What has resulted is a fair amount of data that we have been able to use to help manage the initiative. Often, survey results are shared not only with the CEI Operations and Management Committees and faculty and student champions but also with important external boards and alumni, e.g., the board of trustees of the Kenan Institute and the directors of the Kenan Fund. OIRA leaders have participated routinely in the CEI Operations Committee meetings, which allows them to learn in significant detail the programmatic operations of the different efforts. They also have worked closely with program champions in designing different survey instruments or focus groups that will yield the insights and perspectives to help us evaluate how well we are meeting our objectives.

We have spent considerable time discussing impact: beyond measuring simple inputs and outputs, how can we tell whether we have made a significant difference? Longitudinal studies are too preliminary at this stage, five years out, to be of much help and the longer the studies are continued, the more unreliable they often are in imputing any direct cause to CEI programs. These issues are too complex to review here, but the question of CEI's impact is one that we grapple with every day. We continue to try to assess impact using the best models we can develop. We are proposing a series of intensive focus group studies this spring as the initial five-year initiative concludes as part of this ongoing effort.

This chapter's length precludes the option of discussing all the different elements of the management of CEI. The highlights provided here, though, hopefully offer a sense of the different capacities and efforts that have undergirded the cross-campus initiative. In addition to the close engagement with the private sector in the programs (see below), there were approaches and tactics used in the management of CEI that come closer to business models and proved in this instance to be beneficial: (1) a zero-based budgeting model and a detailed financial management system that tracked not only expenses carefully but also collected cost share from other sources; (2) a primary emphasis on communications and marketing that underlined the need to tell the story of entrepreneurship in order to make it succeed in the university environment; (3) a distinct management structure that captured the university power centers and presented a considerable force behind the effort; (4) an evaluation effort that was not merely window-dressing, but that was used to inform and refine our processes and program content; and (5) a disciplined administrative structure that ensured communication, accountability, and continued creativity. While these elements are not exclusively the domain of entrepreneurship and may be found in one form or another on any university campus, CEI helped the

Kenan Institute reconsider how we conduct large-scale initiatives and how management can employ good business and entrepreneurial principles to make them more successful.

PRIVATE-SECTOR ENGAGEMENT

As previously described, the conceptual model for CEI was based on four overlapping concepts: inspire, teach, connect, and create. For purposes of this chapter, we wish to underscore the *connecting* part of our model, to describe briefly how the private sector is specifically engaged with CEI. Three CEI programs are important in this regard: the minor in entrepreneurship; the Carolina Challenge, our business-plan competition; and Launching the Venture, a two-semester course that supports the actual creation and launch of commercial and social ventures.

Minor in Entrepreneurship

The entrepreneurship minor in the College of Arts and Sciences, housed in the Department of Economics, is one of the great successes of CEI. Designed to provide undergraduates not majoring in business with a solid grounding in entrepreneurship, the minor is now the largest in the College, attracting 100 new students per year, with a total enrollment of 200.

The minor is a four-course sequence with one prerequisite, an introductory course in the principles of economics, and an application essay about the student's specific interests in entrepreneurship. The director of undergraduate studies in the Economics Department and other instructors in the minor review the essays and admit no more than 100 students each year. The first course, Introduction to Entrepreneurship, is a gateway course that provides students basic knowledge about entrepreneurship principles and practice. Afterwards, students are divided among four different tracks: commercial, social, scientific, and artistic. Each track has its own specialized workshop course and a different team of instructors, typically a faculty member paired with an actual entrepreneur from the field. Buck Goldstein, our university entrepreneur-in-residence, has played an active role in bringing entrepreneurs and leading business people into the minor's courses.

During the summer, each student must complete an internship with an entrepreneurial venture. Internships are managed through a full-time coordinator who works with students to identify and secure an appropriate placement. We often comment that entrepreneurship is a contact sport: you cannot learn about entrepreneurship solely through book learning; you must experience entrepreneurship in practice in order to appreciate its complexities and power. Thus, the internships are critical; students return from their summer experience with new and often different insights into the nature and practice of entrepreneurship. Placements are identified and secured mainly through the UNC alumni network, facilitated by a Minor Advisory Working Group, which is composed of alumni supporters of the program. In 2008, 61 companies and nonprofits hosted UNC interns from the entrepreneurship minor.

The response from internship hosts has been encouraging. Several have reported that the minor interns consistently outperformed other college interns and, in a few instances, even recent hires. Placements in the United States are concentrated in North Carolina, New York, and Atlanta, though some have been in other cities and states as well.

Approximately 15 students each year are selected to have their internship experience in China. This unique opportunity was developed to expose a group of students to how entrepreneurship is experienced in Asia and the phenomenon of entrepreneurship migration. Among those who developed the content for the minor, and more generally CEI, there was a strong consensus that an experience in Asia was especially important for budding entrepreneurs. Asians are among the most entrepreneurial people in the world, specifically the Chinese, who have a long tradition of dispersing throughout the region (and the world) to launch and run new ventures. For the past several years, UNC students have worked side-by-side with Chinese entrepreneurs in a variety of firms. Upon returning to school, minor students conclude their study with a capstone course that helps them to integrate their summer internship experience with their other academic studies.

The minor is attracting a diverse group of majors, though it has not achieved the ethnic diversity and gender balance we hope to have eventually.[26] One of the alumni entrepreneurs who has become involved with the program, Julia Sprunt, a former senior executive with Turner Broadcasting, has not only become an instructor in the program but has sponsored the development of a Women's Entrepreneurship Network to support young female entrepreneurs. Meetings of the group are restricted to female students enrolled in the minor and include informal discussions with successful and often prominent female entrepreneurs who share their experiences and the gender challenges they have faced.

The minor also has an active speakers' series that brings to the classroom a range of individuals who speak to different aspects of launching or owning a company or managing a nonprofit. Particular emphasis has been placed on venture financing, with experts in the field bringing their insights to the students and their examination of different case studies. Recent speakers have run the gamut from highly visible entrepreneurs, such as Ted Turner and Stonyfield Farm's CEO Gary Hirshberg, to prominent academics like Harvard Business School's Michael Porter, to local individuals who have achieved extraordinary success through new innovations or ventures. The interaction with the students is extensive and often in small-group settings.

The curriculum for the minor has evolved during the five years. Recently, for instance, a new mini-course in sales was added thanks to the generosity of a donor. (Those who claim entrepreneurship cannot be taught often cite the lack of sales training in university programs as a specific failing.)[27] Entrepreneurs, at the end of the day, have to learn how to sell themselves as well as their product or service.

Carolina Challenge

The Carolina Challenge, our business-plan competition, is the one student-run CEI program. The Challenge is modeled after many business-plan competitions conducted at other universities. During the fall, students, faculty, and staff are encouraged to enroll to compete in a variety of informational meetings held around campus. During the spring, the Challenge offers learning programs to help teams develop their business plans and practice and refine their pitches. The formal competition begins in February and through a series of successive rounds concludes in late March/early April at a finale attended by a large crowd of well-wishers.

At each stage of the competition, a panel of judges is recruited to evaluate the presentations. Local judges are drawn mainly from the Research Triangle Park, but as the competition becomes more intense, the student leaders attract prominent judges from across the country. There is interest in future years in even having a special panel of celebrity judges (entrepreneurs and senior business executives with national name recognition) to help evaluate the winners and bring more visibility to the competition. Judges provide participants extensive feedback on the submitted business plans; some have even become investors in the nascent ventures.

The Challenge takes advantage of business resources in the area through a series of informational workshops they organize for competing teams. The sessions are designed to assist teams in the development of their business plans, from legal organization to venture financing, and to help inform and refine the actual oral presentations so that they are as persuasive as possible. (During the competition, each team has only seven minutes to present its business plan, so there is a premium placed on elegant and succinct expression.) These sessions have led to ongoing partnerships with different service providers in the region, which have expanded their participation in different ways. For instance, a prominent law firm in the area has provided a package of legal services to the final winners of the Challenge.

Launching the Venture

In many respects, Launching the Venture (LTV) picks up where the Carolina Challenge ends and includes a more intensive engagement with the private sector, designed for those individuals who have completed initial preparations for establishing a commercial or social venture and are ready to proceed with implementation. Open to any UNC student, faculty, or staff, the two-module course provides intensive hands-on training, extensive interaction with private-sector experts, and a comprehensive curriculum to take nascent ventures and turn them into reality. Class applications are made available in the early fall; applicants must be committed to starting their business or nonprofit within 12 to 18 months. Typically, 20 to 30 teams are selected after a careful review of submitted materials.

The first module, the Feasibility Phase, continues through the fall and tests the marketability of the targeted product or service and reviews the fundamentals of a good business plan to ensure financial viability of the venture. About 35 coaches, drawn mainly from the private sector, work extensively with the teams throughout this initial phase. Many of the coaches come from the entrepreneur-rich Research Triangle Park and represent key disciplines, such as marketing, technology, and finance. Screened by the director of the program, coaches are matched with LTV teams based on the team's specific needs and the expertise and background of the coach. Coaches are not compensated for their time, but many establish personal connections with the venture team leaders that prove to be mutually rewarding in the future.

Of the original group selected, a smaller group is allowed to proceed to the second module, the Launch Phase, where the goal is to transform the business plan into an actionable document for a self-sustaining venture. The coaches continue to be intimately involved with their teams, but they are now supplemented with a cohort of MBA students, who are assigned to work with the remaining teams. In this intensive stage of the program, there is a legal clinic that is organized and run by regional law firms that cover issues related to legal organization and governance. This year, four law firms are participating in the clinic.

A final, voluntary module, the Venture Finance Phase, helps participants refine their financial models, determine capitalization requirements, and learn about the different kinds of private financing that are available and how to develop a plan to attract it. The clinic is organized by

PricewaterhouseCoopers. Teams of accountants are brought in to work with LTV participants to develop sound financial models and projections for their ventures. Finally, regional equity firms and angel and venture-banking sources participate in this module to provide LTV teams a comprehensive understanding of venture finance and what the options may be for capitalizing different stages of growth.

NOW WHAT?

We believe the key to CEI's success was having an external force—the Kauffman Foundation—spark the cross-campus effort. The institutional and financial barriers for university-wide efforts are high, but given the general tensions surrounding the influence of the private sector in higher education, a cross-campus entrepreneurship program might have been altogether impossible without Kauffman's support. In addition to providing substantial seed funds, Kauffman's imprimatur as one the nation's leading foundations helped to arouse everyone's attention, especially senior administration and faculty, and to legitimize the effort. In the final analysis, the ability to bring different units and schools around the table to develop and coordinate a range of entrepreneurship programs was a direct benefit of the association with Kauffman. No doubt, the prospect of a nationwide competition helped to energize the university as well; rankings and competitions are the bane of most universities, but institutions do respond to opportunities that provide some degree of bragging rights. For these reasons, we hope that the Kauffman Foundation will continue its financial support to cross-campus entrepreneurship efforts. Its leadership is—at least at this juncture—irreplaceable.

What is tantalizing is the realization that we are only scratching the surface of our full potential. Some of the largest opportunities in entrepreneurship at the university are still untapped, particularly in the professional schools. As discussed before, our initial target audience for CEI was the College of Arts and Sciences, which has the majority of students and faculty. We believed it was critical to establish a viable entrepreneurship effort firmly first in the College, the heart of the university. Without infusing the College with an appreciation for entrepreneurship and a more creative, open environment for innovation, the prospects for a longer-term, sustainable cross-campus program would be diminished.

Entrepreneurship tends to blossom more easily in the professional schools, where the idea of specialized training is part of what is expected in graduate education and where students are more emotionally and professionally tied to the workplace. There is much work ahead, we know, to extend our initial successes in the College and expand and intensify our programming with the professional schools to become an even more robust cross-campus initiative.

Any cross-campus effort, though, does run afoul of some harsh realities. Large research universities are dominated by schools and usually strong deans who are rightly charged with protecting the interests of their particular school; in this, Carolina is no different. University-wide initiatives tend to be less popular with deans, who typically view them as underfunded, with intrusive mandates, and as potentially draining needed resources from core school programs. The criticism is often true: cross-campus efforts do not typically have a strong fund-raising infrastructure in place to help secure needed financial resources. These challenges are not unique to entrepreneurship cross-campus programs, of course, but they do underscore just how important the Kauffman grant played in making CEI possible and highlight some of the challenges we will face as we move forward.

Universities are notorious for political minefields and even with the Kauffman national brand and all the success we have enjoyed, UNC has still had to negotiate its fair share of turf battles, personality conflicts, and disagreements over priorities. As with any significant effort, this is to be expected. Any attempt to change the culture of a large organization will encounter resistance. Launching new programs involves hard work and determination. For the most part, these internal complexities have been successfully negotiated over time.

The CEI Management Committee has been instrumental in ensuring that such issues do not derail the larger goal and overall mission of the program; the committee also provides a considerable counterbalance to opposing forces since it includes deans of some of the most powerful schools at the university and works at the behest and blessing of the chancellor. In short, the commitment of these senior administrators led by the chancellor is clearly important to the long-term viability of a cross-campus initiative. If CEI ever retreats to be simply an outreach program of one school, for instance, or loses the public support and imprimatur of the chancellor or provost, its credibility, ability to leverage resources, and impact will be seriously diminished.

Sustainability, as with any university program, then becomes the overriding issue as the initial grant period ends. In retrospect, we wish a dedicated development officer had been hired for CEI right at the onset of the award and for the Management Committee to be more closely engaged with the fund-raising needs of the program. The identification and cultivation of donors is a labor-intensive and time-intensive process. If such work had been initiated at the beginning of the program, CEI would have secured more funds to ensure its future.

In the flush of winning a major award, fund-raising is typically the last thing university leaders want to focus on, but it demands closer attention. There is an unfortunate but widespread belief that entrepreneurship is an easy ask, that there are many donors who would be attracted to this kind of effort, so development efforts tend to be more casual. While entrepreneurship might appeal to some donors, it is always the case that money never simply walks in the door. A good development strategy requires time, dedication of program leaders, and the support of well-qualified professional development staff. An earlier, more comprehensive fund-raising push would have been a more effective and strategic choice.

Kauffman required a 2:1 match for its $3.499 million grant to UNC. This match could be met either with in-kind donations or with new, hard cash donations. UNC met its matching requirement a full year before the end of the five-year deadline, but much of that total was met with in-kind resources. Certain CEI programs, though, did attract significant external funding. The minor, for instance, developed an Advisory Working Group of prominent alumni entrepreneurs to help shape the curriculum and to serve as a vehicle for raising funds. They have already been successful in their early fund-raising efforts and have recently launched a $12.6 million fund-raising initiative to build an endowment and expendable funds sufficient to continue the program permanently.

The Carolina Challenge also has attracted a fair amount of external support, including a sizeable endowment to help fund the prize money awarded each year and the annual expenses for running the competition. Local businesses have provided sponsorships for the final round of the competition that are then used to supplement the annual budget and to pay for the final celebration event when the winners are announced.

These examples of fund-raising success, however, do not provide the funding for the infrastructure and administrative expenses of the larger cross-campus effort. This money will probably be the most difficult to raise since it falls outside of any particular school's responsibility, but it represents some of the most important resources since it supports the management and operations of the larger initiative. While the Kenan Institute has contributed its own infrastructure to support CEI over the past five years, it cannot do so permanently without additional funds.

In the 2009–10 academic year, CEI is losing its organizing principle, the Kauffman Foundation grant, as well as its dedicated stream of funding. It makes for an uncertain time. The external validation of the foundation and the prospect of winning a significant award motivated people to work together on the common effort; with that gone, the university will need to determine how such a cross-campus program will work, what kind of governance structure is needed, and how best to fund its ongoing programs. In short, the university will need to establish cross-campus entrepreneurship as a continuing priority in order for the initiative to succeed and grow.

CONCLUSION

It is difficult not to see in the elevation of Holden Thorp as the chancellor of UNC a strong endorsement of the value of entrepreneurship in the highest ranks of higher education. Thorp was widely known for his entrepreneurial ventures based on his chemistry research and was an early and active participant in CEI. (Thorp's boss, UNC system President Erskine Bowles, is himself a strong advocate of entrepreneurship. In addition to serving as White House chief of staff during the Clinton administration, Bowles also served as head of the U.S. Small Business Administration.)

Having the leader of the university and the university system embrace entrepreneurship as a core function of higher education is indisputably a transforming opportunity for UNC. At the 2007 CEI annual celebration, Thorp provided dinner remarks for the occasion. In his speech, "Keeping the Idea Alive," Thorp unambiguously declared that entrepreneurship is here to stay:

> I'm convinced that weaving entrepreneurship into the fabric of Carolina's teaching and scholarship will redefine higher education as unapologetically rigorous within our traditional disciplines and, at the same time, startlingly pragmatic. This description leverages our extraordinary ability to create knowledge with a relentless determination for doing something with it.

Leaders like Thorp are increasingly common in higher education, a trend that indicates American colleges and universities are beginning to address the challenges of the future by embracing entrepreneurship and thinking creatively about how higher education and the private sector can work together. By being "unapologetically rigorous" and "startlingly pragmatic," universities can—and should—assume a bolder and larger role in the marketplace. While it must retain its fundamental nature as an institution of higher learning, the university misses something when it neglects the power of matching its knowledge-building and innovation-driving capacity with simple die-hard pragmatism—the ability to turn ideas into enterprises. At first, it may be startling, even disruptive, but the entrepreneurial university is here to stay as a force in higher education. We believe it is a good thing.

NOTES

1. See Stanley Aronowitz, *The Knowledge Factory: Dismantling the Corporate University and Creating True Higher Learning* (Boston: Beacon Press, 2000); Derek C. Bok, *Universities in the Marketplace: The Commercialization of Higher Education* (Princeton, NJ: Princeton University Press, 2003); Adrianna J. Kezar, "Obtaining Integrity? Reviewing and Examining the Charter between Higher Education and Society," *The Review of Higher Education* 27, no. 4 (Summer 2004), 429–59; Christopher Newfield, *Unmaking the Public University* (Cambridge, MA: Harvard University Press, 2008); Sheila Slaughter and Larry L. Leslie, *Academic Capitalism: Politics, Policies, and the Entrepreneurial University* (Baltimore, MD: Johns Hopkins University Press, 1997); and *Buying In or Selling Out? The Commercialization of the American Research University,* ed. Donald G. Stein (New Brunswick, NJ: Rutgers University Press, 2004). See also Simon Marginson and Mark Considine, *The Enterprise University: Power, Governance and Reinvention in Australia* (Cambridge, United Kingdom: Cambridge University Press, 2000): "If we continue to subsume the academic functions of the university into its corporate identity, building institutions for the sake of the institutions themselves and losing sight of the fact that it is in teaching, research, and scholarship that universities make their distinctive social contributions, we will impoverish the university as an institution and pave the way for the shift of its academic functions into a generic corporate environment. This might be good for business, but it would not be very good for education." (35)

2. See, for example, the recent controversy at Harvard Medical School as reported by *New York Times* reporter Duff Wilson: "Harvard Medical School in Ethics Quandary," March 2, 2009, http://www.nytimes.com/2009/03/03/business/03medschool.html?_r=1&scp=6&sq=Duff%20Wilson&st=cse; and "Senator Asks Pfizer About Harvard Payments," March 3, 2009, http://www.nytimes.com/2009/03/04/business/04pfizer.html?scp=2&sq=pfizer&st=cse.

3. See Patricia Cohen, "Conservatives Try New Tack on Campuses," *New York Times,* September 22, 2008, http://www.nytimes.com/2008/09/22/education/22conservative.html?scp=1&sq=COnservatives%20Try%20New%20Tack&st=cse.

4. According to the U.S. Department of Education's National Center for Education Statistics, in fall 2008, there were over 18.3 million estimated students in post-secondary degree-granting institutions. Of those,

13.7 million (75%) were in public institutions, 4.6 million (25%) in private institutions.

5. Katie Zezima, "Data Show College Endowments Loss is Worst Drop Since '70s," *New York Times,* January 26, 2009, http://www.ny times.com/2009/01/27/education/27college.html?scp=1&sq=Data%20 shows%20college&st=cse.

6. According to the Council for the Advancement and Support of Education (CASE), there have been 66 fund-raising campaigns of $1 billion or more, the largest being $4.3 billion currently underway at Stanford University. With the recent financial crisis and the dramatic decrease in endowment values, the demand for increased fund-raising will only increase. See Stan Katz, "Universities, Endowments, and the Mega-Rich," *The Chronicle of Higher Education,* September 10, 2008, http://chronicle. com/review/brain storm/katz/universities-endowments-and-the-mega-rich: "Higher-education institutions have been so successful in raising endowment funds that last year [2007] there were 76 colleges and universities with endowments exceeding $1 billion, and another 9 in the $900 million range. And, of course, the largest endowments are huge: As of a year ago, Harvard had $35 billion, Yale $23 billion, and Stanford $17 billion in endowment assets."

7. See John Schwartz, "Dreamers and Doers," *New York Times,* January 4, 2009; Steve Lohr, "A Capitalist Jolt for Charity," *New York Times,* February 24, 2008; and Nicholas D. Kristoff, "Do-Gooders With Spreadsheets," *New York Times,* January 30, 2007.

8. Thomas L. Friedman, *The World Is Flat: A Brief History of the Twenty-First Century* (New York: Farrar, Straus & Giroux, 2005), and Samuel P. Huntington, "The Clash of Civilizations," *Foreign Affairs* (Summer 1993) and *The Clash of Civilizations and the Remaking of World Order* (New York: Simon and Schuster, 1996).

9. One signal that entrepreneurship has arrived on campus and is becoming a respected discipline is the debate over a proper definition. There are many. At UNC-Chapel Hill, we have defined entrepreneurship as the launching of ventures that create value—either commercial or social—and that generate sufficient resources to sustain and grow the venture. See J. Barton Cunningham and Joe Lischeron, "Defining Entrepreneurship," *Journal of Small Business Management* 29, no. 1 (January 1991), 45–61; Robert F. Hébert and Albert N. Link, "In Search of the Meaning of Entrepreneurship," *Small Business Economics* 1, no. 1 (March 1989), 39–49; William Andrews Sahlman, Howard H. Stevenson, Amar Bhide, and Michael J. Roberts, *The Entrepreneurial Venture* (Cambridge, MA: Harvard Business Press, 1999); Hector Rocha and Julian Birkinshaw, *Entrepreneurship Safari: A Phenomenon-Driven Search for Meaning* (Boston,

MA: Now Publishers Inc, 2007); and Peter F. Drucker, *Innovation and Entrepreneurship* (New York: HarperCollins, 1993).

10. See Paula Wasley, "Entrepreneurship 101: Not Just for Business School Anymore," *Chronicle of Higher Education* 54, no. 41 (June 20, 2008).

11. See Kauffman's 2008 report, "Entrepreneurship in American Higher Education," http://www.kauffman.org/uploadedfiles/entrep_high_ed_report.pdf . On the critical role of entrepreneurs in the economy and for job creation, see the foundation's round-up of current research at http://www.kauffman.org/newsroom/research-roundup.aspx.

12. Carl Schramm, "The Broken M.B.A.," *Chronicle of Higher Education* 52, no. 42 (June 23, 2006).

13. The eight original KCI campuses are: University of North Carolina-Chapel Hill; Florida International University; Howard University; University of Illinois at Urbana-Champaign; University of Rochester; University of Texas-El Paso; Wake Forest University; and Washington University in St. Louis. In December 2006, Kauffman awarded a second round of awards to the following institutions: Arizona State University; Georgetown University; Purdue University; Syracuse University; University of Wisconsin-Madison; University of Maryland-Baltimore County; and several northeast Ohio schools in partnership with the Burton D. Morgan Foundation, including: Baldwin-Wallace College; College of Wooster; Hiram College; Lake Erie College; and Oberlin College.

14. UNC-Chapel Hill received $3.499 million from the Kauffman Foundation, which had to be matched by the university 2 to 1, making it an $11 million initiative.

15. In addition to UNC assessments and evaluations, the Kauffman Foundation engaged an independent firm, Mathematica, of Princeton, New Jersey, to conduct ongoing evaluations of the Kauffman campuses.

16. This quotation comes from a statement by former Chancellor James Moeser endorsing CEI and outlining his own ambitions for the initiative at its launch.

17. http:// www.cednc.org.

18. From the final proposal, "Carolina Entrepreneurial Initiative," submitted to the Kauffman Foundation on November 19, 2003.

19. http:// www.cei.unc.edu.

20. Other recent awards include: Most Innovative Entrepreneurship Pedagogy Award, U.S. Association for Small Business and Entrepreneurship, 2004; No. 3, "Top Colleges for Entrepreneurs," *Entrepreneur,* 2005; Entrepreneurial Excellence Award for Community Impact, Council for Entrepreneurial Development, 2005; Global Consortium for Entrepreneurship Centers Award for Excellence in Enterprise Creation for the Launching

the Venture Program, 2007; No. 10, Top Graduate Programs, *Princeton Review* and *Entrepreneur,* 2008; Global Consortium for Entrepreneurship Centers Education Award for Excellence in Specialty Entrepreneurship Education for the Venture Capital Investment Competition, 2008. UNC-Chapel Hill has also recently hosted two prominent entrepreneurship conferences, the 2005 National Consortium of Entrepreneurship Centers Directors Conference and the 2008 Babson/Kauffman Entrepreneurship Research Conference.

21. According to his official UNC biography, Thorp has published more than 130 scholarly articles on the electronic properties of DNA and RNA. He invented technology for electronic DNA chips that is the basis of 19 issued or pending U.S. patents. One invention provides a less expensive blood test to determine if prospective parents carry the cystic fibrosis gene. For his DNA chip technology, Thorp was recognized as one of the Top Innovators of 2001 by *Fortune Small Business* magazine. He also has been adviser, co-founder, or consultant with many small companies, including Novalon Pharmaceuticals, MaxCyte, Osmetech, OhmX and Plextronics. In 2005, Thorp co-founded Viamet Pharmaceuticals, Inc., a biotechnology company targeting metalloenzymes in the fields of infectious disease, inflammation and oncology.

22. See Sarah Avery, "Joe DeSimone—2008 Tar Heel of the Year," Raleigh *News and Observer,* December 28, 2008.

23. Some examples of CEI first-year seminars (and their instructors and discipline) are: "Biologists as Entrepreneurs" (Seth Reice, biology); "Spanish and Entrepreneurship: Languages, Cultures, and North Carolina Communities" (Darcy Lear, romance languages); "Innovation, Entrepreneurship, and Economic Growth" (Maryann Feldman, public policy); "The Entrepreneurial Imagination" (Burton Goldstein, economics); "Organizing and Communication for Social Entrepreneurs" (Steven May, communication studies).

24. The CEI Operations Committee is led by the associate director for administration, Raymond Farrow, and includes the following key staff: John Kasarda, CEI director; Jean Elia, CEI executive associate director; David Oglesby, Patti Harrison, and Karen Stone, CEI financial management; Cyndy Falgout, CEI communications and marketing consultant; Margaret Swanson and Robert Dearborn, CEI administrative support; Jack Walker, CEI information technology specialist; Larry Mayes, CEI evaluation; Lingmei Howell, CEI programs. In addition, representatives from the Minor in Entrepreneurship, including John Stewart, Buck Goldstein, and Genny King, participate; representing the Launching the Venture and Graduate Certificate programs is Ted Zoller; and Jessica Thomas represents BASE, a business accelerator for sustainable enterprise.

25. See, for instance, a recent UNC School of Education newsletter, which highlighted alumni entrepreneurs: Kathryn Williford, "Education Alumni Become Successful Entrepreneurs," *The Carolina Slate* (Spring 2007). The School of Journalism and Mass Communication has hired a new Knight Chair of Journalism and Digital Media Economics, Penelope Muse Abernathy, to help lead the school's efforts to help graduates navigate the dramatic transitions within the journalism industry and identify "this new century's innovative, sustainable forms of news in the public interest." See the school's press release at http://www.jomc.unc.edu/the_news/school_news/penelope_muse_abernathy_803_648.html.

26. In 2007, 67 percent of the entrepreneurship minor students were white and 15 percent were African American or Hispanic. Sixty-four percent were male.

27. See "Education Matters—But Does Entrepreneurship Education? An Interview with David Birch," *Academy of Management Learning and Education* 3, no. 3 (2004): 289–92: "There are three skills that an entrepreneur needs to know and master: selling, managing people, and creating a new product or service. And none of them are taught in the business school. I have never come across a course in any business school called Sales. If you do not have a course on selling how are you going to be helpful to entrepreneurs?" (290).

CHAPTER 3

The Entrepreneurial University in a Triple Helix of Regional Growth and Renewal

Henry Etzkowitz

Very few regions have developed the capability to renew themselves, to move their economy across technological paradigms without experiencing significant gaps. There was a half century gap between the decline of the Boston region's textile, shoe, and machine industries and the growth of the minicomputer cluster. Despite largely missing the personal computer revolution, Boston's transition across technological paradigms in the late 20th century, from minicomputers to biotechnology, was much quicker. Institution-formation projects, such as the invention of the venture capital firm during the 1930s and 1940s, created a regional infrastructure to foster knowledge-based economic development, and made the difference. A well designed university-led project transformed one-off instances of firm formation from academic research at MIT and Harvard into a steady flow of new enterprises as early as the turn of the 19th to the 20th century.

Even Silicon Valley, the global benchmark in high-tech regions, has to struggle to maintain momentum through periodic downturns. In the mid-1990s, Joint Venture Silicon Valley (JVSV), an industry-initiated regional coalition of firms, local governments, and universities, organized a series of public brainstorming sessions. Following a venture capital due diligence model of vigilant selection, JVSV organized Smart Valley, an initiative to develop networking platforms that led to a wave of product innovation. More recently, a pathbreaking development in state science and technology policy has used debt funding mechanisms such as bonds, traditionally utilized for physical infrastructure, to support research and firm formation. Proposition 71, a direct ballot initiative organized by a coalition of university researchers, venture capitalists, and patient advocates, was passed by California voters in 2004, and provides $3 billion for stem cell research and firm formation.

A collaborative process can be identified among university-industry-government both in the incipient stages of growth of a high-tech region and in later stages of renewal. Yet places like Chicago and New York, with great potential given their concentration of research resources, may not realize their full potential due to inability to sustain a collaborative environment. The New York Academy of Sciences attempted to play a convening role in the mid-1990s, but other actors lost interest when the Academy failed to maintain the involvement of the Federal Reserve Bank of New York. The Academy was not taken seriously, acting on its own, in a region where economic actors are preeminent. Nevertheless, despite gaps and lags, new initiatives do appear in New York and elsewhere, with their proponents learning from successes and failures at home and abroad. This chapter provides a framework for the role of the entrepreneurial university in high-tech regional development.

THE NORMS OF THE ENTREPRENEURIAL UNIVERSITY

The entrepreneurial university model can be described in five norms and counter-norms derived from the experience of MIT and Stanford.[1] The creative tension among these norms produces conflicts of interest and obligation and solutions to these problems that integrate new and old academic missions. In the transition to the entrepreneurial university, these norms can also serve as objectives.

1. *Capitalization*. Knowledge is created and transmitted for use as well as for disciplinary advance; the capitalization of knowledge becomes the basis of economic and social development and thus of an enhanced role for the university in society.
2. *Interdependence*. The entrepreneurial university interacts closely with industry and government; it is not an ivory tower isolated from society.
3. *Independence*. The entrepreneurial university is a relatively independent institution; it is not a creature dependent on another institutional sphere.
4. *Hybridization*. The resolution of the tensions between the principles of interdependence and independence is an impetus to the

creation of hybrid organizational formats to realize both objectives simultaneously.

5. *Reflexivity.* There is a continuing renovation of the internal structure of the university as its relation to industry and government changes, and of industry and government as their relationship to the university is revised.

THE ENTREPRENEURIAL UNIVERSITY AND THE REGION

An entrepreneurial university can be either the source of virtually any high-tech region or a consequence of its development. Such a university should be broad enough in its focus to be at the forefront of several areas of advanced science and technology, only some of which have short-term potential for application. If a university is too narrowly focused, say on applied IT, as at Karlskrona/Ronneby in Sweden, the ability to develop alternative knowledge-based sources of economic development may not be available.

Triple helix regions—defined below—may also emerge as the unintended consequences of policies designed for other purposes. For example, the recent emergence of Northern Virginia as a technology region was both a result of its contiguity to the federal government and a consequence of the belief of many that government should decrease in size. On the one hand, the federal government promoted the Star Wars ballistic missile defense system, which required advanced systems development capabilities and complex software. On the other hand, a conservative government wanted to eliminate programs as part of an effort to reduce the size of government. Nevertheless, it still wanted the results of the programs and thus adopted a privatization strategy, generating spin-offs from its laboratories.

A start-up process emerged in the Washington, DC area, formerly a one-industry region based on government, from the government's increasing technology requirements. Firms formed to get government technology contracts wanted to stay close to their customers, the government agencies that were the source of their business. The enhancement of academic capabilities at George Mason University and the development of a northern Virginia extension of Virginia Polytechnic Institute in Blacksburg occurred as a consequence of this government-industry relationship. Northern Virginia is emerging as a triple helix region, led by the presence of government agencies that created a demand for high-tech products and helped create a local industrial and academic base as a byproduct.

A region with an entrepreneurial university at its core can transcend particular technological paradigms and renew itself through new technologies and firms generated from its academic base. The criteria for success are not only the ability to create a cluster of high-tech firms but the ability, over the longer term, to generate additional clusters as earlier successes are superseded. The transition from minicomputers to biotechnology in Boston exemplifies this process of knowledge-based regional renewal across technological paradigms.[2] Relatively few regions have developed the institutional capacity to accomplish this goal. Nevertheless, it is the objective of knowledge-based regional economic development everywhere in the world.

This process may take decades. For example, the firm formation activity that was observed in Silicon Valley in the 1960s and 1970s resulted from initiatives dating from the end of the 19th century of encouraging students from the Stanford engineering school to form firms. It was realized that a great technological university required a support structure of firms. Otherwise, graduates would move elsewhere, and the university would remain a small isolated entity without an industrial base. Stanford University had to take the lead so that there would be a technical industry surrounding the institution.

Transcending the Linear Model

The classic linear model presumed a progression from research to development to innovation and product introduction in which the university was centrally involved only in the first phase, transferring research results with commercial potential. The first step toward an academic entrepreneurial ethos is increased sensitivity to results with practical potential, followed by a willingness to participate in the realization of this potential. This change often occurs through the attention that outsiders pay to academic research.

The entrepreneurial university follows an interactive model of innovation that incorporates linear and reverse linear modes. The original idea was that simply by an infusion of research funds—typically from government—the results would be published and industry would take them up. Now we know it is not so simple a process. Of course, knowledge transfer takes place through publications and the work of graduates, but a more systematic series of mechanisms is required to improve the performance of linearity. There should be people with expertise in transfer on both sides of the equation, on the university side with industrial expertise to find partners in industry, and on the firm side with academic expertise to search universities for useful knowledge and technology. These capabilities must be in place on both sides of the academic-industrial divide if the lateral process is to work well.[3]

The interactive model brings together the two linear models and generates an interaction between them in which basic research questions arise from addressing practical problems and vice versa. The potential of an interactive model became apparent during World War II, when physicists working on engineering problems in wartime research projects like radar, who believed that they had put aside their academic interests, started generating theoretical questions that they would address later. Thus, scientists who had previously opposed federal funding of research, fearing that they would lose their academic freedom, enthusiastically embraced it after the war.

A two-way flow of influence is created between the university and an increasingly knowledge-based society as the distance among institutional spheres is reduced. Universities negotiate partnerships with start-up firms emanating from academic research and invest intellectual and financial capital in exchange for equity in these firms. They also make broad funding arrangements with R&D intensive firms in exchange for preferred access to patent rights and adjunct faculty status for company researchers. The content and formats for teaching, research, and linkage itself are also affected. The assumption of an active role in economic development leaves existing academic missions in place, but it also encourages them to be carried out in new ways.

The development of an assisted linear model of technology transfer (illustrated by Figure 3.1), begins with a liaison office, going a step beyond producing trained graduates and publications that will take knowledge out of the university. Universities have established liaison offices to facilitate contacts, formalizing the process by which firms often make their own contacts through former students and personal connections. An individual liaison officer may take responsibility for organizing interactions between a department or research unit and a group of interested firms. This may take the form of individual meetings, possibly leading to consultation contracts or presentations of a unit's work, typically through graduate student talks, to a group of firms on a regular basis.

University-Industry Relations

In a second stage, knowledge is encapsulated in a technology and moved out by a technology transfer office created to identify, patent, market, and license intellectual property. The technology transfer office operates as a dual search mechanism, pulling technology out of university research groups on the one hand, and finding a place for it on the other. In recent years, universities have explored various ways to add value to early stage

Figure 3.1 Coevolution and Multilinearity of University-Industry Relations

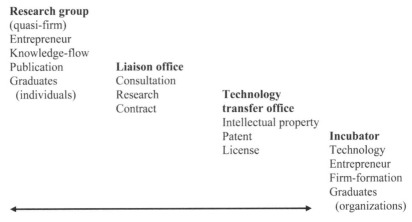

university technologies by conducting marketing surveys, seeking development support, and embodying the technology in a firm.

In a third stage, knowledge and technology are embodied in a firm and moved out of the university by an entrepreneur. Firm formation from academic research was an informal activity for many years, beginning with instrumentation companies arising from work at MIT and Harvard in the late 19th century. The initial formalization of this process took place through the invention of the venture capital firm, which provided an external support structure for firm formation projects that were often initially located in available space in academic buildings. The incubator, a formal organization providing space and other assistance to nascent firms emerging from academic research, was introduced during the early 1980s at Rensselaer Polytechnic Institute, a school previously lacking a tradition of firm formation, and has been widely utilized since.

THE INNOVATIVE REGION

The innovative region is characterized by universities, other science and technology organizations, supporting instruments such as investment funds and angel networks, and organizations to develop regional strategy. The regional innovation environment consists of a set of political, industrial, and academic institutions that, by design or unintended consequence, work to improve the local conditions for knowledge-based development. In this environment, universities, traditionally producers and transmitters of knowledge, also become factors of production.

Such a region undergoes a fundamental transformation to an innovation entity as distinct from a physical geographical area such as a watershed, a cultural area with a linguistic or ethnic group, or even an economic area such as an industrial district or cluster. Regional development was traditionally based on a natural feature such as New York Harbor, the starting point for a global business and financial hub,[4] or the Tennessee Valley watershed, which became the setting for a hydraulic electrification and economic and social development scheme.[5] A region may also emerge as a cluster of traditional firms, as in an Italian or Danish industrial district in shoes or food products, or from new business concepts such as New York City's Silicon Alley multimedia firms.[6]

Regions vary greatly in governance capabilities, with political institutions of various orders from multifunctional governments, such as the German Länder and U.S. states, special purpose districts for transportation, pollution control or business improvement, and quasi-political entities such as high-tech councils that may lack official status. Various actors may play their specialized roles in a regional organizing process. However, if one element is missing or constrained from participating, another may take its part. If a regional government is lacking, a university or industry association may take the lead, for example, in encouraging an industrial district to cooperate with universities or other knowledge-producing institutions. A formal governance structure is no guarantee of organizational coherence in the innovation field, and unofficial structures may serve the purpose better than official ones.

The innovation system concept, presuming coherent structures, has been taken from the nation state and applied to the regional level. However, most regions have significant gaps in their innovation system and need ways to fill these gaps. Thus, it may be best to think of them as environments rather than systems, with some elements in place to foster innovation but not others. Thus, regions may be viewed as thick or thin depending upon the presence or absence of innovation support structures, whether informal or formal. Whether it makes sense for a region to create new organizational mechanisms depends upon whether firm formation is already taking place, for example supported by a network of angel investors, or requires a formal support structure such as an incubator facility to take off. Regions rich in business development requisites such as venture capital and an entrepreneurial culture may appear to have less need to develop explicit organizational mechanisms. On the other hand, regions lacking significant activity may foster regional development by expanding university research capacity in association with transfer mechanisms such as incubators, science parks, and entrepreneurial training schemes.

KNOWLEDGE-BASED ECONOMIC DEVELOPMENT

Route 128 and Silicon Valley have evolved a common model of science-based regional economic development, despite some cultural differences. Continuity in the origins of the model of science-based regional development between Route 128 and Silicon Valley (MIT and Stanford) can be discerned in the work of Vannevar Bush and Frederick Terman, who were, respectively, teacher and student at MIT. The model of science-based economic development from academia through the mechanism of the venture capital firm was transplanted from MIT to Stanford in the early postwar period. Part of the model was transferred because Terman was near MIT during the war as director of the Radar Counter-Measures Lab at Harvard, and had the opportunity to observe MIT's mode of academic development.

In a 1943 letter to the treasurer of Stanford, Terman proposed an intensive replication of the MIT model in northern California. Terman advised his friend that "[from] what I have seen about the way that MIT operates in connection with industry, this is what we have to do as soon as the war is over. We have to form research centers, we have to establish firms. We must make this a central thrust of Stanford if we are to become a major university."[7] The vision that Bush and others at MIT were working from goes back to the ideas of William Barton Rogers. The founder of MIT wrote a report in 1846 propounding the idea of a university, not a technical school, which would be involved in basic research and technological development.

Rogers's idea was that science would infuse industry not merely with low level consulting from engineering design work but with longer-term results of fundamental research. MIT always had a scheme of education broader than merely technical subjects. The goal was to encourage its graduates to take a broad view, appropriate to an organizational leader rather than a technical assistant. Thus, MIT established a humanities department which was oriented to the technical areas. Similarly, when MIT recruited physicists in the 1930s, it recruited the people who had an interest not only in basic research but in the utilization of results. Thus, when Van der Graaf was recruited from Princeton, MIT also arranged to have his patent rights transferred from Princeton to MIT.

Some historians have interpreted the recruitment of basic researchers to MIT during the 1930s as a sign that MIT was moving toward the general research university model in the United States. Actually, Karl Compton, then president of MIT, was recruiting a particular subset of physicists, a subset that had both goals in mind. The integration of academic and business goals is the basis of the entrepreneurial university and knowledge-based regional economic development. The industrial base emanating from a university often retains some of its academic heritage. For example, the biotechnology firms in the Boston and Bay areas, and elsewhere, have a common quasi-academic mode of operation. Advertisements for postdoctoral fellows to work in firms as well as academic laboratories can be found in *Science* and other journals. Common social networks that go back to college and graduate school are sometimes the source for the business and the technical sides of these firms.

Saxenian has emphasized discontinuities of organizational style between these two leading high-tech regions.[8] The issue is structure versus network; vertical organization versus lack of hierarchy. On the one hand, Data General, an old-line minicomputer firm, had a flexible development group in its heyday. On the other hand, the later years of decline at DEC on Route 128 and the recent past of Hewlett Packard, a hierarchical operation in Palo Alto, may not be too dissimilar. As an observer noted, "Resource allocation (a focus on traditional bureaucratic procedures rather than unconventional ways of unleashing new ideas) is just as likely to hobble creativity in large and vibrant Silicon Valley companies as it is in boring, old industrial age companies."[9] The broader significance of this debate lies in the issue of whether these two regions represent unique historical instances or essentially common phenomena.

The implication of the uniqueness hypothesis is that if Silicon Valley and Route 128 were phenomena that arose in particular circumstances, then they may be impossible to replicate. The attempt in the UK to set up science parks may have been misguided, or at least the process often takes longer than many wish to accept. For example, when visitors came from Australia, the UK, and elsewhere to visit the science park at Stanford during the 1970s, the firm formation process they were observing was already the result of 50 years or more of work. The park had originally been built as an industrial park, simply to earn more money for academic development at Stanford. However, the companies that wanted to locate in the park near the university were typically already closely related to the university. The guidelines for the park were soon revised to limit tenants to firms wishing to maintain university links. Thus, the research park was born. The park was the end result, not the starting point, of a process of encouraging the creation of an organizational capacity and ethos to form firms around the university.[10]

Creating the Regional Triple Helix

Europe has announced an ambitious goal of catching up to and surpassing U.S. science-based economic development by 2020. The region has assumed a special significance in this European Union (EU) plan that includes initiatives to develop concentrations of research strengths and bridging mechanisms like the U.S. Small Business Innovation Research (SBIR) program. The EU is constrained by its charter to identify topics not well developed at the national level, and the region meets the EU criteria of adding value where nation states have been relatively inactive. Both declining industrial regions and areas lagging in development have been the focus of attention. The traditional European innovation strategy has been the learning region, based on incremental innovation, emphasizing close relations between firms and customers as the basis for innovation. Building upon existing assets rather than creating new ones is the basic strategy. Universities in a learning region can be expected to focus on traditional university-industry relations such as preparation of trained human capital and on informal relationships such as consultation. Learning regions are more oriented to low-tech than to high-tech, to government-industry relations rather than to university-industry relations.

The U.S. model of discontinuous innovation based on firm formation surpassed the previous innovation fashion of incremental innovation in large firms, characteristic of Japanese corporations, at the turn of the new century. Certainly, the two paradigms are not mutually exclusive. Indeed, combining both approaches is currently the rule. Surely the ultimate objective of initiating start-ups is to grow a reasonable number of these new firms to the scale where they can provide significant employment opportunities and productivity growth. Of course, the goal is also to retain a start-up firm's innovative capacities as it grows large. How to create the conditions to generate a continuous start-up process, at the regional level, is the fundamental issue.[11]

The Triple Helix Spaces

Regional development may be seen as occurring in a series of three non-linear knowledge, consensus, and innovation spaces that overlap and cross-fertilize each other. Knowledge spaces provide the building blocks for technological development, consensus spaces denote the process of getting relevant actors to work together, and innovation spaces denote an organizational invention to enhance the innovation process.

The Knowledge Space

The initial stage is often the creation of knowledge spaces, or concentrations of related R&D activities in a local area, which has been argued to be a necessary condition for knowledge-based regional economic development.[12] These underutilized research resources represent a potential for economic development. For example, the decentralization of laboratories from Mexico City due to the mid-1980s earthquake and subsequent policy measures gave other Mexican regions a research capacity that had heretofore been lacking in most parts of the country. Once the government research institutions were settled in their new regions, they began to take the new setting into account by including local issues in their research programs.

Within specific local contexts universities, governments, and industry are learning to encourage technological innovation through the development of loosely coupled reciprocal relationships and joint undertakings. For this to happen, a region must have some science and technology institutions and must have invented or obtained other necessary kinds of innovation-supporting instruments such as investment mechanisms and leadership to promote new initiatives. As this transition takes place, the traditional meaning of region is transformed. These efforts may start as isolated initiatives, not directly connected to regional innovation. A university may initially become involved in firm formation simply to maximize revenue from technology transfer. However, it typically becomes aware of the regional implications of its efforts and may then take a broader view of its role.

U.S. research universities supported by the growth of federal research funding during the post–World War II era constituted an enormous underutilized resource by the 1960s.[13] Studies showed that only a relatively few successful instances of transfer had occurred in the life sciences, despite evidence of significant discoveries. Publication by itself did not guarantee utilization. An additional series of measures was required to insure use.

A research area can be an instance of underutilized potential because it exists apart from industry or ways of putting this knowledge to use. Nevertheless, there is a potential that can be taken forward through new organizational mechanisms that move research in the direction of economic and social development.

The Consensus Space

Knowledge spaces are transformed from potential to actual sources of economic and social development through the creation of a consensus space, a venue that brings together persons from different organizational backgrounds and perspectives to generate new strategies and ideas. Intersection of different institutional spheres is the basis for creation of a new source of social capital that may then activate development based on untapped intellectual and financial capital resources.

The classic example of a successful consensus space is the New England Council, which brought together governmental, business, and academic leaders during the 1920s and 1930s to analyze the region's problems and

opportunities. Karl Compton of MIT introduced the concept of firm formation from academic research as an economic development strategy. This
approach was based on extending an available focus on new products as
a possible basis of economic development, taking it one step further. The
very process of including actors from these various backgrounds in the
strategy review and formulation process provided access to the resources
required to implement the eventual plan. The participants included members who were able to generate resources to carry out projects once agreed
upon, such as the formation of a venture capital firm. By moving the new-
product approach from the industrial sphere and tying it to the academic
research process, the MIT group, in effect, formulated an assisted linear
model of innovation.

In the late 1970s and early 1980s, the Competitiveness Center of SRI
International advised midwestern states, in industrial decline, how to
organize regional cooperative groups to revive their economies. When the
economic downturn hit Silicon Valley, these policy researchers brought
their model home and helped establish Joint Venture Silicon Valley,
bringing together high-tech company executives, local government officials, and academics for a series of public meetings. Some ideas that came
out of these discussions were then put into practice to develop new high-
technology industry. Smart Valley, a project for computer networks and
information resources to help develop the next level of technology for the
region, formalized some of the informal networks that have been found to
be crucial to the development of high-tech industry in the region.[14]

The Innovation Space

The innovation space may be visualized as a dual set of ladders with
crossbars between them. One ladder is the linear model of innovation; the
other ladder is the reverse linear model of innovation. The crossbars are
the elements that make these models assisted linear models, including the
incubator facilities, the technology transfer offices, the research centers,
the science parks, and so on. For example, on the side of the linear ladder
there is a research center, and on the side of the reverse linear ladder there
is a technology transfer office or incubator meeting the organizational innovations on the other ladder. That is where an innovation space opens
up. Where these movements from both sides occur, the reverse linear side
and the linear side meet and something new results, such as an incubator
with research-oriented firms and close-to-market firms interacting, that
wouldn't have existed without these interactions being encouraged. A
summary of the phases of regional knowledge-based economic development can be found in Table 3.1.

Table 3.1: Phases of Regional Knowledge-Based Economic Development

Triple Helix Spaces	Characteristics
Creation of a *knowledge space*	Focus on collaboration among different actors to improve local conditions for innovation by concentrating related R&D activities and other relevant operations
Creation of a *consensus space*	Ideas and strategies are generated in a triple helix of multiple reciprocal relationships among institutional sectors (academic, public, private)
Creation of an *innovation space*	Attempts at realizing the goals articulated in the previous phase; establishing and/or attracting public and private venture capital (combination of capital, technical knowledge and business knowledge) is central

The regional triple helix spaces are non-linear; they can theoretically be created in any order, with any one of them used as the basis for the development of others. The process of enhancing regional innovation may start with the knowledge space, move to the consensus space, and then proceed to the innovation space in a linear fashion or start from the consensus or innovation space and proceed from there. On the other hand, the process may start in the innovation space, with the development of a project or initiative, directly. For example, an executive of a New York regional development agency interested in promoting incubators said that she could get the necessary information by calling around; an elaborate process was not necessary once her agency had made the decision to act. Action is better than an endless discussion project, and even an initiative taken in a vacuum can be improved, assuming it does not quickly fail and disappear. Other elements, like an effective discussion forum, may be added later to make the regional project more effective.

THE REGIONAL INNOVATION ORGANIZER (RIO)

The question of who will assume a leadership role in resolving innovation crises at the regional level is frequently asked even in countries with strong regional governments. At the regional level, in many countries, there may not be a governmental actor available to take the lead since there are no or only very weak regional governments. Portugal, for example, does not a have a strong tradition of regional government. In this situation the University of Aveiro took the lead in bringing together companies and municipalities, playing the role of innovation organizer. An organization that takes the lead in enunciating a development goal and coordinating cooperation among a group of organizations to carry it out is a Regional Innovation Organizer (RIO). Since governmental boundaries often do not coincide with economic districts, there can be a leadership vacuum.

A company or a university that takes the lead in recruiting partners and managing the interaction among a group of firms in a region may fill this gap. Stanford University, for example, had to take the lead in order to create a technical industry surrounding the university. This process took decades.

Greenfield sites lacking previous development may require different strategies than brownfield sites with previous industrial development. Certainly the constellation of actors will be different, with previously industrialized areas typically having firms in a state of decline that may be too occupied with their own problems to support new firm formation. Indeed, they may oppose it, wanting the resources to save their own companies. On the other hand, greenfield sites may lack actors with industrial experience. In the case described below, the university, as the major available organizational resource, creatively adapted a state government program to local circumstances to stimulate firm formation.

The University as Regional Innovation Organizer

Exurban Long Island lacked an industrial base, and local government was relatively weak. The most significant institutional actor in this far region of New York City, apart from a nearby federal laboratory, was a research campus of the State University of New York (SUNY). Expanding upon a single mode of technology transfer, the patenting and licensing of intellectual property, SUNY Stony Brook has taken the lead during the past two decades in formulating a knowledge-based regional economic development strategy, utilizing local, state, and federal resources.

The New York State science and technology policy of helping local industry through centers of advanced technology at local universities was not relevant to the Stony Brook campus of the State University of New York, located in a greenfield site in Suffolk County 50 miles from New York City. The exurban site was selected to be near the Brookhaven National Laboratory, an asset for a science-based university. The campus was located beyond the zone of suburban industrial development, the exodus of industry from the city having halted well before Stony Brook. Given the lack of industrial development, Stony Brook developed a strategy similar to the one initiated by Frederick Terman, then dean of engineering at Stanford University in Santa Clara County, just prior to the second World

War, which at that time had characteristics similar to Suffolk County during the postwar era.

The presence of a medical school with extensive research capabilities in molecular biology suggested a focus on biotechnology. The technological area for startups selected was one in which the university had special strength. Moreover, a gap was identified in R&D and pilot plant facilities that the university could fill and thereby assist in the development of biotechnology firms. Based upon the observation that such companies typically spend a considerable portion of their start up capital equipping their laboratories and plants, if some needed facilities were provided by the University, it was thought that a Stony Brook location would help attract these companies. Providing firms with access to shared R&D infrastructure was matched by an effort to expand the research capacities of the faculty.

The University adapted an award from the New York State Centers Program to meet its special circumstances as a greenfield site. The Stony Brook Biotechnology Center ran what might be called a pre-Small Business Innovation Research program, directed at uncovering the commercial potential of research findings. For more than a decade, the Center has offered funds to seed new faculty research projects that have some near term commercialization potential. Typically, faculty utilize the funding program to take a basic research finding that originated in their laboratory and examine it from a product-oriented perspective. The Center carved out a key role for itself in the campus technology transfer effort as "a business, economic development and granting center." The presence on the faculty of a professor with previous success in organizing a biotechnology firm provided a significant role model for his peers. Establishing an incubator facility was the next step in the University's regional development strategy of creating high-tech industry adjacent to the campus. Having both spheres available to work in tandem can be the basis for a further stage of mutual development, a coevolution of university and industry exemplified by the following case.

Entrepreneurs as Regional Innovation Organizer

In the Linköping region of Sweden, a regional development initiative originated in a firm moving into the university. In contrast to Long Island, where the academic institution was the only available source of initiative, Linköping had an industrial actor, as well. A group of entrepreneurs created high-tech firms in the region, encouraged directly or indirectly by SAAB Aerospace. The linking element was provided by an industrial liaison officer, appointed by the university, who invited the local technical entrepreneurs to form a discussion group at the university. This entrepreneurs club grew into a project to make university resources available to assist the development of the firms.

In a next step, an academic unit to train students as entrepreneurs, the Center for Innovation and Entrepreneurship, was established in order to encourage a firm formation process from the university to complement the one that had already emerged from industry. Although many technical academics, especially in the engineering sciences, had formed companies, they typically functioned as individual consulting practices, since professors were constrained by the Swedish academic culture from pursuing the practical implications of their research in the direction of firm formation. Students were not similarly constrained from firm formation once an organizational path was opened up.

Student entrepreneurship, encouraged by incubator facilities, was then adopted by regional authorities who supported it as an economic development strategy. Large firms, downsizing their businesses, also contracted with the Center for Innovation and Entrepreneurship to train their employees, who were being laid off, in entrepreneurship and firm formation. The model was transferred to other universities in Sweden and abroad. By utilizing entrepreneurship training capabilities developed at Linköping, the teaching model could be introduced to other universities quickly. Instead of each school developing its own set of courses, it could draw upon a tested model.

In the following case, a state government initiative with business support transformed the knowledge space by creating a critical mass of company and government R&D units that led to up-grading of area universities as well. This knowledge-based regional development process reshaped the identity of the region from low-tech to high-tech and shifted its image from a low-wage to a high-wage area, despite the reality that dual formats coexisted.

Government as Regional Innovation Organizer

The development of the Research Triangle Park in North Carolina was initiated in the 1950s by Governor Luther Hodges in cooperation with three area universities and the North Carolina business community. This prototypical example of the construction of a high-tech region by exerting regional political power at the national level resulted in significant national R&D resources moving to a less research-intensive region. The motivation for high-technology development was the desire to achieve a measure of economic diversification for a state economy narrowly based on tobacco and textiles. Land was obtained for a science park situated between the area's three major academic institutions. Relocation of federal research facilities to the region was an important factor in the park's eventual success.

The Research Triangle Park was the physical manifestation of a successful strategy to attract branch laboratories of federal agencies to the region. This research base was then used to attract smaller R&D laboratories of leading technology firms, such as IBM, to locate in the park. The establishment of an IBM research facility was a key event which led to takeoff. The state's three leading universities were the official locational points of the triangle but hardly the centerpiece of the state's development strategy. In the early years of realizing North Carolina's high-tech ambitions, the universities provided an intellectual and cultural ambiance, making the Research Triangle an attractive residential location for scientists and engineers.

Technology companies considering locating a branch in the south typically think of North Carolina first; its critical mass of federal and corporate labs gives it a competitive advantage in attracting additional organizations. Nor is the original North Carolina strategy easily replicable; opportunities to relocate major laboratories are rare. An important lesson from this initiative was that it took decades to create a science park successfully, undiluted by general industrial ventures. Less patient attempts in other regions gradually became general industrial parks as land was sold and leases were let for plants and professional offices. The park only recently became part of a firm formation dynamic, instigated by firm closures.

Missing Actors; Redressing Regional Imbalances

As triple helix interactions intensify, they may ignite a self-generating process of firm formation, no longer directly tied to a particular university or regional initiative.

This dynamic occurred in Silicon Valley during the 1960s and 1970s as the semiconductor and integrated circuit industries provided the technological base for a personal computer industry. Universities provided a venue for computer hobbyists to exchange ideas, test new products, and take the first tentative steps to firm formation. As the personal computer industry grew, it fed back into the semiconductor industry, expanding the demand for chips and creating a demand for new types of chips such as power-saving models for laptop computers. A demand for software of different type than for mainframe computers was induced, greatly expanding the software industry from an adjunct of the computer industry to an industrial category in its own right.

Innovation in computers and software was no longer tightly tied to Route 128 and Silicon Valley. For example, the business software firm

SAGE was created with loose ties to local university and business networks in northeastern England, a peripheral British region. SAGE grew not through acquisition, by acquiring firms in the UK and then in the US. Nevertheless, since the preponderance of users were in the southern UK, start-ups to provide add-ons to SAGE products tended to locate close to their customers rather than adjacent to SAGE in Newcastle Upon Tyne.

A region may or may not be contiguous with political boundaries, which is at one and the same time a problem in organization and an opportunity for new sources of leadership and organization to emerge. Skåne in southern Sweden has a regional authority, but Silicon Valley does not. However, just as quasi-governance structures, such as Joint Venture Silicon Valley, are created in times of crisis, governmental entities are pressed to take on new functions in the face of adversity. Silicon Valley and the New England region exemplify the former, while the state of North Carolina exemplifies the latter. In Silicon Valley during the recession in the early 1990s, a company played the role of RIO, bringing together area municipal governments, universities, and companies to meet for brainstorming session to create new initiatives.

In Sweden, as in the United States, the concentration of national research resources at a relatively few leading universities is no longer acceptable to other regions now that the role of academic research in creating new firms and jobs has been widely recognized. In the United States during the postwar era, the major research universities were primarily located on the east and west coasts, with a few mid-western exceptions. In Sweden, the Stockholm region was the major concentration, with additional concentrations in Gothenburg and Lund. The research council system of distributing funds primarily to the existing concentrations of research has been supplemented by two additional levels of research funding which have introduced regional criteria as one of the bases for distribution of funds. Research policy has been integrated with regional policy, whether directly as in Sweden or indirectly as in the United States.

CONCLUSION

Early 20th century New England had knowledge spaces, research fields with technological and economic development potential at universities such as MIT and Harvard. The New England Council served as a consensus space where business, governmental, and academic leaders came together to test existing ideas, try out new ones, and develop an analysis that was appropriate to the region's problems and opportunities. Finally, an innovation space was created that we are familiar with today as the venture capital firm.

The premise of governmental activism is that the conditions for high-tech economic growth are not spontaneous creations; rather they can be identified and put in place by explicit measures.[15] As regions formulate knowledge-based innovation strategies, the constellation of actors, and their relative importance in the local political economy, is transformed. With knowledge assuming increased significance as a factor of production, in both high-technology and older manufacturing industries, the traditional elements of land, labor, and capital are reduced in importance with various political consequences, including a leading role for knowledge-producing institutions such as universities in regional growth coalitions.

The transformative role of the entrepreneurial university is the key to setting in motion a self-sustaining process of economic and social development. Regional development is not an evolutionary process beyond human control but is the result of institution-formation projects, such as science cities, to create infrastructure for knowledge-based growth.[16] The ultimate goal is a self-sustaining process of organizational and technological renewal. Instead of resting on a single base that is inevitably subject to creative destruction, an innovative region, with multiple knowledge bases, is capable of creative reconstruction.

NOTES

1. Henry Etzkowitz, *MIT and the Rise of Entrepreneurial Science* (London: Routledge, 2002).

2. See Giovanni Dosi and others, eds., *Technical Change and Economic Theory* (London: Pinter, 1988).

3. Henry Etzkowitz, "The Capitalization of Knowledge: The Decentralization of United States Science and Industrial Policy from Washington to the States," *Theory and Society* 19 (1990): 107–21.

4. Saskia Sassen, *The Global City: New York, London and Tokyo* (Princeton, NJ: Princeton University Press, 2001).

5. Regions shaped by an ethnic or cultural identity (within or across national boundaries such as the southern U.S. states or Kurdistan across Turkey and Iraq) are beyond the scope of our discussion except insofar as protonational identity provides a motivation for economic development, as, for example, in Catalonia and Quebec. See Liah Greenfeld, *The Spirit of Capitalism: Nationalism and Economic Growth* (Cambridge, MA: Harvard University Press, 2001).

6. Wolf Heydebrand, "Multimedia Networks, Globalization and Strategies of Innovation: The Case of Silicon Alley," in *Multimedia and Regional Economic Restructuring*, ed. Hans-Joachim Braczyk, Gerhard Fuchs, and Hans-Georg Wolf. (London: Routledge, 1999).

7. Henry Etzkowitz, *MIT and the Rise of the Entrepreneurial Science* (London: Routledge, 2002), 108.

8. Annalee Saxenian, *Regional Advantage* (Cambridge, MA: Harvard University Press, 1994).

9. Gary Hamel, "Bringing Silicon Valley Inside," *Harvard Business Review* 77, no. 5 (1999): 71–84.

10. Philip Cooke, "Regional Innovation Systems: General Findings and Some New Evidence from Biotechnology Clusters," *Journal of Technology Transfer* 27 (2002): 133–45.

11. Bernard Hofmaier, "Learning Regions: Concepts, Visions and Examples," Halmstadt University College, http://www.hh.se/hss/Papers/papers/hofmaier.pdf.

12. Rosalba Casas, Rebeca de Gortari, and Josefa Santos Ma, "The Building of Knowledge Spaces in Mexico: A Regional Approach to Networking," *Research Policy* 29 (1999): 225–41.

13. See Donald Stokes, *Pasteur's Quadrant* (Washington, DC: The Brookings Institution, 1997).

14. Saxenian, *Regional Advantage*.

15. Richard Nelson, "The Problem of Market Bias in Modern Capitalist Economies," *Industrial and Corporate Change* 11 (2002): 207–44.

16. Louis Albrechts et al., *Regional Policy at the Crossroads: European Perspectives* (London: Jessica Kingsley, 1989).

CHAPTER 4

Technology Transfer, Commercialization, and Proprietary Science

Joshua B. Powers

As has been discussed in the first volume to this series, the enterprise of higher education is changing. The increased competitive environment for students, reduced support from traditional sources of revenue, heightened attention to accountability, and a host of other forces have led many institutions to adopt characteristics and cultures that more closely resemble those of the private sector. Hence, the language and practices of business increasingly permeate mission activities. For example, campuses engage in ongoing strategic as well as tactical planning, enrollments are managed, resources are reallocated towards those activities with stronger marketplace appeal, institutions are branded and marketed, faculty receive performance pay, students are treated as customers, and services are outsourced. To lead such an enterprise, academic and administrative leaders are increasingly expected to bring strong financial management skills, to have the temperament and wherewithal to engage in alumni and stakeholder fund-raising, and to sell and deliver on change.

Among the many changes that are moving institutions to adopt and/or resemble what would normally be characteristic of business is one that is fundamentally affecting the research enterprise. Historically, the archetypical faculty member at a research university toiled at a laboratory bench on a research project of her choosing and published or presented the findings in an academic journal or conference. A private firm would find out about the innovation, adopt it, and a new process or product then appeared for societal consumption. The faculty member was happy because society was served by her lab science, she received tenure and promotion for doing it, and perhaps enjoyed external accolades from her science peers for a new breakthrough. The business that adopted it was happy because the new technology was free and they were able to bring it to market for sale, thereby increasing value for company stockholders.

Today, the historical image of the bench scientist in academe is increasingly seen as quaint, but pedestrian. Increased competition for research dollars, combined with federal and state incentives to expand and to speed the movement of innovation from higher education to consumers, is leading to new norms of practice. Whereas in the past research was viewed as an intellectual commons, freely shared with other researchers and society, today it is increasingly seen as an intellectual property, shared for a price and via a contract.

The purpose of this chapter is to explore the changes that have occurred in the processes of innovation exchange between universities and other researchers, as well as between researchers and society, that are another example of how higher education has become more like a business. In the first section, I discuss the current environment for privatization of research and how academic science is increasingly viewed and handled by those who manage it and those who engage in it. From there, I explore the historical norms of academic science that began with the rise of the research university model and contrast those with the emergent norms of science that are increasingly characterizing its conduct. This discussion follows with an examination of the implications and the normative question of whether adopting a business-like approach to academic science exchange has been beneficial and appropriate. I conclude the chapter with a set of policy and practice recommendations.

21st-CENTURY ACADEMIC SCIENCE

In November of 1944, President Roosevelt wrote to his Director of Scientific Research and Development, Vannevar Bush, requesting his counsel on how peacetime science might be fostered in ways that mirrored the success of the industrial-scientific-government partnership of the war years. In his letter, Roosevelt wrote:

> There is . . . no reason why the lessons to be found in this experiment cannot be profitably employed in times of peace. The information, the techniques, and the research experience developed by the Office of Scientific Research and Development and by the thousands of scientists in the universities and in private industry, should be used in the days of peace ahead for the improvement of the national health, the creation of new enterprises bringing new jobs, and the betterment

of the national standard of living. . . . New frontiers of the mind are before us, and if they are pioneered with the same vision, boldness, and drive with which we have waged this war we can create a fuller and more fruitful employment and a fuller and more fruitful life.[1]

Almost 70 years after Bush submitted his now famous reply, *Science: The Endless Frontier,* the academic science enterprise continues to be one that emphasizes a triple-helix-like relationship between government, universities, and industry in the approach to the discovery and dissemination of knowledge that Bush argued was critical to national innovation.[2] On the funding front, the federal government is the largest sponsor of research on the college campus, providing approximately 60 percent for at least as long as national data have been collected—since 1972 for the current data series.[3] Figure 4.1 provides a perspective on the pattern of academic R&D funding over this 25 year period.

Figure 4.1 Science and Engineering R&D Expenditures at Universities and Colleges, by Source of Funds: FY 1972–2007

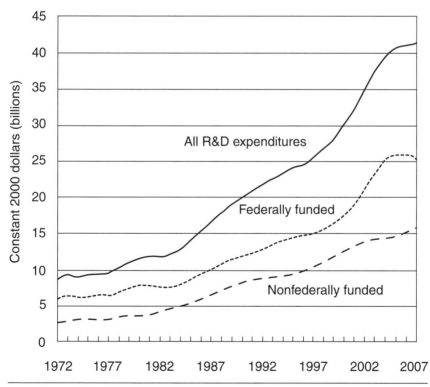

Source: National Science Foundation/Division of Science Resources Statistics, *Survey of Research and Development Expenditures at Universities and Colleges,* FY 2007.

What is noteworthy about this funding pattern is that while federal funding has grown approximately 300 percent in inflation adjusted dollars since 1972, funding from other sources has grown approximately 400 percent. Colleges and universities engaged in R&D activities have substantially ramped up their funding support from alternative sources, most notable from industry, up 22 percent since 2002, with a particular spike upwards in the past two years following a few years where the level of support had declined.[4] Funding from institutional sources, those resources that the institution itself opts to allocate to research, was up 35 percent since 2002 while that from other sources, nonprofit organizations and other nongovernmental entities, was up 30 percent. Research funding from state and local sources increased 25 percent over this same period.

While federal support of academic R&D has been up 39 percent since 2002,[5] this growth has been largely fueled by the latter end of a federal effort to double the budget for the National Institutes of Health from $13.65 billion in 1998 to $27.18 billion in 2003, an unprecedented growth in R&D support for health related research.[6] This growth rate is particularly remarkable given that federal research funding for the Department of Health and Human Services, of which the NIH is a part, is five times larger than the R&D budget of the next largest agency, the National Science Foundation. In more recent years of this decade, NIH funding has leveled while funding for engineering and the physical sciences has been emphasized for national security and economic strength reasons. Yet, after adjusting for inflation, federal funding overall fell for the second straight year, 1.6 percent in 2006 and 0.2 percent in 2005.[7]

The implications of these changing sources and amounts of funding have been significant for the academic R&D enterprise toward a more business marketplace orientation to R&D. First, the growth in industry R&D support reflects the increased emphasis placed on external partnerships for the advancement of innovation. Whereas in the past universities had a more arms length relationship with industry, today the substantial growth in industry-sponsored research has led to the blurring of university and industry lines. Faculty contracted by industry might as often assist with a latter stage innovation project in the firm itself as in the university laboratory.[8] The federal government has also provided incentives for the creation of Industry/University Cooperative Research Centers (IUCRCs) that are designed to foster university-industry collaborations as well as Engineering Research Centers for the same purpose.[9] Furthermore, in direct response to the growth in private, independent contract research organizations (CROs) to conduct clinical drug trials for companies, a growing number of universities have sought to set up their own stand-alone entities affiliated with their medical centers for the conduct of drug trials.[10] Duke University's Clinical Research Institute and others like it are in substantial part responsible for growth rates in industry-sponsored R&D among the top institutions receiving industry funding in recent years.[11] Second, the sheer size and growth rate in health-related funding up until 2003 encouraged a rapid expansion of laboratory space and faculty who were expected to conduct cutting-edge research in their field. Because these dollars were so substantial, going after them represented a clear means of enhancing institutional excellence in research via a strong move up the R&D expenditure rankings, some with the goal of breaking into the exclusive top 100 or top 50 while for others to preserve their top ranking. Many institutions went on an unprecedented spending boom, a market-based response that did not necessarily always align well with an institution's distinct competencies. Thus, as these funds have dried up in recent years, many of these institutions are stuck with expensive facilities and staffing and a limited flow of new grants to keep them afloat.[12] The same spending phenomenon is starting to happen within the engineering and physical science disciplines that have been going after fresh dollars oriented toward homeland security and related activities.

Finally, and most central to the theme of this chapter, academic R&D funding, especially from the federal government, has led to a sea change in thinking about the most valuable asset of any research university, the intellectual capacity of its faculty. As has been widely discussed in both the popular press and scholarly literature,[13] in the late 1970s it became clear that America's position as world economic leader was in question. As a result, federal R&D policy and practice shifted to placing greater importance on the productive utilization of research for specific economic ends. The federal government was concerned that many potential pathbreaking technologies were languishing on the lab desks of researchers, appearing, if at all, in obscure professional journals. The solution, it was believed, lay with creating new incentives for research organizations such as universities to orient their work in practical, market-desired directions. The Bayh-Dole Act of 1980 was a key catalyst for addressing this concern by allowing research organizations such as universities to patent much more easily, and thereby own, the innovations made possible from federal extramural research dollars.[14] As a result of the Bayh-Dole Act and subsequent legislation, many institutions of higher education began pursuing a vigorous technology transfer agenda, including forming specific offices of technology licensing, and encouraging faculty in relevant disciplines— primarily the life sciences, medicine, and engineering—to consider commercialization opportunities for their inventions and letting them share in any licensing royalties.[15] By the late 1980s and early 1990s, higher education was also confronted with considerable resource contraction at both the state and federal levels. Many states experienced budget shortfalls and felt that resources needed to be redirected from such areas as higher education to the prison system, transportation infrastructure, Medicaid, and K-12 education.[16] The federal government also was dealing with a large deficit and chose to reallocate or restrict the growth of funding for student financial aid and the federal R&D funding agencies.[17] Calls for help by higher education officials appeared to fall upon deaf ears since the prevailing view of government policy makers was that higher education needed to downsize, become more productive, and rein in out of control tuition increases.

As a result of these financial pressures, institutions began scrambling to find alternative sources of revenue and found that one of their single greatest assets was their intellectual capital, something that could now be better leveraged as a revenue stream. Thus, not only was commercialization wrapped in the mantra of economic development now legitimate, it might also help address higher education's financial woes. As a result, as noted earlier, institutions turned to industry with greater frequency as a benefactor or partner in the research process.

Further fueling the movement toward commercialization (i.e., patenting and licensing technologies) and away from utilizing just traditional mechanisms for transfer (i.e., publishing and presenting with few or no strings attached to the use of a technology) was the rise of the biotechnology sector. Following the discovery of DNA, researchers were eager to identify new ways to advance health research through the study of this fundamental building block of life.[18] With the discovery and subsequent patenting of recombinant DNA, a process for gene splicing invented by Herbert Boyer and Stanley Cohen in the 1970s, it became clear that biotechnology could be an extremely lucrative pursuit for universities, as evidenced by the licensing revenues that began to flow to the University of California and Stanford University on the Boyer-Cohen patents. When the patents ran out in 1997, the combined revenues for the two institutions reached $255 million.[19] Further encouraging the pursuit of patents on faculty life science discoveries was an important court case, *Diamond v. Chakrabarty*, also decided in 1980, the year that the Bayh-Dole Act was passed. This Supreme Court case allowed, for the first time, the patenting of live, genetically altered organisms, a common outcome from biotechnology related research.

Figure 4.2 shows the growth in academic patenting since 1972. Annual patent data show activity that ranged from 238 to 390 patents per year among all universities in the years leading up to 1980. The decade of the 1980s began a 20-year trend of rapid growth in patenting that peaked in 1999 at 3,340 patents, a year when key changes to patent law created an incentive for speedy filings. Since that time, patent ownership has remained strong, although showing some evidence of a decline in recent years. Nevertheless, in the 25 years following the passage of the Bayh-Dole Act, the number of academic institutions involved in patenting grew from 84 to 190, a 126 percent increase in institutions involved in privatizing research.[20]

Although actual patent issues appear to be falling recently, survey data collected from the Association of University Technology Managers (AUTM) suggests that the propensity to patent has continued to increase, as evidenced by annual growth rates in both invention disclosures (inventions shared with the campus technology transfer office) and new patent filings.[21] What is revealing is not only the steady increase in invention disclosures and patent application activity, but also the change in proportion between the two. In summary, in 1992 universities generally patented just under 30 percent of the inventions disclosed to their technology transfer offices (about 1 in 3); by 2006, they were seeking patents on over 60 percent of the disclosures (about 2 of every 3). This proxy measure of an institution's orientation toward patenting, and by extension, its orientation toward privatization, is significant. Whereas in the past universities and their faculty inventors were more willing to transfer technologies to the marketplace for free, today it appears that they are increasingly interested in doing so for a fee, as would be expected from a technology license to recoup patent costs and to ensure a future revenue flow from royalties on product sales. Furthermore, judging by the start of a drop-off in the actual awarding of patents, some of these patent applications may be of questionable legitimacy (i.e., federal patent examiners judging them to not be patentable, possibly due to infringement on another patent or falling outside

Figure 4.2 Academic Patenting: 1972–2005

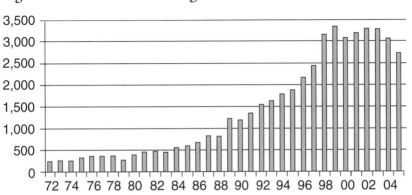

Source: United States Patent Office.

of the bounds of what may be considered patentable). Previous research has also shown that the quality of patents in recent years has declined in relation to patents from previous years, possibly due to universities trolling deeper into their research pool for patentable technologies but likely as a result of new and smaller university entrants to patenting.[22]

Regardless of the explanation, it is clear that universities feel considerable pressure to patent as a visible sign of their commitment to economic development. Furthermore, there remains a powerful belief that a strong patenting program will eventually lead to a blockbuster patent and financial windfall. Success stories through royalty flows or stock sales such as from Gatorade at the University of Florida ($100 million in licensing revenues to date and averaging about $4 million per year), Taxol at Florida State University ($200 million), and Google at Stanford University ($350 million) act as a strong inducement for universities to pursue patents aggressively, despite the research that clearly shows few universities enjoy blockbuster success.

NORMS OF ACADEMIC SCIENCE

Thus far in this chapter, I have mapped the current landscape for commercialization and the forces that have led to the growing orientation towards privatization, or what Slaughter and Leslie[23] label academic capitalism. Etzkowitz[24] refers to this contemporary entrepreneurial environment for the conduct and dissemination of research as the second revolution in American higher education, the first being the rise of the research university model itself in the late 19th century. At that time, universities shifted from a focus on cultural preservation to the creation of new knowledge to benefit society. Today, universities are shifting from a model of basic knowledge dissemination to one that emphasizes a participative role in the creation of actual products and new enterprises that serve the targeted goals of practical and nearer term societal benefit and economic development.

To understand the current context in which the university commercialization phenomenon has emerged, it is first necessary to explore the larger issue of academic entrepreneurship and its historical roots. Contrary to popular perception, higher education has experienced periodic calls for greater relevance even early in its history. The *Yale Report* of 1828, for instance, while noted for its vigorous defense of the classical curriculum, recognized that there were significant challenges to the academy for increased practical relevance, including increased accommodation for business interests.[25] However, it was during and after the Civil War period that greater university ties to commercial interests and activity were more formally forged. America was in an expansion mode and needed a citizenry educated in the ways of practical science, both agriculturally and industrially based.[26] As such, with the advent of the Morrill Land-Grant Act of 1862 and subsequent legislation, specific institutions were established or directed in each state to focus on the need for a practical education for the working classes. A primary manifestation of this effort was the creation of agricultural extension and mechanical arts programs at these institutions with the goal of meeting the agrarian and industrial needs of society.[27]

By the turn of the 19th century, a number of university-based research laboratories had also been formed. Based on the German research university model, a number of these laboratories were funded by large philanthropic foundations interested in the ultimate application of university research.[28] Some of the largest of these at places like MIT and the University of Michigan had established strong relationships with industry by the early part of the 20th century.

During this early 20th century growth period in academic research, however, few institutions were engaged in patenting and licensing activity, and where they were involved, it was typically at arm's length. For example, in 1912, Frederick Cotrell, Professor of Chemistry at the University of California-Berkeley and considered the father of the academic-sourced patent, developed a process for reducing pollution from power and manufacturing plants. Believing that industry would be given more incentive to adopt the technology if it was patented, he did so, but formed an independent entity, the Research Corporation, to manage the patent. In his view, "A danger was involved . . . particularly should the experiment prove highly profitable to the university. The danger . . . was the possibility of growing commercialism and competition between institutions and an accompanying tendency for secrecy in scientific work."[29] Another example from this period comes from the University of Wisconsin. Henry Steenbock, Professor of Biochemistry, developed a process in the early 1920s by which milk was subjected to ultraviolet light that in turn raised its vitamin D content. Knowing that raising the vitamin D content of milk could be of immense benefit to children suffering from the scourge of rickets, he approached the university to set up a separate and independent nonprofit organization to manage the patent he had received on the technology and to handle the mechanisms of licensing it to industry. The Wisconsin Alumni Research Foundation was formed in 1925 to do so, one of the first of its type directly affiliated with a particular university.[30] To that time, the few academic patents in the United States that were filed were being handled by the Research Corporation noted above. Most universities, however, eschewed patenting, believing that "knowledge wrested from nature in universities ought to be bestowed upon the world free of charge, not exploited for profits by the universities."[31]

Although linkages to business and industry existed and the land-grant institutions in particular were actively engaged in activity related to economic development, particularly in the area of agriculture, the research engines of America's colleges and universities really did not move into high gear until World War II. Additionally, it was not industry providing the bulk of the financial support for academic R&D but rather the federal government. As the United States faced the daunting task of waging a world war, Vannevar Bush of the Carnegie Institution persuaded President Roosevelt that the scientific brainpower of America's universities could be brought to bear for developing the military technology needed to defeat Germany and Japan.[32] The enormous resources provided led to the development and refinement of radar, atomic energy, and aeronautics, all produced through the coordinated efforts of academic researchers.

This auspicious beginning ultimately led to a formalized government policy of support for basic research in higher education and the establishment of federal agencies like the National Science Foundation and the National Institutes of Health, major sources of research funding that continue to this day. The tacit agreement with the federal government up until the late 1970s was that scientists would be given considerable autonomy to pursue research streams with little requirement of practical application or economic relevance.[33] Thus, the massive infusion of federal dollars into academic R&D activity dwarfed any industry-sponsored research occurring during this period.[34]

With the rise of the research university model in the latter part of the 19th century and the professionalization of collegiate faculty in the early part of the 20th century, the conduct of science began to take on certain fundamental characteristics. Merton[35] codified the ethos of science that emerged with his description of four fundamental norms undergirding academic science. The first of these, universalism, captured the importance of recognizing that science should be evaluated on its merits and not on subjective criteria such as the reputation or social standing of the researcher. The blind review process of publication is perhaps the most apparent manifestation of this value set. Specifically, a researcher's work is ostensibly evaluated on its own and without consideration of the person who produced it. The second norm, communality, articulated as a value that no person owns knowledge. Thus, academic scientists should be willing to freely share their data and discoveries with others, all in the name of advancing knowledge. Furthermore, they have the obligation to communicate those findings widely, as manifested in the expectation of publishing their work in academic journals and doing so in a timely basis so others can build upon their work. The third norm was entitled disinterestedness. The intent of this value was that a researcher should conduct his work separate from personal motives. In other words, the academic scientist should selflessly pursue truth wherever it may lead in the name of advancing science and not as a means of personal gain. The last norm, organized skepticism, captured the importance of public and open critique of research findings, allowing others to attempt to replicate results and/or to build on the ideas. The most readily apparent manifestation of this norm is the process of presenting papers at academic conferences where others can openly question and explore the merits, opportunities, and implications of new research findings.

While these four norms continue to be present in various forms today, some have suggested that there has been an emerging set of norms that are altering what has undergirded the historic conduct of academic science. Mitroff's[36] study of the Apollo moon project offered a language to describe these counter-norms. In contrast to universalism, for instance, he argued that the forces of particularism are also at work. Particularism, he suggested, has led some to judge the quality of scientific work not on its own merits, but in part on the reputation of the individual or group presenting it. The fact that researchers with a known reputation tend to have enhanced chances at landing a major federal grant, for instance, is one high profile example of particularism. A second counter-norm that Mitroff articulated was solitariness. In contrast with the belief that ideas and knowledge are universally shared and owned by all, solitariness suggested that scientists sometimes do seek to protect their findings jealously and not share their source data. An unwillingness to share data best ensures their ability to maintain a stream of research and safeguard future credit for discoveries. Self-interest, in direct conflict with its traditional norm, disinterestedness, was the third counter-norm that Mitroff identified in academic science. Self-interest, as might be inferred, values the pursuit of new knowledge not for its own sake but for personal gain from such efforts in whatever form that might come—personal accolades, financial rewards, and the like. Thus, particular streams of research might be pursued because they are perceived in the field as more important, cutting-edge, have potential financial gain opportunities, and/or lead to certain valued benefits like access to resources to build a larger and more complex lab. Mitroff labeled the final counter-norm organized dogmatism, or the practice by which academic scientists would promote or trumpet their own findings, theories, and innovations over those of others, and not for sound research-related reasons. Hence, this counter norm affirms that a researcher's key ally becomes his agent, who spins out regular releases to the popular press in the hopes of landing a feature story on his work, or the researcher practice of criticizing others' work simply because it is perceived as a threat to one's own.

As the forces for commercialization have grown in intensity, the counter norms are increasingly reflected in the academic research enterprise and with at least some negative implications.[37] For example, an increasing body of work has found evidence of growing secrecy in science.[38] Others have noted faculty reticence to jeopardize their resource flows from industry and thus a willingness to accept publication restrictions or delays, often so that patent protections for which they and an industry sponsor might ultimately benefit can be filed.[39] This practice has extended to pre-publication review or ghost writing by contracting firms, especially for studies involving drug trials.[40] Faculty themselves are withholding data from colleagues, primarily to preserve their scientific lead[41] or to increase the chance of obtaining needed resources to advance their research.[42] Furthermore, it is common for faculty to have consulting arrangements, board positions, or an equity stake in a company that has licensed their technology.[43] Other researchers have reported growing scientific misconduct,[44] calling into question the legitimacy of published findings and in some cases, even serious breaches in human subject protections.

A growing body of literature has studied these forces and noted how they are manifested in academic faculty and their institutions in terms of a growing tolerance or ambivalence about conflicts of interest.[45] Campbell[46] offers some useful examples in her study of university-industry conflicts such as faculty or institutional stock ownership in licensee companies, the powerful influence of corporate sponsors of research, faculty serving in company management posts while simultaneously serving as a faculty members, and faculty and institutions placing profiting on intellectual property over the pursuit of research free of financial motives.

A few high-profile conflict of interest cases are illustrative of the effects of privatization. In 1989, two researchers at the University of Utah, Stanley Pons and Martin Fleischmann, claimed to have discovered a practical process for cold fusion. To much fanfare, they and the university held press conferences announcing their discovery to the world but refused to share the exact techniques used in their experiment so others could seek to replicate it. Although the underlying reasons for their reluctance to share the results are still debated, it was certainly in part due to efforts by the researchers and the university to pursue intellectual property protections and a $25 million grant from Congress to advance their project. Ultimately, others were able to attempt cold fusion replications but without success, and Pons and Fleischmann were ultimately discredited, with some considering them to be frauds.

A high-profile conflict of interest case that occurred at the University of Pennsylvania in 1999 involved the death of a human subject enrolled in a genetics experiment. The 18-year-old boy from Arizona had enrolled in a clinical trial in which genetically altered viruses were infused into his liver in an experimental therapy designed to treat his rare liver disease. He had a massive negative reaction and died. A subsequent investigation revealed that the lead investigator held patents on parts of the procedure and stock in the company that was commercializing it. In the course of the investigation, it was also revealed than neither the Federal Drug Administration nor the human subjects in the trial had received information that monkeys had died in previous animal studies using the therapy, or information that other human subjects had experienced serious toxic reactions. This finding led the federal government to shut down or restrict clinical research at 20 major research institutions, and Health and Human Services Secretary Donna Shalala labeled the problem deeply troubling and not an isolated incident.[47]

Conflicts of interest stemming from commercialization are not limited to faculty researchers but also include institutions. For instance, the University of Wisconsin came under considerable fire when it patented a technique for harvesting stem cells from monkeys, a process that had enormous potential therapeutic benefit, given their ability to grow into human organs or tissue. The concern was that the patent was too broad and limiting to others for the conduct of research. The University of Wisconsin had successfully received a patent covering all lines of embryonic stem cells for primates (including humans), along with the actual method for isolating them, and then licensed the patent to a single company, the Geron Corporation. The industry and research community was outraged, given the onerous licensing provisions ($5,000 licensing fee) plus royalty payments and reach-through provisions that gave the University of Wisconsin first rights to any commercialization opportunities that developed from the work of others using their stem cell lines.[48] After considerable pressure from the NIH and bad press, the University of Wisconsin partially backed off by reducing the number of stem cell lines that Geron could use exclusively and the most onerous of the provisions required of academic researchers desiring to use the lines for research.

Another noted conflict of interest case involved Boston University and its much ballyhooed start-up company, Seragen. In the early to mid-1990s, President Silber believed that this one company and its specialized approach to cancer research had the potential for enormous breakthroughs and thus, by extension, for greatly enriching the university's bottom line through stock ownership appreciation and institution prestige. His infectious enthusiasm for the firm ultimately led him, with Board of Trustees and other senior university officer compliance, to invest millions of the university's endowment into this one company, at one point reaching $85 million, 1/5 of the entire endowment at the time. This choice was astounding given the historical conservatism of universities and care in diversifying financial risk. As has been true for many biotechnology companies holding great initial promise, the company failed to achieve its goals, lost over $150 million, and was ultimately sold, an outcome for the university that resulted in its losing 90 percent of its investment.[49]

Among the emerging controversies associated with privatization of research has been the growth in contractual exchange between institutions and researchers as regards the sharing of new innovations for the purpose of follow-on research and innovation. In the past, the exchange of data, materials, and research processes typically occurred via a simple phone call between researchers, a mailed package, or an e-mail or letter in which the source researcher agreed to share freely what was desired. Today, this exchange is increasingly conducted via a signed contract called a Material Transfer Agreement (MTA), reviewed by the legal staffs of both institutions, that spells out the finer points of how the requested items, information, or material can be used, especially as it may lead to potential future patenting opportunities. Of particular note have been reach-through provisions by which original inventors and their institutions have the right to royalties that may accrue from the downstream researcher's work and/or to prevent the downstream researcher from patenting based on the original inventor's work. This heightened attention to a formal, legal relationship governing what was once a collegial, informal exchange process, coupled with the belief that one's research has the potential for personal financial gain, has led some to express concerns that these transaction costs are hindering, rather than facilitating, the advancement of science.[50]

To date, very little research has been done on this subject. What has been done on MTAs specifically shows some evidence that they do not have a negative effect on follow-on patenting,[51] although the research did not explore delays in research per se. Related studies, however, have found reason for concern. Campbell et al.,[52] in their national study of geneticists, found that 35 percent of researchers did feel that withholding of materials or information had increased in recent years and that approximately one half had been denied access to materials at least once by fellow researchers in the past three years, with 12 percent stating that they had denied requests from other researchers. Much research is still needed on this phenomenon to understand its actual effects more fully, but nevertheless, it does suggest cause for concern regarding the complexities of contractual exchange on research findings and the emerging profit motive in which it is embedded that characterizes practice in the for-profit business sector.

IMPLICATIONS

Research on the technology commercialization phenomenon in higher education has in recent years become quite extensive. Not only has there been considerable empirical work that has emerged, but some have written helpful literature reviews to provide a framework for making sense of it.[53] Nevertheless, the question as to whether or not higher education's adoption of a business and market-based model for knowledge exchange has been good for science or society continues to be debated. Within what I label the positivist camp are those that point to the rapid and visible expansion of technological innovation from universities to business as evidenced by growth rates in patenting and licensing. Others have pointed to new forms of university-industry interaction that have facilitated the growth of technology clusters and start-up companies, some of which have gone on to considerable success in terms of products on the market and employment growth. Still others note how incentives have served to nudge, if not shove, universities and their research faculty toward a greater orientation to serving society's articulated needs. The majority of persons from the positivist camp have tended to come from the business or science disciplines that are closer to the marketplace or that frame issues from a business orientation.

By contrast, those in the critical camp have pointed out the very real limitations of academic capitalism as manifested in conflicts of interest but also conflicts of commitment and conflicts of internal equity. As evidence, they point toward high profile violations in human subject protections, evidence of misdirected faculty efforts toward their firms or firm-related work above their academic responsibilities, the abuses of graduate students caught in the tangle of proprietary industry-sponsored research, and resources being directed to more market-oriented disciples and away from the social sciences and humanities. Others discuss the heightened issues at what is essentially ground zero in the debate, the commercialization of basic life science related technologies, especially in genetics and genomics that all affirm will be the source of significant breakthroughs in health and health care. These critics express strong concern that bottling up these platform technologies through exclusive licenses with singular companies hinders science via restrictions on access by other researchers, a building block of our academic research enterprise in the United States. The critical camp of researchers tend to be located in those disciplines less closely aligned with the marketplace (e.g., education) or that take a particular lens on the study of the phenomenon (e.g., ethics, public policy).

What is clear from the literature, however, is that the historical norms guiding the conduct of academic research are changing and in ways that have had negative implications and potentially may have others that have so far not been adequately explored. We know, for example, that proprietary science has led to increased secrecy, conflict of interest concerns, and increased power by industry to drive the university research agenda. These outcomes appear to reflect a movement away from the historic norms of academic science that most point to as having been a fundamental driver of national innovative achievement in the United States. It has also been evident that in this era of resource contraction, researchers and their institutions have sought to move their mission efforts increasingly toward their contribution to regional, state, and/or national economic development, one of the few places where obtaining new funding flows has received traction. Thus, many universities are forming or expanding patenting and licensing operations, business incubators, research parks, and university-business partnerships in part because those are visible manifestations of societal relevance, even though some of those evidentiary measures of achievement are of questionable utility. For example, is a university that patents more technologies a better steward of the public trust than those that patent fewer? Are the numbers of new jobs created a reasonable benchmark of institutional contribution if it costs a particular threshold amount to achieve those new jobs? Should licensing income received be an appropriate rubric for measuring contribution? If it is, when income goals are not achieved, as is true for most institutions, does that mean technology commercialization has failed or that the current efforts of technology licensing practitioners to downplay such a rubric are a clever ploy to justify their existence in some other way? These and questions like them remain under-studied and worthy of future inquiry to better answer the issues surrounding higher education's adoption of a business model for knowledge exchange.

POLICY AND PRACTICE RECOMMENDATIONS

Given that the appropriateness of proprietary science has not been resolved, while at the same time troubling evidence exists as to its negative effects, I offer a set of policy and practice recommendations. First, national and state policymakers should conduct an audit of their economic development policies to see if they may be stimulating suboptimal institutional behavior and an overemphasis on revenue generation as a goal of technology licensing. For example, targeted grant programs designed to stimulate regional development may lead an institution to set up its own stand-alone technology commercialization office and/or business incubator. Pooling resources with other institutions or outsourcing this work to larger, established programs might be a wiser investment of resources. Policy makers should better adapt economic development expectations based on institutional mission, location, and R&D activity levels, and hold institutions appropriately accountable in light of those context differences. Furthermore, policymakers also need to be realistic about the chances that a given program can ever realize a net positive return. Subsidizing the commercialization enterprise, in philosophically the same way that R&D activities are funded, is necessary if the public benefits purpose of the Bayh-Dole Act is to be better achieved, namely, increasing the number of technologies developed with public funds and to speed their movement into the marketplace.

Second, technology commercialization practitioners and their institutional leader champions have much that they can do to ensure greater integrity of process and appropriate practice. In 2007, 11 major research universities and the Association of American Medical Colleges (AAMC) proposed a nine-point framework for licensing practice (AUTM, 2007). This document emphasizes clarity of language in licensing contracts that seeks to preserve key values of academic science such as broad access (a preference for non-exclusive licensing or, if exclusive, only in narrow fields of use), institutional control over the publication of research on a licensed innovation (limited publication delays and the right to publish findings, regardless of their impact on a company's bottom line or reputation), the minimization of reach-through rights (patent owners should not automatically insist upon the rights to own further improvements or to expect downstream royalty flows from improvements), and proactive safeguards in the arena of conflicts of interest (unfortunately left vague, but a principled first step). A recent study of licensing agreements suggests that much work is needed to improve in these areas.[54]

On the institutional front, it is critical that institutions also move toward greater transparency of process. Proprietary science has led to increased secrecy, not only by researchers as noted above but by institutions as well. Licensing contracts and related agreements that institutions have with industry are considered by most to be confidential. Yet, as recipients of substantial amounts of public money and as a function of their social contract for science responsibilities, they should make greater disclosure as regards licensing practice. For instance, royalty sharing arrangements, stock equity shares held by the university and the inventor, and publication right terms should be publicly disclosed. At present, this information is not revealed and is often redacted from contractual documents that are available through entities like the Securities and Exchange Commission. Thus, for example, it is impossible to know if the conflict of interest thresholds expected for disclosure by the NIH are being adhered to—5 percent ownership stake or higher in a company or $10,000 or more a year in income from a firm for which the fruits of an academic researcher's federally-sponsored research are being used/developed. Transparency such as this can do much to ensure the integrity of academic science.

CONCLUSION

Niels Reimers, the architect of Stanford's approach to licensing recombinant DNA technology and what instrumentally led to the emergence of the biotechnology industry, summed up their licensing goals for recombinant DNA in this way:

> Our objectives were to develop a licensing program consistent with the public service ideals of the university, to encourage the application of genetic engineering technology for public use and benefit, to minimize the potential for biohazardous development, and, finally, to provide a source of income for educational and research purposes.[55]

This milestone technology license from a university was one that insisted upon broad access by many while also enabling a revenue flow to the institution that benefited the conduct of future research. The key to the future success and management of proprietary science will be for institutions to insist upon such a model, the reduction of emphasis on revenue generation, and vigilance in ensuring that basic academic principles are not compromised.

NOTES

1. Vannevar Bush, *Science: The Endless Frontier* (Washington, DC: National Science Foundation, 2000), 1.

2. Henry Etzkowitz, "The Norms of Entrepreneurial Science: Cognitive Effects of the New University-Industry Linkages," *Research Policy* 27 (1998): 823–33.

3. Ronda Britt, "Universities Report Continued Decline in Real Federal S&E R&D Funding in FY 2007," *InfoBrief* (Washington, DC: National Science Foundation, 2008).

4. Britt, "Universities Report."

5. Ibid.

6. Jennifer Couzin and Greg Miller, "NIH Budget: Boom and Bust," *Science* 316 (2007), 356–61.

7. Britt, "Universities Report."

8. Jerry G. Thursby and Marie C. Thursby, "Industry Perspectives on Licensing University Technologies: Sources and Problems," *Industry and Higher Education* 15 (2001): 289–94.

9. Roger L. Geiger, *Knowledge & Money: Research Universities and the Paradox of the Marketplace* (Stanford, CA: Stanford University, 2004).

10. Marcia Angell, *The Truth About the Drug Companies* (New York: Random House, 2004).

11. Adam Linker, "Duke, NCSU Among Leaders in Corporate Research Dollars," *Triangle Business Journal*, January 11, 2008, 1.

12. Jennifer Couzin and Greg Miller, "NIH Budget: Boom and Bust," *Science* 316 (2007), 356–61.

13. Derek Bok, *Universities in the Marketplace* (Princeton, NJ: Princeton University Press, 2003); Richard R. Nelson, "Observations on the Post-Bayh-Dole Rise of Patenting at American Universities," *The Journal of Technology Transfer* 26 (2001), 13–19; Sheila Slaughter and Larry L. Leslie, *Academic Capitalism: Politics, Policies, and the Entrepreneurial University* (Baltimore, MD: Johns-Hopkins, 1997).

14. Norman E. Bowie, *University-Business Partnerships: An Assessment* (Lanham, MD: Rowman & Littlefield, 1994); Slaughter, *Academic Capitalism*.

15. Irwin Feller, "Technology Transfer from Universities," In *Higher Education Handbook of Theory and Research, Vol. 9*, ed. J. Smart (New York: Agathon. 1997), 1–42.

16. Don Hossler et al., "State Funding for Higher Education: The Sisyphean Task," *Journal of Higher Education* 68 (1997), 160–90.

17. Slaughter, *Academic Capitalism*.

18. Martin Kenney, *Biotechnology: The University-Industrial Complex* (New Haven, CT: Yale University Press, 1986).

19. Maryann P. Feldman, "Where Science Comes to Life: University Bioscience, Commercial Spin Offs, and Regional Economic Development," *Journal of Comparative Policy Analysis* 2 (2004), 346.

20. Joshua B. Powers, "Patents and Royalties," in *Privatization and Public Institutions of Higher Education: Implications for the Public Trust*, ed. D. Priest and E. St. John (Bloomington, IN: Indiana University Press, 2006).

21. Association of University Technology Managers, *AUTM Licensing Survey: FY 2006* (Deerfield, IL: AUTM, 2007).

22. David C. Mowery and Arvids A. Ziedonis, "Academic Patent Quality and Quantity Before and After the Bayh–Dole Act in the United States," *Research Policy* 31 (2002): 399–418.

23. Slaughter, *Academic Capitalism*.

24. Etzkowitz, "The Norms of Entrepreneurial Science."

25. Frederick Rudolph, *The American College and University: A History* (Athens: University of Georgia, 1990).

26. Christopher J. Lucas, *American Higher Education: A History* (New York: St. Martin's Griffin, 1994).

27. National Association of State Universities and Land-Grant Colleges, *What is a Land Grant College?* (Washington, DC: NASALGUC, 2000).

28. Roger L. Geiger, "Organized Research Units: Their Role in the Development of University Research," *The Journal of Higher Education* 61 (1990): 1–19.

29. David C. Mowery and Bhaven N. Sampat, "Patenting and Licensing University Inventions: Lessons from History of the Research Corporation," *Industrial and Corporate Change* 10 (2001): 317–55.

30. Charles Weiner, "Universities, Professors, and Patents: A Continuing Controversy," *Technology Review* (1986 February-March): 33–43.

31. Daniel J. Kevles, *The Physicists: The History of a Scientific Community in Modern America* (Cambridge, MA: Harvard University Press, 1995).

32. Gary W. Matkin, *Technology Transfer and the University* (New York: American Council on Education, 1990).

33. Henry Etzkowitz, Andrew Webster, and Peter Healey, *Capitalizing Knowledge: New Intersections of Industry and Academia* (Albany, NY: State University of New York, 1998).

34. Gary W. Matkin, "Technology and Public Policy: Lessons from a Case Study," *Policy Studies Journal* 22 (1994): 371–83.

35. Robert K. Merton, "A Note on Science and Democracy," *Journal of Legal and Political and Sociology* 1 (1942): 115–26.

36. Ian I. Mitroff, "Norms and Counter-Norms in a Select Group of the Apollo Moon Scientists: A Case Study of the Ambivalence of Scientists," *American Sociological Review* 39 (1974): 579–95.

37. Derek Bok, *Universities in the Marketplace.*

38. Teresa Isabelle Daza Campbell, "Public Policy for the 21st Century: Addressing Potential Conflicts in University-Industry Collaboration," *The Review of Higher Education* 20 (1997): 357–79; John P. Walsh, Charlene Cho and Wesley M. Cohen, "Science and the Law: View from the Bench: Patents and Material Transfers," *Science* 309 (2005): 2002–3.

39. David Blumenthal et al., "Withholding Research Results in Academic Life Science," *JAMA* 389 (1997): 454–59.

40. Marcia Angell and Arnold Relman, "Patents, Profits, & American Medicine: Conflicts of Interest in the Testing & Marketing of a New Drug," *Daedalus* 131 (2002): 111.

41. Karen S. Louis, Lisa M. Jones and Eric G. Campbell, "Sharing in Science," *American Scientist* 90 (2002): 304–7.

42. Kenney, *Biotechnology*.

43. Elizabeth A. Boyd and Lisa A. Bero, "Assessing Faculty Financial Relationships with Industry," *JAMA* 284 (2000): 2209–14.

44. Judith P. Swazey, Melissa S. Anderson and Karen S. Lewis, "Ethical Problems in Academic Research," *American Scientist* 81 (1993): 542–54.

45. Melissa S. Anderson and Karen S. Louis, "The Graduate Student Experience and Subscription to the Norms of Science," *Research in Higher Education* 35 (1994): 273–99; Michael E. Gluck, David Blumenthal, and Michael A. Stoto, "University-Industry Relationships in the Life-Sciences: Implications for Students and Post-Doctoral Fellows," *Research Policy* 16 (1987): 327–36.

46. Teresa Isabelle Daza Campbell, "Public Policy for the 21st Century," 357–79.

47. Jennifer Washburn, *University Inc.* (New York: Basic Books, 2005).

48. Ibid.

49. David Barboza, "Loving a Stock, Not Wisely but Too Well: The Price of Obsession with a Promising Start-up," *The New York Times,* (September 20, 1998), 3 (1, 13).

50. Michael A. Heller and Rebecca S. Eisenberg, "Can Patents Deter Innovation? The Anticommons in Biomedical Research," *Science* 280 (1998): 698–701.

51. David C. Mowery and Arvids A. Ziedonis, "Academic Patents and Material Transfer Agreements: Substitutes or Complements?," *Journal of Technology Transfer* 32 (2007): 157–72.

52. Eric G. Campbell et al., "Data Withholding in Academic Genetics," *JAMA* 287 (2002): 473–80.

53. Barry Bozeman, "Technology Transfer and Public Policy: A Review of Research and Theory," *Research Policy* 29 (2000): 627–55; Frank T. Rothaermel, Shanti D. Agung, and Lin Jiang, "University Entrepreneurship: A Taxonomy of the Literature," *Industrial and Corporate Change* 16 (2007): 691–791.

54. Joshua Powers, "Ethical Conflicts and Public Responsibilities: Commercialization in the Academy," in *Understanding and Achieving Higher Education for the Public Good*, ed. P. Pasque, N. Bowman, and M. Martinez, (Kennesaw, GA: Kennesaw State University Press, in press).

55. Niels Reimers, "Tiger by the Tail," *Chemtech* 17 (1987): 464–71.

CHAPTER 5

Ongoing Challenges in University Involvement in R&D for Industry

Ronald A. Bohlander

The role of universities in research for the private sector is gradually increasing[1] due to companies shopping for innovation, encouragement to universities to spur economic development, and shifting availability of funding from the public sector. A number of universities are credited as being at the center of vital communities of new businesses founded on technologies first advanced on campus. University research is applauded when it is quickly and efficiently translated into working technology in industry rather than sitting idle for years in the library. Nevertheless, university involvement in research for the private sector gets mixed reviews. Some people inside and outside of academe feel uneasy about university agreements that are exclusive to individual industry research sponsors. Some find it difficult to reconcile such agreements with the university's historic mission to advance knowledge for the general public good.

In 2002 the author wrote an essay for the Sam Nunn Bank of America Policy Forum on "Commercialization of the Academy,"[2] in which he observed that expectations for economic spin-off from universities were too high to forgo research for industrial application. The question could no longer be *whether* to conduct university research for industry, but how to manage it in such a fashion that it is both effective and consistent with evolving public and academic values. He examined experiences with the management of industry research in the context of his experience in the Georgia Tech Research Institute, which is embedded in a university and dedicated to applied engineering R&D. Such institutes help move cutting-edge technology out of academia into applications for clients in a way that can be examined and tested, and in this context some of the challenges in working with industry come into sharp focus.

There are some important limitations on a university's engineering work, particularly for clients in the private sector. Since 1997, the U.S. Internal Revenue Service (IRS) has articulated rules that have essentially eliminated work for hire agreements between research universities and the private sector. This was a relatively new development at the time of the author's earlier essay, and the university community was still adjusting policies and practices in response. Significant adaptation in university contracting and licensing has occurred since that time, and the present essay will, among other things, examine how these federal regulations have been understood and accommodated in managing R&D and technology transfer programs for industry today. Pivotal are the rights to intellectual properties developed through sponsored research in non-profit universities.

At the same time, industry's outlook on intellectual property has also taken some new directions. Gone are the days when corporations seek to command within their own walls all the inventive steps necessary for their new products. A spirit of collaboration and exchange of intellectual property has opened up between corporations and other organizations in the interest of more rapid product innovation. Futurists[3] over the last couple decades connected the dots between three related trends: the proliferation of widely dispersed knowledge creation, the appearance of powerful networked computing/designing power available to masses of people, and the desire for more personalization and faster innovation in products. As a result these visionaries heralded a resulting rise of wider participation and collaboration in new product definition and production, involving cooperating corporations, suppliers, customers, and other third parties. Henry Chesbrough[4] and others have chronicled this paradigm shift with accounts of corporate experiences in what has come to be termed open innovation. Not surprisingly, universities are among those organizations industry turns to for inspiration and collaboration in innovation. Experience with structuring and managing such relationships will be the subject of the following essay.

THE PROMISES AND CHALLENGES OF OPEN INNOVATION

The transition from closely held corporate innovation to more open strategies was driven not only by the advantages of these new approaches but also by the breakdown of the means of protecting technology within corporate enclaves. Chesbrough enumerates at least four factors that now cause technologies to move outside of the companies that develop them:

- Increase in numbers of workers well educated in technology, some of whom migrate to other companies or start their own
- Companies create substantially more ideas than they can use, and some of these ideas may be useful elsewhere, thereby creating a market pull to free them up. This pull is sometimes answered by the initiating company making a deal, or sometimes by employees taking the ideas to market in a spin-off
- The rise of venture capital willing to fund businesses founded on new technologies and business models
- Increasing technical capabilities of suppliers and other business partners to make contributions of their own in creating innovation within the total business model surrounding a product

Even when attempts to hold technology secrets closely work for awhile, the rapid pace of technology development from so many fronts makes technology ownership fleeting at best and calls forth new strategies focused on forging business relationships and applying technology creatively in new business models.[5]

To capitalize on such factors, rather than merely endure them, companies have employed a number of tactics, including:

- Paying greater attention to developing open standards that create greater value for customers and more opportunities for multiple companies, that is, making the pie bigger;
- Putting more emphasis on the integration of products used in customers' businesses, opening up connections to other companies' products;
- Understanding better where customers obtain value (or could obtain value) from one's expertise;
- Unbundling products and offering different combinations of component technologies in new markets, including even one's competitors;
- Licensing technologies to other companies both as a revenue stream and as cross-licensing defense;
- Teaming with customers or suppliers in jointly developing new products and processes;
- Following fast with technologies pioneered by innovators in other companies;

- Broadening company research expertise to focus not only on the internal conduct of research but also on the evaluation of research conducted elsewhere;

- Developing corporate programs for incubating startup technology ventures inside a company, for creating spin-off companies to take peripheral new ideas to market, and for making investments in independent new ventures in other companies;

- Developing complementary processes for evaluating and acting on opportunities to acquire (or reacquire) technology ventures developed outside; and

- Establishing joint or satellite research enterprises with other organizations, including also national laboratories and universities.

Numerous advantages have been realized from such tactics, including faster time to market, increased revenues from multiple value streams, and in many cases even simply corporate survival. Case histories for all of these have been described elsewhere and generally need not be further elaborated here. Worth further discussion are the roles of university organizations in relation to open innovation in the corporate sector.

Universities are created with a purpose of advancing knowledge, so an obvious place for companies to look for ideas is to universities with cutting-edge technology innovations relevant to their products. Notable historical examples include:

- An IBM research center located next to Columbia University to spur and involve an early instance of a distinct university computer science faculty unit;

- Utilization by IBM of core computer memory invented by a faculty member at MIT;

- Major influence on worldwide automobile manufacturing from a research program on lean manufacturing principles led by MIT;[6]

- Influence of Stanford University research in the creation of multiple spin-off companies in what came to be known as Silicon Valley. Similar instances of this effect appear near many other universities, including Columbia and MIT.[7]

These and many other examples affirm the potential value of university work as part of commercial wealth creation and in each instance have depended on remarkable individual initiatives outside of the paradigms of the time. When one tries to generalize ways to broaden the possibilities of partnerships between businesses and universities, two challenges become clear.

The first of these concerns intellectual property ownership. While the idea of open innovation involves lowering intellectual property trade barriers between companies and other organizations, such trade is still marked by clear exchanges of valuable property rights. Trade involves the exchange of considerations, not a free-for-all in general. Universities have historically been conflicted over the idea of knowledge ownership. With the advent of Bayh-Dole legislation,[8] universities were encouraged to seek patents on inventions arising from their research funded by the federal government, and as a result, universities now point with pride to rather large patent portfolios. Still, when it comes to carving up ownership rights to pieces of knowledge, there are deep concerns in academic communities, analogous to concerns about fences in the range wars of the old west. While universities wish to facilitate the translation of knowledge into useful objects for the communities they serve, they also have to preserve their freedom to continue to explore and not sell off their access to future areas of inquiry. While the Bayh-Dole Act is the best known federal statement on university patenting, it applies principally to the commercialization of research originally funded by the federal government. It does not answer questions of ownership of research funded in other ways such as through industry sponsorship. In 1997 the Internal Revenue Service entered the picture to articulate rules consistent with tax exemptions in university business that also helped preserve the essential character of universities as sources of knowledge for the common good. Section 2 of this chapter will be devoted to a discussion of how universities have used these rules to guide their transactions with industry around research and intellectual property ownership for mutual benefit.

As an aside, the rise of notable open source software products like Linux does not diminish or dodge the importance of intellectual property ownership questions;[9] it just sets out an alternative discipline. Some universities have innovated by placing special emphasis on creating open source intellectual property—for example, the University of California at Berkeley.[10] Open source represents a distinct branching off from mainstream models of open innovation. It still involves a discipline of exchange and careful attention to the maintenance of licenses that specify obligations of a developer when creating subsequent derivative works. Such licenses often specify, for example, that software improvements or new software products incorporating open source material must themselves remain open source and subject to the same license terms as sources from which they are derived. Thus ownership is not ignored, but rather specified to be held and preserved in common. Businesses that make use of such products must carefully take account of such terms and build suitable business models that earn value not necessarily from the sale of licenses to the open source objects but rather from services or other complementary products used with the common property.

The second challenge in building fruitful university-industry relationships is a matchmaking dilemma (i.e., how to acquaint companies with the offerings of particular university researchers both in terms of results already achieved and perhaps more importantly in terms of research potential). Industry's knowledge of results already achieved is to some extent a matter of their tracking published literature, which is extensively indexed and cross-referenced in indices, published papers, and search engines. Dedicated programs of tracking relevant research across the world are important activities for industrial research departments. Nevertheless, knowing everything that is going on is more easily said than done, and there is at least the worry that some vital nascent breakthrough has been missed in the modern explosion of published material. The other problem with relying on published literature for innovation tracking is that once published, that part of the know-how is either in the public domain or already the property of someone else. That may be quite acceptable if one's business innovations depend on novel marketing and business models and not so much on unique technology. But often companies search for advantages based on unique technology. How is a company to know what it should be most interested in concerning *potential future research* at a given university? A range of strategies to improve the chances for meaningful encounters between university and industry personnel will be explored in section 3 of this chapter.

THE PIVOTAL PLACE OF INTELLECTUAL PROPERTY AGREEMENTS IN UNIVERSITY–INDUSTRY RESEARCH RELATIONSHIPS

The impact of the Bayh-Dole Act, mentioned earlier, was felt soon after its passage in the form of stepped up licensing of federally funded research results. In contrast, the influence of new Internal Revenue Service regulations on intellectual property disposition came to the university scene with much less notice at first. IRS Revenue Procedure 97–14, published in 1997,[11] was noticed early on by those universities most active in industry-sponsored research. But five years later, at a forum on the Commercialization of the Academy, eight out of 13 papers mentioned the effects of Bayh-Dole and only one discussed the effects of IRS regulations. Since that time, university policies concerning intellectual property rights allowed to industrial research sponsors have been heavily influenced by these regulations. More recently, the IRS issued a revised edition, Revenue Procedure 2007–47,[12] to clarify some ambiguities in the original version over how

Bayh-Dole rights might affect application of the Revenue procedures. The main thrusts concerning industry-funded research were unchanged.

Many misunderstand the IRS regulations and infer that the IRS took the initiative to limit university activities, supposedly in an effort to keep the universities pure and true to their mission to expand knowledge unfettered. The actual limitations were put in place by the U.S. Congress in the Tax Reform Act of 1986 and, ironically, the purpose of the cited IRS revenue procedures was to establish a safe haven in which universities could operate without running afoul of the provisions of this legislation. These included limitations on tax exempt bonds such that no more than 5 to 10 percent of the proceeds of the bonds issued to institutions could be directly or indirectly used to benefit private business purposes. Since universities often finance buildings or other facilities through tax exempt bonds, they might not be entitled to tax exemptions if more than 5 to 10 percent of the research conducted within the facilities benefited business sponsors. Thus, the cited revenue procedures stipulate that business sponsorship of research will not be counted as "private business use" of facilities funded by tax exempt bonds if the following safe haven conditions are met:

> A research agreement relating to property used for basic research supported or sponsored by a sponsor [does not result in private business use] if any license or other use of resulting technology by the sponsor is permitted only on the same terms as the recipient would permit that use by any unrelated, non-sponsoring party (that is, the sponsor must pay a competitive price for its use), and the price paid for that use must be determined at the time the license or other resulting technology is available for use. Although the recipient need not permit persons other than the sponsor to use any license or other resulting technology, the price paid by the sponsor must be no less than the price that would be paid by any nonsponsoring party for those same rights."[13]

The essential stipulations in the above are that:

- The work sponsored by industry must fit the IRS definition of basic research, which is "any original investigation for the advancement of scientific knowledge not having a specific commercial objective"
- The sponsoring company may be offered an exclusive or other license to technology developed under the company's sponsorship but only on the same terms and for a competitive price such as would be offered to any other entity

- Such a license may not be pre-sold. Any license agreement can be entered into and a price determined only after the development is far enough along that the value of the development can be fairly determined. This means that the cost of a license cannot be built into the initial contract or sponsorship agreement.

Universities take these safe haven rules very seriously, since losing tax exempt status for their bonds would be a very serious risk. In practice, universities seeking new tax-free bond programs are certified by examiners to be compliant with the conditions for tax exemption. So they are subject to careful scrutiny concerning compliance at the point that a bond program is set up. If in later examinations a university was found to be noncompliant and the issued bonds lost their tax exemption, then investors would have cause to seek compensation from the university. Getting future bonds would also be problematic or create added expense.[14] As will be discussed later, there is not complete agreement among all stakeholders as to the weight of these risks or whether the IRS position is challengeable, but suffice it to say for now that universities seldom if ever take that risk.

Several tactics are possible in principle for accommodating industry work while remaining compliant with the cited IRS regulations. Such tactics include:

- Carefully limiting industry sponsored work to be carried out with facilities not financed with tax exempt bonds so that the details of the cited IRS regulations need not apply; or
- Preparing contract research agreements for use with industry that are consistent with the conditions set out by the IRS.

Attention has been given by some universities to the first strategy, although one can see from their experiences that the tracking of what research is done where becomes cumbersome and complex.[15] In national forums between industry and university leaders, the industry side has sometimes urged that such strategies be used more often in order to permit greater flexibility in intellectual property terms in research agreements. However, complexity of tracking in such matters is further compounded by the university's encouragement of faculty to engage in collaborative interdisciplinary research crossing many boundaries within the university. Thus, tracking and ensuring that any given research is done only in a neatly definable section of university facilities is problematic, and many universities have opted to just keep things simple and write research agreements that are consistent with the IRS regulations.

In any case, a scan of policies in use by major research universities today indicates that most now work from agreement templates that meet the standards of IRS Revenue Procedure 2007–47. Such research agreements commonly begin with a clear statement of purpose consistent with basic research and then

- Define intellectual property in such a way as to clarify that which is owned by the sponsoring company through actions solely by their personnel, that owned by the university through actions solely by university personnel, and that owned jointly through collaborative efforts;
- Grant the company a right of first refusal to negotiate an exclusive license (in an appropriate field of use and subject to any existing third party rights) to any university-owned intellectual property developed as part of a research agreement funded by the company—and with the same access also for the university's rights in any joint intellectual property;
- Assert that any such license shall be negotiated in good faith on fair and reasonable terms after notice of disclosure of the creation of intellectual property and within reasonable limits on the time for exercising the company's option to negotiate such a license; and
- Retain certain licenses for the university to enable ongoing research and educational activities.

The above may represent a kind of current equilibrium in university-industry contracting, but that is not to say that everyone is satisfied with this state of understanding.

There are still significant expressions of discontent both inside and outside academe. An interesting "Dialog between a Major State University and a Major Global Company Headquartered in the United States" has been released by the School of Engineering of Iowa State University and illustrates commonly heard complaints from industry.[16] Among the points brought out in this paper are the contrasting and difficult to resolve positions summarized in Table 5.1.

The bottom line from such dialogs is often a feeling in industry that universities should be more flexible in reaching accommodation with industry on IP terms and should partner with industry in challenging the IRS positions that constrain university policies. The fact this has not happened to any significant degree is sometimes taken to mean that universities are either very risk averse or actually prefer positions consistent with the IRS Revenue procedures. Both views are true to some degree.

Table 5.1: Contrasting Views of Contracting and Licensing Terms

University Positions	Industry Responses
1. Intellectual property (IP) rights are often a sticking point with industry. Industry expectations of owning the IP created by their funding of university research are unrealistically based on customary work for hire relationships with commercial contractors.	Universities' expectations are colored by their strong reliance on federal funding which grants them liberal IP rights. Foreign universities do not have these expectations and may soon displace U.S. universities as resources to U.S. industry.
2. Companies say they fund research projects at the university and therefore deserve to own the resulting IP, but they are really only funding the marginal costs of the next steps after a great deal of prior work has been funded by the university or others. Companies come to the universities because the latter have developed valuable expertise not possessed by the companies.	This is a red herring. The companies also bring a great deal of experience and understanding of important problems and background methodologies to such engagements. While the expertise of the universities is the attraction, there are also offsetting risks from dealing with universities which may have difficulty producing practical results.
3. University policies and procedures must conform to U.S. tax and export regulations and therefore the universities must restrict attention to basic research, must publish openly, and cannot pre-sell intellectual property.	These claims are exaggerated because the IRS Revenue Procedures are not tax law and have not been tested in the courts. Moreover, universities do not take enough advantage of the opportunity to place their industry research in facilities that were not built by tax free bonds or ones where the bonds have matured and are no longer at issue.
4. Further on that last point, the university is unable under U.S. tax policies to set license terms until the technology is ready to use.	Companies fear universities will be unrealistic in their assessments of the business values of their contributions and it may be impossible to come to mutual agreement. This impasse may not be realized until the research and patent costs have already been met by the companies. At the point when a university is finished with their part of the development cycle, the technology will often still be a long way from ready to use and the company will be faced with risky decisions the university may not fully appreciate.

(Continued)

Table 5.1: Contrasting Views of Contracting and Licensing Terms (*Continued*)

University Positions	Industry Responses
5. Exclusive licensing is an adequate substitute for patent assignment and one with a good track record in product commercialization.	True, but there are some circumstances where assignment would be preferable so that a company's in-house patents can be better coordinated with those arising from funded university research.
6. A university's retention of patent rights encourages its faculty to work with industry on patentable inventions because, among other things, the university inventors can share in the rewards from license revenue.	True, as far as that goes, but it disincentivizes the company to encourage any more invention within the university context than absolutely necessary and can choke off long term collaborations.

First on the risk: there may indeed be some technical merit to questions about the foundations of the cited IRS revenue procedures, though one must remember that the Congress and not the IRS is the source of the underlying restrictions. IRS revenue procedures are only a safe haven from the full application of the Tax Reform Act of 1986. Questions about tax law will not be resolved by the present essay and are in any case quite complex legal issues.[17] Failing to find a simple alternative path through the legal maze, university policy makers are not ready to risk accepting unrestricted work-for-hire terms. For one thing the risks that they would take in pushing that envelope are not mere business risks commensurate with the scale of a particular research contract, but are more fundamental risks to the credit and reputation of the university which could embroil them in years of litigation. Furthermore, it is not as if a brave university can gain so much benefit from advertising that it is now willing to lead the way and challenge generally accepted practice by accommodating work-for-hire terms. That advertisement might not only bring industry calling but could also hasten a government challenge and tie up the university's assets for the duration. Thus normal business exhortations to grasp risks in view of greater rewards are a stretch in this context. The appropriate venue for challenges to U.S. tax policies or laws would be through a joint initiative by university-industry coalitions. Some of these will be described later and some attention has been given to this topic, but without any conclusions to date.

A significant reason that these issues remain unresolved is that a clear picture has not yet emerged of a better set of rules than those expressed in the IRS revenue procedures. Universities appreciate some protective boundaries because their business is fundamentally to accomplish one intellectual achievement after another, indefinitely. Selling off rights to these in a succession of intellectual property deals is a very delicate matter because researchers' future access to foundational intellectual property can be threatened, as can their access to future research sponsorship. The fact that any given research outcome might be patentable in its own right does not mean that to practice it will not infringe patents on previous work.[18] So at the very least universities are conditioned to be careful about intellectual property management and to try to maintain rights to access the intellectual landscape to which they have contributed. This is not to say that the IRS revenue procedures cited here by themselves guarantee to protect such access. They do not necessarily do that because permitted exclusive licenses could be written in such a way that they would lock up access to needed intellectual property just as much as outright patent assignments would. However, the opportunity is there for negotiation of more measured IP terms, especially since the implications of any new technology might be better understood later in an engagement than at the outset. It used to be that universities also relied upon "experimental use" exceptions to protect them from claims of patent infringement when they practiced previously patented technology in new research. Recent court decisions have held that a university is not automatically afforded this protection because it is seen to be in the *business* of conducting research and receives rewards for engaging in this business.[19] Thus universities have begun to include explicit terms in licenses that provide them with future access to the research subject matter.

To be sure, members of university communities are themselves conflicted over IP issues. Many university researchers rail against their contracting or technology licensing offices over their handling of proposed deals with industry sponsors. Some of the commonly experienced tensions are sketched in Table 5.2.

The common thread running through faculty, university, and industry concerns is a wish for expeditious negotiations that are as fair as possible to all interests but avoid exhausting the parties' patience. Most of the contrasting views in Tables 5.1 and 5.2 can be brought to an acceptable common ground through better communication and understanding of respective needs.

The thought that industry and academe should come together at a high level to work on systemic improvements in relations is something that has borne fruit in several forums, including:

- *Government-University-Industry Research Roundtable* (GUIRR) sponsored by the U.S. National Academies. Its mission is "to convene senior-most representatives from government, universities,

Table 5.2: Possible Contrasting Outlooks of Faculty and Their University Administrators in Charge of Contracting and Licensing

Faculty Concerns	Administration Perspective
The contracting or licensing office is taking too long or being too picky about IP terms. There is a risk this important research contract opportunity will be lost if the industry sponsor loses patience.	The company may be asking for terms that are out of bounds and time is needed to explore possible alternatives. Today's deals can impact tomorrow's possibilities and require due care.
Sometimes faculty members see no great patentable breakthrough as possible in the next proposed research and advise that there is no harm in assigning patent rights when there may be none in any case. This approach is urged to expedite closure of a deal.	It is difficult to guarantee no discoveries will be made without awkward language in the contract. Still sometimes very simple terms can be agreed with a promise to renegotiate if the assumptions prove incorrect. Negotiators try to avoid precedents that can cloud future negotiations when assumptions about inventions are different.
Conversely, some faculty members express surprise and dismay when the contracting or licensing office grants a sponsoring company customary rights to consider licenses from sponsored work. Some faculty members prefer to maintain proprietary control of their own inventions or, at the other end of the spectrum, to make sure they are in the public domain.	Such missed expectations principally signal a failure of communication. Assumptions are sometimes made, in the absence of sufficient communication, that it is ok to apply generally accepted terms in the interest of expeditious negotiation of the agreement.
Sometimes a concern arises after a license is negotiated. Faculty members may feel the university has sold the license too cheaply.	Administrations can be caught between conflicting expectations of the stakeholders, making ideal solutions difficult. Again, failures to understand all the expectations of all the stakeholders in a timely way can be involved in this predicament.

and industry to define and explore critical issues related to the national and global science and technology agenda that are of shared interest; to frame the next critical question stemming from current debate and analysis; and to incubate activities of ongoing value to the stakeholders. This forum will be designed to facilitate candid dialogue among participants, to foster self-implementing activities, and, where appropriate, to carry awareness of consequences to the wider public."[20] Under this larger umbrella the following important focused program has emerged:

- *University-Industry Partnership* or the *University-Industry Congress 2003–2006* morphed into the *University-Industry Demonstration Partnership* (UIDP) in 2006. The UIDP and its predecessors have been important forums though which university and industry leaders from a wide spectrum of institutions have developed important principles and tools to support working together on research and innovation.[21]

- Another forum is the *University-Industry Innovation Summit* sponsored by IBM and the Ewing Marion Kauffman Foundation and involving six major research universities and four major information systems corporations that met in 2005 and 2007 to develop consensus principles for collaborative research and the development of open source products.[22]

Two key documents[23] prepared by the National Council of Research Administrators (NCURA) and the Industrial Research Institute (IRI) as part of their participation in the first two forums above set out key principles for finding paths through the issues already discussed in this section.

The first and most important of these principles is that "a successful university-industry collaboration should support the mission of each partner. Any effort in conflict with the mission of either partner will ultimately fail." Merely telling the other party that something one side wants is legal (or worse, that the other side is being unreasonable) does not meet the spirit of this test. Such comments may help clear the air as part of a full and frank dialog, but ultimately common ground must be sought in which each side's essential must haves are identified, refined, and accommodated as far as possible. Reference 23 provides a lengthy list of needs typical of universities and companies, among which are:

For universities

- Educate students year after year;
- Perform research year after year;
- Publish to advance knowledge available to the public;
- Meet high standards of compliance with federal and state laws to preserve public trust;
- Perform work for multiple research sponsors fairly and consistently.

For companies

- Earn a return on research investments, including those placed at universities;
- Have engagements and projects completed in a timely manner relative to company needs;
- Conclude agreements enabling profitable commercialization.

As will be seen in the following discussion, the exact expression of the must haves depends on where the intended relationship is in a spectrum of possibilities, but in any case the hope is that prompt and honest appreciation of each side's mission constraints and desirable outcomes can lead to common ground in contracting and license agreements. Given the rise in recent years of industry-sponsored research at universities to over $2.6 billion, there is a lot of evidence that people can get to yes.

The second principle, listed in Table 5.3, points to the need for the parties to take long views and appreciate the value to both sides of really substantive relationships. This means that both parties should take university-industry relationships seriously enough to invest in the requisite expertise. This does not come easily in the present situation. In 2007, industry funding to universities, while growing, was still only 5.4 percent of total university research funding. This tends to mean that a relatively small fraction of university resources is directed at industry contracting and a commensurate small fraction of the faculty's time involves experience with industry contracting. Meanwhile, industry's investment in research at universities has represented only about one percent of their total research expenditures (internal and external). It should be no wonder then that there are familiarity gaps and misunderstandings between such parties. If the degree of mutual involvement is to increase significantly, both cultures need to invest in programs to build understanding in their people about the other culture. Personnel exchanges and cross-hiring can of course help

Table 5.3: Guiding Principles for University–Industry Endeavors

Guiding Principle #1: A successful university-industry collaboration should support the mission of each partner. Any effort in conflict with the mission of either partner will ultimately fail.

Guiding Principle #2: Institutional practices and national resources should focus on fostering appropriate long-term partnerships between universities and industry.

Guiding Principle #3: Universities and industry should focus on maximizing value resulting from collaborations by streamlining negotiations and measuring results.

but are not silver bullets. It takes time for transplants to become accepted, adapted, and informed representatives of their new culture, and there is a limit to how many deals can flow through them. Georgia Tech has taken two significant steps in these regards. First, it has formed an industry contracting group as a separate department staffed by contracting officers with significant industry experience. Secondly, to foster a wider experience base in the faculty, this author and others have developed internal courses for faculty covering industry contracting principles and intellectual property decision making.

Yet even these steps will not be sufficient by themselves without additional programs to expand active participation by faculty in interchanges with industry and in active development of new research programs for this sector. Such experiences for the faculty are necessary not only to build their knowledge of relevant business practices but also to build their confidence about what works. University administrators and faculty alike often make the mistake of supposing that getting the right contracting, licensing, and technology transfer people and policies are the only keys. Those arrangements help a great deal but faculty are on the front line in making contacts, understanding sponsor needs, explaining technical possibilities, and setting expectations. It is difficult to make progress from the university side in building relations with industry without providing a substantial boost to the faculty's know-how in industry relations. Years of success in federal grant and proposal writing have built the necessary experience with the federal funding sector. Increased mentoring, training, and relationship-building opportunities are needed now for prospective faculty and industry collaborators and for people in their respective support structures.

The third and final principle from the NCURA-IRI study (Table 5.3) emphasizes the importance of reducing aggravation and the time needed for contracting and licensing negotiations. Data have been gathered as part of the UDIP that indicate that 80 percent of contracts are successfully negotiated in five months, but surely in many cases that is long compared with the time frame of the opportunity. Furthermore, that time is often spent in uncomfortable wrangling that works against the potential relationship. What can be done?

Many universities have introduced and make use of Master Agreements (MAs), an analog to the Basic Ordering Agreements (or Indefinite Delivery/Indefinite Quantity contracts) common in federal research contracting. An MA is negotiated by a university at the beginning of a potentially long term relationship with a particular industry partner where an area of work is contemplated that may involve many steps. Such an agreement covers the basic terms and conditions that will govern all work to be performed. Terms pertaining to particular tasks (the statement of work, performance period, cost, and any exceptions to the basic terms that are required for the particular task) are described in subsequent individual Task Order Agreements which are negotiated as they are needed. MAs get most of the dialog about terms and conditions out of the way in the beginning of relationships and expedite contracting for the university-industry parties as they move through the later Task Order stages. They put the parties in a frame of mind to think in terms of a longer term relationship. And they allow work to be defined in clear increments in which there is less guesswork and thus diminished risk on both sides.

As was mentioned earlier, patterns are emerging for some consistency in starting terms for contracting and licensing across different universities. Near consensus by research universities about how to handle the rules set out in IRS Revenue Procedures and the emergence of some standards in licensing have tended to create some familiar and consistent starting points in negotiations. But in the end, one must remember that there is no one perfect answer that fits all situations, so it is also helpful to have guidelines for how to consider special features.

Some intriguing insights have come out of one of the projects of the UIDP, namely, one devoted to the development of a software tool called TurboNegotiator[24] that aims to provide industry-university contract negotiators with guidance in *customizing* contact and licensing terms. It has an interview section that helps the negotiating parties place their situations in a multi-dimensional space marked by answers to questions covering:

- Nature of research—fundamental or applied?
- Nature and extent of contributions of each party
- Nature and likelihood of desired outcomes—deliverables, patents?

Once both parties mutually understand their engagement space, they can be led to consider the most relevant contract options from a library of possibilities and can also be provided with further in-depth explanations. The hope for this tool is to provide a platform for common training and to facilitate quicker mutual understanding of options. Since it arises from a forum involving wide participation from many respected universities and companies, the worry over whether a best practice has been missed will be avoided. To date TurboNegotiator has been released to the UIDP members for beta-testing and results in practical cases are eagerly awaited. There is also a public access site, http://turbo.sitesetup.net/, which offers a growing list of papers expressing consensus understanding reached by the industry-university project team about many issues concerning research and related agreements.

THE MATCHMAKING DILEMMA IN FACILITATING UNIVERSITY–INDUSTRY RESEARCH RELATIONSHIPS

The foregoing section has discussed some pivotal issues that need resolution in any research contract to be concluded between a given company and a given university. One of the underlying factors highlighted is that the two organizations are fundamentally different in nature. A university is unlike a for-profit corporation in many ways; for example, it tends to be more grassroots-oriented than most corporations. Someone once said that a major research university is just a collection of thousands of research and educational entrepreneurs who share only a common parking-lot problem. The resulting diversity of research interests is both a blessing and a challenge for corporations searching for help with a particular problem.

Most major research universities have developed spotlights to help with this challenge. It is recognized that investments in new faculty and research facilities have more impact if they are focused in a few topical areas. The choice of these may be the outgrowth of formal strategic planning based on an assessment of national and regional needs and unique complementary building blocks already found at the university. Or they may arise serendipitously from the advent of major new external overtures and investments. Flowing from such choices are numerous press releases and publications that invite attention to new research centers, new distinguished faculty members, and so forth, which can result in significant notice from industry.

University research centers, particularly ones focused on industry needs, are another way of creating not only valuable research agendas but also communities of two-way familiarity that deepen company contacts with host universities. Some research centers have been spurred by federal investments through such programs as NSF's Industry/University Cooperative Research Centers program, which began around 1980[25] and helped to get a broad range of companies thinking about how they could better utilize university communities to tap valuable ideas.

Nevertheless, one still hears puzzlement today from companies seeking more effective strategic ties to selected universities or seeking simply to discover some missing technological ingredient for a particular product opportunity. "How do we find out where to go in the university for X?" or "What does the university have that we should be interested in?" In large research universities, each of the thousands of faculty members have things they are presently funded to be working on, things they are thinking about, and things they used to work on and would be glad to go back to. Ask university people what their core competencies are and it is hard to get a succinct list. The culture of universities, even with a great deal of attention to multidisciplinary research, still reinforces individualism in a way that opens up many lines of investigation. With a kaleidoscope like this, there are not necessarily crisp answers to the questions posed above, even if one knew all one wished.

Perhaps in simpler times the self-indexing nature of university departments, organized around degree subjects, would be a place to begin. If one had a question that seemed to be about electronics, one would start by talking to the department of electrical engineering, or maybe physics. However, the drive to be ever more multidisciplinary has created two phenomena that complicate this strategy. First, most departments of instruction now span wide areas of subject matter. Schools of mechanical engineering, for example, are apt to include experts in some aspects or applications of electronics, such as electronics in industrial controls and the mechanics of electronic packaging. Secondly, interdisciplinary centers have become commonplace in the university and create alternate affiliation identities for the faculty therein. Knowing where on a campus to visit, let alone who to visit, is hard.

Some experimental programs have been created to assist companies when they need more than their existing contacts and searches of the World Wide Web and campus websites. For example, Georgia Tech has initiated a Strategic Partners Office to serve a number of important bridging functions. Professionals staff the office to help companies find their way in the Institute and to facilitate introductory meetings with individual researchers. In cases where a major strategic alliance is contemplated and unfolds, the office can stay in touch with engagements in multiple departments to assist with coordination and problem resolution. Alliances that mature are generally understood to take root in deepening relationships and mutual respect between industry champions and faculty leaders. Nevertheless, an office focused on strategic relationships can provide some additional glue and can spot and help resolve potential issues that may otherwise interrupt the flow of good results. However, one should not expect this sort of thing to mature into a top-down model of operational management, which would be inconsistent with typical university cultures. It is better to see it as a complement, not a new order.

There are also third-party groups apart from universities and companies who are interested in match making. Section 1 mentioned the important influence of venture capital firms (and related earlier stage investors) as catalysts for open innovation. VC firms are intensely interested in new technology and business possibilities, though they know that university discoveries often need more work. Says the Stevens Institute at the University of Southern California in a recent white paper, "Venture capitalists are eager to share stories of their successes, but they are also vocal about their disappointment dealing with universities. They view academia as a rich potential source of lucrative deals, but are often frustrated by how difficult it is to identify, extract, and develop ideas into thriving businesses."[26] Intermediaries have grown up with the mission to act as a bridge between technologists and people in the business sector. Sometimes called innovation capitalist firms, they invest their time and expertise in digging out market-ready ideas and then offer their vetted discoveries to the marketplace that can realize the potential. Universities are among the places such firms scour to find possible nuggets. A number of different styles of matchmaking have been identified and some guidance has been provided concerning how to engage such services most effectively.[27]

It will be interesting to see how emerging social network tools may provide additional methods to discover and explore research relationship opportunities. This may give the parties a feeling of more control over the choices they will make than they may feel they have with middlemen matchmakers, but there are several challenges, among which are:

- Knowing how to set and operate filters so as to get more wheat than chaff; and
- Knowing how much to share in the open (that is not already published) while looking for persons who might be interested.

Ultimately success will come down to establishing mature, quality relationships between people with common research and development interests, and these will succeed best when both parties are experienced and confident about building the relationships.

CONCLUSIONS: HOW TO BUILD A SUSTAINED UNIVERSITY RESEARCH PROGRAM SUPPORTED BY INDUSTRY

This essay has explored the way universities and their partners organize to engage in research exchanges as part of open innovation. The promise of university creativity has attracted about $2.6 billion total research funding annually from industry but, as noted earlier, this represents only a little over 5 percent of total university research funding. Some hopeful signs for future growth appear to be:

- The university and corporate communities realize they are very different types of organizations with fundamentally different missions. They have come to agreement that successful contracts must be consistent with the missions of both parties or they will fail. Deeper dialog is taking place about a range of acceptable terms that lie within currently tested legal norms. Future clarifications of national tax policies and laws may expand the possibilities though clarity about the form of better rules has not yet been reached.

- Both industry and university leaders (including faculty) want to shorten the time and aggravation it takes to get agreements. Hope of progress comes from substantive experiments such as those around the TurboNegotiator project.

- It is recognized as critical that people in industry and the university gain experience and confidence in working with one another.

The author was recently asked, "What does it take to build a university program with sustained industry funding?" He concluded there are 3.5 necessary things that are consistent with the discussions earlier in this essay:

1. Select a few areas of technology and application know-how in which the faculty group can excel and for which industry has a compelling need. Do not just settle for things that come up as isolated inquiries. Choosing good initiatives (markets) will require careful analysis of faculty interests and resources with an appreciation of important needs in society and commerce. The faculty's aim may have to morph to new enthusiasms as they understand better the critical sore points and issues in the outside world to which they can give attention. Build a mutual appreciation of these goals with early involvement of prospective industry partners. In fact, innovate in creating communities of industry that can get to know the faculty group and get past the matchmaking hurdles. Furthermore, be prepared to consider not only the research the university can do but also complementary services that can create innovative business models from the perspective of both parties.

2. Build the expertise and confidence of the faculty team and its supporting staff in dealing with industry. Make sure that they lead from what they can do and do not waste energies ruing what they cannot change. The issues to master are not all in the contract terms at the start of the engagement. Just as important is having a sharp sense of the clock speed in industry and of the form of the deliverables that will enable a given company sponsor to make best use of the results. What does the sponsor have to have, and when? Invest in training and mentorship.

3. Build a program that multiple companies can support. It is very difficult to break out of the five percent industry research funding part of the ladder without engaging more than one company. Successful large programs can be built for a time on the support of just one company and that can feel good while all is well. But relationships often rest on company champions and when these people leave their positions or their companies, relationships can quickly evaporate as part of a company's customary need to change the furniture to suit the new leaders. Plural funding of research programs provides a buffer against changes in particular sponsors, but it also presents a challenge to manage the integrity and expectations of each individual engagement in relation to the whole. Consortial funding of research may also need to be considered as an option. Keep in mind that a relationship of trust is central to serving multiple sponsors in related areas of research. To the extent that long term singular relationships do mature, invest the time of senior university leaders in reinforcing relationships with company people as high as possible in the organization.

3.5 Make special arrangements to involve small and start-up businesses. They are often working at the cutting edge of new technology and business models. On the other hand they have to be very careful with money and often do not have the resources by themselves to sustain a substantive research effort. Plan to find and tap supplemental research funding, such as from economic development agencies, where possible to make sure that the university can sustain a business model including this cambium of commerce.

In the third workshop of the Chemical Sciences Roundtable, Christopher Hill charted out five eras with characteristically different understandings between industry and universities over research and development.[28] These were the pre-World War II era, postwar era through the 1960s, the post-oil embargo era after 1973–74, the competitiveness crisis of the 1980s, and the present era of industrial restructuring beginning in the early 1990s. This was the era in which open innovation became a widely-accepted expectation and the possibility of vital university contributions to industry was glimpsed. As this essay has tried to show, there remains the opportunity of really capitalizing on this possibility, for those determined to do so.

NOTES

1. National Science Foundation, "Universities Report Continued Decline in Real Federal S&E R&D Funding in FY 2007," InfoBrief Science Resource Statistics, NSF 08–320, August 2008, http://www.nsf.gov/statistics/infbrief/nsf08320/nsf08320.pdf; President's Council of Advisors on Science and Technology, *University-Private Sector Research Partnerships in the Innovation Ecosystem*, November 2008, http://www.ostp.gov/galleries/PCAST/past_research_partnership_report_BOOK.pdf; Robert Killoren and Susan B. Butts, "Industry-University Research in Our Times," published by the National Academies as background for their project "Re-Engineering Intellectual Property Rights Agreements in Industry-University Collaborations," June 26, 2003, http://www7.nationalacademies.org/guirr/IP_background.html.

2. Ronald A. Bohlander, "Pushing the Envelope in University Involvement with Commercialization," presented at the Sam Nunn Bank of America Policy Forum on *Commercialization of the Academy*, Emory University, April 5–7, 2002 and published in *Buying In or Selling Out: Essays on the Commercialization of the American Research University*, ed. Donald Stein (Piscataway, NJ Rutgers University Press, 2004), 75–88.

3. See, for example, Alvin Toffler, *Powershift: Knowledge, Wealth, and Power at the Edge of the 21st Century* (New York: Bantam, 1991); Stephen L. Goldman, Roger N. Nagel, and Kenneth Preiss, *Agile Competitors and Virtual Organizations: Strategies for Enriching the Customer* (New York: Van Nostrand Reinhold, 1995).

4. Henry Chesbrough, *Open Innovation: The New Imperative for Creating and Profiting from Technology* (Boston: Harvard Business School Press, 2006); *Open Innovation: Researching a New Paradigm*, ed. Henry Chesbrough, Wim Vanhaverbecke, and Joel West (New York: Oxford University Press, 2006).

5. Henry Chesbrough, *Open Business Models: How to Thrive in the New Innovation Landscape* (Boston, MA: Harvard Business School Press, 2006).

6. James T. Womack, Daniel T. Jones, and Daniel Roos, *The Machine That Changed the World: The Story of Lean Production* (New York: Harper Perennial, 1991).

7. Scott Shane, *Academic Entrepreneurship: University Spinoffs and Wealth Creation* (Cheltenham, Gloucester, UK: Edward Elgar Publishing, 2004).

8. Council on Governmental Relations, *The Bayh-Dole Act: A Guide to the Law and Implementing Regulations*, Monograph, 1999.

9. Steven Weber, *The Success of Open Source* (Cambridge, MA: Harvard University Press, 2004).

10. University of California-Berkeley Academic Senate, "Report by Senate Task Force on University-Industry Partnerships," October 2008, http://academic-senate.berkeley.edu/pdf/TF_UIP_report-Final1.pdf.

11. U.S. Internal Revenue Service, Revenue Procedure 97–14, May 16, 1997, http://www.unclefed.com/Tax-Bulls/1997/Rp97-14.pdf.

12. U.S. Internal Revenue Service, *Internal Revenue Bulletin 2007–29* concerning Revenue Procedure 2007–47, July 16, 2007, http://www.irs.gov/irb/2007-29_IRB/ar12.html.

13. U.S. Code, Title 26, Sections 141 and 145. See for example http://www.law.cornell.edu/uscode/html/uscode26/usc_sec_26_00000141----000-.html, and http://www.law.cornell.edu/uscode/html/uscode26/usc_sec_26_00000145----000-.html.

14. Council on Governmental Relations, *University Industry Research Relationships,* Brochure published August 2007, http://www.cogr.edu/docs/UniversityIndustryBrochure.doc.

15. For example: Amy Kweskin, Craig McCurley, Richard Chirls, and Diana Hoadley, "Issues in Sponsored Research: Funding, Regulations, and Strategies to Cope," from the Proceedings of the Treasury Symposium for Higher Education 2007, San Antonio, Texas, sponsored by the Treasury Institute for Higher Education, February 12, 2007. http://www.treasury institute.org/resourcelibrary/Symposium_2007/15.pdf; RTI International, "Intellectual Property and Technology Commercialization in North Dakota: A Study for the North Dakota Department of Commerce and the State Board of Higher Education," Project 0210102.00, July 7, 2007, http://www.legis.nd.gov/assembly/59-2005/docs/pdf/ec071906 appendixh1.pdf.

16. Ted Okiishi and Ken Kirkland, "Dialog Between a Major State University and a Major Global Company Headquartered in the United States: Working with Industry on Sponsored Research Agreements," April 11, 2006, http://www.eng.iastate.edu/papers/IPdialog.pdf.

17. Joint Committee on Taxation Staff, "Present Law and Background Relating to Tax Exemptions and Incentives for Higher Education," JCX-49–06, Scheduled for a Hearing Before the Senate Committee on Finance on December 5, 2007. See http://www.house.gov/jct/x-49-06.pdf.

18. There is sometimes a mistaken expectation that a patent allows one to do the thing that is patented. If this were true one's next patentable invention would protect the inventor. However, in actuality, a patent only allows the inventor or assignee to prevent others from practicing the invention. The assignee must still respect the claims of all prior patents still in force. Thus improvements on prior patents are not necessarily clear of the thing improved.

19. AUTM, The Association of University Technology Managers, "In the Public Interest: Nine Points to Consider in Licensing University

Technology," March 6, 2007, http://www.autm.net/AM/Template. cfm?Section=Nine_Points_to_Consider.

20. U.S. National Academies, "Government-University-Industry Research Roundtable: Policy and Global Affairs, Mission Statement," http://www7.nationalacademies.org/guirr/About_GUIRR.html.

21. Merrilea J. Mayo, "University-Industry Demonstration Partnership," July 2006, http://uidp.org/UIDP_Intro.pdf; Roberto Peccei, Larry Rhoades, Susan Butts, and Bob Killoren, "Re-Engineering the University-Industry Partnership: From the University-Industry Congress to the University-Industry Demonstration Partnership," October 12, 2006, http://www7.nationalacademies.org/guirr/UIDP_Intro.ppt.

22. Ewing Marion Kauffman Foundation and International Business Machines Corporation, "Open Collaboration Principles," December 2005, http://www.kauffman.org/uploadedfiles/open_collaboration_principles_12_05.pdf; International Business Machines Corporation, "University-Industry Collaborative Research Principles," June 2007, http://www-304.ibm.com/jct01005c/university/scholars/collaborativeresearch/docs/FreeParticpantUsePrinciples_2 007.pdf.

23. National Council of University Research Administrators and Industrial Research Institute, *Living Studies in University-Industry Negotiations: Applications of the Guiding Principles for University-Industry Endeavors,* published by NCURA, April 2006 and available through the National Academies, http://www7.nationalacademies.org/guirr/Living_Studies.pdf; National Council of University Research Administrators and Industrial Research Institute, *Guiding Principles for University-Industry Endeavors,* published by NCURA, April 2006 and available through the National Academies: http://www7.nationalacademies.org/guirr/Guiding_Principles. pdf.

24. James J. Casey, "The University-Industry Demonstration Partnership: An Incremental Improvement to University-Industry Collaboration," in *Legal Framework for E-Research: Realizing the Potential,* ed. Brian Fitzgerald (Sydney: Sydney University Press, 2008). http://ses.library. usyd.edu.au/bitstream/2123/2681/1/LegalFramework_Ch13.pdf.

25. Denis O. Gray, "Creating Win-Win Partnerships: Background and Evolution of Industry/University Cooperative Research Centers Model," in *Managing the Industry/University Cooperative Research Center: A Guide for Directors and Other Stakeholders,* ed. Denis O. Gray and S. George Walters (Columbus, OH: Battelle Press, 1998). See also http://www.ncsu.edu/iucrc/PurpleBook.htm.

26. Krisztina "Z" Holly, "Venture Capital—University Interface: Best Practices to Make Maximum Impact," Stevens Institute, University of Southern California white paper, February 3, 2009, http://stevens.usc.

edu/docs/vcstudy.pdf and http://stevens.usc.edu/read_article.php?news_
id=424.

27. Satish Nambisan and Mohanbir Sawhey, "A Buyer's Guide to the
Innovation Bazaar," *Harvard Business Review* 85, no. 6 (June 2007):
109–118.

28. Christopher T. Hill, "Partnerships in Research: The Evolution
of Expectations," Proceedings of the Third Workshop of the Chemical
Sciences Roundtable titled Research Teams and Partnerships: Trends in
the Chemical Sciences (Washington, DC: The National Academies Press):
chap. 2, 21–27.

CHAPTER 6

An Industrial Perspective on University Technology Commercialization Practice

Albert Johnson

The comments that follow reflect my personal opinion concerning patents and know-how generated by university laboratories via sponsored research (funded by industry, foundations, and government) and related issues. They are intended to encourage thinking and discussion in academic and industrial communities having an interest in the subject.

First, I will share background observations from my university and industry employment, as well as some history as premises for my comments. Then I will outline current observations and opinion, followed by some points for future discussion.

HISTORY AND BACKGROUND

Industry and academe have a longer history as partners and collaborators than many people realize. The relationship between industry and academe is longstanding and has coevolved with the impact of the resultant technologies.[1] In the 1890s, scientific research at major universities was largely a major input for what was then high tech industry—namely, electrification, telegraphy/telephony, and chemical inputs and processes for agriculture and steel. The dominant, vital industries of the time were machine tools, firearms, clocks, sewing machines, hardware, agricultural implements, bicycles, steel, electrification, and telegraphy/telephony. Universities founded by philanthropic industrialists (i.e., Stevens Institute of Technology) and either funded (University of California) or transformed

(Rutgers College of New Jersey forming the Rutgers Scientific School) by the Morrill Act of 1862 and the Hatch Act of 1887 were instrumental in—and in some cases responsible for—creating transformative technologies and transferring those to industry. The Morrill and Hatch acts laid a foundation facilitating systematic creation and dissemination of commercially important technologies, in part through technology transfer and in part through development of scientists, technologists, and entrepreneurs who either created companies or went to industry.

Over a century has passed since enactment of the Morrill and Hatch acts, and science now underpins innovation in virtually every major industry. Microelectronics, biotechnology, advanced materials (for instance, tires, specialty fabrics, polymers), telecommunications, plastics and high-performance chemicals, Computer Numerical Controlled (CNC) machine tools, civilian aircraft, and computers (hardware and software) are but a few. Further, accumulated wisdom and understanding in the social sciences motivates and underpins much innovation in services and informatics (Google, YouTube, MySpace).[2] The understanding, maintenance, and development of our globalizing society depends more on the physical and social sciences than ever before in human history; the sciences accelerate and in some cases enable the development. Innovations in physical sciences, together with services and informatics, are major factors in the endowment and future potential wealth of individuals and, in turn, nations.

The evolution of modern industries and their associated technologies in the United States has much to do with the creation and development of U.S. universities as institutions of science a century or so ago. These industries and technologies also owe much to ongoing federal commitment to research performed not only in universities, but also in federal labs and, to an extent, in industrial and small business innovation research. The National Science Foundation, National Institutes of Health, and many military and civilian federal departments sponsor and conduct scientific research.[3]

Companies producing various products and services conduct some research internally, and orchestrate the efforts of others via sponsorship and open innovation.[4] They approach commercialization—the transformation of a body of work or knowledge into profitable economic use—by way of syndication of resources needed to create products and services for the markets with which they are familiar and to which they have access. Conversely, venture capitalists are primarily factors in commercialization of technologies developed with the funding and at the risk of others, largely from universities (entrepreneurs, not necessarily graduates) and small companies that are grantees of the Small Business Innovation

Research and Small Business Technology Transfer programs in various government agencies. Largely, venture capitalists neither sponsor nor conduct scientific research; rather, they approach commercialization by syndication of the financial and social resources needed to create products and services.

Universities, government, and companies share a central role in developing and exploiting the sciences, and an understanding of how that role is shared requires that we consider notions of process in technology commercialization. Notions of process help in understanding, from an industrial perspective, how to balance competition and collaboration among and across institutions.

NOTIONS OF PROCESS

One example of how commercialization can reduce to a process is demonstrated by the Missouri University of Science and Technology (formerly the University of Missouri—Rolla).[5] In this process, invention disclosures are vetted for patentability, and the university decides whether to proceed based on a combination of patentability and marketability. If it decides to proceed, the university obtains a patent and notifies the research sponsor. There are some issues with this process. For one, depending on the sponsor, it may be of benefit to the university to confer and collaborate with the sponsor much earlier in the process than their post-patent notification. Another issue is that in cases where the innovations are taking place in domains that another party has patented extensively, the prior patents may make it very difficult for the university to proceed, as the value of its IP ownership may be relatively low due to others' legitimate ownership interests.

However, the main point here is that commercialization can reduce neatly to a process, and this is one example. In dealing with a university, it is critically important to get at least a general sense of its commercialization processes to determine whether it is commercially appropriate to conduct sponsored or collaborative research with the institution.

Taking a macro look at the relationship between academic technologies and their commercialization, the conventional wisdom is that universities and government play the major role in basic research, and industry plays the major role in market-driven technology development and commercialization. In 1999, while serving as vice provost of Columbia University, Michael Crow described that conventional wisdom during a keynote address at a NASULGC conference. Crow was talking about Linton Freeman's "Three Phases of Science Policy," and in his expansion stated the phases as follows:

- *Phase I: Military S & T Policy.* Science policy is directed towards military purposes, promoting the development of new weapons systems for global superiority and the modification of existing technology for local regional application.
- *Phase II: Commercial S & T Policy.* Science and technology policy is devoted to developing and maintaining the national economy, focusing on key technology industries; there is a national strategy that targets specific interests for either direct or indirect technology development and protection; trade policies, financial policies, and/or government-financed research institutes assist in technology development.
- *Phase III: Comprehensive S & T.* The national objective is to use science and technology for sustainable growth, environmental quality, and general quality of life.[6]

At the time, Crow claimed that the Vannevar Bush policy no longer worked, meaning that the Bush allocation model of resource distribution (peer review) is subject to reevaluation because of a new focus and new politics that bring in a range of constraints and increased oversight on universities. The new politics change the impact and effectiveness of the Bush model. Although his comments were made in 1999, Crow's view has held to a certain extent, but while universities are very important in this new science policy, there is ongoing political and economic tension. In a nutshell, the political tension arises when both land-grant and private universities are working to influence state government policies that impact their mission, and economic tension arises between universities competing for the same commercialization grants or customers (in the macro sense) as well as among educators (within or across academic institutions) who favor or oppose taking money from industry for any purpose. Consequently, universities have not been and should not ever be expected to become unanimous in this policy movement.

Crow further claimed that research leaders in universities needed improved political sophistication inside and outside of the university, and that it would become even harder to manage within the academic research enterprise due to a divergence of priorities between the institutions and their faculties. He also claimed that due to this divergence, effectively there are economic spies on campus.[7] There is also insider trading in technologies and commercialization opportunities, and economics and attentions are influenced by venture capitalists who have no knowledge of university culture but want university products. Universities evolve and adapt slowly and have complex internal policies. Crow argued that those that are flexible and act fast would survive, those that do not will not likely survive as research universities in this new environment, and those that survive must guard against becoming arrogant. Another informed perspective on this divergence is offered by Derek Bok in *Universities in the Marketplace: The Commercialization of Higher Education*.[8] This book is a fairly well-balanced commentary on factors that university leadership and polity should consider concerning the complex issues that arise in various university relationships with commerce, not only in technology commercialization.

The current issues that impinge on sponsored research affairs at universities in the United States prove, to some extent, that Crow was right, and they invite other questions. The process perspective gives us a way to systematically understand and perhaps address those issues—whether in a commentary such as this or, from an industrial perspective, in preparation to create and negotiate some sort of syndication of universities and small businesses toward a commercialization goal. Let us look further at those issues.

ISSUES

So, how do universities engage in technology development? From the university's perspective, what issues are involved with the commercialization of those technologies? Since universities generally do not engage in product manufacturing, their policies generally seem focused on one or another form of technology push—in which they use government money to generate technologies that then can be marketed to industry and venture capitalists. The two comments shown in Figure 6.1 point to some of the difficulties in the process.

Many in technology transfer claim successes, and many point to failures in such technology push efforts. The quote from Young Kim outlines a challenge presented by this philosophy—finding economic use for nascent technologies can be very difficult. Recall Crow's comments about divergence of priorities between institutions and their faculties; one dimension of that divergence arises from the fact that manufacturing is not an institutional priority for universities, and another arises from how well-informed

Figure 6.1

- *With university research, you're starting with a piece of technology that can be thought of as the solution. Then you have to find the market problem, which is no trivial exercise.*
  —Young Kim, Georgia Tech/GTronics
- *Commercializing a medical device typically takes three to five years and $25 million in funding . . .*
  —Steve Kennedy, Georgia Tech/Orthonics

the focus of academic research is with respect to technical challenges that are socioeconomically meaningful. These dimensions are important for many professors who engage in technology development, however, because it is via manufacturing or service delivery that the value of their innovations is realized for society and the economic wherewithal for their rewards are generated. More simply, universities do not manufacture things, and consequently the technology push means that a venture investor or a going company has to be found that will license that technology and make a business of it. It also means that the university's researchers may get very little feedback. Feedback is important not only for improving the technology implementation or motivating and informing improvements, enhancements, or new directions for investigation, but also for ways to refine the science toward initial utilization. Further, making a technology push business work is enormously expensive.

The quotation from another person in a Georgia Tech spin-off, Steve Kennedy, suggests that commercializing a medical device is not cheap—typically three to five years and 25 million dollars in costs. Another source, the *Economist* magazine's December 2002 Technology Quarterly, asserted, "A dollar's worth of academic invention or discovery requires upwards of $10,000 of private capital to bring to market. Far from getting a free lunch, companies that license ideas from universities wind up paying over 99 percent of the innovation's final cost."[9]

Compounding the technology push problem is the talent issue. Scientific research at universities depends, in part, on retaining researchers who are as much talented proposal writers as they are talented technologists. Their ability to write grant proposals that are funded by third parties—government or industry—is very important to keep the grant money flowing in. The NSF's 2001 survey found, for instance, that in the biological and health sciences, most doctoral recipients leave academia, and of those in academia many are not on a tenure track (see Figure 6.2). One reason for this is that the predominant growth in university research positions is in grant-funded, so-called soft money positions. Soft money means, of course, that the university scientists fight for lab space and raise money for their own salaries via grants. When I was a university administrator, I noticed that it pays universities to keep (up to space constraints of the physical plant) as many grant-generating professors as they can, if only because the university keeps and uses the overhead that is charged against the grants that the professors pull in. Unless they become chaired, or at least tenured and funded, they are somewhat marginal employees with respect to the university in the sense that they are supported by soft money. The more professors at that margin are chasing and getting grant money, the more overhead the university earns and keeps to pay for other expenditures. This is neither right nor wrong; it

Figure 6.2

> - *50 percent or fewer of biological and health sciences doctoral recipients are employed in academia, and an even smaller percentage of those are tenured or on tenure track.*
>   —2001 survey, National Science Foundation
> - *There is growth in less stable, soft-money positions, which lack the guarantees of tenure track, leaving scientists to fight for lab space and raise their own salaries via grants.*
>   —http://www.fasebj.org/cgi/reprint/03-0836lifev1

is just how universities cover expenditures that are usually strategic (or at least related) to their mission but usually do not attract grants or gifts.

One concern with this state of affairs in some circles is that government funding for research, except in the life sciences, is decreasing. The decreases mean that some of these scientists will have to go; they are not tenure track, and funding decreases mean that they are not all going to get by.[10]

Soft money and other constraints put a practical limit—a ceiling—on the number of scientists that can be employed in universities. Therefore, if one believes that universities are the natural home for all scientific development, a couple of consequences follow (see Figure 6.3). One is that the size of that home—universities in the United States, taken together—defines and caps the limit of scientific development in the nation. Any reduction in soft money instantly shrinks the aggregate size of that home, and the shrinkage persists for some time to come because new scientists are not created instantly. If one compares the size of the U.S. university research enterprise and its production of scientists against that in the Pacific Rim (China, Japan, India, Singapore, Malaysia, and such), comparing the current size and rate of change in the population and output of the science component of U.S. universities against that of the Pacific Rim universities and institutes, one can argue that the United States has already constructively lost the scientific talent generation tournament.[11] The rate of change is more important than absolute size, given the underlying demographics. Further, when one is evaluating this argument, it is important to be careful about any representations of quality, or lack of quality, among newly-minted scientists in the Pacific Rim that are made by people who are not on those scientists' Ph.D. committees.

One way to resolve this issue, or at least to remain competitive, would be for a resurgence of the U.S. industrial research laboratory to take place. However, one issue with that resurgence is that the need for industrial research labs tends to follow manufacturing and consumer

Figure 6.3

> • **Bridges to Independence** *cited lengthening postdoc apprentice terms and other hurdles to becoming an independent academic principal investigator—suggesting that there are not enough faculty positions to employ the available pool of employable scientists*
> —http://www.nap.edu/books/030909626X/html,
> National Research Council, 2005.

markets—whether for capital, durable or consumer goods and services—and so does product development. Much manufacturing, for economic and strategic reasons, has largely moved from the United States to overseas. This is especially true in basic industries such as steel and bulk commodity chemicals. I perceive this to be a central issue of structural socioeconomic change in the United States, and it is a direct impediment to the growth of U.S.-based industrial research labs.

One dimension of strategic thinking about technology that has always intrigued me was taught to me by Dr. Mary Shaw in the brief time we simultaneously worked at the Software Engineering Institute of Carnegie Mellon University under Angel Jordan in the late 1980s. Professor Shaw taught me that the technologies that are useful to people, in most domains, arise from converging threads of invention. A number of technologies, representing in many (if not most) cases a number of patents and areas of know-how, are incorporated within any one product. This holds true even in pharmaceuticals; although a compound's patent can have enormous economic value, the delivery systems (pills, infusions, injections, devices) enable the compounds to be useful to people—and those delivery systems are not necessarily reinvented with every new compound. What this means is that interdependence among transformative (new to the world) and enabling (incremental and supplementary) technologies is important. With a transformative academic technology that is a candidate for commercialization, there are potentially any number of infringement (because potentially more than one academic is working on a similar or substitute technology) and freedom to operate (because other companies and academics hold the rights to complementary, supplementary, or substitute technologies) issues.[12] The ability to use converging threads of invention depends in no small way, then, on the ability to manage the concomitant intellectual property issues.

Another problem is that the interests of universities and industry may be divergent. The Association of University Technology Managers (AUTM) web site states that the primary objective of academic technology transfer professionals is enabling the development and commercialization of academic research findings. That can be read to mean that the primary objective of university technology transfer has little to do with supporting the existing industrial base that is generating the wherewithal—the taxes—largely funding the work that universities desire to commercialize. It may be difficult to interest industrial managers and executives in collaborative research with universities if the situation is read this way. In addition, there are substantial efficiency issues with respect to university technology development. If one is to believe the AUTM averages, at the 142 universities surveyed in 2001, it takes $10 million in research spending to get one patent issued and one signed license agreement. That research spending does not begin to cover the expenses of safe and effective commercialization of a technology, whether transformative or incremental in nature.

Based on informal conversations with other technology managers, I have learned that a company maintaining internal fundamental research is on average 10 times more efficient at technology development via generating patents than any of the universities participating in that AUTM survey. Granted, this is informative but indefinite—because of differences in patenting in different domains, as well as differences in patenting preferences among inventing organizations in each domain.[13] The apparent inefficiencies of university-based technology development are a problem for universities themselves, as well as for their industrial partners. If universities are engaging, in part, in the development of patentable technology in order to build income streams that are independent of donors' influence (unrestricted income), the inherent inefficiency of their research further constrains technology development in two ways. First, if other factors (funding and staffing) are equal between competing labs, the university labs would likely suffer in comparison, which makes it harder to build a defensible intellectual property estate, due to their legitimate education and service requirements. Secondly, the direction of resources toward building a royalty-paying IP estate may attract internal scrutiny from powerful interests in the university, not to mention an adverse change in tax treatment. A further complication is that the efforts to build that estate can put them in direct economic competition with potential collaborators.

Some of the so-called inefficiency would seem to be due to the understandable tendency at universities to use relatively broad definitions of categories for allocation of restricted support. In other words, money granted to research activity at universities is indeed spent on research, although it is internally taxed for institutional and departmental overhead. Moreover, it is often the case that the things that money gets spent on have utility beyond their primary or initial research purpose, but the value of that utility is not directly counted in the assessment of the relationship between income and output. This adds to the appearance of inefficiency, although it definitely helps universities support their broader educational and outreach missions. Another complication is that at some universities, a professor's salary is deemed to be related to instruction and service, and so is not counted in their R&D spending. Be that as it may, combining this inefficiency observation with the apparent interest of the AUTM-stated university objective, one could argue (hopefully not successfully) that as concerns technology development, research universities are spending an awful lot of federal and state tax money to achieve a low, marginal return for a dwindling customer base.

These issues, taken together, seem to buttress the argument that in spite of the increase in success as measured by royalty income or patent issuance, commercial technology development may not be one of the university's primary functions in the U.S. economy, and that it is past time but hopefully not too late to discuss in earnest the ways and means of encouraging commercially appropriate university collaboration with what remains of the U.S. industrial base. Here are some observations, with kernels of ideas to motivate discussion toward such collaboration.

OBSERVATIONS AND DISCUSSION

The history, process, and current issues lead toward many opinions— not in any particular order—about the factors that affect universities' technology commercialization practices, as well as items an industrialist might consider concerning working collaboratively with them.

Career Environment

First, let us consider the academic's career environment. Given the way academic research institutions seem to be run and the way researchers in them seem to be rewarded, in order to continue doing research in their fields, I suspect that more academics need either to generate royalty income streams or intentionally plan an orderly, entrepreneurial exit from academia. But exit to where? Industrial labs, at least in the United States, are under significant pressure for many reasons:

- Multinational, globalized firms continually move manufacturing to lower cost regions, and those regions have been outside of the United States for quite some time. What's more, firms operating outside the United States face pressure and incentive to use their domestic universities. The pressure comes from the relation of those universities to their respective governments, in pursuit of the socioeconomic value of the spillovers from conduct of industrial research. The incentive comes from the value of an educated workforce and consumers for production and demand.

- Commercial research operations do not necessarily survive mergers or acquisitions that lead to rationalization of company operations;
- Incremental innovations that many labs excelled at are sometimes no longer economically demanded;
- Risk management is leading many customer-facing firms to focus on coordinating innovations of others rather than trying to generate radical innovations from within and calling the process open innovation.

So, part of the problem for an academic researcher is that an orderly, entrepreneurial exit from academia might not be feasible—or at least, it might not make use of their personal investment in developing their technical expertise.

One might further suspect that increasingly the firms able to find and commercialize technologies from academia are not going to be domiciled in the United States, if only because of the greater growth rate in population and middle class affluence outside of the United States. Many of the research inputs—human capital and research tools—are increasingly within reach of universities outside of the United States, and are now more than ever a strategic focus for them.

The Industrial Base

Continuing with the notion that more university professors need either to generate royalty income streams in order to continue doing research in their fields or intentionally plan an orderly, entrepreneurial exit from academia, we must consider the industrial base; research has always *followed and not led* manufacturing. Given the economically motivated movement of manufacturing, not only for consumer goods but now increasingly for capital equipment, from the United States to the Pacific Rim, the U.S. industrial base is in competitive decline. That is, the incumbents are under severe competitive pressure, and new investment is not confined to the United States.[14] Since location of research and development activity has followed manufacturing throughout the history of global industrialization, it is safe to assume that much industrial research will follow the manufacturing investment, and the resultant spillovers will accelerate development of the science and technology base in universities domiciled in communities where investment occurs.

It is not apparent that this shift in private investment has had an impact on universities in the United States, but it will, not necessarily by way of disinvestment in U.S. universities but rather by comparatively larger investment in universities outside the United States by their countries' governments and industry interested in leapfrogging U.S. socioeconomic development. This is a problem because portions of the U.S. industrial base are in continued decline, leading to the increasing possibility that the firms able to find and commercialize academic technologies are not going to be domiciled in the United States. Again, firms domiciled outside the United States face pressure and incentive to use universities local to their domicile.

Promises to Customers

As mentioned earlier, companies that are engaged in open innovation approach commercialization—the transformation of a body of work or knowledge into profitable economic use—by way of syndication of resources needed to create products and services for the markets with which they are familiar and have access. I also mentioned that venture capitalists approach commercialization by syndication of the financial and social resources needed to create products and services. Whether company or venture capitalist, this commercialization requires the ability to make confident promises to customers about their privileges for using technology that is embodied in the products and services they buy. This is generally called freedom to operate, the ability to make, use, or sell a product or service such that no third-party intellectual property is infringed. The problem is that the intellectual property licensing terms that some universities often present to companies for company-sponsored research, although consistent with what they are permitted to do under Bayh-Dole, are neither consistent with the economic models of many firms contemplating sponsoring their research, nor with the need those firms have to promise their customers that the technology embodied in those products and services can be used without later discovering economic responsibility to one or more third parties.

Freedom to operate[15] is an active issue for the universities, foundations, and companies involved in creating and selling innovations because the innovative activity makes the issue more than merely legal. It is also a strategic, operational, and technical issue, and can be very difficult to assure. Consequently, business decision makers, faced with the possibility of contract terms that leave uncertainties in freedom to operate, will, more often than not, suspend or terminate negotiations with a university if the contract terms under discussion imperil that freedom. In many industries, the act of technical collaboration with a university can easily taint a business's intellectual property estate. Sometimes, to avoid such taint means that the industrial partner will require a nonexclusive royalty-free right to use whatever is created during the research agreement, if only to assure that an obligation is not created by the honest collaboration and exchange between their industrial scientists and the university scientists under contract. This can be especially important in situations where others in the company are working independently (apart from the contracted collaborators) on innovations in technical areas similar to those anticipated under the collaboration agreement.

Intellectual Property Dilemma

Given the need to generate royalty streams for personal and professional reasons, it is no surprise that there is wrangling over intellectual property rights well ahead of any inventive activity. This presents a dilemma in that although the IP terms that some universities often present to companies for company-sponsored research are allowable under Bayh-Dole, those terms are not usually compatible with the economic models of firms in many industries that are contemplating sponsoring research. The wrangling discourages industrial engagement in sponsored or collaborative research because it increases both the cost and the risk of the engagement well beyond the expected reward. Most research, although necessary to inform us all about the topics of interest, does not yield new intellectual property.

Further, the risk of tainting their intellectual property estate, not to mention the commercialization risk, is so large for many companies that some intellectual property ownership terms allowable under Bayh-Dole and regulations in some states are unwise for a company to accept. The risk of taint appears when some interaction between a university's and a company's researchers is required to inform, motivate, or conduct a sponsored research project. Without securing IP rights in advance, the interaction itself could taint the company's intellectual property. The commercialization risk arises when a company, having sponsored research at a university with an option to license the resulting intellectual property, finds one or more show-stopping problems. Typically, these are that the terms offered make commercialization unprofitable or that the intellectual property itself is inadequate for confident commercialization because of the claims or prior art of others.

Consequently, for many firms the need to negotiate intellectual property terms prior to conducting sponsored research is very strong, and the motivation of many universities to agree to such terms can be very weak unless the university faculty and administration are more interested in the spillovers—which can be substantial—than the research results. A series of annual reports from Pennsylvania State University, for instance, indicates that spillovers from research can be considerable. An analysis of Penn

State's performance by the Pittsburgh accounting firm of Tripp Umbach found that every dollar spent on research—in 2005, that was $638 million—generates $3.22 for the Pennsylvania economy. It may well be that the value of the spillovers, at $3 per $1, rivals the value of the intellectual property generated.

Collaborate or Compete?

The wrangling over intellectual property may have a more grave consequence, because it pits companies engaged in scientific research, both small and large, in direct competition with many universities' research organizations. The shame of this is that due to the realities of the global research environment, industrial and academic scientists, especially in the physical sciences, need each other more now than they have at any time in the past. Their professional survival and intellectual development depends on this, due to *ephemeralization*.[16] Buckminster Fuller coined the term to describe the use of science and technology in creating more value with ever less weight, time, and energy. The communication capacity increase that glass fiber provides compared to copper cable is an example of effective ephemeralization. One strand of optical fiber will carry as much information as the old copper Atlantic undersea cable—from about 180 centimeters in diameter to about half a millimeter in diameter, an ephemeralization of several orders of magnitude.

Why is this important? Because scientific activity creates and motivates much ephemeralization. Moreover, more scientists are alive today than have lived and died in all recorded history to this point, and the tools available to those scientists for research and development have never been more powerful. The computing power in a PDA (personal digital assistant—an iPhone, a BlackBerry, or other common device) was a desk-full very recently, a roomful not long before that, and only theoretically anticipated when electronic computers with stored programs were developed. Desktop computers are much more powerful than those PDAs, and other tools for scientific investigation have improved apace—for instance, the advent of microchemistry in the late 1970s and early 1980s that had such a strong impact on research, engineering, and instruction. In the social sciences, the impact of advanced tools on archaeology has been dramatic, to say the least. These include nondestructive dating technologies such as paleogeomagnetism, fluorine-based fossil dating, and others, and also more recently the use of a number of digital technologies to facilitate field excavations. In the social sciences, increasing access to greater computational power has led to greater use of tools for statistical and combinatorial analysis,[17] giving social scientists much greater ability to innovate in the field.

Since there are more scientists alive and working today than ever before, ephemeralization means that with such tools they are able to discover and harness more about the physical, biological, computing, and social sciences than at any earlier time in history. They can work increasingly more effectively alone or as distributed asynchronous teams, in a global environment where shrinking effort and resource requirements per unit of output lead to reducing the elapsed time between research inception and publication of results. In order to maintain and develop scientific skill in such a rapidly changing environment, interaction with scientists in and among universities is very important for staying aware of and advancing the state of the sciences. The actual interactions depend on the context and purpose. In many interactions, industrial and academic scientists collaborate in person by visiting each other's offices and laboratories, working together on technical papers for publication in refereed journals, at conferences, and sometimes on books; initially these collaborations create work statements to plan research activity, then per that plan they engage in collaborative work. The necessary interaction, however, in and of itself accelerates ephemeralization no matter where it is on the spectrum of engagement between nominal professional camaraderie and major collaborative effort.

Academic and industrial scientists, at a minimum, share interesting problems and effective and relevant techniques in order to develop and deliver technologies that are useful to people. Technical and professional associations such as the Association for Computing Machinery, American Chemical Society, American Ceramic Society, IEEE, and others facilitate appropriate sharing of problems and solutions via their meetings and the professional friendships that result. The sharing is necessary in light of ephemeralization, and industrial history shows that it has been a major factor in developing and maintaining U.S. competitiveness and socioeconomic security, as well as in improving science and technology worldwide.

Why? Because with the speed and diffusion of development in science and technology combined with scientists' personal preferences as to lifestyle and challenges, communication and networking among scientists is necessary in order to develop some of the technology we need. Some scientists prefer working in industry, and others prefer academe. Those preferences need not prevent the communication necessary to advance the state of the sciences and the arts. Collaboration among those scientists and across those bounds can be very helpful in improving the human condition, and it has to be done in ways that respect each scientist's contribution while also maintaining the viability and freedom to operate of the organizations they are part of, as well as the value that each represents.

However, it is not possible to initiate and establish the necessary collaborations if academia and industry are fighting over intellectual property rights in industrially sponsored research, or if practices within academia affect innovation.[18]

For Further Discussion

In order for industrial firms to maintain internationally competitive business models, they must make decisions that do not threaten their freedom to operate. Some firms actively manage intellectual property to maintain that freedom. Because intellectual property can be a tool as well as a barrier, applied differently in different industries and situations, options for different approaches for ownership, licensing, and sharing must be available to universities and firms—especially if scientists in those organizations have the need or desire to collaborate.

A further issue relates to trust among university and industry partners, which is difficult to establish and very easy to lose. Trust issues are common between organizations—and the interface between universities and industry is not immune to such issues.[19] Taken together, the need for independence of action combined with the need for trust in cooperation and collaboration presents a formidable barrier to university technology commercialization practice. That barrier is more problematic now because of the integral role that university-industry collaboration has played in developing many important technologies.

One way to address the trust issue is to look at the relative strength of the institutions. In relative terms, what does each partner bring to the collaboration in terms of know-how, prior art, or other assets to invest in the technology opportunity and subsequent commercialization? Further, do industry norms or conditions influence the anticipated terms of collaboration—as to publications, intellectual property, and applicable law? Do others competing in the same technology space have similar assets or face similar burdens? What are the relevant objectives and constraints?

Another dimension to consider in addressing the trust issue is the challenge of introducing new technologies to the market. Specifically, consider the problem of developing markets for new, advanced materials. Two market levels have to be addressed. One is the immediate customer base—the

Figure 6.4

Think hard about how much industrial freedom to operate can be provided by technologies originating in the university setting.

people who will make things out of the new materials for end users—and the other is the large, heterogeneous group of industrial and individual consumers. In the immediate customer base, there is extensive work to be done to build interest and trust across the different companies that potentially can use the new material. It may be effective, for instance, to work with end-product manufacturers for whom the new material enables creation of a completely new market area or a competitive foray into an existing market in order to increase their existing share or increase their profitability given their current share. In either case, it is likely to be necessary not only to create the new material to reliable specifications but also to pioneer the processes by which the end products might be made. Then the entity making the new material can offer strong inducements to customers to use it—inducements including technical information and support, as well as samples for market trials, lifetime testing, and quality control. Another inducement the material producer can offer is promotion to help create primary demand, such as 3M's promotion of Thinsulate and DuPont's promotion of Kevlar. Such promotion would involve media advertising, direct sales, and technical support services. So, the share of revenue available to reward innovation collaborators is probably proportionate to the contribution those collaborators make to advancing and supporting the technology, not just inventing it, in no small way due to the investment of time and attention required to help the product succeed in a crowded competitive marketplace. Naturally, the viewpoint and valuation opinion of a company executive will differ from that of a university technology transfer executive.

One might argue that the problem of creating and introducing new materials to the market is a boundary case for technology transfer from lab-to-market. Unlike pharmaceutical compounds that provide functional benefits largely independent of other things except for delivery systems, new materials provide functional benefits to the extent they are incorporated into other things. It is a well-known case, however, and the realities as outlined above strongly suggest that universities are not well equipped to do much if any of it unless the salient distraction from and distortion of their social and educational missions that would obviously result can be reasonably managed.

Yet a way to address that challenge might be for interested sets of university and industrial partners to jointly create a process to generate technologies. To be complete, the process has to address systemic issues a priori. The partners probably need a flexible process, or at least a somewhat different process for each industrial/technological domain (example domains might be advanced materials, pharmaceuticals, electronics, software) in which they wish to collaborate over the long term. Current state policies may make it difficult for some universities to put the master agreements in place that would support such long-term collaboration, and current university faculty may have more than a little to say about the wisdom of such relationships. Guidelines for establishing such partnerships and processes might be worth discussion, if only because of the potential for economic benefit from local and regional spillovers such as seem to be enjoyed by Penn State. The university-industry technology creation process also needs to vary depending on the nature of the innovation—is it an incremental change to or extension of something in the market, a creation of something new-to-the-world, or a step-change in a science that creates a platform for later innovations? Is the problem at hand that a new technology is in search of a use or that there is an opportunity to invent something that relieves suffering, avoids cost, or improves the quality or joy of life?

The role of venture capital investors should also be reconsidered by university technology transfer offices. One example of venture investment in new technology can be found by looking at information technology companies. Brad Burnham of Union Square Ventures asserted that historically the defensibility of IT company margins has been based on intellectual property—usually patents, sometimes copyrights. From the late 1970s until the late 1990s, many venture backed start-ups contributed key components to the IT infrastructure we all now depend on. These businesses needed big R&D investment and often were in product development several years before they hired their first sales or marketing people. Once they were ready to go to market, they distributed their products through major equipment companies that sold a broad range of products to a large base of customers. Because it was usually easy for any given major equipment manufacturer to copy the innovation of a start up, solid intellectual property protection was the only way to protect and maintain margins of these businesses and hence provide good returns for their investors.

As the technology infrastructure business matures, however, the nature of defensibility changes, and so the things that matter to venture capitalists in terms of research and development should also tend to change—probably to include asset creation and some notion of operational impact. Those changes may subsequently have an impact on how deals are structured and valued, especially if the technology was developed in a university setting and not only the inventor but also the technology transfer office has to be reckoned with. Time will tell; the know-how, prior art, or other non-financial assets that venture investors can bring may have some influence, but it is not apparent how many venture capitalists have an effective combination of all those assets to contribute to start-up firms except that those intangible assets they do have tend to govern the ventures they will fund.

From a company perspective, then, it would not be a waste of time to consider assessing, perhaps aggressively, the monetary value of the know-how, prior art, sales, marketing, and technical service that can potentially be brought to bear on any given deal. In some cases, the university counterparts will be well aware of those values and prepared to give them appropriate credit; in other cases, they will not. A discussion concerning the strengths that different investors possess might help university technology transfer offices improve their marketing results.

Another discussion topic might be whether flexible sponsored research terms might help universities control the size of their research organizations by becoming de facto outplacement for competent researchers who for whatever reason choose not to or fail to make tenure. Although discussion of the concept would probably be difficult, this might be a compassionate way for universities to deal with faculty who invent but do not earn tenure. At the same time, the university could generate residual income from technologies developed while under university patent assignment agreements.

CONCLUDING COMMENTS AND QUESTIONS

There is room for change in university-industry technology relationships, although the changes may or may not increase the amount of university-industry engagement in developing technologies that are useful to people. This is a serious, perhaps grave, issue. The challenges facing our world are amenable to improvements based on advances in the physical and social sciences. If one assumes that the key challenges are things such as increasing size and density of cities in the newly industrialized countries, the advancement of information technology, cost reductions and access improvement for health care, expansion of a global middle class, and continuing substitution of machinery for labor, all of those challenges are addressable via intelligently applied technologies. However, there seem to be other problems that affect our ability to improve university-industry engagement in meeting these challenges.

One problem is what seems to be, in some cases, a strategic and intentional disengagement between universities and established companies. I suspect that the roots of this issue run very deep. Assume, for a moment, that industry is, in general, a mechanism and means by which society improves the standard of living. That improvement requires a spectrum of things that can be created through imagination and invention, and delivered by new and existing industry. To paraphrase remarks by George Whitesides of Harvard University during a 2008 symposium at Corning Incorporated celebrating the 100th anniversary of their industrial research laboratory, societies have needs and wants: while satisfying the needs is definitely more urgent, satisfying the wants is usually more profitable. Whitesides's observation begs us to ask, regarding this strategic disagreement, many questions. How does the needed long-term problem-solving to address global concerns appear in business plans of organizations—companies—that can make and do what is needed? Why do many businesses seem to want *options* for new products and services with only the narrowest sense of *strategic alignment*? Why do some technology transfer offices in universities take a similar, narrow view? Could it be that intentional disengagement between universities and companies due to wrangling over intellectual property rights impedes and delays addressing urgent societal needs?

Some say that another problem is that research for industry diverts or dilutes university research resources, to the detriment of scientific discovery to generate the knowledge for technology platforms that will address urgent societal needs. In many major research universities this is an active question.[20]

We need to repair the bridges between universities and industry in order to obtain more of the benefits of economically appropriate approaches to addressing true societal needs, not just the profitable attainment of societal wants. One group working on this issue is the University-Industry Demonstration Partnership. One unique aspect of the UIDP is that it has implemented a relatively open, project-based approach to pairing leaders from academia and industry to lead teams working on understanding and resolving the myriad systemic issues that hamper collaborative research, especially concerning required contracts and administration. The UIDP provides a forum to expose and resolve relevant issues outside of the context of one or another contract negotiation so that the legitimate contract interests do not cloud or conflict discussions of the equities or merits. It also enables university and industry leaders of sponsored research to learn about and expand their interactions across industrial contexts. That is, they become informed, in one forum, about the cross-industry and cross-university impact of one or another general matter of preference held by a type of university (say, public or private) or in an industrial sector (say, advanced materials or pharmaceuticals). This broad participation in UIDP really helps people understand or at least comment on whether those matters of preference (running versus upfront royalties, for instance) have a beneficial or adverse impact in other types of universities or companies.

Again, this is a discussion not clouded by the competing interests the parties would have if they were in the middle of a contract negotiation. In general, participants in UIDP are working to improve key aspects of the quality of sponsored research in the United States: to learn by sharing experiences, embracing needed changes, and achieving full involvement across research universities and industrial sectors.[21]

Many business relationships for industrially sponsored research at universities are fractured, but not totally broken. However, in order for those fractures to heal so that we are all strong again, experience and common sense offer some useful guidance. One piece of advice, especially for industry representatives who are new to technology transfer from universities, is that industry should not expect to appropriate intellectual property developed apart from their financial or intellectual input, and should expect some give-and-take to determine how to effect that transfer. And, in turn, university administrators who are relatively inexperienced should be warned that if the effort needed for that give-and-take appears on the verge of becoming a resource sink, the quality and quantity of attention they get from their industrial counterparts will become rather low if not vanish entirely. In many industries, the contribution of a given technology may be so relatively small or marginal that a running royalty truly may not make economic sense for either party.

Further advice: universities should not expect to appropriate financial or intellectual input from industry to aid generation of intellectual property that inures solely to the university's IP estate. For industrial partners with active research organizations, the risk of taint is palpable. If it is important for a university's technology community to access a strong industrial technology community, it is not unreasonable for it to trade intellectual property rights for that access so that its industrial partners can avoid the taint, simultaneously maintaining healthy collaborations and commercial freedom to operate.

In closing, those involved in sponsored or collaborative research ought to think strategically about building frameworks for shared perspective. If the objective in the university is to build an IP estate, then the university must be prepared to bear the costs alone and be warned that the costs may always exceed the income. It may be that product sales are necessary to build the organization that can put up with those costs, including maintenance of the patents and know-how needed for effective technology transfer and management—which most universities would find not only difficult, but also perhaps a violation of their not-for-profit status. Likewise, if the objective in companies is to conduct technology invention and development without stimulating interactions with outside scientists, there is a risk that they will be overtaken by ephemeralization and competition for brains, instead of leveraging both by establishing strategically and economically reasonable relationships with universities that are strong in the technologies desired. As far as the parameters are concerned, including the type of research and an assessment of its value, it really boils down to the company's business model, the university's business model, and whether appropriate collaboration can be built between the two. If so, a contract or even a master agreement should be achievable. If not, then not, because the university and company are then effectively in competition, and neither in anticipation of nor working toward collaboration.

It has been said repeatedly that commercial technology development may not be a university's primary job, and that negotiation of involvement frequently tests the patience of industrial partners and often results in disengagement. That is, with universities, industry is dealing with a type of organization that is obviously an academic enterprise but that also is increasingly playing by competitive rather than collaborative business rules. The universities I deal with are mostly businesslike, although there is room for improvement both in my organization and in theirs. Further, there are legitimate disagreements between universities and companies—not solely the companies and universities I negotiate with, but also those I have learned of via working with people in the Industrial Research Institute, UIDP, and NSF—as to the terms for university engagement in sponsored research toward technologies to be utilized in a product or service.

Finally, it might be a good idea for the IRS and federal and state governments to consider whether—in light of international competition, global needs (not wants), and national priorities such as the America Competes Act—it would be beneficial to amend or rescind the laws and procedures that restrict universities' flexibility in negotiating terms and conditions for industrially-sponsored research contracts. The IRS has already taken a step in this direction by replacing IRS revenue procedure 97–14 with 2007–47. This helps because it increases negotiating flexibility somewhat to address the priorities and constraints that are unique to industrially sponsored research at universities utilizing bond-financed facilities. If federal and state governments want to see the university research enterprise remain strong, and those governments are not prepared to fund all of it, then they need to consider further modifying or reducing legal restrictions so that sponsors can negotiate research participation in strategically and economically sensible ways.[22]

Growing and expanding from their role in industrializing a young nation in the late 1800s, university research laboratories became an integral part of the development, defense, and lifestyle of the United States of America. Scientific research—both industrial and academic—has been a vital resource for leveraging technological interdependence into socioeconomic strength. Current policy and custom in some cases has improved and in other cases has damaged symbiosis between academe and industry. The need for linkage between university research and industry is especially pressing now, since we are faced with technology challenges not only domestically but internationally. The linkage needs to preserve academic and industrial institutional independence while permitting the variety of needed and meaningful interactions that achieve greater good. Going forward, we need to encourage a rebirth of academic-industry symbiosis by formally and informally encouraging their research communities to collaborate in commercially and academically appropriate ways—to build on the technologies and lessons of the past, to collaborate and resolve our present urgent needs, and to grasp and secure our future with confidence.

NOTES

1. For a more complete treatment see Scott Shane, *Academic Entrepreneurship* (Cheltenham, United Kingdom: Edward Elgar Publishing, 2004).

2. See research literature concerning how and why people communicate and build social networks. A reasonable place to start is Linton Freeman, *The Development of Social Network Analysis* (Vancouver, Canada: Empirical Press, 2004). This book provides an overview of ideas and literature in the field. Freeman also offers access to his recent publications via http://moreno.ss.uci.edu/.

3. For more about this, see http://merrill.ku.edu/publications/1998 whitepaper/keynote.html. This is a vital speech by Michael Crow, now President of Arizona State University, given when he was vice provost at Columbia University.

4. See Henry Chesbrough, *Open Innovation* (Boston, MA: Harvard Business School Publishing, 2003). Chesbrough outlines a paradigm for interinstitutional collaborative research and development. See also http://www.haas.berkeley.edu/faculty/chesbrough.html. The idea Chesbrough promotes here is that companies should more freely license inventions created by others and more freely license out their inventions in order to enable and accelerate the innovation process.

5. A process flowchart is available at http://ecodevo.mst.edu/info/ceo_tto_process.html.

6. Michael Crowe, "Science and Technology in the United States: Trading-in The 1950 Model" in *New Technology Policy and Social Innovations in The Firm*, ed. Jorge Niosi (London: Pinter Publishers Ltd., 1994), 47–49.

7. See http://blog.wired.com/27bstroke6/2007/11/fbi-drafts-univ.html for an explanation of this phenomenon.

8. See Derek Bok, *Universities in the Marketplace: The Commercialization of Higher Education* (Princeton, NJ: Princeton University Press, 2003). A review of the book can be found on the American Library Association Web site, http://www.ala.org.

9. "Innovation's Golden Goose," *Economist,* 365:3.

10. To see evidence of the decrease, and track this funding, see the series of reports from the American Association for Advancement of Science (AAAS), at http://www.aaas.org/spp/rd/guidisc.htm. See the left hand side of the page for AAAS reports on the topic.

11. For details, please see the OECD's reports on science and technology talent. One link is http://www.oecd.org/dataoecd/41/0/17130709. pdf; this is but one of a series of reports on the topic.

12. For a good look at an example of a relevant infringement, take a look at the *Duke News* article, http://dukenews.duke.edu/2002/12/cell pro.html, recounting a Johns Hopkins University lawsuit that stopped one of another university's licensing opportunities.

13. One good paper on the topic can be found on the Web at http://student.ulb.ac.be/~tcoupe/patents1.pdf. The author, Tom Coupe, is an assistant professor at the Economics Education and Research Consortium at the National University of 'Kyiv-Mohyla Academy' which is located in Kyiv, Ukraine. Part of Tom's ongoing research focuses on the "economics of science." The article cited takes a systematic look at patenting by U.S. universities and concludes that the universities have decreasing returns to scale from patenting activity.

14. For an example of capital equipment for semiconductor manufacture, see http://www.advantivtech.com/prm/.

15. One perspective on the freedom to operate issue can be found at http://www.iphandbook.org/handbook/ch14/, a chapter of a book from the Public Intellectual Property Resource for Agriculture (PIPRA).

16. For a brief explanation see http://www.nous.org.uk/ephem.html, and for primary explanation see R. Buckminster Fuller, *Nine Chains to the Moon* (Philadelphia, PA: Lippincott, 1938).

17. For another good introduction to analysis of social networks see S. Wasserman and K. Faust, *Social Network Analysis: Methods and Applications* (Cambridge, UK: Cambridge University Press, 1994).

18. See Janet-Rae Dupree, "When Academia Puts Profit Ahead of Wonder," *The New York Times,* September 7, 2008, NY Edition: BU-4. See also Jennifer Washburn, *University Inc.: The Corporate Corruption of Higher Education* (New York: Basic Books, 2005).

19. A useful treatment of this topic is the recent anthology edited by Christel Lane and Reinhard Bachmann, *Trust Within and Between Organizations: Conceptual Issues and Empirical Applications* (New York: Oxford University Press, 1998).

20. See, for example, Donald T. Hornstein, "Accounting for Science: The Independence of Public Research in the New Subterranean Administrative Law," *Law and Contemporary Problems,* 227, http://www.thecre.com/quality/2005/20050901b_quality.html.

21. For more information about UIDP, see http://www7.national academies.org/guirr/UIDP_Intro.pdf and http://www.uidp.org. If your organization is involved in industry-university collaborative research in the United States, most likely your organization would benefit from UIDP membership and the UIDP would invite you to inquire.

22. There is also active discussion about the impact of Bayh-Dole; the least I can say is that although it seems to work well for pharmaceutical research, further discussion of it is unavoidable, and it would not be inappropriate to consider clarifications consistent with the overarching needs of universities and research sponsors to increase research in the physical sciences. One approach that might be interesting to discuss is what happens if a federal requirement stipulates that private sponsors get treated, for IP ownership purposes, no worse than government sponsors—which would then likely require de minimus granting of a non-exclusive royalty-free license to sponsors if only because that is what the law says the government, as sponsor, gets.

CHAPTER 7

Developing and Sustaining Academic-Corporate Alliances

Cynthia C. DeLuca and David J. Siegel

If we wanted to devise an elaborate scheme whereby the academy might be slowly and surreptitiously remade in the image of the corporation, we could hardly do better than to use industrial partnerships as the prototypical delivery system for business ideas and practices that would ultimately cinch the extreme makeover. What better way to diffuse commercial orthodoxy than to introduce it subtly, almost imperceptibly, into the academic bloodstream and—most ingenuous of all— to involve academics themselves as the agents of their own culture's destruction and the architects of its replacement by one more genial to the economic imperative?

***

If we wanted to devise a scheme whereby academic work might be moved into the public domain for further development and application, we could hardly do better than to use industrial partnerships as the delivery system of choice for inventions, discoveries, and promising new ideas that have the potential to radically improve human and societal well-being. What better way to promote the academic ethos than by joining our intellectual capital with external sources of financial support, expertise, and other critical resources for the diffusion of innovation in the public interest?

***

These two oppositional perspectives fairly crystallize the peril and promise of academic-industry partnerships. On the one hand, we can read partnerships as hasteners of the academy's worst fears: that we will come to be valued simply as the handmaidens or order-takers of big business or that we will even be transmogrified into some version of corporations ourselves. On the other hand, partnerships can be read as enablers of our best hopes: that the important work performed in colleges and universities will make a bigger difference in the world.

In this chapter, we examine the phenomenon of academic-corporate partnerships.[1] We briefly take note of the popularity of this form of organizing, identify major reasons for the explosive growth of partnerships, and review prominent criticisms of partnership arrangements involving academic institutions. We then advance an argument that at least some of the controversy surrounding these relationships is built on unchallenged assumptions about what academic and industrial parties want or expect out of their relationships with each other. The fundamental question of what academic and corporate leaders view as the major factors involved in developing and sustaining productive alliances between the sectors was the subject of a study whose findings we present here for the first time. We use these findings to talk back to the literature on partnerships and then discuss several relevant implications for partnership formation and development. In our concluding comments, we make a case for greater attention to specificity and particularity in seeking to understand the conduct of partnerships between academic and business enterprises.

THE RISE OF PARTNERSHIPS

By almost any measure, academic-industry relationships are on the rise, most notably in the life sciences and biomedical research.[2] In the nearly 30 years since passage of the landmark Bayh-Dole Patents and Trademarks Act of 1980, which permitted universities to retain title to patents generated from federally supported research, ties between universities and industry have intensified as calculated by growth in industrial funding of academic research and development, the number of licenses granted to industry, the amount of licensing income produced, patent applications filed, and the number of published research articles jointly authored by academic and industrial partners.[3] Patent applications filed by American universities numbered 250 before 1980; by 1998, there were 4,800 such applications.[4] University licensing income rose from $123 million in 1991 to just over $1 billion in 2002.[5] Industry's share of total investment in biomedical research alone grew 30 percent (from 32% to 62%) in the period from 1980 to 2000.[6]

The 21st century is predicted to be the age of interorganizational alliances,[7] and these alliances will be—already are, in many cases—deeper and more strategic than the philanthropic sponsorships that character-ized earlier generations of academic-corporate relations.[8] As just one prominent example of the scope of modern-day relationships, in 2007 the University of California-Berkeley and British Petroleum (BP) final-ized a 10-year, $500 million contract to establish the Energy Biosciences Institute to discover and develop alternative energy sources, with an emphasis on biofuels.[9] This deal includes the University of Illinois at Urbana-Champaign and the Lawrence Berkeley National Laboratory as strategic partners.

Both in the United States and abroad, university-industry partnerships are viewed by government officials and policymakers as a vital component of national innovation systems. Innovation policies emphasizing the for-mation of linkages between universities and industrial organizations are a feature of most industrialized economies,[10] and recent studies of these arrangements in Ireland, Germany, Japan, Malaysia, and Algeria suggest that academic-corporate relationships are a rapidly accelerating global phenomenon.[11]

As most scholars and observers are quick to point out, academy-industry relationships (AIRs) cover a number of forms of linkage, in-cluding technology transfer, spin-off companies created from academic research, science parks, consulting, and licensing.[12] Ties captured under the banner of AIRs can be individual (at the level of the researcher) or institutional (at the departmental, unit, or other administrative level). The research literature and popular media are dominated by examples of scientific partnerships, but these belie a robust portfolio of additional types of partnership that have social policy agendas and other public purposes at their core. Cross-sector social partnership is one designa-tion given to this emerging form to distinguish it from its more familiar counterparts.[13]

WHY THE GROWTH?

The proliferation and institutionalization of academic-industry partner-ships can be understood as emanating from three sets of factors: (1) the American university's history of engagement in regional and national eco-nomic development, (2) the establishment of federal and state policies to encourage intersectoral alliances, and (3) the stream of mutual benefits that flows to the two sectors—industry and the academy—and to the general public. All of these are underscored by the reality that single organizations or sectors simply lack the capability to solve many technical or social prob-lems on their own and therefore seek alliances with other collectivities to accomplish complex tasks.

A Tradition of Economic Development

American higher education has a long history of involvement with industry. In fact, for as long as scientific research has been conducted in U.S. universities, it has developed largely in concert with industrial and commercial priorities,[14] intertwined as these are with broader national interests. The disciplines of biology, chemistry, engineering, and medicine were some of the first to secure industrial ties.[15] Land-grant institutions, which grew out of the Morrill Act of 1862, were always "expected to work with agriculture and industry to contribute to economic" aims,[16] and utilitarian science in the public interest quickly became a defining feature of these new institutions. A number of schools developed agricultural extension centers and industrial research centers to facilitate the application of academic research to regional priorities.[17] In 1940, a study by the National Research Council claimed that "50 U.S. companies were supporting 270 biomedical research projects in 70 universities."[18] By the late 20th and early 21st centuries, references to economic development had become commonplace in college and university mission statements and a complement to the traditional triumvirate of teaching, research, and service.

Federal and State Policy

The modern era of academic-industry relations is generally recognized to have begun in 1980. Key pieces of federal legislation that year led to the current model of academic-industry cooperation and particularly to increased academic participation in national economic development. The most influential of these were the Bayh-Dole Act and the Stevenson-Wydler Technology Innovation Act of 1980. The Stevenson-Wydler Act stated:

> Many new discoveries and advances in science occur in universities and Federal laboratories, while the application of this new knowledge to commercial and useful public purposes depends largely upon actions by business and labor. Cooperation among academia, Federal laboratories, labor, and industry, in such forms as technology transfer, personnel exchange, joint research projects, and others, should be renewed, expanded, and strengthened.[19]

Opinion is divided about the net effect of these congressional acts. One view is that they have been successful in promoting the utilization of inventions arising from federally funded research and stimulating the formation of academic-industry partnerships. Another view is that they have had a corrosive influence on the academy by encouraging for-profit decisions on academic research agendas.

From a macro (national) perspective, AIRs are viewed as crucial to innovation, economic development, and prosperity.[20] State-level policies have also helped to merge knowledge-intensive firms and research universities in the service of technology-based economic development,[21] most notably through the development of enterprise corridors and clusters. These federal and state policy initiatives are supplemented (and sometimes superseded) by informal alliance networks,[22] institutional policies, and even the enterprising behavior of independent faculty members eager to connect with industry peers.

The Flow of Benefits

Without question, the most straightforward rationale for partnership initiation and development has to do with the direct and indirect benefits that flow to participants. For universities, industry offers research funding, employment opportunities for graduating students, and access to industry skills and facilities.[23] For industry, universities offer capabilities in basic scientific research whose complexity and costs have outstripped the R&D capacity of firms.

National Science Foundation (NSF) studies and the National Academy of Engineering (NAE) have determined that universities and industry advance knowledge and technology in a number of ways. Research support, cooperative research, knowledge transfer, and technology transfer are vectors used to describe specific types of relationships between academic institutions and industry.[24] Research support in the form of money and equipment is one of the most common exchanges between universities and industry. Cooperative research can be conducted through institutional arrangements such as an individual or group interaction between industry and university employees, use of facilities at either partnering institution, or informal collaborations.[25] Knowledge transfer involves activities in the development and use of knowledge, including cooperative extension and education, consulting, student training, economic development, joint publications, and exchanges of personnel. Finally, technology transfer focuses on academic-industry research and the push to move scientific discoveries to industry for economic development or the public good.

Industrial funding of academic research and development in science and engineering (S&E) fields alone totaled $2.3 billion in 2005, according to the National Science Foundation. This represents 5 percent of total R&D funding for research in academic science and engineering, down from a high of 7.4 percent in 1999. Federal funding of academic research totaled $29 billion in 2005, which represents 64 percent of total academic R&D support.[26]

Revenues from licensing provide another source of income. However, these revenues tend to be dominated by a handful of very lucrative home run or blockbuster inventions in the biomedical sciences. For example, Emory University's total licensing income of $585 million in 2005, which led all universities that year, included a $525 million lump-sum payment by Gilead Sciences and Royalty Pharma for all of the intellectual property rights to an HIV-AIDS drug developed by Emory researchers.[27]

Patents and licenses are not the only indicators of technology transfer, though, and neither are they deemed to be the most important; surveys of industrial R&D managers during the 1980s and 1990s revealed that these were rated as less important channels for the exchange of knowledge than jointly authored articles, conference presentations, and other more informal and non-contractual interactions with university scientists.[28] Student hiring, corporate philanthropy, consulting opportunities, advisory board memberships, and exchanges of research materials are among the other flows precipitated by academic-industry linkages.[29] According to the Council for Aid to Education, corporations gave $4.8 million to higher education in 2007, or 16 percent of total support for colleges and universities. Many corporate donations—particularly those that help to build a new program, fund scholarships for students, or name a physical space such as a classroom—involve not just a direct transfer of funds to beneficiary institutions but sweeteners in the form of board seats, preferred scheduling for campus recruitment, access to faculty, access to research results, campus presentations, participation in curricular development, naming opportunities at sponsored events, and other active participation in governance, operations, and academic policy.

In addition to the tangible rewards that come from academic-industry commercialization efforts, there are symbolic ones.[30] For example, universities can project themselves as engines of economic development, commensurate with public expectations and pressures, which in turn has the effect of granting legitimacy to institutions and their members (which, to complete the cycle, results in material benefits).[31] In general, academic-corporate alliances—although not without problems for the cultures of either entity—represent a pragmatic response to various external conditions, including reductions in government spending on higher education, national innovation and economic development priorities, public calls for more engaged universities, and escalating costs of scientific research.

The preponderance of benefits received by partners in AIRs suggests that the only substantive issue for debate is not whether to develop and expand linkages between higher education and industry, but how. Nevertheless, there remains profound skepticism, criticism, and concern about these ties, mainly in academic quarters.

CRITICISMS OF THE ARRANGEMENT

Corporations and universities have never made for easy bedfellows, and some variation of cultural incompatibility is typically held to account for the tension. Essential differences between the two cultures are often described in terms of an academic emphasis on intrinsic values and a corporate focus on extrinsic values, with academics aspiring to create public knowledge and gain peer esteem while industry seeks to develop a competitive advantage through proprietary knowledge.[32] Whatever the causes, the two sectors have always tended to regard one another with some degree of suspicion and trepidation.

It is not surprising, then, that so much of what has been written about university interactions with industry is of a polemic character; there exists quite a healthy culture of critique surrounding the dangers of what is variously referred to as corporatization, commercialization, and commodification, including the related question of how closer ties with business enterprises compromise the academy's traditional values and commitments. Scholars have weighed in on whether and to what extent the academic ethos is being replaced by a new entrepreneurial or market ethos that also travels under the name of academic capitalism.[33] Concerns about compromised research objectivity, a devaluation of the academy's role as social critic, threats to the already delicate socioecological balance that relies on differentiation for its overall effectiveness but that is being increasingly challenged by forces of homogenization, and a host of similar ills have been described in several prominent books.[34] As just one example, the provocatively titled *Buying In or Selling Out: The Commercialization of the American Research University* poses the question of what exactly is represented by this phenomenon of closer ties with business and industry.[35] Overall, there is a pervasive fear that the work of the university—considered vital in itself—is rapidly coming to be seen only for its instrumental value vis-à-vis corporate interests and that it might, over time, be wholly absorbed by and organized according to the business agenda.

The potentially negative consequences of AIRs are richly detailed in academic and popular media. Major issues include financial conflicts of interest, suppression of or lack of access to research results, pro-industry biases, and various conflicts of commitment that pose a threat to traditional academic values.

For example, it is not uncommon for researchers or for institutions themselves to take equity stakes in spin-off companies created from faculty

inventions or discoveries.[36] A cross-sectional survey of AUTM (Association of University Technology Managers) members in 1999 revealed that
15 percent of faculty held equity in 10 or more start-ups that were supporting research at the same institution, and 68 percent of institutions
surveyed held equity in businesses supporting research conducted at the
same institution.[37] Roughly one-quarter of academic biomedical investigators receive research funding from industry, and about one-third of
investigators have personal financial ties with corporate sponsors.[38] These
ties have led to worries about the ethics of publication of scientific
research in which principal investigators have a vested interest in the
outcomes. Krimsky and colleagues found that 34 percent of articles in
14 high-profile journals were authored by scientists with a financial interest
in the outcome.[39]

Academic-industry relationships are also criticized on the grounds that
they impede open access to—and open sharing of—scientific research.
Reports show that academic researchers are occasionally denied access to
industry-sponsored research results or materials in order for firms to protect trade secrets or block competition.[40] In their meta-analysis of 37 studies
that addressed the extent, impact, and management of financial relationships involving scientific investigators, academic institutions, and industry,
Bekelman and colleagues found that between 12 percent and 34 percent
of researchers had been denied such access.[41] A recent survey of geneticists
reveals that data withholding is on the rise,[42] and evidence also exists to
support the claim that industry may obstruct publication of studies with
unfavorable results[43] or require publication delays of significant duration.[44]

There is also evidence of bias toward sponsoring firms' drugs or procedures[45] or other incidences of pro-industry conclusions yielded from
industry-sponsored research. For example, several studies have revealed
that industry-sponsored research in the biomedical sciences in particular
yields results or conclusions that are favorable to industry.[46]

Corporate influence over the academic research agenda presents itself
in other ways, too. Studies in the biomedical sciences have shown that
researchers with ties to industry are more than twice as likely to consider
commercial implications in their selection of research topics.[47] Critics warn
that industry sponsorship facilitates a general shift in focus from basic to
applied research in universities, which are currently responsible for about
one-half of all basic research conducted in the United States.[48] Finally,
adapting to the demands and expectations of the private sector may require an investment of time and effort that increases the faculty workload
and diverts attention from customary professorial duties.[49]

All of these entanglements contribute to an erosion of public trust in
institutions of higher education and have prompted the establishment

of guidelines to support sponsored research collaborations between academe and industry. A 2006 report issued jointly by the National Council of University Research Administrators and the Industrial Research Institute emphasizes that furtherance of each partner's core mission should be the determinative factor in decisions to enter into research agreements. The interests of universities and industry in sponsored research arrangements are also represented by a number of associations, including the University-Industry Demonstration Partnership (UIDP), the Government-University-Industry Research Roundtable (GUIRR), and AUTM. The UIDP, convened by the National Academies, aims to "enhance the value of collaborative partnerships between universities and industry in the United States"[50] by sharing best practices and developing tools that streamline agreements.

Various mechanisms—formal and informal, centralized and dispersed—have been developed for the management of risks and the mitigation of corrosive effects of industrial relationships. In the field of medicine, for example, several professional organizations—the Pharmaceutical Research and Manufacturers of America (PhRMA), the American Medical Association, and the American College of Physicians—have adopted codes of conduct to regulate physician-industry relationships.[51] Watchdog organizations occasionally play an active role in questioning the wisdom and integrity of AIRs. When the Energy Biosciences Institute was announced, Greenpeace, Essential Action, and the Foundation for Taxpayer and Consumer Rights collectively raised the question of whether public universities should be in league with "giant oil companies that are contributing massively to climate change."[52] Finally, calls have been sounded for the establishment of institutional centers for responsible innovation (CIRs) and institutional conflict-of-interest review groups in order to foster increased accountability, transparency, disclosure, and oversight of activities associated with AIRs.[53]

Collaborations with industry can and do have some deleterious effects on academic institutions. But there is also a prevailing assumption that universities are being dragged into such relationships reluctantly and that corporations are to blame for a reordering of academic values. University administrators and scientists, however, are often the ones courting relationships with industrial partners in order to realize financial or reputational gain from the arrangement.[54] As research costs continue to escalate (an estimated $45.8 billion spent by universities on R&D in 2005, according to the National Science Foundation), academic-industry alliances are likely to play an ever more vital role and need to be better understood at every stage of the partnership life cycle in order to improve their functioning. Indeed, among the most dangerous threats to the academic enterprise is a largely unspoken one that strikes right at the heart of our identity as a community of truth seekers: the threat that we will substitute untested hunches for actual knowledge about our industrial counterparts, their motivations, and their preferred mode of working together.

DEVELOPING AND SUSTAINING ALLIANCES

So common have partnerships become that we have ceased to show much interest in their specific, intricate stories. Hence, many assumptions, inferences, and outright fallacies—some of them shaped by stereotypes and misunderstandings—take hold. For example, many academics are under the impression that businesses want to control higher education or at least bend it to serve narrow corporate financial interests. Meanwhile, many businesspeople believe that academic researchers want only to pursue arcane agendas based on personal curiosity rather than on commercially viable prospects. Much is unknown or based on tenuous (and often outdated) data.

Those who have operated on the boundary between the sectors recognize that the common characterizations are—as usual—reductive and misrepresentative, but entrenched images still exert a powerful force on the imaginations of these camps and on the possibilities for successful partnership. Failure to grasp the true motivations, needs, or core values of partners can lead quite naturally to problems in any joint venture.[55] Not knowing our prospective partners can lead us to exaggerate their intentions, motives, and the size and shape of the threat presented by our involvement with them.

In the grand tradition of questioning assumptions that is one of the academy's enduring values, we ought to open our suppositions to inspection and further detailed scrutiny. How well, for example, do we understand the factors involved in developing and nurturing academic-corporate alliances from the perspective of experts—academic and corporate leaders—involved in their implementation? Despite a body of literature saturated with references to university-industry alliances, there is surprisingly little empirical research dealing with these factors. To be sure, there is plenty in the way of best practices shared in popular books and articles on the subject of partnership and collaboration.[56] For example, nearly every guide to partnership formation and development emphasizes the importance of compatibility or fit between partnering organizations, and it is typically recommended as an important first step in the collaborative process that partners make an effort to assess the congruency of their missions, purposes, values, expectations, requirements, and strategic directions.[57]

Much of what we know is codified in *prescriptive* formulas for successful partnerships. Few studies angle at learning what these two sectors actually seek from each other or how relationships might be structured to protect the integrity of partnering entities while generating value for both sides.

THE STUDY

In an attempt to supplement anecdotal insights with data from the field, we undertook a research project to understand how leaders experience academic-corporate relationships, what they expect out of such interactions, and what they deem to be instrumental to partnership effectiveness. Specifically, we investigated the views of university-industry experts so that, through consensus, specific factors leading to the development and sustainability of partnerships could be identified.[58]

Method

The Delphi Technique, a data collection method developed by the Rand Corporation in the early 1950s, was chosen for this study because it is designed to facilitate communication and refine and draw upon the collective opinions and expertise of a panel of experts. Seven academic and seven industry experts participated in a three-round Delphi study. The academic leaders came from research universities and were predominately senior-level administrators—one was a chancellor, one was a vice president, one was an associate vice president, two were associate vice chancellors, and two were directors of economic development. Corporate leaders involved in the study were members of international companies based (or having subsidiaries based) in the United States. Industry respondents held executive positions within the companies—one was president and chief executive officer, four were vice-presidents, one was a director of people and organizations, and one was a director of intellectual property and licensing. These academic and industrial experts were asked to come to consensus in the identification of factors in developing and sustaining academic-industry partnerships.

A review panel consisting of members of the academic and industrial communities who have worked with—or are currently working with—academic-industry partnerships was formed to review the questions to determine whether we had achieved the stated purpose and to address concerns of possible bias in interpreting the Delphi experts' responses.[59] Two review panel members were from universities affiliated with the Research Triangle Park of North Carolina. The Research Triangle Park was created in 1959 through a public-private partnership involving business, academe, and state government. One of the top priorities of the Research Triangle Park is to develop and sustain collaborations among Duke University, North Carolina State University, and the University of North Carolina-Chapel Hill. Additionally, there are extensive efforts to encourage companies to locate their R&D facilities within the Park. Currently, there are 136 companies in the Research Triangle Park, with total employment of more than 37,600 people and combined annual salaries of more than $2.7 billion.[60] The review panel was used in each round to review all instruments utilized in the study.[61]

The first round of the study posed two open-ended questions to respondents. The questions as presented were: *What are the factors involved in developing an academic-industry partnership? What are the factors involved in sustaining an academic-industry partnership?* The second round presented the data collected in Round 1 and allowed the panel of experts to rate items on a five-point Likert scale (numeric ranges: 5 = "Strongly Agree" to 1 = "Strongly Disagree") and provide written comments on items in the instrument. After each round of questions, summary data in the form of mean responses for each statement and interquartile ranges (IQR) were computed and relayed to the panel of experts in the subsequent round of questions. The factors with a mean of 3.5 or greater were considered a consensus-reflecting agreement and were included in Round 3 of the study. Round 3, the final round of the Delphi study, was intended to determine consensus on those factors retained from Round 2. This round gave the experts an opportunity to accept or reject each factor retained from Round 2 and achieve final consensus. The data from the Round 3 instrument were analyzed using a chi-square nonparametric test. Each factor was placed in a table to indicate the number of responses made to accept or reject the factor. A probability value (p) was determined for each factor using the chi-square test with one degree of freedom. Any factor with a probability value higher than .05 was eliminated from the final list of factors.

Key Findings

In the first round, responses from each panelist ranged in number from 4 to 10 for each question. After the raw data were analyzed, edited for replication, and similar items were grouped together, 45 factors in *developing* and 44 factors in *sustaining* academic industry partnerships were identified. These factors were presented to the expert panel in Round 2, and factors receiving less than a 3.5 rating were considered (for purposes of this study) unimportant in developing or sustaining a partnership and were deleted from the subsequent round. It is worth noting that a significant number of the factors that were eliminated challenge notions of academic-industry partnerships that are frequently presented in the literature.[62] As just one example, exchange of resources is cited in extant research as a critical factor in academic-industry partnership; however, the experts in this study reached consensus that this factor was relatively unimportant to partnership development and sustainability.

In the final round, the experts identified 25 factors considered to be essential for developing an academic-industry partnership (see Table 7.1), and 26 factors were identified for sustaining such a partnership (see Table 7.2). Each of the 51 factors met the established statistical criteria (p-value $< .05$) and was approved by the review panel. These factors represented a cluster of related knowledge, skills, and attitudes for developing and sustaining an academic-industry partnership.

Table 7.1: Final Factors Identified in Developing Academic-Industry Partnerships (Question #1)

Factors

Reciprocity—something to gain for both/all parties

Mutual respect, trust, openness, and confidence in the relationship

Establishing clearly understood and agreed upon objectives

Execution of win-win research contractual agreement which meets both partners' needs

Memorandum of agreement or contract as needed

Creation of an action plan

Technical expertise

Team leaders identified for each partner

Flexibility

Agreement as to how any profits resulting from the collaboration would be shared

Willingness of academic side to understand the real-world conditions of private industry

Assignment of key objectives and associated tasks to designated individuals within the academic-industry partnerships

Relationship between key people in the business and the institution of higher education

Identification of a single go to person within each partner's structure to channel all communication

Agreement as to how the teams involved in the partnership would be kept informed

(Continued)

Table 7.1: Final Factors Identified in Developing Academic-Industry Partnerships (Question #1) (*Continued*)

Factors

Identification of management sponsors from industry who have the ability to establish such projects within their companies, and who have the ability and means to see the projects through to completion

Academic research capabilities relevant to industry partner and applications

Inclusion of licensing and royalty elements which address patent ownership and publishing rights

Development of a research plan and associated budget, including key objectives, associated tasks, and timing

Agreed upon communication plan, including written report types (high level or detailed, timing, distribution), meetings (telephonic or in person, frequency, process – i.e., minutes and action items) and methods for troubleshooting to solve unanticipated events

Information on how collaboration would be funded

It should encompass existing research strength, focus area, and capabilities of the academic unit or group

Consistency with the university's mission

Strengthening of faculty scholarship as a result of the engagement

Enhancement of the education experience for involved students

Analysis

The final factors addressed many of the conflicts of interest and barriers to the development and sustainability of academic-industry partnerships that have been reported in the literature. The barriers most commonly cited in the literature from the industry perspective include inadequate communication, unstable infrastructure for collaborations, lack of responsiveness by universities to short-term business pressures (such as quarterly earning reports), lack of knowledge about partners, and lack of strategic planning.[63] From the university perspective, key problems with industry partnerships have included publication delays, biases in reporting research results, denial of access to research, perceptions of disparity in overall budget allocations to departments involved in industry partnerships, and adverse effects on the productivity of faculty involved in industry collaborations or neglect of the faculty's traditional academic responsibilities.[64] In the final round of this study, a statistical analysis of the responses indicated a particularly high level of consensus on the importance of factors such as *a budget that covers the actual cost of the partnership*; *frequent and open*

Table 7.2: Final Factors Identified in Sustaining Academic-Industry Partnerships (Question #2)

Factors

Maintaining trust, openness, and confidence

Team leaders are accountable for making sure that research plan and timelines are followed

Effective delivery of research, services, and programs from the university

Sustained commitment from the leadership of the company

Developing methods of evaluating progress of the projects and determining their true value at completion

A clear understanding (by both parties) of roles, responsibilities, scope of work, and a statement of mutual expectations

Frequent and open communication

Regular reporting of results, issues, and successes

Candid discussion and understanding of outcomes

A budget that covers the actual cost of the partnership

Periodic assessments, including modifications and adjustments

Team leaders (or designees) are responsible for assuring communication plan is followed

A vision and agreed upon timetable, with actions, monitoring, reporting, and occasional face-to-face interactions

Team leaders ensure action is taken when troubleshooting is necessary (both project-related and if there are problematic interpersonal relationship issues building)

Focused team with clear priorities

Retention of the champions/lead contacts from both higher education and industry

Maintaining relevance of research to solving industry's problems

Continued clarity on the joint relationship, ensuring that the needs of both parties are being met

A relationship not solely dependent upon a single person from each partnering entity

Results; reciprocity

Constant attention to the relationship

Action is taken to ensure team members meet timelines

Funding stability and long term commitments

Positive leverage—the partnership achieves more than the university could accomplish in isolation

Partnership behaves like two equals rather than one being subordinate to the other

The active participation of senior leadership from participating organizations *communication; regular reporting of results and the continued clarity of the joint relationship; effective delivery of research, services, and programs from the university; and strengthening faculty scholarship as a result of the engagement.*

It should also be noted that the identification of final factors by the expert panel did *not* support the criticism that collaborations would lead to an erosion of public interest concerns in academic research (as long as one is of the view that industry serves the public interest at least in part through the development and distribution of its products and services).[65] Rather, it emphasized a high degree of consensus about factors such as maintaining the relevance of research to solving industry's problems. And, in fact, it supported research showing that collaboration would enhance knowledge production and would also turn knowledge into a product that has a commercial value or a practical application that would improve the health and living standards of society.[66]

Public policies have been credited as the catalysts for innovation and knowledge production collaborations between academic institutions and industry.[67] This study's findings suggest that public policies have fundamentally impacted the partnership experience of respondents by introducing issues of intellectual property and patents into the mix. Such issues are often viewed as a barrier to successful partnerships; however, the responses obtained in this study suggest that leaders in these alliances recognize the challenge and proactively manage issues surrounding proprietary information as a critical factor in the development and sustainability of a partnership. For instance, in the subjective round of the study, Round 1, there were seven factors that addressed the issue of proprietary information (in other words, privately owned knowledge or data, such as that protected by a registered patent, copyright, or trademark). The terminology used in the responses emphasized the importance of understanding and clearly establishing strategies for handling proprietary issues as an initial step in the collaboration; examples included "*establishment* of rights to intellectual property," "*rules* for rights to publish results," "*requires* inclusion of licensing elements," "*must address* patent ownership and publishing rights," and "*protection* of proprietary information."

As a specific policy, the Bayh-Dole Act has been given credit for providing the incentive for many universities to establish technology transfer offices and other infrastructure in order to take a more commercial approach to technology transfer. These offices are designed to protect the university's intellectual property and promote the transfer of academic discovery to industry for public benefit. They have also increased the scope and complexity of academic-industry partnerships. Findings from this study support observations in extant literature[68] that technology transfer offices provide a sense of equity and standardization between collaborating organizations. For example, expert references to *the identification of management sponsors who have the ability to establish such* (collaborative research) *projects and the means to see the projects through to completion* and *the inclusion of licensing and royalty elements which address patent ownership and publishing rights* point to the importance of structural capabilities and expertise that can facilitate mutually beneficial relationships.

The benefits to industry of R&D partnerships are apparent in recent studies that have highlighted a significant increase in productivity for companies that partner with academic institutions.[69] In the pharmaceutical industry, for example, there is a significant correlation between new drug patents and academic pharmaceutical partnerships.[70] In fact, in one study tracing the historical origins of 32 innovative drugs, it was discovered that "universities alone made a major contribution towards half of the drugs discovered."[71] Our Delphi study involved two pharmaceutical companies, and the experts from these companies gave high ratings to a number of factors that are essential for successful research and development collaborations and, specifically for pharmaceutical companies, in the drug development process. Among these factors were *development of a research plan . . . including key objectives, associated tasks, and timing*; *effective delivery of research services and programs from the university*; *regular reporting of results*; *academic research capabilities relevant to industry partner and applications*; *inclusion of licensing and royalty elements which address patent ownership and publishing rights*; and *reciprocity*. These responses highlight the importance of developing a collaboration that enhances the two-way flow of knowledge leading to mutually advantageous results.

This study produced little evidence that universities are focusing on technology transfer solely as a revenue generating concept. Rather, the results indicate that the core mission of universities still remains education and the generation and dissemination of new knowledge to be shared with the public. Throughout the study, factors such as *consistency with the university's mission, strengthening faculty scholarship as a result of the engagement,* and *enhancement of the education experience for involved students* received high ratings. The consensus reached in this study supports the observation in the literature that when partnerships are integrated into the mission of the university, interaction between the partners is stronger and more likely to succeed.[72]

As noted earlier, the different cultures of universities and corporations present challenges to the development of successful partnerships between the sectors.[73] In our study, the major cultural difference had to do with time. Industry leaders consistently gave a higher rating to the following four factors: *action is taken to ensure that team members meet timelines, quick turnaround time, establishing and maintaining meeting times,* and *periodic assessments.* Issues that involved administrative detail, such as timely reporting structures, were rated as less important by the academic leaders. This issue of time orientation has been discussed in recent research, and it has been concluded that business organizations "often take a short-term perspective on R&D activities while timeframes are longer-term and less defined for researchers in universities."[74] The findings in this study were consistent with scholarship pointing to cultural differences between universities and corporations; however, there was also evidence to suggest that each partner is aware of the attendant challenges and is taking steps to manage cultural divergence.

Finally, our findings did not support the assumption, detailed in much of the literature on AIRs, that universities are becoming more like businesses. The final factors that reached consensus (for example, *strengthening of faculty scholarship as a result of the engagement, enhancement of the education experience for involved students,* and *consistency with the university's mission*) indicate that academics remain motivated by the quest for knowledge and understanding and that the primary responsibility of higher education is of a traditional academic—rather than a commercial—nature.

Implications

Leaders of academic institutions and industrial organizations understand the growing importance of collaboration between the sectors, yet the data to support these partnerships are limited. The factors identified by the expert panel serve as a foundation for future research into academic-industry collaboration. Building upon the factors identified in this study, additional research and discussions may aid in the development of strategies for future academic-industry partnerships.

The missions and goals of universities and industries remain different, of course, and will therefore continue to create challenges in developing and maintaining successful partnerships. However, this study reveals a conscious effort by representatives of each sector to understand the other's cultures, values, and missions. The 51 key factors are by no means exhaustive, but their identification through this iterative process shows that these sectors are working to create synergistic relationships that respect and even leverage essential cultural and operational differences. Perhaps most importantly, the simple act of asking academic and corporate leaders to announce and come to agreement on the factors they view as instrumental to healthy collaborations has value as a tool for generating higher levels of trust and understanding between the sectors. As such, a modified Delphi technique like the one employed in this study can be adapted for use by academic and industrial partners as an initial intake to learn of the areas of convergence and divergence in partner views of what will make the interaction effective. Baseline data in this regard may be helpful in forming a responsive collaboration and adjusting it down the road to better adhere to original intentions and preferences.

A VOTE FOR SPECIFICITY

It should be emphasized that this study's findings may not translate across organizational contexts. Indeed, given the idiosyncratic nature of relationships, specific partnership practices tend not to travel very well beyond their particular local circumstances.[75] The population from which the sample was drawn includes only research universities and major companies that have a focus on the research and development of new technologies (and that support collaborative efforts between academic institutions and industry). Although methodologically sufficient for the purposes at hand, the results cannot be generalized to all types of academic institutions and industry stakeholders. Moreover, the opinions of the experts are not necessarily generalizable to all academic and industry administrators. A different set of factors would be expected to arise if the study were focused on small private institutions and community colleges that partner with industry or on smaller start-up companies that partner with academic institutions. As just one example, well-established firms tend to be more product-oriented than nonpublic start-up firms, which tend to be more focused on the science and technology.[76] Further study is needed to refine and verify results across a diverse sample of institutions.

This generalizability disclaimer is in the service of a larger point. There is enormous variety in the world of partnerships, much more than is acknowledged in the academic and popular press. Not all collaborations are focused on the commercialization of science and technology. Still, there is a tendency to use the scientific or technological partnership as representative of all partnerships (this despite a highly variegated landscape of interactions characterized by different forms, purposes, exchanges, and degrees of formality), and there is a notable tendency to lump firms together instead of making appropriate distinctions on the basis of relevant attributes such as size, stage of development, product portfolio, and motivations. The focus of research and commentary has been disproportionately on the 20 institutions reporting the highest R&D expenditures in science and engineering.[77] Additionally, it is well-known that corporate ties are not distributed evenly across campus; they tend to be concentrated in professional schools and in the hard sciences. Countless unremarkable interactions fly beneath the radar but are nevertheless part of a vast continuum of involvement. More attention should be paid to the expectations and experiences of university and corporate collaborators in these lesser documented instances.

It is also the case that the term *partnership* has become overworked, and the danger in this, as with all instances of language that has lost its descriptive power, is that highly discrepant notions of working together may be obscured. The language of collaboration may be so familiar that we no longer think critically about its premises. What do partners even have in mind when they think about partnership? What are the operating images of partnership they use, and how do these images have a shaping influence on their judgments of partnership in the abstract or of particular partnerships? Analysts and leaders may benefit from deconstructing the constitutive elements or activities of partnership and treating these as variables worthy of examination in their own right.

CONCLUDING THOUGHTS

Strong ties between universities and industries appear to be one of the answers to a multifaceted set of global challenges. One should not be unrealistic about what is possible through partnerships, but they can offer a source of abiding hope that many large-scale problems are being—or will be—addressed by mutually concerned parties. In order to maximize their value, however, we need a more precise way of observing and describing them.

Attempting to understand the dynamics of partnership on their own terms—without too much reference or recourse to accumulated wisdom—is important for practitioners and scholars alike. Problems often arise from (1) misreads of a partner's (or prospective partner's) intentions or wishes, (2) guesses substituted for knowledge of what partners want, with some of these guesses based on inferences or stereotypes, (3) imputing to particular organizations characteristics that are held to be true of whole sectors, (4) extrapolating incautiously from previous alliance experiences, and (5) a belief that rationales for involvement or expectations for involvement are static instead of evolving (and therefore not in need of continuous monitoring or updating).

Many of these problems can be avoided simply by not taking things for granted; we would be better served to enter into collaborations with a certain posture of humility and curiosity. Asking questions of partners and allowing for surprises (rather than short-circuiting the learning process) may go a long way toward improving the conduct of cross-sector interactions, our satisfaction with them, and the outcomes associated with them. The asking and answering of questions about motivations and desires within a partnership constitutes an important part of relational work, helping to build and solidify relationships and offering occasions to demonstrate responsiveness to the stated wishes of partners.[78]

One of the overlooked and underappreciated benefits of academic-industry collaborations is that they provide opportunities for those of us in the academy to challenge what we think we know about business organizations. Not all corporations are out to control universities. In fact, successful academic-industry partnerships appear to be built on an appreciation for the *distinct* missions of universities and firms.[79] Far from trying to co-opt universities, corporate partners recognize and desire the complementary value provided by institutions that are distinctly non-commercial in their value structure, culture, and orientation.[80]

The argument here is simple: we ought to take better advantage of opportunities to know industrial partners better than we do. This is one of the nontechnical outputs of partnership that should be actively encouraged and managed, and it can be achieved at no additional cost. In the end, we'll find that we're not just talking about academic-industry relationships but about how institutions of higher education engage all manner of controversy, otherness, and the unknown. We are always the best version of ourselves when we are coming at a problem or challenge not by taking others' word for it but by testing the matter for ourselves. While we have yet to apply this principle in the realm of academic-industry relations in any concerted way, there exist abundant opportunities to do so. If the collaborative form of organizing is to become even more of a fixture in the future, as has been predicted, then it is incumbent upon us to work with our cross-sector counterparts to shape our alliances in ways that simultaneously preserve our uniqueness (and therefore our integrity) and multiply our impact through joint efforts.

NOTES

1. We write from the perspective of boundary spanners, both of us having spent our professional lives in universities, in corporations, and as developers of academic-corporate partnerships.

2. See, for example, David Blumenthal, "Academic-Industrial Relationships in the Life Sciences," *The New England Journal of Medicine* 349, 25 (2003), 2452–9; Zach W. Hall, "The Academy and Industry: A View Across the Divide," in *Buying In or Selling Out: The Commercialization of the American Research University,* ed. Donald G. Stein (New Brunswick, NJ: Rutgers University Press, 2004), 153–160; Walter W. Powell, Jason Owen-Smith, and Jeanette A. Colyvas, "Innovation and Emulation:

Lessons from the Experiences of U.S. Universities in Selling Private Rights to Public Knowledge," *Minerva* 45, (2007): 143–59.

3. Manuel Crespo and Houssine Dridi, "Intensification of University-Industry Relationships and Its Impact on Academic Research," *Higher Education* 54, (2007): 61–84.

4. Eyal Press and Jennifer Washburn, "The Kept University," *Atlantic Monthly* 285 (2000): 39–54.

5. Association of University Technology Managers, *AUTM Licensing Survey: FY2002 Survey Summary,* The Association of University Technology Managers, Inc. (2003).

6. Justin E. Bekelman, Yan Li, and Cary P. Gross, "Scope and Impact of Financial Conflicts of Interest in Biomedical Research: A Systematic Review," *Journal of the American Medical Association* 289 (2003): 454–65.

7. James E. Austin, *The Collaboration Challenge: How Nonprofits and Businesses Succeed Through Strategic Alliances* (San Francisco: Jossey-Bass Publishers, 2000).

8. Merle Jacob et al. "From Sponsorship to Partnership in Academy-Industry Relations," *R&D Management* 30 (2000): 255–62.

9. "Master Agreement Dated November 9, 2007 Between BP Technology Ventures Inc. and The Regents of the University of California," http://www.energybioscienceinstitute.org/images/stories/pressroom/FINAL_Execution_11-9.pdf.

10. Taran Thune, "University-Industry Collaboration: The Network Embeddedness Approach," *Science and Public Policy* 34 (2007): 158–68.

11. Will Geoghegan and Dimitrios Pontikakis, "From Ivory Tower to Factory Floor? How Universities Are Changing to Meet the Needs of Industry," *Science and Public Policy* 35 (2008): 462–74; Georg Krücken, Frank Meier, and Andre Müller, "Information, Cooperation, and the Blurring of Boundaries—Technology Transfer in German and American Discourses," *Higher Education* 63 (2007): 675–96; David W. Edgington, "The Kyoto Research Park and Innovation in Japanese Cities," *Urban Geography* 29 (2008): 411–50; Mohammed Saad, Girma Zawdie, and Chandra Malairaja, "The Triple Helix Strategy for Universities in Developing Countries: The Experiences in Malaysia and Algeria," *Science and Public Policy* 35 (2008): 431–43.

12. Melissa S. Anderson, "The Complex Relations between the Academy and Industry: Views from the Literature," *Journal of Higher Education* 72 (2001): 226–46.

13. John W. Selsky and Barbara Parker, "Cross-Sector Partnerships to Address Social Issues: Challenges to Theory and Practice," *Journal of Management* 31 (2005): 849–73.

14. Henry Etzkowitz and Andrew Webster, "Entrepreneurial Science: The Second Academic Revolution," in *Capitalizing Knowledge: New Intersections of Industry and Academia,* ed. Henry Etzkowitz, Andrew Webster, and Peter Healey (Albany: State University of New York Press, 1998), 21–46.

15. Hall, "The Academy and Industry: A View Across the Divide."

16. Lori Turk-Bicakci and Steven Brint, "University-Industry Collaboration: Patterns of Growth for Low- and Middle-Level Performers," *Higher Education* 49 (2005): 61–89, 70.

17. Ibid.

18. Blumenthal, "Academic-Industrial Relationships in the Life Sciences," 2452.

19. "Stevenson-Wydler Technology Innovation Act of 1980," http://www.csrees.usda.gov/about/offices/legis/techtran.html.

20. Georg Krücken, Frank Meier, and Andre Müller, "Information, Cooperation, and the Blurring of Boundaries—Technology Transfer in German and American Discourses," *Higher Education* 63 (2007): 675–96.

21. Roger L. Geiger and Creso Sá, "Beyond Technology Transfer: U.S. State Policies to Harness University Research for Economic Development," *Minerva* 43 (2005): 1–21.

22. Powell, Owen-Smith, and Colyvas, "Innovation and Emulation."

23. David Blumenthal and Eric G. Campbell, "Academic-Industry Relationships in Biotechnology Overview," in *Encyclopedia of Ethical, Legal and Policy Issues in Biotechnology,* ed. Thomas H. Murray and Maxwell J. Mehlman (New York: John Wiley & Sons, 2000): Frieder Meyer-Krahmer and Ulrich Schmock, "Science-Based Technologies: University-Industry Interactions in Four Fields," *Research Policy* 27 (1998): 835–51.

24. National Academy of Engineering, *The Impact of Academic Research on Industrial Performance,* (Washington, DC: National Academies Press, 2003).

25. Michael D. Santoro and Alok K. Chakrabarti, "Corporate Strategic Objectives for Establishing Relationships with University Research Centers," *IEEE Transactions on Engineering Management* 48 (2001): 157–63.

26. National Science Foundation, "Industrial Funding of Academic R&D Rebounds in FY2005," http://www.nsf.gov/statistics/infbrief/nsf07311/nsf07311.pdf.

27. Association of University Technology Managers, *AUTM Licensing Survey: FY2006 Survey Summary,* The Association of University Technology Managers, Inc. (2007).

28. David C. Mowery et al., "The Growth of Patenting and Licensing by U.S. Universities: An Assessment of the Effects of the Bayh-Dole Act of 1980," *Research Policy* 30 (2004): 99–119.

29. Powell, Owen-Smith, and Colyvas, "Innovation and Emulation."

30. Ibid.

31. Paul J. DiMaggio and Walter W. Powell, "The Iron Cage Revisited: Institutional Isomorphism and Collective Rationality in Organizational Fields," *American Sociological Review* 48 (1983): 147–60.

32. Dasgupta Partha and Paul A. David, "Toward a New Economics of Science," *Research Policy* 23 (1994): 487–521.

33. Sheila Slaughter and Larry L. Leslie, *Academic Capitalism: Politics, Policies, and the Entrepreneurial University* (Baltimore, MD: Johns Hopkins University Press, 1997).

34. See, for example, Derek Bok, *Universities in the Marketplace: The Commercialization of Higher Education,* (Princeton, NJ: Princeton University Press, 2003); Jennifer Washburn, *University, Inc.: The Corporate Corruption of American Higher Education* (New York: Basic Books, 2005); Eric Gould, *The University in a Corporate Culture* (New Haven, CT: Yale University Press, 2003); David. L. Kirp, *Shakespeare, Einstein, and the Bottom Line: The Marketing of Higher Education* (Cambridge, MA: Harvard University Press, 2003).

35. Donald G. Stein, ed., *Buying In or Selling Out? The Commercialization of the American Research University* (New Brunswick, NJ: Rutgers University Press, 2004).

36. Crespo and Dridi, "Intensification of University-Industry Relationships and Its Impact on Academic Research."

37. Lori Pressman, "AUTM Licensing Survey, FY 1999: Survey Summary," Association of University Technology Managers (2000).

38. Bekelman, Li, and Gross, "Scope and Impact of Financial Conflicts of Interest in Biomedical Research."

39. Sheldon Krimsky et al., "Financial Interests of Authors in Scientific Journals: A Pilot Study of 14 Publications," *Science and Engineering Ethics* 2 (1996): 395–410.

40. Bekelman, Li, and Gross, "Scope and Impact of Financial Conflicts of Interest in Biomedical Research."

41. Ibid.

42. Eric G. Campbell et al., "Data Withholding in Academic Medicine: Characteristics of Faculty Denied Access to Research Results and Biomaterials," *Research Policy* 29 (2000): 303–12.

43. Bekelman, Li, and Gross, "Scope and Impact of Financial Conflicts of Interest in Biomedical Research."

44. Washburn, *University, Inc.*

45. Lise L. Kjaegard and Bodil Als-Nielsen, "Association Between Competing Interests and Authors' Conclusions: Epidemiological Study of Randomised Clinical Trials Published in the BMJ," *BMJ* 32 (2002): 249–53.

46. Bekelman, Li, and Gross, "Scope and Impact of Financial Conflicts of Interest in Biomedical Research."

47. Ibid.

48. Geiger and Sá, "Beyond Technology Transfer."

49. Crespo and Dridi, "Intensification of University-Industry Relationships and Its Impact on Academic Research."

50. "University-Industry Demonstration Partnership," http://uidp.org/UIDP_FAQ.html#P42_4738.

51. Eric G. Campbell et al., "A National Survey of Physician-Industry Relationships," *New England Journal of Medicine* 356 (2007): 1742–50.

52. "Letter from Essential Action, Greenpeace USA, and the Foundation for Taxpayer and Consumer Rights to U.C. Board of Regents & President," http://www.essentialaction.org/ebi/.

53. "Report on Individual and Institutional Financial Conflict of Interest," American Association of Universities Task Force on Research Accountability (Washington, DC: AAU, 2001); David H. Guston, "Responsible Innovation in the Commercialized University," in *Buying In or Selling Out,* ed. Donald G. Stein, 161–174.

54. Norman E. Bowie, *University-Business Partnerships: An Assessment* (Lanham, MD: Rowan & Littlefield, 1994).

55. Hall, "The Academy and Industry: A View Across the Divide."

56. See, for example, Austin, *The Collaboration Challenge.*

57. Ibid.

58. Those interested in the full study may wish to consult Cynthia C. DeLuca, *An Analysis of the Factors Involved in Developing and Sustaining Academic-Industry Partnerships* (Unpublished doctoral dissertation, East Carolina University, 2008).

59. Nicholas Nash, "Delphi and Educational Research: A Review," ERIC Document Reproduction Service, ED 151 950 (1978).

60. "Research Triangle Park," http://www.rtp.org/main/.

61. Mary A. Meyer and Jane M. Booker, *Eliciting and Analyzing Expert Judgment: A Practical Guide* (New York: Academic Press, 1990).

62. Bronwyn H. Hall, Albert N. Link, and John T. Scott, *Universities as Research Partners,* National Institute of Standards and Technology, United States Department of Commerce, NIST-GCR 02–829, (2002).

63. Richard M. Cyert and Paul S. Goodman, "Creating Effective University-Industry Alliances: An Organizational Learning Perspective," *Organizational Dynamics* 25 (1997): 45–57.

64. Hall, Link, and Scott, *Universities as Research Partners*.

65. David Ervin et al., "University-Industry Relationship: Framing the Issues for Academic Research in Agricultural Biotechnology," Proceedings From an Expert Workshop Sponsored by the Pew Initiative on Food and Biotechnology and the U.S. Department of Agriculture's Initiative for Future Agriculture and Food Systems Project Public Goods and University-Industry Relationships in Agricultural Biotechnology. Charles Hammer Conference Center, November 19–20, 2002, Research Triangle Park, NC.

66. See, for example, David Blumenthal et al., "Relationships Between Academic Institutions and Industry in the Life Sciences—An Industry Survey," *The New England Journal of Medicine* 334 (1996): 368–73; Irwin Feller, "Technology Transfer from Universities," in *Higher Education: Handbook of Theory and Research*, ed. John C. Smart (Edison, NJ: Agathon Press, 1999): 1–43.

67. Blumenthal et al., "Relationships"; Feller, "Technology Transfer from Universities"; Philip H. Phan and Donald S. Siegel, "The Effectiveness of University Technology Transfer: Lessons Learned, Managerial and Policy Implications, and the Road Forward," *Foundations and Trends in Entrepreneurship* 2 (2006): 77–144.

68. Phan and Siegel, "The Effectiveness of University Technology Transfer."

69. Susan K. Finston, "The Relevance of Genetic Resources to the Pharmaceutical Industry: The Industry Viewpoint," *The Journal of World Intellectual Property* 8 (2005): 141–155; Wendy H. Schact, "R&D Partnerships and Intellectual Property: Implications for U.S. Policy," CRS Report for Congress, Congressional Research Service, December 6, 2000; Coopers and Lybrand L.L.P., "Growth Companies with University Ties Have Productivity Rates Almost Two-Thirds Higher Than Peers," *Trendsetter Barometer,* January 26, 1995, 1.

70. Robert Kneller, "The Origins of New Drugs," *Nature Biotechnology* 23 (2005): 529–30; Janice M. Reichart and Christopher-Paul Milne, *Public and Private Sector Contributions to the Discovery and Development of 'Impact' Drugs,* Tufts Center for the Study of Drug Development, White Paper (2002).

71. Jaye Chin-Dusting et al., "Finding Improved Medicines: The Role of Academic-Industrial Collaboration," *Nature Reviews Drug Discovery* 4 (2005): 891–97.

72. Dina Biscotti et al., "University-Industry Relationships: Framing the Issues for Academic Research in Agricultural Biotechnology." Report of Workshop, "University-Industry Relationships and the Public Good: Framing the Issues in Agricultural Biotechnology," November 19–20,

2002 (2003); Pablo D'Este and Pari Patel, "University-Industry Linkages in the UK: What Are the Factors Determining a Variety of Interactions with Industry?" *Science and Technology Policy Research,* www.sussex.ac.uk/spru/documents/d-este-paper.doc; Edwin Mansfield and Jeong-Yeon Lee, "The Modern University: Contributor to Industrial Innovation and Recipient of Industrial R&D Support," *Research Policy* 25 (1996): 1047–58; Kristi M. Tornquist and Lincoln A. Kallsen, "Out of the Ivory Tower, *Journal of Higher Education* 65 (1994): 523–39.

73. G. William Dauphinais and Colin Price, *Straight From the CEO: The World's Top Business Leaders Reveal Ideas Every Manager Can Use* (New York: Simon & Schuster, 1998).

74. Cyert and Goodman, "Creating Effective University-Industry Alliances"; Ashok K. Gupta, S. P. Raj, and David Wilemon, "A Model for Studying R&D, Marketing Interface in the Product Innovation Process," *Journal of Marketing* 50 (1986): 7–17; Carolin Plewa and Pascale Quester, "Key Drivers of University-Industry Relationships: The Role of Organizational Compatibility and Personal Experience," *Journal of Services Marketing* 21 (2006): 370–82.

75. Powell, Owen-Smith, and Colyvas, "Innovation and Emulation."

76. Ervin et al., "University-Industry Relationship: Framing the Issues for Academic Research in Agricultural Biotechnology."

77. Turk-Bicakci and Brint, "University-Industry Collaboration."

78. Jody Hoffer Gittell, "A Theory of Relational Coordination," in *Positive Organizational Scholarship: Foundations of a New Discipline,* ed. Kim S. Cameron, Jane E. Dutton, and Robert E. Quinn (San Francisco: Berrett-Koehler Publishers, 2003), 279–95.

79. Hall, "The Academy and Industry: A View Across the Divide."

80. David J. Siegel, "Minding the Academy's Business," *Academe* 92, no. 6 (2006): 54–7.

CHAPTER 8

Academia, Industry, and Government: Building Bridges

Tom McMail

This chapter is essentially divided into two complementary parts. In the first part, I focus on research collaborations involving corporations and universities. I begin by highlighting some of the key similarities and differences in these entities' modes of operation. I then introduce the federal government as an additional partner in the innovation process; together, academe, business, and the federal government form a research community value triangle that offers mutual benefits to each sector consistent with its scope and priorities.

In part two, I suggest that higher education's traditional role as educator—not just its role in cutting-edge research—is a critically important driver of innovation that benefits industry and society in general. In other words, qualified graduates can be understood, on one level, as the products and services that colleges and universities produce. Distance learning, in particular, is radically transforming how this is accomplished. It offers distinct advantages (in access and flexibility, for example) and challenges (in evaluations of quality, for example) to both higher education and industry. Moreover, it suggests an emerging business model for higher education in which external stakeholders—such as corporations and government—play a more important role as investors and advisors, commensurate with the value they expect to receive from the outputs of academe.

BUILDING EFFECTIVE COLLABORATION MODELS

Some fundamental similarities, as well as profound incompatibilities, confront collaboration between industry, government, and the higher educational ecosystem in North America, and each sector would do well to keep in mind the others' basic modes of action, expectations, and raison d'être. To be fair, to enable better collaboration, some businesses and institutions are making progress in this area, although they may need to continually remind themselves to see things through each other's eyes, focusing on their key areas of common interest: research, education, and policy.

THE RATE OF CHANGE

First of all, there are differences in perspective relating to timeframe. Industry must change and adapt quickly to competition in the marketplace. To academia, which bases decisions on careful deliberation and input from many sources, the corporate rate of change seems to exemplify progress on steroids. To industry, on the other hand, the rate of change in academia can seem glacial, even in the best of times.

The reasons for this impedance mismatch become obvious when examined closely. Businesses, when they fail to compete, die, or at least suffer serious decline in profitability that can lead to their eventual demise. The output of businesses (their products) must always be in high demand, must be useful, and must solve important problems for people, and they must do so better than the competitor's products do.

Universities, in contrast, may persist in their patterns for much longer periods without significant change. Degrees and other certifications are major products of institutions of higher learning. These usually remain in high demand by those seeking to advance their careers, and are regularly required by many businesses for positions requiring particular types of training or expertise. The demand for degrees changes over time and from field to field, but demand generally increases over time. While the percentage of occupations requiring degrees is increasing from decade to decade and is now becoming a critical roadblock to prosperity,[1] disruptions in industrial trends may also lead many individuals to return to college to update their current expertise or change the course of their careers by obtaining training for different disciplines altogether. These disruptions may occur as a result of competition, changes in technology, globalization, or outsourcing.

Research, the other product of the higher education system, can also be of significant value to industry. Some major corporations maintain extensive R&D departments or even whole divisions devoted to research activities, including Hewlett Packard, Intel, Microsoft, Proctor & Gamble, the automotive companies, and, of course, the big pharmaceutical companies such as Merck, Eli Lily, GlaxoSmithKline, and many others. While industry sees academic research as a source of great ideas for new and innovative products, academia sees industry as a funding source for basic research.

ORGANIZATIONAL CONTEXT

Although they are often mutually appreciative, both higher education and industry are somewhat mismatched in their goals. While academic researchers are interested in the advancement of science, corporations are seeking to increase both their profitability and their survivability. When there is a decline in funding from public sources such as the National Science Foundation (NSF) in the United States, academic researchers are motivated to find replacement funding from industry. Whereas NSF does fund basic research, corporations are usually interested in more applied types of innovation, or at least innovation with fairly direct applicability. It is important for both academia and business to better understand each other's motivations and objectives in order to produce appropriate and satisfying quid pro quo collaborations.

Companies which retain their own R&D groups occupy a special status and can maximize the benefit derived from academic research collaborations by establishing links between the internal corporate researchers and their counterparts in academia. This occurs in many situations quite naturally, since many practitioners in the same discipline may have crossed paths in their academic careers. Over a number of years of collaboration with academia, the most effective and productive research outcomes undertaken by Microsoft's External Research group have involved continued close participation of Microsoft researchers with their academic counterparts. This makes so much sense that many may consider it obvious, but since it is one of the most important factors for predicting success in this sort of collaboration, it is worth highlighting.

Corporations are organized to enable certain kinds of activities, and although academia may engage in similar activities, its basic organization is quite different. Both entities are structured hierarchically, but in academia, faculty members have much more freedom than their corporate counterparts. Peer review and consensus are the basis for arriving at well-considered positions in the world of higher education, and this explains why it can take so long to arrive at decisions. Although good ideas are sent up through the hierarchy in the corporate world, decisions are often made at the top and must be followed by those lower in the organizational structure. The degree of top down-ness varies, of course, from corporation to corporation, but it is safe to say that companies usually depend less on consensus and opinion from groups of lower level managers and other employees, while academia is quite responsive to its faculty committees.

THE DYNAMICS OF HIERARCHIES

Both top-down and bottom-up dynamics exist in both the academic and business worlds, although there is serious difference in emphasis between the two. Sometimes the introduction of a new dean or president at a university is used to shake things up from the top down and provide the leadership and vision necessary to inspire serious change that is too important to remain languishing in committees. Once the new leader has managed to get most of the faculty leadership to buy into the new vision and accept him or her as a credible agent of change, things settle down and much of the decision making reverts to the committee model once again.

Business leaders brought in to drive change usually have more power and ability to transform things and less need to enlist the support of everyone, although many do try to promote buy-in by creating compelling arguments for the new path. It is certainly better to transform a company's approach with the support of lower level managers and employees than to achieve progress by fiat alone. However, it is not as important for incoming business managers as it is for new deans in academia. Employees have important reasons for getting in line, since their job security may be at risk; tenured faculty members do not have the same degree of anxiety.

Some businesses and universities are becoming increasingly aware of each other's context. Hewlett Packard, Intel, Microsoft, IBM, and Google are among high tech companies that have been actively engaging with academia in ways that support university objectives as well as those of the corporation. The University of California-Berkeley, Stanford, The Georgia Institute of Technology, and Harvard are just a few of the many universities now actively embracing industry in ways that seek to understand business needs and motivations while meeting the objectives of higher education. Some of the various contexts within which academia and industry tend to view their activities are summarized in Table 8.1.

Many schools maintain internal industrial relations departments to handle interactions with the business world. In the early 1990s, many of these were primarily focused on obtaining funding from industry for research or capital projects. Capital projects—the fund-raising initiatives undertaken by universities to raise money from alumni, philanthropies, corporations,

Table 8.1: Business and Academia Have Overlapping, Interesting and Different Perspectives

	Business	Higher Education
Motivation for organizations	Profit and competitiveness	Status and ranking
Motivation for individuals	Financial rewards and perks	Recognition
Products: tangible	Material goods	Degrees and certification
Products: process-oriented	Services	Research
Motivation for research	Innovative, competitive products	Answering interesting questions
Requirements for research	Out-of-the-box thinking	Continued funding
Internal competition	Continual peer challenges	Tenure is the objective

and other donors—can leave industrial representatives with the idea that academia is only interested in money, rather than true collaboration. Often, the request for funding has no meaningful quid pro quo, which is generally a deal-breaker for business representatives. This perspective does not lead to useful attitudes toward future collaborations. Having a new building appear with the donor's name chiseled in granite may be appealing to philanthropists and individual donors interested in legacy, but corporations may be more interested in productive collaborative relationships.

Government activities contribute significantly to many of the inherent dynamics of industrial-academic relations, and without examining these, the picture of research collaborations would be incomplete. Governmental and quasi-governmental organizations in the United States are numerous, many with names familiar to the general public, while others remain more obscure. These include the National Science Foundation (NSF), the National Academy of Science (NAS), the National Academy of Engineering, the National Institutes of Health (NIH), the Department of Defense (DOD), the Department of Energy (DOE), the Department of Homeland Security (DHS), the National Aeronautic and Space Administration (NASA), and the Office of Naval Research (ONR). In Canada, the primary organization is the National Research Council (NRC); in the European Union, it is the European Research Council (ERC); and in Japan, it is the Japan Society for the Promotion of Science (JSPS).

The billions spent by governments to keep their national and regional competitiveness high usually overshadow the contributions of industry investors in research by one or two orders of magnitude. There are interesting relationships among the three sectors that are mutually reinforcing, although these dynamics are not often articulated explicitly.

RETURN ON INVESTMENT

To understand motivational mechanisms better and to extend this interpretation into all three segments (business, academia, and government), it is useful first to examine how each views the concept of Return on Investment (ROI). For industry, ROI is connected to financially favorable outcomes, and as mentioned earlier in the context of R&D, it is intended to measure how funds spent turn into profitable new products that make the corporation more competitive. For academia, research is driven for the most part by individual investigators who are pursuing questions that are of burning interest to them and to their chosen discipline. This means that they are, for the most part, highly motivated, focused, and following their individual passions. Government is looking for advantages that can help contribute substantively to the greater good for the nation and its citizens, whether related to security, health, economic development, or the environment. Based on an understanding of the various contexts for ROI, it is possible to engage in productive discussions and negotiations that would otherwise be intractable. The outlooks of industry, academia, and government can be better understood after reviewing the summary insights in Table 8.2 focusing on focusing on ROI.[2]

It is important to understand the power of these perspectives to truly appreciate negotiations across the domains. For instance, a corporate representative must keep financial ROI in mind when discussing collaboration with academic researchers, but must also remain aware that the researcher is intent on pursuing research of interest. Research of interest, in this sense, refers to following the next steps in the current research investigations, which may be interesting but orthogonal to the business desire to turn the resulting innovation into profitable products for the marketplace. Ideas that are exciting scientifically may not directly align well with corporate desires to produce something from them, and often do not align naturally without some effort.

Table 8.2: Stakeholders in the Academic Ecosystem Have Significantly Different Expectations

Return On Investment (ROI)	
Different Audiences	**Different Definitions**
Industry	Return on investment
Academia	Research of interest
Government	Results of importance

RELATIONSHIP MANAGEMENT

Relationship is the term used to describe these interactions, and although they are one of the most important advantages needed to un-tangle the web of cross-purposes, relationships are unfortunately one of the most misunderstood words in this context. It is *extremely* important for those engaging in collaborative undertakings of this sort to develop relationships *built on trust*. When Person A wants Person B to do some-thing that is low on B's priority list in order to fulfill one of A's goals, A may need to do something that is low priority for her but important to B in order to make it work. For instance, at times a company may sponsor a conference that does not directly enhance its own ROI, while a fac-ulty researcher may adjust his research goals somewhat to provide more practical and immediately applicable value for the corporate interests. This is not unlike some of the productive compromise on which many successful marriages depend. I may have only passing interest in ballet, while my spouse is not all that excited about action movies, yet we may attend both, enjoy them more than either of us would have imagined, and, in the end, have derived additional enjoyment from going with a companion.

This phenomenon may seem obvious to some but bears emphasis be-cause of its importance and the fact that understanding of it is tacit and rarely made explicit in industry/university relationships. There are several fundamental principles necessary for this relationship dynamic to work well as it pertains to industry and academia.

1. *Effective relationships are built on trust,* especially when dealing with participants from different domains who have different expectations.

2. *Listening carefully* is required in order to be trusted. It is impor-tant to hear all the things that the other is saying and understand them and keep them in mind throughout all interactive dealings. Such a partner is said to get it.

3. *Follow through is essential.* Requests for information, honest feed-back on the real appeal of certain proposals, and ideas for further connection must receive crisp and clear response. In this sense, trust grows from dependability. Ultimately, items 2 and 3 are needed to result in item 1 (trust).

4. *Maintaining consistent connection* is critical. Roles in industry change much more quickly than in academia. Key contacts leave organizations and disappear to outsiders much more frequently in the business world than in higher education.

More collaborative possibilities come into being when trust is established. For instance, it becomes possible to float ideas for confidential, informal review before presenting them for formal proposals and negotiation.

Whenever things break down in communications, it is exceedingly important to have a trusted go-to person to contact in order to find out the real story and how to proceed. This saves many relationships between corporations and academia but is also not well documented. The truth about relationship management is that it sounds to some business people like a form of group therapy rather than an operationally definable set of processes for achieving collaborative goals. Some industrial organizations that engage in collaboration with academia have removed the widely accepted and understood term *university relations* from their titles. Regardless of whether relationship management is mentioned explicitly or engaged in as a more subtle art of engagement, its importance remains extremely high for productive connections between industry and academia, which they ignore only at their own peril.

DOMAIN COMPLEXITY

The players in the industrial/academic milieu operate within complex environments, in which each player occupies different roles at different times, for different reasons, and in different contexts. Each academic and corporate entity has multiple identities and concomitant webs of relationships which relate them, one to the other. For example, to academics collaborating with Microsoft, the corporation has many unique personas. The company and its research division have been referred to by faculty on various occasions as:

- The world's largest software company
- The world's largest CS department
- Collaborators in research
- Industry partner in policy

Similar sets of identities are routinely assigned to a wide number of companies and academic entities. Indeed, on a practical front, depending on the roles and context, academics may view *any* corporation as:

- A means to connect to their corporate researchers
- A funding source
- Partners in educational policy
- Important for validating ideas about research and education to funding agencies

DIVERGENT WORLD VIEWS

Since the perspectives of academia and industry can diverge so widely, it is important for each to remember how to speak the other's language. Industrial representatives must remember that academics are primarily motivated by recognition and that funding is important but secondary (despite prevalent corporate wisdom). Most importantly, academics do not want to be marketed to! It is considered insulting and abusive; anything that smacks of direct corporate marketing to academics sends them running in the opposite direction. Discussions about a company's products, even if relevant, must be informational only and undertaken in the context of the problem to be solved rather than as a tool for sales. There are companies that take the opposite approach and lay out the means for collaboration by telling partners: "Focus on these areas, use our tools and products, and follow these other guidelines." Although it might sound abrupt, this approach, although not as collegial, is appreciated by many for its directness and clarity.

Academics sometimes hold corporate partners in higher esteem if there is potential for:

- Connections with company researchers and shared thought leadership.
- A respectful approach of company personnel, long-term commitment, and staying power.
- Funding of riskier research.
- Valuable programs the corporations may sponsor.

Despite the complexity of roles and motivations, the perspectives of industry, business, and government are nevertheless fairly simple to articulate:

- Industry is interested in business goals, R&D, profit, and image.
- Academia is chartered to drive education and basic research.
- Government is concerned with funding the right things for the benefit of the nation, as well as formulating and promulgating policy.

INDUSTRY SPEAKING TO ACADEMICS

The most effective, proven approaches for companies to connect meaningfully with academics are those that engage in intellectual curiosity and shared challenges. Corporate representatives are most effective when they adopt a collegial demeanor, rather than a corporate persona. Honesty, consistency, and credibility are paramount in interactions. Dropped programs are problematic and indicate to universities that the industrial partners do not know what they want or are afraid to persist in pursuing it. We must remember that researchers, academic and corporate, usually think of themselves much more as colleagues than as competitors. Clarity on the part of the industrial partner is essential in aligning goals; academics know that there is always a quid pro quo and are suspicious when they don't hear one. The industry interest is not always directly related to new inventions and profitability. If reasonable, academic research goals can often be adjusted to create a win-win situation.

ACADEMICS SPEAKING TO INDUSTRY

Some academic researchers are very responsive to connections with corporations and understand corporate concerns and the need for information. Industrial partners are very interested in status updates and progress reports, even if they are not directly overseeing projects. This is understandable; it is only common sense that they would want to track the progress and success of projects they may have invested in quite heavily. They can be even more attentive in this respect than some government funding agencies.

Academics who ignore status reports, execute them haphazardly, or provide them late are showing that they do not understand or appreciate corporate culture and business motivations, and they do so at their own peril. Industry partners ignored this way can perceive this unresponsiveness as an indicator of a don't care attitude or an interest in money but little respect for collaboration, or, in some cases, simple disrespect. Progress reports are common in business and good ones must be supplied by academic partners if they are to be taken seriously. In reality, academic researchers are interested primarily in furthering their work, and those funds can come from the university, from corporate partners, from foundations and philanthropies, or from government agencies (which tend to provide larger blocks of money). Funds from industry often come with some expectations of one sort or another. These are often paid attention to but sometimes ignored, which can be interpreted by some as disdain for the funder. Whether this is an intentional slight or not, it is a not a good way to ensure that the researcher will be held in high esteem at funding time for future projects.

Understanding the motivation of industry is a topic that has been examined in depth, and much of what was known 10 years ago is still valid in terms of the importance for preparing for rapid change, transformations in the workforce, and styles of doing business.[3]

GOVERNMENT

The interlocking motivations and mutually-reinforcing activities of industry, academia, and government are not to be underestimated. They can be best illustrated as a value triangle in which value flows between each pair of nodes.

Upon examination, it is easy to see how academia, industry, and government are inextricably woven together in a web of mutually beneficial activity. Industry provides recognition and some funding for projects in academia, and at the same time this helps government agencies see what is really important commercially to the nation, or at least which projects may have enough practical application to be seen as having more immediate value than other research.

Academics benefit from this validation and the resultant increase in funding, and in turn provide industry with some very capable graduates to assume roles of importance in the corporation. In addition, academic innovation is the source of many ideas for new products. Government benefits by seeing which academic research areas might be the best to contribute to, as a function of what corporations are already investing in. Corporations and academia both benefit from this appreciation because government agencies may react by funding, at a higher level, projects that might otherwise have gone unnoticed and that are important not only to the academic researchers but to industrial partners. In this way, businesses enjoy a multiplier effect whereby government agencies sometimes fund areas of research at a rate that is many times higher than those that businesses are able to provide. Government, in turn, benefits from academic expertise for its important policy formation and other decision making processes. These dynamics can be traced in the following illustration (Figure 8.1), in which the arrows indicate the flow of value of various types from one entity to another.

A COMMON THREAD: THE SEARCH FOR INNOVATION

One thing that government, academia, and industry have in common is that all three are highly motivated to leverage the advantages afforded by access to cutting-edge innovation and new ideas. Government is most eager to obtain from academia, among other things, technology for the military, new methods for reducing environmental impact, and insights which inform new directions for developing effective policy in the future. The problems with which government leaders are concerned provide many challenges that academic researchers are eager to attack, not just because these are initiatives that may be well-funded in the future, but because they provide compelling intellectual challenges.

Figure 8.1 All Three Sectors Benefit from a Value Network Based on Mutual Benefit

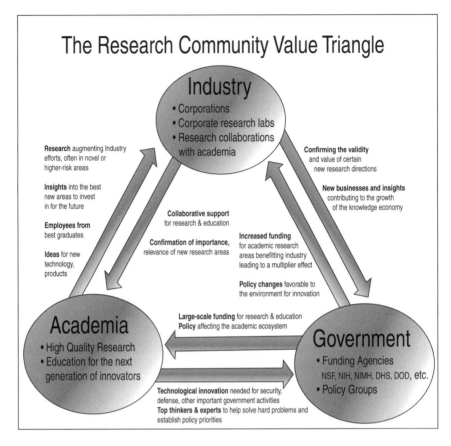

Similarly, industry provides good ideas and tough problems for academic investigators to focus on solving. Even though academics do receive funding from both government and industry, it would be inaccurate to characterize their interest as only about the money. Setting aside for a moment all mention of funding, it is of significant interest to academics that the real-world concerns of industry and government supply an endless list of possibilities for them to apply their theoretical findings to solving much more concrete types of problems. Moreover, researchers in academia, industry, and government all belong to similar professional and intellectually related networks.

Problems that are difficult to solve sometimes become more tractable when approached from a different perspective. Corporate R&D groups find that academic research is interesting when it applies entirely different methodologies and approaches to solving comparable problems, sometimes with dramatic results unachievable by other means. For similar reasons, academic researchers also find the work of corporate researchers interesting.

INTELLECTUAL PROPERTY

The intellectual property produced as a result of collaborative research innovation has become an area of increasing focus in academia and industry. This topic, which was not scrutinized nearly as closely 20 years ago, has grown in importance in direct proportion to the increasing need to solve difficult problems and the increasingly large investments required to achieve them. The legal ramifications can be quite complex, and today enormous care is taken to ensure that the proper agreements are in place to protect the inventors and manufacturers, as well as the institutions. Indeed, some innovations can result in the generation of millions in profit for whomever the agreement favors. However, the results of research are not always predictable, or it wouldn't be called research. In North America, corporations routinely engage with university legal departments that are highly motivated to make sure that their institutions and innovators receive all that they deserve, especially if their contributions result in highly profitable inventions.

In fact, each university legal department has a different approach and different set of criteria for entering into these types of agreements. Because of this, corporate legal departments must be prepared to sometimes enter into protracted negotiations with universities for intellectual property (IP) that is of unclear value until it is tested further. Some university legal departments that are more aware of technology development and entrepreneurial investment paradigms are easier for corporations to work with than others which may be interested in protecting everything, at all costs.

There are companies that are focusing more of their IP collaborations in the European Union than in North America specifically for the reason that North American universities are more difficult to deal with regarding questions of IP ownership. Although some university partners are flexible and ready to negotiate, there are others who are convinced that some of their research IP is worth more than it actually is, which makes negotiation much more difficult. In some cases, it is hard to tell how much IP is worth until it is developed further, and some university legal departments err on the side of being too careful; that is, they protect innovation *just in case* it may turn out to be worth much more than anyone had imagined. To be certain, there are no villains in these scenarios, but clearly changes need to be made to ensure both protection and flexibility.

Some companies only collaborate in a format similar to work-for-hire. Others provide a number of different possible IP agreements that could be executed, depending on the situation, the individual project, the degree of uncertainty, and the development requirements. It is easy to see examples in which corporations have asked, alternately, for results to be placed in the public domain, or to be made available through nonexclusive license, in order to have the right of first refusal if licensable IP is created as a result of the research or contractual work-for-hire.

Making available a range of agreement types is clearly beneficial to corporations and universities that are flexible and adaptable in this way. However, these types of agreements are not standardized, and they vary significantly from school to school and company to company. The difficulties of IP negotiation in this environment are well-known and widespread. Today the negotiation for rights to an idea or invention often take so long that they are no longer valuable at the time the deal is signed. Universities and corporations would do well to standardize around a core set of agreement types, which could then be adapted easily to specific situations, and in this way speed up the rate of productive collaboration and maintain clear lines of ownership without losing control of key rights to intellectual property or potential profits.

EDUCATION AND INNOVATION

The responsibility of academics as educators is at least as important as their role as drivers of research and innovation, and may be changing significantly as the demand for specialized training and lifelong learning increases. Government looks to higher education as a source of national competitiveness, and the universities in North America still remain the most respected in the world. Corporations look to colleges and universities as a source of well-educated individuals to recruit for staffing their new initiatives. Individual citizens look to higher education as a means to better themselves, enable upward mobility, obtain better jobs with higher pay, and achieve an overall higher standard of living.

This educational component, which is so important to all sectors of society, has for some time and even at the time of this writing been experiencing a massive transformation. A much higher proportion of the workforce needs some form of higher education or continuing education today than ever before as we move from a manufacturing-based model to a knowledge economy. Yet, the old paradigm of colleges and universities does not lend itself to readily educating everyone. The model of professors lecturing students in buildings made of brick and mortar simply does not scale to serving the entire population. It would be impossible to hire enough professors and build enough buildings to meet the need in this manner.

Distance education has arisen to fill this need and is changing the mix of learning opportunities available. Today, students can attend elite universities if they can meet the requirements and have sufficient cash or loans to sustain them, or they can attend a variety of other institutions, including private and state universities and colleges, community colleges, and technical schools. These are all expensive in varying degrees and show no signs of getting cheaper. All except distance education require physical presence—that is, attendance at classes in some physical location—in order to progress toward degrees or certification.

THE APPEAL OF DISTANCE EDUCATION

Distance education breaks many aspects of the traditional educational model simultaneously. First and most obviously, it does not require a physical location. That is, students and teachers need not be in the same place at the same time. This immediately tears down many barriers. Older students who are reeducating themselves for new roles and for new jobs can remain in their homes and do not have to commute long distances to acquire the knowledge and training they need. This is especially valuable for people who already occupy a job and may also be simultaneously raising a family.

The most significant variables to evaluate in terms of effectiveness for a particular educational model are: (1) its success in getting students where they need to go with their career/life trajectories, and (2) the value the education provides in preparing the student for a particular role that is important in the job market.

Given these preconditions, there are several aspects of distance education that are particularly challenging to both academia and the corporate world. First of all, distance education introduces a simple economic model of commercially available certification without some of the traditional hurdles. No longer can universities assert that only those students who live at the school or nearby should seek degrees, abandon all other life responsibilities, and meet in person with their professors and instructors. There is also the problem that some online schools provide a learning experience of questionable value, leading some traditional academics to disparage them as diploma mills.

HOW DISTANCE EDUCATION CAN WORK

There is certainly some value in meeting people face-to-face that cannot yet be replicated in virtual interactions. Some of these limitations are no doubt inherent in the distance education model, but some may be overcome soon through the use of technologies and platforms that enable interactions allowing participants to feel as if they were actually there. When this point is reached, some of the advantage of being there on campus is somewhat diminished. These types of advancements are quite attainable.

The Massachusetts Institute of Technology (MIT) has made all of its courses available online. This has not diminished traditional enrollments at MIT one iota. Part of the reason for this disparity rests in the idea that there are two kinds of MIT education; one obtained online, and another, "real" MIT education, obtained in person, onsite. So far there is no decrease in interest in MIT degrees obtained on-campus. This is largely because (1) on-campus degrees are considered by many to be the "real" MIT degrees, (2) the distance MIT education is still considered inferior (and is even branded differently), and (3) there are many visionary educators at MIT that one simply must see in person to be inspired by them.

Another interesting aspect of the distance education equation that is particularly compelling is economic in nature. If people don't have to attend classes as they did in the past to obtain degrees, for some the existing schools could diminish in attractiveness and at some point even become close to irrelevant. Until recently, it has been possible for established universities to be dismissive of online educational institutions, like the University of Phoenix, as degree mills that miss the important components of scholarly inquiry and turn education into a readily available commodity for consumption by anyone interested who can pay the fees (much lower than traditional costs) and do the work (considered inferior or less rigorous by some). The inference here is that graduates of online institutions have received a somewhat inferior education that might have been considerably easier so they may not be as qualified as others who have managed to survive the challenges of the traditional model.

Interestingly, because of their particular situations—including age, marital status, and location—many of those who engage in online forms of education are more highly motivated than traditional college freshman and sophomores. Many of them are older, really know what they want, are more dependable in terms of doing the work and finishing it, and overall, are more motivated to succeed. Distance education offers these driven individuals a learning paradigm that is convenient, flexible, relatively non-disruptive, and much less expensive.

THE BUSINESS OF HIGHER EDUCATION AND ONLINE DEGREES

Viewing higher education as a business when discussing distance learning can be liberating in a number of ways. The distance model makes a higher degree seem like much more of a readily accessible commodity available to everyone than a privilege for an elite minority. If people can do it, regardless of where they are, why shouldn't they be allowed to? Deficiencies in the primary education system, especially in the United States, ill-prepare students for the rigors of higher education. Highly motivated individuals, especially students returning for another go at the system, are nonetheless extremely enthusiastic and very likely to succeed, often even making up for poor preparation in grade school and high school. At some point, the differences between some forms of traditional higher education and distance education may become indistinguishable. When this happens, the value of extremely expensive university educations will diminish except for special cases. Indeed some traditional academics have shared in confidence that many laugh at the University of Phoenix, but we should really sit up and pay attention to what they are doing.

It is also illustrative to note that traditional universities are always asking for money by holding capital fund-raising drives, asking alumni repeatedly for donations, and engaging with industry, governmental agencies, and philanthropies to obtain ever more. Yet online universities are profitable and are not generally asking for money. Indeed, now that this has been noticed fairly widely, many traditional universities are offering online courses and degrees, and this may help to ensure that they are not left out of a major paradigm shift, if and when it occurs. It helps to view education as focused on learners rather than on teachers or institutions. For instance, much is said about how institutions of higher learning could be improved. These institutions are delivery systems for conveying learning, experience, and degrees to those initially less knowledgeable. This is a focus on the enterprise of higher education and those who drive its goals, the teachers.

In reality, much of the learning that takes place today involves the students teaching themselves, or at least teaching each other. Institutions famous for producing highly successful graduates are involved in a bit of self-fulfilling prophecy. Students who are smart, focused, and driven enough to gain entry to top-tier schools have all the ingredients for success and would probably succeed if they attended that school, another type of school, or perhaps if they attended none at all. The selection process identifies candidates who are highly likely to succeed, based on their previous accomplishments, personality type, vision, and drive. For a school to claim that it produces top graduates ignores the possibility that they are the kind of people who would have been successful with or without the benefit of the school. However, investing in a high priced education produces *credentials* that are widely recognized and which therefore ensure the likelihood of obtaining good jobs.

Table 8.3: A Disciplined Process for Implementing and Improving Distance Education

Three-Step Success Cycle for Distance Education

1. Procurement and preparation of the resources necessary to meet the distance education goals.
2. Delivery of instruction using the best practices from education, business and research.
3. Analysis of the results of distance education to gauge achievement of the goals.

Certification is another matter. Any thoughtful person would hesitate to be operated upon by a brain surgeon who had neither a degree nor residency experience. Degrees attest to competency, yet certification itself is (curiously) looked down upon in academia as a somehow inferior type of educational outcome, to be conferred by lower institutions teaching process but not *real* education. It may be time for some of these prejudices to disappear as well.

Distance education is still today considered inferior to location-based education, but even this disparity may not persist for long. Much systematic research and applied work has been done to address the reasons for the differences and recommend changes that increase the value of distance education. A good example of a clear and disciplined methodology can be seen in the approach of distance education specialists Cavanaugh & Cavanaugh,[4] who articulate 3 steps in a cycle that will ensure success, included in Table 8.3.

The systematic analysis and evaluation process has enabled them to produce an exhaustive list of success factors to attend to in order to make distance education work (see Table 8.4). Although much has been written on the subject, it would be difficult to find a more thorough analysis.[5]

DISTANCE EDUCATION AND EMPLOYMENT OPPORTUNITY

The foregoing discussion of distance education has major implications for academic-corporate relations, in the sense that industry is a consumer of talent that is cultivated to a large extent in institutions of higher education, both traditional and online. Clearly, employers generally accord lower value to degrees acquired online than they attribute to credentials obtained in more traditional ways. Acceptance of these new degrees varies significantly, however, depending on several important parameters which also reflect a change in the educational landscape, both culturally and technologically.

Table 8.4: A Thorough Listing of What Is Required for Successful Distance Education

The 44 Distance Education Success Factors

Institutional policy	Qualified staff and faculty	Focus on content and students	Student independence; self-assessment
Strategic plan	Community involvement	Relevant and important skills and knowledge	Peer review of student work as a professional experience
Stakeholder Analysis	Informed faculty	Structured information in motivating context	Student portfolios to showcase accomplishments
Financial commitment	Instructor time	Social strategies for student comfort, control, challenge	Varied assessments; accurate view of student abilities
Team support	Instructor training	Fast feedback from instructors to students	Open-ended assignments to increase thinking skills and reduce cheating
Technology infrastructure	Course design and delivery	Consistent and accessible design throughout each course	Secure online testing
Program standards	Well-designed materials	Highly interactive activities for student engagement	Ongoing course evaluation by students
Program review	Student orientation, training	Authentic communication among students, instructors and experts	Evaluation of program by students and faculty
Effective communication	Access to resources, instructors	Course activities designed to maximize student motivation	Review of program outcomes and components by all stakeholders
Student services	Technical support	Activities focused on high-level cognitive skills	Program accreditation
Information privacy	Technology plan	Development of applied technical skills	Student independence through opportunities for self-assessment

As recently as 2005 a strong bias against distance education was evident. A Dallas-Fort Worth TV station ran a story in December 2005 entitled "The Value Of An Online Degree." in which they interviewed students and reviewed some trends.

> Online degrees are one of the fastest growing trends in higher education, but can you land a good job with a diploma from a virtual school? Audrey Lawrence is getting a degree online. She says, "It's a great alternative and it's the only alternative for me." With a full-time job, Audrey had trouble getting to classes at a traditional campus. Online, she can set her own schedule. "As long as you log on before midnight, you're okay for attendance for that day."
>
> Audrey is one of 300,000 students earning an education completely online. A recent survey of about 500 human resources training managers found that 63 percent of employers are fine with an online education. Scott Gallagher of Eduventures points out, "That means 4 in every 10 employers are looking at online degrees with some degree of skepticism." Prospective college students are also wary. Only a third of those surveyed think online programs are on par with face-to-face learning. Working students, like Audrey, disagree. "My employers were great and they were very supportive and never once did anyone try to persuade me not to do the online." Most traditional schools offer programs both on campus and online. Online programs tend to target working adults, and schools claim it's a major misconception that the courses are easy. Maureen Brown of Lesley University says, "A good online program is usually more rigorous than face-to-face." If you are considering an online degree, make sure that the school and the program is accredited. Also, online classes are not cheap. Costs are comparable to private universities.[6]

However, since that time, the boundaries are blurring in several ways. First of all, at the time of this writing, most, if not all, traditional institutions are including some distance education as part of their offerings. Obtaining a degree from a well-known and respected institution that provides at least part of its material online is now an accepted (and in some cases, from the learning process perspective, preferable) delivery method. A school that can produce decent graduates who experience a mixture of on-site and distance learning will quite often see their graduates hired by industry. It is becoming increasingly difficult to understand (from the outside) exactly how much of the learning these students are experiencing belongs in the category of distance education. 10 percent? 30 percent? 90 percent?

Some professionals share privately that on average, distance students, in their response to questions, are noticeably inferior to those who have been educated in more traditional formats. It is interesting to speculate whether this is an inherent discrepancy in the efficacy of the two educational models or that the social interaction and give-and-take debates of the classroom are not being translated effectively into the new medium.

The reputation of the school is still obviously very important, and the experience that interviewers have had with potential employees from these schools influences their hiring and recruiting decisions in the future. To date, traditional schools are looked upon favorably, and applicants who do not draw attention to the online nature of the education they may have obtained from them can do as well as those who attended all classes in person, all the time, at the same institution. Even if students obtained as much as 90 percent of their education online from an accepted institution, they could be looked on favorably, as long as they do not unnecessarily draw attention to the fact that much of this degree was obtained while wearing pajamas. This can be done simply by limiting the use of the term online in interviews.

This is a trend that will continue, with more and more schools offering online education, and the contrasts between on-site and online education will continue to diminish. As computer and communication technologies advance and are implemented in ways more effective for the educational process, these distinctions will become even more blurred. Consequently, the distinctions between the two modes of education are likely to diminish in importance for industry recruiters.

THE IMPORTANCE OF LEARNING TECHNOLOGY

Since the year 2000, much emphasis has been placed on technology for learning, but so far no breakthroughs or silver bullets have been found. A number of technologies have been experimented with, including electronic whiteboards, Tablet PCs, distributed devices, new forms of teleconferencing, and a number of systems for enabling both traditional and virtual classrooms are being examined. Academics continue to experiment with various models, and when the ultimate configurations are found, the new functionality and connectivity will greatly empower higher education, resulting in much wider availability of quality interactive learning for both traditional on-site formats as well as the next generation of distance education. There is a commonly held belief that may be based either on fact or imagination that states that traditional on-site education is always superior to connections which are more remote. Rigorous research is needed into what those differences, if they exist, might actually be and how to mitigate them through the optimal use of technologies for creating better tele-presence, graphics, and collaboration tools. These solutions are close at hand and, when found, will transform how education is presented, transmitted, and visualized.

INCREASING CROSS CULTURAL UNDERSTANDING

Academia has started to view itself more as a business in recent years, and its forays into distance education have reinforced the impression. This is nonintuitive for traditional higher education models, but the exercise of casting educational components in a business framework can go a long way toward helping the understanding of how corporations must operate, how academia is similar in some ways and not in others, and how the sectors can cooperate in light of these different contexts. Companies are basically responsible for producing products and services to sell in the marketplace to create profit. Universities produce products and services too, in one sense, in the form of qualified graduates. But here the similarity ends. Qualified graduates are not actually a product that can be created and sold, but the certification that they are qualified and experienced enough to be hired as reasonably proficient practitioners in a certain discipline is in fact an item that *can* be sold, which is purveyed in the form of degrees. In a sense, the students (and those who may be investing in their education) are buying education that results in degrees which will get them, hopefully, the kind of employment opportunities they are looking for. At this point in the analysis, it is natural from the academic standpoint to ask, "Why doesn't industry invest more directly in this process, since it has so much to gain from the outcome?" In reality, however, the customers are actually the students, who are well served by the transaction if their education is capable of making them as well prepared for the jobs they seek as it purports to be. The corporation and the school have some value transactions occurring, but it is often not explicitly articulated. First, the school, based on its reputation and the past successes of its graduates in employment, is providing some assurance to the corporation by awarding degrees to the capable ones. However, in highly volatile times the market and industrial needs change rapidly, and it is important for businesses to let universities know what they are looking for now in graduates for the next generation of company initiatives. Figure 8.2 illustrates these dynamic and interconnected motivations and the value that is transferred thereby.

It is worth noting that the value exchanged directly between schools and companies is rarely articulated as explicitly as is shown in this diagram. The fact remains that companies can sometimes rest assured that an applicant who has a degree from a certain school must also have the requisite expertise, and conclude that his likelihood of success is probably fairly high.

Figure 8.2 Degrees: Representing Higher Education in an Economic Context

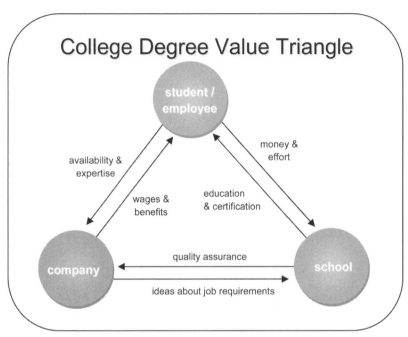

In order to stay aware of how well this educational preparation actually is, some schools are straightforward in their queries, and may even ask plainly, "Are we doing a good job—are our graduates still turning into great employees for you?" Indeed, companies have intuitions about how employees graduated from certain institutions tend to turn out, and their tendency to hire heavily from certain schools attests to this. Much of the back-and-forth communications between schools and companies occurs in advisory board meetings and other confidential settings. To be able to answer definitively these questions of how well students are prepared for industry jobs, a longitudinal study would need to be performed, examining how well graduates from specific schools do during their careers over a course of years. Someone should consider starting one soon, because the benefits would be broadly felt.

STAKEHOLDERS IN THE ACADEMIC ECOSYSTEM

Besides companies, students, and schools, there are other entities involved in the business of higher education, including citizens and the government that represents their interests.

All of these are stakeholders in the outcome of the educational process, and, indeed, in the other outputs of higher education, including research. Each stakeholder has a vested interest in the products of higher education and has something to gain and something to lose depending on how the interrelated dynamics are managed. If the stakeholders are visualized as participants sitting around a table and working things out, the metaphor works fairly well.

ADVISORY ORGANIZATIONS AND CONSORTIA

Advisory boards can be an effective mechanism for academics and industrial representatives to ask each other direct questions that would be considered impolite or indiscreet in a broader, more open setting. In this way, they can understand the thinking behind the decisions that would otherwise remain inscrutable. Corporate entities that deal with academia routinely sponsor advisory board participation by their counterparts in higher education in order to provide greater insights into how to work better together. This is another way in which trusted relationships provide a good way to facilitate cooperation between industrial and academic sectors. Universities, too, often host industrial advisory board meetings to make sure that their activities are in alignment with the overall thrust of industrial development.

Governmental organizations often invite key representatives from industry and academia to help inform the decisions they make. Policy making is the activity that brings together a confluence of interests, and it is the means by which at least some coordination among all these stakeholders can be achieved. To issue a paper on educational or research policy, the participation of representatives from government, industry, and academia is essential for producing recommendations that are complete, inclusive, and broadly applicable. For instance, government is interested in higher education policy that not only benefits citizens but ensures national competitiveness in the broader global marketplace. This could influence recommendations to executive leaders as well as legislators and result in actions that could ultimately affect everyone.

Professional associations can often span many domains. The Association for Computing Machinery (ACM) is a good example, with a membership spanning a number of academic domains, practicing professionals in the computational disciplines, and governmental members, and it maintains many special interest groups (SIGs) to support activities in an increasingly wide number of areas of computing activity. There are as many other examples of these types of organizations as there are disciplines and interest groups (too numerous to mention here). This illustrates how significantly the activities of the academic ecosystem are facilitated by networks of professional relationships, further complicated by the fact that each is an integral component of other networks, thus ultimately constituting a network of networks of relationships.

SHARED TOPICS OF URGENT INTEREST

There are a number of pressing issues of high concern to all three components of the academic ecosystem, including academics, industry, and government. Higher education and business have a crucial role to play in these discussions and can leverage their alignment, where it exists, to advocate change effectively. For instance, sometimes a funding agency is the organization needed to initiate action in a certain area. In such a case, when academia and industry speak with one voice, it becomes easier to influence the governmental group to take appropriate action.

Conversations about the most pressing issues are important opportunities to garner wide support for urgently needed policy change that requires involvement and support from all sectors to enact. Some of these topics are enumerated below.

MISMATCH BETWEEN K-12 EDUCATION AND HIGHER EDUCATION OPPORTUNITIES

In the United States, the curious imbalance between the quality of K-12 education and the standards expected by institutions of higher education has increased significantly. The odd situation now exists in which the top institutions of higher education are located in the United States, while American primary and secondary education are the worst in the developed world. American students have the best colleges available but are not prepared to attend them. This is a disparity that cannot long be endured by a nation before it loses competitiveness and economic stability, let alone its preeminence in thought leadership. This is a topic that has been examined by cross-segment organizations and study panels, but it will not be resolved without a major governmental initiative supported by all sectors.

NEW PEDAGOGIES AND LEARNING MODELS

The whole process for learning is changing rapidly, and new ideas are desperately needed. The fact that transformational new models must be figured out *now* cannot and should not be underemphasized. It is clear that technology is part of the equation, although technology has not been as revolutionary in its impact as might have been hoped. Eliminating the differentiation between distance and on-site education, as we have seen, is another of the challenges that should be met soon. Academia, industry, the research community, and the appropriate governmental organizations should band together and invest heavily in a grand challenge to address this issue as a matter of national innovation policy.

A NEW MODEL FOR RESEARCH
AND COLLABORATION

New, better standards for dealing with collaborative research between academia and industry are very important. Right now, the means for dealing with IP are outmoded and unresponsive. New, productive, and beneficial collaborations that could be occurring are not, often because of long and unproductive negotiations. This is a job to be addressed by leaders and legal departments in both academia and the corporate world.

Beyond collaboration, what happens to the relationship between industry and academia as higher education begins to operate like a business itself? Do they each become more like competitors than collaborators? In reality, higher education is already a business, but one that is not often examined in the same way that most businesses are scrutinized.

In some cases, universities have created organizations focusing on achieving some profit from the business application of the research findings that originate from their domains. One way of doing this is to foster startups, and to do so, academic institutions must operate more like venture capitalists. MIT, Berkeley, and Stanford have all been involved in this way for years and have developed specific models to embrace an increasingly businesslike model for academic innovation futures.

Keith McGreggor heads up the new technology evaluation and promotion organization known as the Georgia Tech Enterprise Innovation Institute[7] (colloquially known as GaTech Venture Lab). McGreggor comes from a long background in innovation with Apple and Bell Labs and has connections with many in the field, including industrial researchers. The intent of the organization is to identify outstanding innovation occurring throughout diverse and scattered pockets and silos at the university and apply strong triage that can turn them into startups or other ventures yielding increased value to Georgia Tech. An increasing number of universities have been engaged in similar ways, and many professors simultaneously teach, do research, and head up external startups where this is possible.

Where all of this is headed is still somewhat uncertain, but one thing is known: the general direction favors increased innovation everywhere and at the same time a strong growth of businesslike sensibilities and approaches in academia.

PIPELINE AND GENDER EQUITY ISSUES

Pipeline and gender equity issues are of equal concern to all segments; the issues directly involve academia, industry, and governmental bodies, and all of these must be involved in crafting new policy to address them. The K-12 education problems in North America are only one component. Ultimately, the unavailability of suitable candidates for technical positions in industry is a serious problem that is not improving with time. When industry cannot find enough employees for certain jobs, this sometimes is offset by an increase in immigration of qualified professionals from other regions. It is clear that this situation could be mitigated if more applicants were available domestically. For instance, it was noted at the Government University Industry Research Roundtable (GUIRR) discussions held at the National Academy of Science in Washington, DC[8] that an increase in the availability of qualified computer scientists emerging from the ranks of U.S.-born women and other minorities would greatly alleviate this situation. Women and minorities are proportionately underrepresented in these fields and, if motivated, could greatly compensate for the current lack of supply. This motivation must come from multiple sources, including new recruitment policies in industry, government-sponsored scholarship programs, and academic initiatives designed to attract and retain women and minorities.

THE PROPER USE OF RESEARCH FINDINGS

It is becoming increasingly important to make correct decisions about how best to solve really important problems. Scientific knowledge has at times been ignored or even suppressed by politicians when the objective facts conflict with cherished beliefs and political dogma. It is no longer acceptable, for instance, to ignore phenomena such as global climate change or metrics which predict severe economic upheavals just because they do not fit the wishful thinking and world view of one political system or another.

There are many examples of this tendency to ignore facts because they are incompatible with obsolete theories. For example, at the time of this writing, economies worldwide are experiencing an enormous disruption caused by underregulation of key financial institutions, which was based on the concept that free markets can and always do correct themselves, based on some sort of inherent equilibrium. One of the foremost proponents of this view in the United States, former Federal Reserve Board chairman Alan Greenspan, has now admitted that the basis of his economic theory was wrong, and that the assumption that businesses always act in their own best self interest was false and based on ideological preconceptions which helped lead to the implosion of the financial system.[9]

The primacy of documentable, irrefutable, and scientifically verifiable facts in making important decisions must be reinstated and continually emphasized in order for real progress to be made. Much that is decided must be based more on crisp facts rather than general suppositions and ideology. Higher education is the source of much of the research that provides the irrefutable body of facts required for really objective decision making. Academia and industry, as well as citizens, must lead in the demand that government pay attention to all the pertinent verifiable facts available.

These are only five of the important issues which form the basis for policy-making that requires the participation of all segments of the academic ecosystem, including universities, governmental officials, and concerned industries. There are many more.

THE MELDING OF TWO CULTURES

Higher education and the corporate sector have in the past been organized in very divergent ways, with different objectives and dynamics determining their functions in society. As challenges increase and economic pressures impact academia, the time has come for these institutions to adopt some of the approaches that have become useful in the business world. Academic culture need not adopt all of the practices of the business world to become more effective, but several are promising and provide insights for possible further expansion:

1. *Higher education and industry move at different speeds* and have other incompatibilities. Both should continue to work hard to analyze issues from each other's perspective.

2. *It is important to consider academic organizations with economic models* to clarify how higher education creates value, what its products are, and how they can be optimized.

3. *The delivery of education as a business is a growing trend* driven by widespread need. Higher education must integrate the best of distance and traditional models.

4. *The outcome of academic research is of great value to industry and national economies.* New business models and agreements are needed to quickly enable useful applications.

5. *Higher education and industry share many goals and objectives* and should continue to combine their advocacy to ensure timely and appropriate governmental response.

NOTES

1. "Adding It Up: State Challenges for Increasing College Access and Success," The National Center for Higher Education Management Systems and Jobs for the Future, November 2007, http://www.makingop portunityaffordable.org/wp-content/adding_it_up/Adding_It_Up.pdf.

2. Ellen Levy, Director, Silicon Valley Connect, www.businessinno vationfactory.com/weblog/archives/2007/10/post_6.htmtl.

3. D. Oblinger and Anne-Lee Verville, *What Business Wants from Higher Education* (Phoenix, AZ: American Council on Education Oryx Press Series, 1998).

4. T. Cavanaugh and C. Cavanaugh, "The 44 Distance Education Success Factors," http://www.drscavanaugh.org/distlearn/44_dl_success_factors.htm.

5. Ibid.

6. Ginger Allen, "The Value Of An Online Degree," CBS 11 News, Dallas-Fort Worth, December 16, 2005, http://cbs11tv.com/business/Online.Degree.College.2.492528.html.

7. See more about the Georgia Tech Venture Lab at: http://innovate.gatech.edu/.

8. Educational Paradigms for Homeland Security, GUIRR, 2004. See http://www7.nationalacademies.org/guirr/GUIRR_Annual_Reports.html. These topics were also discussed at the Globalization, Competitiveness and Workforce Roundtable Meeting, February 3–4, 2004, Washington, DC.

9. "Greenspan Admits 'Mistake' that Helped Crisis." Associated Press, October 23, 2008.

CHAPTER 9

The Paradox of For-Profit Higher Education

Vicente M. Lechuga

When Jones International University was accredited by the North Central Association of Colleges and Universities in 1999, a minor frenzy ensued among some within the higher education community, including the American Association of University Professors. At issue was whether the school should be considered an institution of higher learning given that it offered courses on only a single subject at the time—business administration—and had just a handful of full-time faculty with little to no academic freedom.[1] Additionally, many argued that because the institution operated as a business whose goal was to turn a profit "off of the backs of [their] students,"[2] awarding it regional accreditation was a slap in the face to private nonprofit and public universities whose view of education was based on the notion of preparing individuals for democratic participation to serve the public good. This debate prompts us to consider the changes that have taken place in how colleges and universities operate; they are increasingly behaving like business enterprises that seek to maximize efficiency and increase revenue generation.[3]

Jones International, along with numerous other for-profit colleges and universities (FPCUs), has reshaped the paradigm from which higher education institutions operate. One could even argue that they have created a new business model that takes into account revenue generation, organizational efficiency, employers and the job market. Several factors point to the recent success of FPCUs. For-profit institutions function in a niche market that provides education to working adults in need of specific training and skills to remain viable in an increasingly competitive job market. Unencumbered by conventional models of how institutions of higher learning are organized and managed, FPCUs have restructured the nature of how colleges and universities operate. They view knowledge as a private good, a commodity from which to generate a profit. Education is no longer thought of as a public good that can only be delivered by private nonprofit and public universities. Moreover, the notion that educating individuals takes place within the confines of a physical classroom is no longer the norm. FPCUs were among the first to provide postsecondary education to working adults and other previously underserved populations through the use of technology and the Internet, now a staple of many traditional postsecondary institutions. Shared governance, the norm that traditional universities follow, is all but eliminated in favor of more hierarchical decision-making forms. Through a unique combination of market savvy and educational innovation, FPCUs have reshaped the function and purpose of postsecondary education.

This chapter explores the many facets of for-profit higher education to provide readers with a fundamental understanding of the sector and the institutions that comprise it. I do not intend to suggest that all for-profit colleges and universities (FPCUs) are alike; they are not. The common thread amongst these institutions is that they operate in two separate arenas with differing priorities and foci—the for-profit business sector, and the nonprofit higher education sector. The nonprofit higher education sector traditionally focuses on serving the public good by acting as sites for the free expression of ideas, as well as arenas for knowledge creation, and its dissemination. Conversely, the for-profit business sector provides students with the knowledge and skills sets to enter the job market and remain competitive while at the same time serving their owners and investors. By examining this clash of cultures that exists within the FPCU sector, one can begin to understand the complexities involved with offering education for a profit. I begin by providing a brief history of for-profit postsecondary education in the United States prior to providing a current context from which readers can view for-profit higher education. I then move into a discussion of the philosophic paradigm from which FPCUs operate.

SETTING THE STAGE

The roots of proprietary schools can be traced as far back as 1660 when local masters (proprietors), early Dutch settlers typically trained as clergy, tutored individuals in English and mathematics for a fee.[4] These evening schools provided a basic form of instruction that played an important role in early America. Colonial colleges provided the type of education to support the development of an educated upper social class, which focused on the four learned professions—law, medicine, education, and the clergy. Proprietary schools filled a void. As the need for skilled workers during the industrial revolution increased, they offered occupational training that focused on market demands and the needs of society at that time (e.g., manufacturing, engineering, and agriculture).[5] Not unlike the present, proprietary education provided training to support the growing public demand for skilled labor. As Charles Dabney, president of the University of Tennessee in 1899, noted in reference to the need for agricultural education, "A vigorous demand arose for the sciences and their application to the arts of life. The old college was not meeting the new demands."[6]

Not unlike the proprietary institutions of the past, the current breed of for-profit institutions fill a similar educational void; they develop academic programs based on the needs of businesses and employers. The need for knowledgeable business managers, for example, fueled the development of MBA programs in the proprietary sector. Business courses at for-profits such as Cardean and Walden University have become a staple of FPCU degree-granting curricula. More recently, the University of Phoenix began offering the doctorate in education (Ed.D.) as well as establishing nursing programs to take advantage of the increased demand for terminal education degrees and the skilled nursing shortage, respectively. Yet regionally accredited, degree-granting institutions are not the norm in the proprietary sector. A majority of FPCUs offer less than 2-year certificate programs in such areas as automotive repair, cosmetology, and real estate.[7] With the exception of community colleges, these types of educational programs do not exist at traditional private nonprofit and public colleges and universities (TCUs); enter for-profit higher education.

FPCUs AND THE HIGHER EDUCATION MARKET

Our higher education system is continually being shaped by the growing knowledge economy. Many consider the U.S. higher education system to be amongst the best in the world. College attendance rates are among the highest in the world, and the proportion of adults attending college has risen dramatically over the past two decades.[8] Nevertheless, our colleges and universities face an uncertain collective future. In an increasingly globalized society other nations are catching up in higher education, as they have in other fields. Within the last few decades "the U.S. share of the global college-educated workforce has fallen from 30 percent to 14 percent, notwithstanding a very large increase during the same period in the fraction of Americans entering college."[9] Our colleges and universities are a deeply engrained element of our history and culture. The 3,000 to 4,000 institutions with which we are so familiar are structured and governed, virtually without exception, as public or private, *not-for-profit* organizations. For-profit higher education, however, is on the rise. Just as higher education outside of the United States is gaining on U.S. higher education, for-profit higher education is gaining ground on not-for-profit or traditional higher education in the United States.

Forces affecting all of higher education fuel the emergence and growth of the FPCU sector. Spending on higher education makes up nearly 2.3 percent of U.S. gross domestic product (GDP) and about 40 percent of all spending in the education industry as a whole, which totaled $1.04 trillion in 2006. This places the education sector among the three largest with regard to our GDP.[10]

For-profit colleges and universities have grown rapidly from a small base to one that is significantly outpacing the growth rates of the traditional nonprofit institutions. FPCUs grew from about 0.4 percent of all degrees granted in 1974, to 4 percent of all degrees granted in 2000, and about 6 percent of all degrees granted in 2006.[11] Although they enroll a miniscule percentage of the college-student population, FPCUs substantially outnumber traditional (private nonprofit and public) colleges and universities in terms of number of institutions. Of the Title IV eligible colleges and universities[12] in the United States, 40 percent are for-profit institutions, of which the majority, 52 percent, are less-than-2-year career colleges offering vocational training.[13] Since 2003–04, enrollments at FPCUs increased by 17 percent, and nearly half of all students attending a for-profit during 2005–06 were enrolled at institutions that offered bachelor's, master's, and/or doctoral level degrees.[14] FPCUs have grown in enrollments partly due to their collective focus on workforce preparation, despite their relatively high price in comparison to public colleges and universities.

An increased need in human capital and a more skilled workforce has contributed to the rapid growth and economic success of the for-profit higher education sector. The U.S. Department of Labor predicts a significant increase from 2008 through 2016 in occupations that require postsecondary training. Jobs requiring an associate's degree are projected to be in most demand, with a projected increase of 19 percent.[15] The area that will see the largest growth is information technology, more specifically network systems and data communication analysts and computer software engineers.[16] Because FPCUs align their academic offerings to meet the needs of employers and the market, it is fair to argue that they will focus their efforts on filling the needs of the job market, especially those that will be facing high growth, such as nursing, information systems, business, and several health related fields. In short, FPCUs will continue to play a large role in training the next generation of workers, and of importance to academe is an understanding of the framework within which they operate.

THE BUSINESS OF FOR-PROFIT HIGHER EDUCATION

A New Paradigm

For-profits did not develop within the established boundaries of traditional colleges and universities; instead, they chose to operate at the margins of the higher education community. The shift towards a knowledge-based economy has increased the demand for higher education, which has provided an impetus to create new ways to market and deliver it.[17] FPCUs have quickly filled this void, and until only recently, experienced tremendous growth in enrollments, revenue, and earnings.[18] As businesses, for-profits are willing to make what could be considered risky capital investments that allow for growth. Even among the most wealthy traditional colleges and universities—those with billions of dollars in endowment monies—decisions about capital investments toward such things as construction to alleviate or expand enrollments take years to come to fruition. Moreover, endowment spending is relatively conservative to the degree that lawmakers have considered imposing federal minimum spending requirements.[19]

As with most business enterprises, for-profits are concerned with what their competitors are doing while simultaneously focusing on what they can do to capture a larger share of the higher education market. Rather than simply focusing on their competitors, FPCUs follow market trends and the needs of employers. For-profits have conceived of new ways to manage educational costs, deliver services, and have restructured the roles of faculty and administrators. Their organizational forms are nearly impossible to utilize within the traditional private nonprofit and public higher education sector. As a consequence traditional institutions are slow to innovate, make decisions, and adapt to new ways of thinking. While they serve, by far, the majority of the college-going population, TCUs are not known for their ability to adapt to change quickly. Moreover, the increasing need for continuing and life-long education has created the potential for increased revenue generation and profit, and with that comes the need to maximize organizational efficiency and effectiveness. FPCUs, not TCUs, have quickly capitalized on the growing niche market of students seeking additional training and skills to remain competitive in an increasingly knowledge-based economy and have focused much of their recruiting efforts towards individuals who tend not to be the focus of TCUs.

Diversity of Institutional Type

Although often discussed by scholars in academe as a single monolithic type, FPCUs are growing in variety as well as in size. Kinser[20] notes that although the FPCU realm consists of an array of institutional types, "the academic and organizational models employed by for-profit colleges and universities are poorly understood." Much of this confusion stems from the manner in which FPCUs are discussed as one-dimensional institutions that operate under a corporately-owned structure. The University of Phoenix, the FPCU that is most familiar to the public, is not indicative of how FPCUs operate; their organizational model is the exception rather than the norm. Nevertheless, increased competition among FPCUs as well as with traditional colleges and universities makes an understanding of FPCU institutional types important.

Ownership type. There are a number of ways to categorize the types of for-profit colleges and universities. One method is with regard to their ownership status. The largest for-profit education providers are publicly traded conglomerates. These institutions are set up as corporations whose shares can be bought and sold on the open market. The University of Phoenix, which is owned and operated by the Apollo Group, is an example of one such entity. In contrast, the majority of FPCUs are privately held organizations owned either by a single individual, a family, or by corporate investors. FPCUs can exist in many forms: as a single-campus institution, multi-campus institutions operating solely within a particular region of the United States, multi-campus institutions with campuses nationwide, or as Internet-only institutions.

An alternative taxonomy that can be utilized takes into consideration curricular offerings. A number of FPCUs are designed to educate students for mid-level and senior management positions in such fields such as business and education. Others provide vocational training for students interested in paraprofessional occupations such as HVAC technicians (Heating, Ventilation, and Air Conditioning), dental assistants, or administrative office managers. Many FPCUs offer academic programs at the associate degree level, whereas others offer graduate and professional degrees. Differences in institutional type with regard to academic and curricular offerings should not be overlooked because they provide a context from which to critically examine the role that for-profit institutions play within the larger realm of higher education.

Accreditation. Obtaining accreditation by a national or regional accrediting body is of great import to FPCUs for two reasons: (1) for-profits are aware of the importance of accreditation in sending a message to potential students about the quality of education they provide,[21] and (2) without accreditation from a national or regional accrediting body that is recognized by the U.S. Department of Education, FPCUs are unable to participate in Title IV financial aid programs. Although accreditation poses a major barrier to entry for for-profit postsecondary institutions, many FPCUs recognize that without it they would be unable to operate, since FPCUs obtain 90 percent of their revenues from student financial aid.[22]

A majority of FPCUs hold national, as opposed to regional, accreditation. The major difference between the two is that national accrediting agencies tend to focus on specific programs of study such as those accredited by the Accrediting Commission of Career Schools and Colleges of Technology (ACCSCT). Given that career-oriented programs are the focus of most FPCUs, national accreditation seems an appropriate fit. Debates persist about whether national accreditation provides the standards of quality associated with regional accreditation. National accrediting standards, such as those associated with the ACCSCT, are quite stringent and set high standards of quality control.[23]

Less common are FPCUs that hold regional accreditation, the same type that most TCUs hold. Kinser found that most of the FPCUs that hold regional accreditation "have relatively traditional academic models and faculty roles. More than 60 percent of the institutions describe their faculty in traditional terms and employ a traditional academic calendar (quarter, trimester, or semester)."[24] The Education Commission of the States conducted a study regarding regional accreditors' perception of for-profit institutions.[25] Among the findings, the study revealed that the overall approach for accrediting proprietary institutions is no different from the approach used to accredit nonprofit institutions; most accrediting agencies do not have separate standards of quality that pertain to for-profit institutions.[26]

Challenges of Functioning in a Nonprofit Realm

Definition of higher education institutions. FPCUs compete with traditional colleges and universities to offer a service which has traditionally been provided by public and nonprofit institutions, and also compete for Title IV federal financial aid monies if accredited by an agency recognized by the Department of Education. Their for-profit status, however, dictates that they operate under different conditions from traditional institutions and, as such, are designated as a separate type of postsecondary institution by the U.S. Department of Education. In other words, two different definitions of what constitutes an institution of higher education exist—one for TCUs and the other for FPCUs. The different definitions have implications for the types of federal dollars for which institutions qualify.

FPCUs argue that because they offer a service similar to that of traditional colleges and universities, there ought to be a single definition that classifies all postsecondary institutions similarly. Those in the traditional higher education sector argue that FPCUs are fundamentally different because they view education as a private commodity and, consequently, should not be classified under the same definition. Tensions lie in the fact that the manner in which FPCUs provide their "product," postsecondary education, inevitably places them at the margins of the higher education sector; but the nature of the product itself and the push for a single definition of a higher education institution also places them directly inside the confines of the traditional higher education sector—the community of which they claim not to be a part.

Regulatory conditions. The higher education regulatory environment is different for FPCUs, partly because FPCUs are defined as a separate type of institution and, as such, are treated differently from public and private nonprofit TCUs due to their status as profit-seeking organizations. The Career College Association (CCA), the national lobbying association for many FPCUs, continues to push for a single definition of a higher education institution, arguing that such a step would eliminate much of the confusion that multiple definitions cause. Those who oppose a single definition argue that the inherent differences between nonprofit and for-profit colleges and universities necessitate separate classifications and contend that dual definitions will appropriately direct federal resources to institutions that serve private investors as well as students.[27] In the 2008 Reauthorization of the Higher Education Act, FPCUs continued to be defined by a separate definition that focuses on their for-profit status, and applies only to the distribution of Title IV programs funds.

The regulatory environment continues to challenge the position that FPCUs currently occupy within the U.S. higher education community. This, however, has not slowed their growth. Increased demand for postsecondary education in the United States has opened up new markets for proprietary higher education organizations. The regulatory environment for these organizations can be more favorable in certain states that provide FPCUs relatively easy entry into their higher education markets, while other states are more cautious. In 2006 six states, including three with the largest number of FPCUs—California, Florida, and New Jersey—conducted regulatory reviews or investigations into the activities of several FPCUs. Similarly, the New York State Board of Regents endorsed proposals "designed to provide greater oversight of new for-profit colleges and those undergoing a change of ownership."[28] Students are at the heart of these challenges. Advocates for tighter regulation argue for more oversight to protect students from unscrupulous institutions aiming to take advantage of them and the financial aid monies they bring. Those who favor fewer restrictions argue that increased oversight will stunt the growth of new programs and campuses, resulting in fewer students being able to enter higher education.[29]

Reaching Out to Marginalized Groups

For-profit colleges and universities deliberately target their product to specific populations that are often overlooked or somewhat excluded from traditional higher education (e.g., full-time employees, adults with families, students of color). For example, for-profit *degree-granting* colleges and universities enroll a much larger percentage of students who are employed full-time, 42 percent to be exact.[30] FPCUs also provide a point of entry into higher education for many low-income students and students of color who would otherwise be excluded from higher education. Two-year for-profit degree granting institutions enrolled the highest proportion of dependent students, 37 percent to be specific, with family incomes of less than $25,000.[31] The percentage of minority enrollments at FPCUs significantly outnumbers those at TCUs; nearly 43 percent of students attending for-profits are minorities. Additionally, in 2003 nearly 61 percent of Hispanics attending a 2-year FPCU graduated, whereas 44 percent of Hispanics attending 2-year private nonprofits and 18 percent attending public institutions graduated from those institutions during that same time (2008). In 2005–06, 37 percent of students enrolled at FPCUs were minorities, compared to 25 percent at public institutions and 20 percent at private nonprofit colleges and universities.[32] Six of the top 10 institutions producing minority graduates with bachelor's degrees in Computer and Information Science were FPCUs, with DeVry Inc. topping the list. Moreover, of the top 10 institutions awarding Master of Business Administration degrees to minorities, four were FPCUs according to Borden, Brown and Majesky-Pullmann.[33] These are impressive numbers considering that for-profit colleges and universities enroll only 5.5 percent of all students attending college in the United States.

Academic Dimensions

Curricular offerings. In most cases, FPCUs develop curricula that respond to the needs of the local labor market. They perform market research, meet with local employers, and assess their potential customer base to formulate data-driven decisions prior to creating a new program and making a financial investment. Similarly, courses and programs are eliminated if enrollments decline beyond a certain level or are simply not offered because local market conditions do not demand them. Advisory boards consisting of faculty, administrators, and employers provide input and help to drive the nature of the training and skill sets the institution will provide so that students can receive an education that is current and relevant to the job market.

FPCUs draw faculty from local employers, thus creating a *virtuous circle model*.[34] Students who attend for-profits learn from an employer-influenced curriculum that is taught by faculty from specific career fields. Just as employers depend on for-profits to supply a well-trained workforce for their organizations, FPCUs rely on employers to provide them with faculty who provide real world knowledge and experience to their students. Both create what can be referred to as an *interdependency cycle* in which the success of one facilitates that of the other.

Knowledge. Faculty members at traditional institutions possess a great deal of education and training related to their discipline. One the one hand, the knowledge base from which faculty teach students is grounded in their theoretical expertise. FPCUs, on the other hand, regard knowledge differently. The market highly influences the knowledge and skill sets that students receive; FPCUs regard knowledge as revolving around the needs of employers and businesses. As such, courses are designed and academic programs are developed to fit those needs.

As will be discussed shortly, faculty members who work at FPCUs are, more often than not, practitioners who teach courses that are directly related to their full-time jobs. For-profit institutions rely on faculty members to convey their professional work experience to students as part of the educational process. Given that the knowledge faculty members impart is practical rather than theoretical in nature, their approach to teaching by focusing on applied learning is regarded highly. Although faculty members may utilize theoretical frameworks to support course content, their knowledge base is rooted in their experiences. As a consequence, knowledge—as defined by for-profit institutions—is skill-based, practical, and applicable.[35]

Faculty work. Faculty, historically the primary asset and expenditure item in higher education, are utilized and deployed at FPCUs in a manner that is distinctly different from traditional universities. Because research is not a function of faculty work at FPCUs, the role that faculty play is more akin to faculty working at community colleges—teaching is the primary focus. Faculty members fill specific roles that are functions of needs-based analysis of the market, course and program design that reflects those needs, and instructional staffing that minimizes expenditures. It is not uncommon for scholars to point to a lack of faculty involvement in governance activities, a lack of control over the curriculum, and a limited amount of academic freedom as attributes that apply to all faculty members employed at for-profit institutions. While this may hold true for some, such blanket statements paint an inaccurate and monolithic image of for-profit postsecondary education providers and their faculty.

Similarities do exist with regard to faculty work at TCUs and FPCUs. For example, faculty members at for-profit institutions may teach courses, design curricula, and in some cases participate in committee work and chair dissertations. For-profit institutions, however, view faculty work differently. Faculty responsibilities are unbundled, meaning that teaching, curricula writing, dissertation chairing, and administrative duties are separate activities. Part-time faculty members are hired to perform specific tasks and can choose their work activities—whether it is developing a new course, teaching a class, sitting on a curriculum committee, or a combination of all three. Each task is a separate responsibility, and faculty members are compensated on a per-task basis. In addition, the nature of faculty work is highly influenced by external forces and profit generation.

Governance and decision-making. The unbundling of faculty work and the use of part-time faculty have disadvantages. More specifically, when faculty members are hired simply to teach one or two courses, their role limits their ability to determine course content and program goals. The organizational culture of for-profit colleges and universities is shaped in many ways by corporate culture. Decisions are made quickly, are driven by market research and other data, and reflect the needs of consumers. However, faculty members often are not involved in the decision-making process. Faculty engagement in the university community is minimized to the extent that shared governance is not the norm at FPCUs. One can argue that many faculty members from traditional institutions are not heavily engaged in their university community and are more focused on their own endeavors. The major difference, however, is that faculty at TCUs can choose whether or not to be engaged.

Considering outputs over inputs. For-profit institutions concern themselves more with student outputs than with inputs. Traditional colleges and universities typically measure the academic characteristics of students before making admissions decisions. It is quite common for traditional universities to consider an individual's SAT or GRE scores, as well as their high school or undergraduate grade point average. Rather than focusing on standardized test scores and prior academic performance, for-profit institutions place a higher value on what their students learn once they are in the classroom. Although admissions standards are admittedly weak, an educational approach that focuses on mastering core competencies is a critical difference between faculty work at TCUs and FPCUs. In the current climate of accountability, traditional institutions would be well served to establish learning outcomes and place more of a focus on measuring whether students meet certain competencies. Calls for increased accountability in higher education may place TCUs in a position where they may be forced to measure specific outcomes, without the option of determining what those outcomes are. By focusing on an outcomes-based educational model, FPCUs have placed themselves ahead of traditional colleges and universities in that respect.

Contextualized academic freedom. Academic freedom remains a fundamental tenet of academia that frames faculty work at traditional nonprofit colleges and universities. At FPCUs, academic freedom is contextual, and is interpreted to mean freedom within the classroom environment; in many cases, it is of peripheral concern because it is not an essential element that defines how faculty work is structured at these institutions.[36] As a consequence, the characteristics that frame faculty work at FPCUs place these institutions in a fundamentally different stance with regard to serving the public from that of nonprofit public and private institutions to the extent that FPCUs consider the dissemination of knowledge their only concern. At institutions that utilize a standardized curriculum, such as the University of Phoenix, administrators at central headquarters in Arizona design and evaluate course outlines from which faculty members teach. Faculty members have little leeway in the topics they teach and cannot stray into areas that are not part of the prescribed course plan. At other institutions faculty can design their own courses within certain limitations established by the institution's accreditation director.[37] Still, one could argue that academic freedom in the classroom is a non-issue when teaching students particular skills such as those necessary to prepare tax documents or repair computer equipment.

The intersection of education and profit. As previously discussed, faculty work is highly influenced by market conditions, but there are other factors that shape the roles and responsibilities of faculty work life at FPCUs. Because faculty members are taken from the workplace, they often teach part-time and are allowed to choose the courses they would like to teach. This approach provides student with real-world learning experiences while lowering the institution's instructional costs. At numerous institutions, faculty members are trained to teach in-house, which allows FPCUs to maintain quality control in the classroom while socializing faculty into culture of accountability. Scholars have begun to address numerous issues concerning for-profit institutions,[38] and there are many unanswered questions yet to be addressed. What can be said about the philosophical approach from which FPCUs operate is that, in essence, for-profit institutions are compelled to meet the needs of two distinct sets of customers—the students they enroll and the employers that will employ them. Inevitably, questions arise about the role FPCUs play in serving the public good as a result of the competing set of constituencies they serve.

FPCUs AND THE PUBLIC GOOD

The discussion of the public good as it has been conceived in general is complex. There is general agreement that individuals require a postsecondary education to enter the job market. Consequently, some will argue that postsecondary education is not only a public good; rather, it is increasingly becoming a private benefit. The extent to which education is considered a public good is debatable, as a consequence of the advanced training needs of the citizenry. Some argue that the purpose of higher education, when defined by teaching students, is only part of the function of a postsecondary institution, and the additional tasks (i.e., research, free exchange of ideas, and academic freedom) are central to the public good. The question here focuses on whether traditional definitions of the public good fit or do not fit the needs of our knowledge economy and society in general and the extent to which for-profits are linked to the social good.

Tierney argues that definitions of the public good in general, and with regard to higher education, change over time: "What the country expected of postsecondary education in the late 19th century when largely one class of people received a degree is different from what we ought to expect in the kind of country we inhabit in the 21st century."[39] One of the functions of TCUs has traditionally been to prepare citizens for participation in a democratic society and provide the citizenship function of liberal learning. Those in the for-profit sector acknowledge that they do not serve students in this capacity; their sole purpose is to provide a practical education to customers. Similarly, one also must recognize that many TCUs do not serve their students in this capacity. What is in question is the extent to which FPCUs should be allowed to partake of public (Title IV)[40] funds, if at all. Much of this concern stems from the public reputation FPCUs have gained in the recent past.

Points of Concern

During the 1980s proprietary colleges were synonymous with the fly-by-night institutions whose motive was to defraud the federal government of financial aid monies. As a consequence the U.S. Department of Education imposed tighter restrictions on how financial aid dollars could be used to avoid further abuse by unscrupulous proprietary institutions and their owners. Today, FPCUs are considered quite reputable; yet some well-known FPCUs have also been accused of questionable practices. Institutions such as the University of Phoenix, Career Education Corporation, ITT Technical Institutes, and others have been or are currently being investigated by various branches of the federal government—the Justice Department, Securities and Exchange Commission, and the Department of Education. The University of Phoenix, for example, was accused of recruitment violations and improper use of Title IV monies. DeVry Inc. was accused of questionable student loan practices by the State of New York. Career Education Corporation was investigated by the Security and Exchange Commission for non-compliance issues related to overstated enrollments and manipulation of financial statements and is under investigation by the Justice Department. And most recently, in 2007 the California attorney general threatened to file suit against Corinthian Colleges for alleged misrepresentation of their job placement statistics.

The growth and success of the for-profit higher education sector has not gone unquestioned. It is unfair to suggest that traditional colleges and universities have not faced similar challenges, but given the relatively small student market FPCUs serve, the extent to which accusations and allegations have been made against them are, proportionally speaking, much greater. Such incidents contribute to the widespread skepticism among many in the traditional higher education sector. Moreover, some within academe view FPCUs with slight contempt because of their profit-seeking motives. Heller suggests that for-profits ought not be considered "institutions of higher education" because they do not focus on serving the public good; instead, they are accountable to corporate boards and private investors.[41] Others argue that FPCUs do contribute to the public good through increased tax revenues and employment rates.[42] Still, questions remain.

Questions Regarding Quality

Educational quality, which in and of itself is difficult to define and measure, is an unknown at FPCUs. Although FPCUs design courses and curricula with measurable learning outcomes in mind, the degree to which learning takes place in the classroom is unclear because faculty are held accountable for a student's ability to successfully complete a course.[43] Moreover, academic freedom, as previously discussed, is non-existent, which is problematic in courses and academic programs leading to a bachelor's, master's, or doctoral degrees. Furthermore, the tension between academic and corporate decision-makers inevitably is linked to the tension between academic quality and financial culpability. The question here is whether for-profits opt for the former over the latter, or vice versa. This is not to suggest that FPCUs lack academic quality; the majority of for-profit institutions are evaluated and vetted by national and regional accrediting associations. Rather, my intent is to offer the various criticisms FPCU face from detractors, most of which are based on the idea of education as a tool for profit generation.

A Clash of Values

The main issue that plays a role in the resistance to for-profits by critics is the inevitable conflict of values that exists when a good or service, which has been traditionally provided by private nonprofit and public institutions under the pretext of serving the common good, is offered by an organization whose focus includes generating a profit from it. FPCUs consider themselves businesses that trade in the market of postsecondary education, separate from the traditional private nonprofit and public colleges and universities.[44] Consequently, they function within the realm of commerce and organize their operations as such. The kind of education they provide is pertinent to this discussion as well (i.e., skills-based training). At issue is whether the *type* of organization that provides this form of education is relevant, so long as the end result is an educated workforce. The response by those who view for-profits favorably is, of course, no. If a higher education institution can provide society with an educated work force, then the fact that the institution is doing this to generate a profit is irrelevant. Skeptics, on the other hand, question whether training should be synonymous with education. And their response is inevitably, yes. Institutional type and profit motives should matter. They argue that FPCUs are fundamentally different from traditional colleges and universities. In other words, critics view for-profits with reservations since their values do not mirror those of traditional higher education institutions. One should not overlook, however, that their organizational culture is bound to differ since they operate under rules and regulations that do not apply to traditional colleges and universities (who function under 501(c)(3), tax exempt status).

FINAL THOUGHTS

There are advantages and disadvantages associated with the for-profit educational business model. Many of the multi-campus FPCUs, for instance, take advantage of opportunity cost savings associated with creating and distributing curricula. Similarly, part-time faculty are used as a cost-saving tool of the FPCU educational paradigm since expenses related to full-time employment, such as retirement accounts, health benefits and vacation time, apply to only a small proportion of full-time employees. In some instances part-time faculty are often paid on a fee per assignment basis either to teach courses, design curricula, and/or participate in developing new academic programs.

By taking advantage of postsecondary educational demands pertaining to the growing need for skilled labor, FPCUs provide services to specific employment markets as needs arise. Traditional colleges and universities are slow to meet these demands, on which FPCUs can capitalize. For example, a growing demand for individuals with specific information technology certifications emerged over a decade ago; employers sought Microsoft Certified Systems Engineers, Certified Novell Administrators and other similarly qualified individuals. Since traditional colleges and universities, with the exception of community colleges, were neither interested in nor able to provide this type of training, FPCUs began offering certification training and reaped the benefits of this untapped market. Their ability to adapt to changes in the job market, coupled with the use of innovative educational delivery methods and services, allows for-profits to identify new markets and provide the necessary training business and employers seek.

To be sure, FPCUs make up a small proportion of the postsecondary landscape in terms of student enrollment; about 5 percent of college students enroll at FPCUs. Yet, one cannot overlook the rapid growth of the FPCU sector over the last decade. The growth rates of FPCU enrollments have outpaced those of TCUs by a wide margin. Between 1998–2003, for-profit enrollments at less-than 4-year programs increased by 80 percent, while enrollments in degree-granting academic programs increased by 91 percent.[45] FPCU enrollment growth increased at seven times the rate of traditional colleges and universities, 10.4 percent versus 1.4 percent.[46] With tremendous growth and success, however, comes increased scrutiny by the government and the general public. FPCUs have grown rapidly, significantly outpacing the growth rates of the traditional nonprofit institutions. Although the current breed of FPCUs differs from their TCU counterparts, forces affecting all of higher education—and, indirectly, all of society—fuel their emergence and growth. In other words, FPCU enrollment growth is partly due to their collective focus on workforce preparation, despite their relatively high price in comparison to private nonprofit and public institutions.

For-profit colleges and universities also capitalize on the general public's recognition that individual earnings are enhanced through the acquisition of additional knowledge and skills. Both individuals and businesses recognize the value of increased education and are increasingly willing to invest greater proportions of their own resources in schooling. While society is eager to increase the educational levels of its citizenry, budgets are heavily constrained by competing fiscal demands. When examined in this light,

FPCUs are a natural consequence, rather than an external intrusion, of environmental forces. Additionally, their growth has been aided in part by their structure as for-profit businesses, their responsiveness to changes in demand of specific labor markets, federal student aid monies, and for some, their corporate structure that provides additional access to investment capital.

In pursuing their sense of success, FPCUs raise the same public policy issues which have been common across all of higher education for some time—issues such as access, selectivity, completion, and the like. At the same time, they are raising and responding to new issues more directly associated with workforce employability and regional economic development. Although seemingly quite different from traditional colleges and universities, FPCUs are filling in the labor force training gaps and responding to the social, political, and economic forces that are acting on all of society. From an historical perspective, FPCUs are responding to and fostering the demands for enhanced skills and the needs of employers, while simultaneously tapping into new student markets, similar to the forces that created public community colleges and land grant institutions. Differences between FPCUs and traditional institutions are of growing interest to many, especially within the context of our emerging knowledge economy.

NOTES

1. David L. Kirp, *Shakespeare, Einstein, and the Bottom Line: The Marketing of Higher Education* (Cambridge, MA: Harvard University Press, 2003).

2. Ibid.

3. David Breneman, Brian Pusser, and Sarah E. Turner, "The Contemporary Provision of For-Profit Higher Education: Mapping the Competitive Market," in *Earnings from Learning: The Rise of For-Profit Universities,* ed. David W. Breneman, Brian Pusser, and Sarah E. Turner (Albany, NY: SUNY Press, 2006), 3–20; Eric Gould, *The University in a Corporate Culture* (New Haven, CT: Yale University Press, 2003); Kirp, *Shakespeare, Einstein*; Frank Newman, Lana Courtier, and Jamie Scurry, *The Future of Higher Education: Rhetoric, Reality, and the Risks of the Market* (San Francisco: Jossey-Bass, 2004); Sheila Slaughter and Gary Rhoades, *Academic Capitalism and the New Economy: Markets, State, and Higher Education* (Baltimore, MD: Johns Hopkins University Press, 2004); Lawrence C. Soley, *Leasing the Ivory Tower: The Corporate Takeover of Academia* (Boston: South End Press, 1995); Jennifer Washburn, *University, Inc: The Corporate Corruption of American Higher Education* (New York: Basic Books, 2005).

4. Robert F. Seybolt, *The Evening School in Colonial America* (Urbana, IL: University of Illinois, Bureau of Education Research, 1925).

5. Richard S. Ruch, *Higher Education, Inc: The Rise of the For-Profit University* (Baltimore, MD: Johns Hopkins University Press, 2001).

6. Charles W. Dabney, "Agricultural Education." (Monographs on Education in the United States, 1899), 602.

7. U.S. Department of Education, National Center for Education Statistics, *Postsecondary Institutions in the U.S.: Fall 2002 Degrees and other Awards Conferred* (Washington, DC, 2003).

8. Ibid.

9. National Center on Education and the Economy, *Tough Choices or Tough Times: The Report of the New Commission on the Skills of the American Workforce* (Hoboken, NJ: Jossey-Bass, 2007), 16.

10. Jeff M. Silber, "Equity Research: Education and Training" (New York: BMO Capital Markets, 2006).

11. Ibid.

12. Title IV eligible colleges and universities are those who qualify to receive federal financial aid dollars, for example Pell grant monies, federally subsidized and unsubsidized student loans, and so on.

13. U.S. Department of Education. National Center for Education Statistics, *Postsecondary Institutions*.

14. JBL Associates, Inc., *Economic Impact of America's Career Colleges* (Washington, DC: Imagine America Foundation, 2007).

15. U.S. Department of Labor. Bureau of Labor Statistics, *Tomorrow's Jobs 2006 and Projected 2016: Occupational Handbook* (Washington, DC, 2003).

16. Ibid.

17. Andreas Ortmann, "Capital Romance: Why Wall Street Fell in Love with Higher Education," in Breneman et al., *Earnings from Learning*, 145–66.

18. Ibid.

19. Doug Lederman, "Higher Ed Acts Gets Hairier," *Inside Higher Ed.com* (February 6, 2008), http://www.insidehighered.com/news/2008/02/06/hea/.

20. Kevin Kinser and Daniel C. Levy, "For-Profit Higher Education: U.S. Tendencies, International Echoes," in *The International Handbook of Higher Education*, ed. James Forest and Philip Altbach (Dordrecht, Netherlands and London: Spring Publishers, 2006), 107–20.

21. Breneman, Pusser, and Turner.

22. William G. Tierney and Guilbert C. Hentschke. *New Players, Different Game: Understanding the Rise of For-Profit Colleges and Universities* (Baltimore, MD: Johns Hopkins University Press, 2007).

23. Elise Scanlon and Michael S. McComis, "Accreditation and Accountability: The Role of For-Profit Education and National Accrediting Agencies," in *Higher Education's Expanding Market: For-Profit Colleges and Universities as Schools and Businesses,* ed. Guilbert C. Hentschke, Vicente M. Lechuga, and William G. Tierney (Albany, NY: SUNY Press, forthcoming).

24. Kinser, 73.

25. Education Commission of the States, *Report from the Regions: Accreditors' Perceptions of the Role and Impact of For-Profit Institutions in Higher Education* (Denver, CO, 2000).

26. Ibid.

27. Donald E. Heller, "Not All Institutions are Alike," *The Chronicle of Higher Education* (November 2003): B7.

28. Xiao B. Yuan, "Disputes Over Regulating For-Profit Colleges Come to a Head in California," *The Chronicle of Higher Education* (August 2006): A20.

29. Ibid.

30. U.S. Department of Education. Education, National Center for Education Statistics, *Postsecondary Institutions in the U.S.: Fall 2002 Degrees and other Awards Conferred* (Washington, DC, 2003).

31. Sarah K. Goan and Alisa F. Cunningham, U.S. Department of Education, National Center for Education Statistics, *Differential Characteristics of 2-Year Postsecondary Institutions* (Washington, DC, 2007).

32. U.S. Department of Education, National Center for Education Statistics, *Postsecondary Institutions in the United States: Fall 2006 and Degrees and other Awards Conferred, 2005–2006* (Washington, DC, 2007).

33. Victor M. H. Borden, Pamela C. Brown, and Olivia Majesky-Pullmann, "Top 100 Undergraduate Degree Producers: Interpreting the Data," *Diverse Issues in Higher Education* 24, no. 8 (2007): 9–21, 31–45, 37–61.

34. Tierney and Hentschke.

35. Vicente M. Lechuga, "Assessment, Knowledge, and Customer Service: Contextualizing Faculty Work at For-Profit Colleges and Universities," *Review of Higher Education* 31, no. 3 (2008): 287–307.

36. Vicente M. Lechuga, *Changing Landscape of the Academic Profession: The Culture of Faculty at For-Profit Colleges and Universities* (New York: Routledge, 2006).

37. Ibid.

38. Gary A. Berg, *Lessons from the Edge: For-Profit and Nontraditional Higher Education in America* (Westport, CT: Greenwood Publishing Group, 2004); Kirp, *Shakespeare, Einstein*; Brian Pusser and Sarah T. Turner, "Non-Profit and For-Profit Governance in Higher Education,"

in *Governing Academia,* ed. Ronald G. Ehrenberg (Ithaca, NY: Cornell University Press, 2001), 235–57; Washburn.

39. William G. Tierney, "The Public Good in a Changing Economy," in *Higher Education's Expanding Market: For-Profit Colleges and Universities* (Baltimore, MD: Johns Hopkins University Press, 2007).

40. Title IV funds.

41. Heller.

42. Tierney and Hentschke.

43. Lechuga, "Assessment, Knowledge, and Customer Service."

44. Tierney and Hentschke.

45. U.S. Department of Education, National Center for Education Statistics, *Postsecondary Institutions in the U.S.: Fall 2002 Degrees and other Awards Conferred* (Washington, DC, 2003).

46. Tierney and Hentschke.

CHAPTER 10

Applying Business Insight and Strategy within the Academy: An Idea Whose Time Has Come

Brent D. Ruben, Kathleen M. Immordino,
and Sherrie Tromp

Higher education *is* a business. We don't produce widgets like a manufacturer, nor do we sell tangible products like Wal-Mart or services like a Hyatt hotel. But, indeed education—particularly higher education—is very much a business, and that business can be described as the production, dissemination, translation and use of ideas, and the cultivation of learning and learners.

The business-like character of higher education could have been (and often was) overlooked in earlier times when we enjoyed many of the privileges of a monopoly. What we did, and how and for whom we did it, were largely matters that were self-determined by the academy—and most specifically, by the faculty—in this respect, at least, *the faculty truly was the university*.[1] Scarce resources, new competitors, heightened institutional aspirations, decreased public funding, spiraling tuition costs, the consumerism movement in healthcare, and a host of other interrelated developments ushered in a new scrutiny and critique of our once-sacrosanct academy.[2] This critique brought charges of insularity and resistance to change and a new consumerism with heightened expectations for service and marketplace responsiveness, and more generally, demands for greater attention to the needs and requirements of higher education's "customers."[3]

In recent years, it has also become increasingly clear that many of the external constituencies who fund and regulate our activities embrace a business model.[4] Even in the assessment of the quality of our academic work, for example, the traditional provider-side view of academic excellence, is no longer considered sufficient. Many of us can remember when it was assumed that the quality of an academic program could largely be determined by a review of the *credentials of the faculty and the resources and opportunities afforded* by the institution. In the contemporary context, the assessment of quality is presumed to extend beyond the quality of scholarship and instruction. It now focuses equally, also, on the consumption-side of the equation—on *outcomes* and *benefits derived* by students and other constituents that we serve.[5]

For those who have worked within colleges and universities during the past two decades, it has been difficult, if not impossible, not to notice the many changes—small and large—that have come to the academy. Today, as one peruses the higher education print and online publications, or listens to the discourse at faculty or administrator meetings, there is no mistaking our increased and increasing attention to the concerns of higher education-as-a-business, so aggressively eschewed by many not that many years ago.

Few of us within the academy have experienced a rush to embrace the business perspective. Obviously, each sector is unique in a number of respects, and the argument that higher education is different, unique, special, and privileged is very well known, well rehearsed, and often replayed within the academy to the point where it is quite familiar to all of us.

The point of our introductory comments is not to persuade readers that higher education institutions do or should conform in every respect to other businesses. We do believe, however, that viewing academic units as *organizations which function in and depend upon marketplace interactions* provides a useful lens for higher education.[6] The idea we hope to advance is that colleges and universities—and the higher education sector, more generally—have a number of similarities to other industries and businesses, and especially to healthcare[7] and the public sector.[8] We advance this perspective because we believe that we in higher education can benefit from thinking more broadly about our programs, departments, colleges, universities and systems as organizations with stakeholders operating within a complex and dynamic marketplace of ideas and resources. We think this enlarged view will enable us to benefit quite directly from a variety of themes, strategies and tools that have been useful in business and applied in other sectors.

Unlike Wal-Mart or Hyatt, the business of higher education requires highly engaged customers; customers who must function interactively with our institutions for us—and them—to be successful. A high level of interaction with constituents is necessary for all facets of the higher education mission. First and foremost, effective interaction is required for the instructional component of our mission, where active collaboration with our beneficiaries is indispensable to successful teaching-learning outcomes.

The business/organizational/marketplace model is also applicable with regard to the research and scholarly mission component of colleges and universities. Here our primary customers are our colleagues in the research and professional communities of our disciplines—and again, the success of our work depends upon establishing and maintaining effective producer-consumer information interchange to contribute to the advancement of knowledge. Activities in this domain also account for a substantial amount of the operating resources for many institutions, and the economics of sponsorship conform even more obviously—though some would say, regrettably—to a traditional business model.

A marketplace perspective can also be applied to the service and outreach facet of college and university work. It's probably fair to say that our goal in serving the interests of our communities is both altruistic and pragmatic. We believe in the value of such work as a part of our institutional missions, and we hope our contributions will engender greater understanding, appreciation, and support for our institutions, and higher education.[9]

Speaking more generally, the purposes of higher education are best served when our relationships with our constituencies and communities exhibit this pattern of engaged interaction between "providers" and "consumers." For students, this model envisions the cultivation of informed and lifelong learners who value both education and the institution(s) which serve this function for them and society at large. Similarly, the research component of our business model assumes the generation of useful information that continues to expand the boundaries of knowledge, and our public service and outreach work imagines a society that understands values, integrates and uses ideas generated from the academy, and in turn helps to shape the agenda and provide financial and moral support for our work.

HEALTHCARE, PUBLIC SECTOR, AND HIGHER EDUCATION ORGANIZATIONS

The challenge of seeing an intersection between its traditional practices and the practices of business is not restricted to higher education. Despite a reluctance similar to that seen in higher education, healthcare and public sector organizations have faced the same challenge to adopt a more business-like approach to appropriate aspects of organizational life. Business and marketplace perspectives have played an influential role, particularly in the last decade, in both the healthcare and public service sectors, both of which have a good deal in common with higher education institutions. In these sectors, as in higher education, business success—judged in terms of mission fulfillment and economic viability—requires active, engaged and collaborative relationships between providers and consumers. Paralleling higher education's ultimate goal of enabling lifelong learning/learners, healthcare's goal is to facilitate a lifelong commitment to health and health-promoting/maintaining behavior; fundamental to both models is the production, dissemination, and adoption of information and knowledge that makes this possible. Likewise, at the highest level the purpose of public sector organizations is to provide the essential services that enable the effective and efficient functioning of society. Its goal—again paralleling higher education—is to provide those services needed for lifelong support of its constituents through the variety and scope of the functions it provides. The changing nature of society, combined with changing demographics and increasing demand for services, insures that public sector effectiveness relies on constant interaction with constituents and beneficiaries.

As healthcare and public sector organizations have increasingly embraced a business perspective, so too, can higher education benefit by applying some of its basic insights and strategies. In the following sections we describe six such themes and three strategies which we believe have particular relevance for the challenges we face in the academy.

THEMES

Mission, Vision, Goal, and Action Plan; Clarity and Alignment

Perhaps the most fundamental tenets of organizational excellence in contemporary business thinking are that there must be a clear and shared sense of mission and aspirations for an organization, and that measurable, aligned goals and action plans need to be established, effectively communicated, and implemented to advance those purposes.[10]

These principles seem obvious enough, but even in leading corporations where their centrality has been recognized for some time, effectively developing, articulating and integrating them into everyday organizational practice is a challenge.

Applied to higher education, this implies that the purposes and aspirations of an organization—a program, department, college, university or system—need to be understood and shared by faculty and staff, at least, and ideally also by students, and other key external constituencies—on campus and beyond. An implication of this notion is that the organization ought to have collective purposes and aspirations that are something more than the simple sum of the personal mission, aspirations, and goals of the individuals who work within the unit at a particular point in time, which often seem so much the preoccupation with the academy.

If leading corporations find it a significant challenge to achieve these collective perspectives, imagine the result from an independent survey of faculty and staff members in your unit where questions such as the following are asked:

- What is the purpose of our department?
- How is the department distinctive when compared to other departments within this institution, or to departments at other institutions?
- Thinking about the department in 4–5 years, what should be its defining characteristics?
- What needs to change to fulfill these aspirations?
- What are the 3–5 most important goals that need to be pursued by the department during the next two years in order to advance the department toward its five-year aspirations?
- How can the department organize itself most effectively to pursue these goals?

The ideal of course, would be that the survey results reveal a high level of intersubjective agreement on each question. This could happen only if there had been systematic processes in place to discuss these issues and develop common perspectives on them. What level of consensus would you expect to see in the answers within your unit? Obviously, the results of this kind of activity are not merely of academic interest. To the extent that there are shared perspectives on these issues, it is possible to focus scarce departmental resources and faculty and staff energies in these common directions, and considerably increase the probability of fulfilling aspirations. The alternative is an all-too-familiar one for many of us.

Monitoring Effectiveness and Efficiency of Programs and Services

Another basic theme of sound organizational practice is the regular review of programs and services, and the operational processes associated with them, to assure that they are as effective, efficient, cost-effective and client-satisfying as possible.[11] Ideally, this monitoring process is a systematic one, whereby the most mission-critical programs, services, and processes are carefully documented, reviewed, and refined on a regular basis. The notion is that regular reviews, streamlining or elimination of steps, and the use of technology result in refinements that lead to increased effectiveness and substantial savings in time and resources.

An element of the review process is the consideration of whether all current programs and services are mission-appropriate and mission-critical. Particularly with limited resources, it also becomes essential to determine which programs and services provided by any organization are critical to the mission and aspirations, and which are optional, peripheral or no longer essential. Activities that may have been initiated during lush times often lead to mission and vision drift, and become extremely burdensome—and mission and vision diverting—during more difficult times.

Key questions for this review include:

- Does each program or service we provide have an essential value to our mission, aspirations or goals?
- Are those that are less essential still needed?
- To what extent do some programs and services that could be considered optional draw resources and energies that could better be invested in mission or aspiration-critical activities? Could these programs or services be eliminated, or done by or in collaboration with, another organization?

In the context of higher education, this theme and these questions would direct attention to the establishment of a systematic process for regular review of all core activities to be sure that effective and efficient procedures are in place, that once developed these are well-documented so that procedures don't have to be reinvented by each new administration, committee, and individual assigned to a particular area of responsibility. Examples in an academic context might include a periodic review of systems for initiating and approving new courses, allocating support and travel funds, scheduling courses, communicating academic requirements, coordinating multisection courses, developing hiring plans, welcoming and orienting new colleagues, assessing learning outcomes, supporting faculty scholarship and research, or recruiting and training coadjutant faculty. Once documented, these processes can be periodically reviewed, evaluated, streamlined where possible, and radically altered or eliminated if they are no longer appropriate.

One of the questions above relates to the need to be cautious about the outsourcing of core functions within higher education such as instruction, research, or service/outreach. The issue here has to do with the risks of creating the perception that anyone can do it. To the extent that that this occurs, those outside the organization may begin to question the extent to which the unit's mission is distinctive, value-adding, or necessary.

Program and service review, documentation and appropriate standardization is an area in which we believe many units within higher education have a great deal to learn from the practices in leading corporations. Particularly at the department level, we in the academy often have a tendency to operate in quite informal, casual and idiosyncratic ways. Our cultures are largely oral, and we often retain and share operational information through word-of-mouth rather than through more formal documentation. While there are some perceived niceties associated with the casual approach, this operating style can lead to substantial reworking and waste of time and resources. It also, perhaps unintentionally, privileges those who have been around longer within the culture—and who know more through experience—and puts newcomers at a tremendous disadvantage as they struggle through a trial-and-error socialization process.

Measuring Progress and Outcomes

A concern with measuring and monitoring outcomes of various kinds is a tradition in business and healthcare. Beyond providing a yardstick for evaluating effectiveness, such approaches have other values for the sectors and organizations that employ them. They help to create focus, clarify and operationalize goals, energize employees, and provide the basis for telling the organization's story to internal and external publics.

Measurement—or what might more broadly be termed *assessment*—consists of three basic steps:

- Establishing goals
- Developing methods to evaluate the extent to which these goals are being met
- Using the resulting information to plan and implement improvements

Depending on the sector and the organization, some goals, methodologies, and improvement strategies are obvious. When the goals are financial, for instance, their articulation and measurement are straightforward—though the ways in which the resulting information can be used to close the loop for improvement may well be less obvious.

Beyond standard financial reporting systems, and much-maligned reputational and ranking systems, our approaches to assessment of all kinds have historically relied heavily on personalized professional judgment. A number of factors come into play in this regard. It can be difficult to clearly identify and agree upon our goals, and the measurement of success relative to these is even more complex. But, it is also true that we manage to address similarly complex questions in our own scholarly research with considerable effectiveness and far less lament.

For any number of good and perhaps not-so-good reasons, higher education is not a standard-setter when it comes to the measurement of the impact of our own work. We continue to struggle to develop models and methods in which we can have confidence. Where we have made an effort to measure our effectiveness—such as scholarship and research—the emphasis has been upon publication counts and calculations of dollars generated through grants; we struggle to identify more meaningful measures of impact. With regard to teaching-learning, we have traditionally relied on scholastic accomplishments and, more recently, peer ratings coupled with student evaluation. Here, too, there is obvious room for improvement.

With regard to organizational assessment, questions like these might be asked:

- What would it mean to be an effective program, department, institution, system?
- How do we know if we meet these standards?
- How would the information that comes from this assessment process be useful in leadership, planning, priority setting and resource allocation?

In the area of teaching/learning outcomes assessments, where mounting pressures for assessment have helped to create and/or underscore the pressing need to become more systematic and standardized in our assessment approaches, typical measurement questions are these:

- What are the instructional goals of our program, department, and institution?
- How will we know if these goals are being achieved?
- What measurement methods are appropriate (valid, reliable, useful)?
- How can we ensure that the resulting information is useful and used in planning and improvement of teaching and learning outcomes?

Assessment of either type begins with the clarification of goals—for an institution, school, department, or program. This is followed by the development of a system of information- and evidence-gathering to determine the effectiveness of the institution or department in achieving its goals. In this phase, criteria, indicators, and information-gathering tools are identified or developed, and implemented. This is the measurement component of the assessment process. The resulting information is used to document successes and to identify gaps in the effectiveness of the unit or institution's work. This information may be useful to institutional, departmental or programmatic reviews; for the accrediting process; or for updating other external constituencies or stakeholder groups. Over time, the information can also be useful to guide a review and refinement of the goals and more fundamental directions of the organization and its activities, and for educating internal and external publics about achievements, accomplishments and progress—for telling the institution's, program's, or department's story.

Learning through Benchmarking Peers, Competitors, and Leaders

Fundamentally, benchmarking consists of comparing approaches, practices, performance and processes in order to facilitate organizational assessment, innovation, or improvement.[12] It has also been described as "a structured approach for looking outside an organization to study and adapt the best outside practices to complement internal operations with new, creative ideas."[13] Thus, benchmarking can refer to comparisons at various levels. It can be used to refer to rather specific comparisons like how many times phones are allowed to ring before being answered at peer, competitor or leading service centers, at one extreme, or to an examination of the processes through which strategic planning is conducted, at the other extreme.

The paradigm of comparison and information sharing in organizational development has found its way into other organizational settings such as healthcare,[14] human resource management,[15] and in academic settings.[16] Benchmarking studies look to financial issues[17] and, just as prevalent, focus on organizational relationship processes often associated with human resources management, training and development, organizational knowledge, and how these areas impact organizational performance.[18]

Within the context of higher education, benchmarking can take the form of internal, competitive, and generic comparisons.[19] Internal benchmarking refers to units within the institution making comparisons. Looking outward, competitive and generic benchmarking have as their goal the identification of best practices of other organizations. The first of these involves comparisons with direct competitors, while generic benchmarking involves organizations that are not direct competitors but, rather, share similar organizational practices and procedures—for example, those in other sectors such as healthcare, government, or business. Benchmarking against organizations in these other sectors can result in significant insights about operations that are not exclusive to higher education. We might consider what a campus public safety function could learn about incident management from a local or state police emergency management unit, or what a residence hall might learn from the operations of a long-term stay hotel facility.

One of the most typical goals of benchmarking is assessment—that is, to provide information that allows an organization to judge the effectiveness of its own activities or performance compared to others. To illustrate with a very simple example, suppose that surveys of students relative to their satisfaction with computing services on a particular campus reveal that 65 percent of first-year students are "extremely favorable" or "somewhat favorable" in their rating of computing services. What, exactly, is the significance of this finding? Unfortunately, it is of little value for assessing performance without having a context in which to interpret the finding. Benchmarking provides that context. Comparisons with peers, competitors, or leaders, provide the basis for interpreting one's own results in a meaningful manner. If comparable, competitor or leading computer services departments at similar institutions achieve a rating of 50 percent on these criteria, then we arrive at quite a different conclusion than if others' average ratings were at the 80 percent level.

Innovation is a second primary value of benchmarking. Comparing one's own organization to others can provide new insights into ways of thinking and working, and inspire and motivate useful and profound change. Organizational leaders often report that some of their most creative organizational insights come from benchmarking what might seem the least likely comparisons. Thus, for example, members of a product-oriented organization might find they are stimulated by new ways of thinking about customer service through comparisons with a service-oriented business. Or, university administrators might find the basis for innovation in faculty recruitment by benchmarking with private-sector research and development organizations.

Within the academy comparisons can be made at the level of an institution, department, program, workgroup, or specific process. And one may compare across academic, support or administrative units. At an institutional level of analysis, one might examine recruiting relationships with junior colleges (inputs), organizational approaches to strategic planning (internal processes), and student placement and faculty productivity (outputs). Or, at a lower level of analysis, a university computing services department could benchmark vendor management (inputs), the management of on-campus computer labs (internal processes), or approaches to assessing student, faculty or staff satisfaction with services (outputs). Or, an academic department could benchmark approaches to recruiting top graduate students (inputs), methods for assisting faculty with research and publication, or providing professional development for staff (internal processes), or student satisfaction (outputs). As noted earlier, these comparisons can be with other higher education organizations, or with other sectors. For instance, in the case above, the computing services could benchmark against other higher education institutions, or with computing organizations in private-sector, government, or healthcare organizations.

Among the fundamental issues considered in benchmarking are these:

- With whom should our programs, departments, colleges, university or system be compared? Who are our peers, our competitors, those we seek to become more like, the leaders in the field?

- How do our approaches/processes/methods/results compare to those of these other organizations?

- Can we adopt or adapt others' approaches/processes/methods/results?

Developing and Valuing Leaders

Within higher education, business schools and other professional programs offer a variety of programs and courses focused on leadership. These offerings respond to the widespread recognition of the importance of competent and skilled leadership as a component for organizational effectiveness. While we offer these courses to others, we are typically not overly active consumers of these offerings ourselves.

The inescapable conclusion that one reaches after considering this state of affairs is that sectors other than higher education seem to be more aware of the importance of developing and valuing leadership and leaders. Within the academy there is the general sense that any smart person can be a good leader. This seems to follow from the equally questionable view that all that is required to build and maintain an excellent program, department, or institution is a collection of distinguished scholars and professionals.[20]

Within leading businesses, a great deal of attention is devoted to identifying, cultivating, and rewarding leaders. These efforts grow out of a recognition that the competencies required for outstanding leadership—like those required of outstanding organizations—are neither obvious nor naturally occurring even among individuals who are bright and well-educated.[21]

Beyond the issues related to the identification and cultivation of individual leadership competencies are organizational issues, related to professional development, leadership development programming, meaningful performance review, coaching, and succession planning—areas typically receiving considerably less attention in higher education than in other sectors.

- How effectively do we convey our regard for effective leader-ship and effective leaders—at the program, department, college, institutional levels?
- How do we attract, recruit, train and reward such individuals?
- What programs are in place to support professional and leadership development?

Telling the Story

Good work often goes unnoticed. Substantial attention within lead-ing corporations is directed toward assuring that their products and ser-vices are of an appropriate quality to promote the kind of image and reputation that leads to customer loyalty, repeat and referral business. There is also a recognition that cultivating a desired identity within the marketplace may require, additionally, more focused communica-tion efforts. The awareness of the importance of getting one's story out has long driven attention to activities such as branding, marketing, public relations, and other forms of purposeful and targeted external communication.

There is little doubt that higher education as a sector—and colleges and universities and programs—face a substantial public communication chal-lenge. We are not nearly as well understood and appreciated as we would like to be. For example, we are often seen as overly detached and uninter-ested in others' questions, needs and perceptions. And, while many within the academy see our purpose as substantially broader than preparation for a particular job, some of our constituencies have difficulty fully under-standing or embracing these more abstract facets of our mission—research and traditional liberal arts education, for example.

It is probably time for the academy to begin thinking more creatively about how best to articulate our purposes and value as a public good, and more specifically how to clarify and disseminate our understandings of the vital roles we know that we play for our students, our communities, and society at large.

Whether one thinks about higher education as a whole, or particular institutions, or units within these institutions, some questions to focus our thinking are these:

- What *is* our story?
- How is that story unique, special, compelling?

- What benefits do we provide for our students, the marketplace, our communities, our disciplines and professions, and other specific constituencies?
- To whom does the story (or stories) need to be told?
- How best can we reach those groups?
- How can we monitor the effectiveness of these communication efforts?

Other Themes

We have selected six themes that are well developed in leading businesses, and we believe, largely underdeveloped in higher education. As they are important in their own right, they are also examples of the potential value of paying closer attention to the development of concepts and ideas in business and other sectors. There are other areas one might choose as well, among them leading change initiatives; valuing service excellence; addressing the need for effective internal communication; and crisis management.[22]

STRATEGIES AND TOOLS

The ability to move forward and consider how these themes can be applied in higher education also requires appropriate strategies and tools. In this section we will provide brief overviews of three strategies and tools that have been developed and are widely used in business, and increasingly in healthcare and public sector organizations, as a means of addressing a number of the themes discussed above. Depending upon the way they are implemented and utilized, each of these three strategies, (1) Scorecards/Dashboards, (2) Strategic planning, and (3) Baldrige-based organizational assessment, have the potential to address all of these themes.

Scorecards/Dashboards

As indicated above, one of the pervasive themes of contemporary organizational learning theory and practice is the emphasis on *information* and *measurement* for evaluating and enhancing excellence.[23]

Traditionally, business and industry have measured organizational performance using a financial accounting model that emphasizes profitability, return on investment, sales growth, cash flow, or economic value added. The need for external accountability and standardized measures for financial comparison across corporations continues today. In recent years, however, questions have increasingly been raised regarding the exclusive reliance on these measures. There is a growing sense that these financial performance indicators, used alone, fail to capture many of the critical success factors required for external accountability and are of limited value for addressing internal management needs.[24]

Many major corporations now couple financial indicators with other measures selected to reflect key elements of their mission, vision, and strategic direction. Collectively, these cockpit or dashboard indicators, as they are sometimes called, are used to monitor and navigate the organization in much the same way a pilot and flight crew use the array of indicators in the cockpit to monitor and navigate an airplane. The usefulness of these indicators extends beyond performance measurement per se and contributes also to self-assessment, strategic planning, and the creation of focus and consensus on goals and directions within the organization.

One approach that addresses this need systematically is the balanced scorecard developed by a study group composed of representatives from major corporations, including American Standard, Bell South, Cray Research, DuPont, General Electric, and Hewlett-Packard.[25] As described by Kaplan and Norton, scorecards translate the mission and strategies of an organization into a comprehensive set of performance indicators that serves as a framework for measurement and management. The measures represent a *balance* between external measures for shareholders and customers, and internal measures of critical business processes, innovation, and learning and growth. The measures are *balanced* between outcome measures—the results of past efforts—and the measures that drive future performance. And the scorecard is balanced between objective, easily quantified outcome measures and subjective, somewhat judgmental, performance.

Organizations that adopt this approach report that they are able to use it to:

- Clarify and gain consensus about vision and strategic direction
- Communicate and link strategic objectives and measures throughout the organization
- Align departmental and personal goals to the organization's vision and strategy
- Plan, set targets, and align strategic initiatives
- Conduct periodic and systematic strategic reviews
- Obtain feedback to learn about and improve strategy[26]

One company executive describes the approach and critical questions it addresses this way: "A balanced business scorecard is an information-based management tool that translates our strategic objectives into a coherent set of performance measures. We start with the vision. What are the critical success factors to attain our vision? What are the key performance measures to measure our progress against those success factors? What are the targets, initiatives, and what is the review process to ensure that this balanced business scorecard is the key management tool to run the businesses? And, finally, how do we tie in the incentives?"[27]

In higher education, scorecards and dashboards can similarly provide critical information across a number of key areas. Doing so requires the same attention to balance. In the same way that the focus in business was, in the past, solely on financial indicators, the traditional measures associated with the academy have resulted in an emphasis on faculty credentials and facilities provided—student, faculty, and institutional quality and achievement.[28] These measures focus on inputs and outputs, rather than on the value added. As the demand for measurement and assessment become more widespread from a variety of stakeholder groups, the emphasis has shifted. It is now more centered on presenting a broad spectrum of measures that consider all aspects of a college or university. At the highest levels, this may generate consideration of the fundamental purposes of the institution, such as: What does it mean to be a graduate of this institution? What constitutes an undergraduate education?

There are three primary uses for scorecards or dashboards and the measures/data they represent: to assess performance, to guide strategic planning, and to determine improvement priorities. All three of these uses rely on the comparison of information to assess change. The process of developing and implementing measures can establish a baseline for future comparisons internally within the institution, or for benchmarking. It can also be used to share the stories of the organization's successes.

The scorecard or dashboard itself is a communication mechanism that can be used to convey information efficiently and effectively to various audiences, but the value results from the balance and appropriateness of the measures they display. There are a number of issues to be considered in developing measures, including the scope, the intended use, the audiences, and whether the process will be centralized or decentralized. Factors to consider are:[29]

- Institution-wide criteria, while important, may not provide the best measures of academic and administrative departments, which have different roles in accomplishing the mission of the college or university
- Broad-based or generic measures may fail to capture what is unique about a particular institution, department, or program

- Qualitative information, which can be extremely valuable, is often overlooked when selecting measures because of the difficulty of measurement
- Traditional measures may not have predictive value
- Centralized control of the measurement process, while in many ways a traditional approach to academic institutional measurement, may limit engagement and ownership by the community at large
- Emphasis only on academic measures can obscure other factors that are important to various stakeholders

Developing Scorecard or Dashboard Measures

The process of developing a scorecard or dashboard can take place within a department or program, but is often most successful when it is done as a facilitated effort involving various individuals who meet in a workshop format or in a series of meetings. It begins with identifying the critical participants and engaging them in determining what to measure and why, how to use results, and in selecting appropriate comparisons. Measures can be developed at many levels: the institution, a campus or a department/program. Consider as an example the development of a set of dashboard measures for an administrative program that supports student success. Who will be involved? Who has the necessary information? Leaders, faculty, staff, and students all have perceptions of the mission and key indicators of success. What steps will be taken to insure that the perspectives of all of the important constituent groups have been considered? Once the participants have been identified, selecting measures for a scorecard or dashboard involves a four step process.

Step 1: Examining key concepts. Higher education, like any other field, generates many different types of data and information, and the tendency in the early stages of developing measures is to work from the information that is already being collected. For example, a program might already count the number of students who use their services on an ongoing basis, but it should not be assumed that this data belongs in the dashboard simply because it is readily available. The process of identifying the measures for the dashboard should actually begin with asking a set of questions to establish a context for the information:

- What is our mission/vision? What are the goals we are trying to accomplish?
- What is important to our key stakeholders?
- What are our most important programs and services?

- For whom do we provide them?
- How do we judge our success?
- How do we know if we are making progress toward our goals?
- What information do we need to tell the story of this institution/ program? The last question takes into account the fact that success will be defined not only by those within a program, but by others outside the institution whose support is critical to its success, and who may have different definitions of success. Parents, for example, may consider their student's satisfaction with residence life as important as academic success in judging the quality of the educational experience.

Step 2: Selecting measures. Based on the information obtained by examining these key concepts, the participants in this process can begin to identify the measures that will advance their understanding of the accomplishment of the mission and goals of the program. There is no hard and fast rule as to how many measures should be used, but they must be sufficient to answer the question of whether, how, and how much progress is being made. A variety of measures can be considered and those selected should reflect four categories: activity (a quantitative reflection of the work accomplished), quality (an assessment by staff, faculty, students or other stakeholders as to the quality of the services provided), benefit and satisfaction (an assessment by stakeholders of their satisfaction with the services provided), and impact (the effectiveness in advancing the core mission or vision).[30] For example, a student leadership program might address the categories of measures in the following way:

- *Activity.* The number of students each semester participating in the student leadership program.
- *Quality.* An assessment by faculty members of the quality of coursework for the leadership program.
- *Benefit and Satisfaction.* The level of satisfaction expressed by the students who participate.
- *Impact.* The degree to which the leadership knowledge of the students increases after participation in the leadership program and its activities, and/or an assessment of their competence in student leadership roles.

The measures selected must be aligned with the larger mission of the institution, department, or program.

Step 3: Establishing a plan for collecting data. Determining how to collect data and the extent of data collection is largely a matter of balancing
benefits and resources. The concept is to collect the information you
need to assess the measure selected, but not to make it so burdensome a
process that it doesn't happen, or that it costs more (in time, effort, or
dollars) than the value it brings to the measurement process. The first
step is to examine what data the program already has. It is very likely
that much of the information that can be of use already exists, although
it may not be available or compiled in the manner called for by those
who selected the particular measure. Some examples to consider as data
sources are organizational self-studies, benchmarking, interviews/focus
groups, and student/faculty/staff surveys.[31] There may, however, be data
which do not currently exist. The question becomes how best to collect and how to maximize the value of the data while minimizing the
disruptive nature of collection. For example, several different programs
within a department may wish to collect information about satisfaction
and breadth of experience from graduating students. In such a case, a
consolidated survey of graduates with questions from multiple departments is more likely to produce results than are multiple surveys sent to
the same individuals.

Step 4: Reviewing and disseminating the information. Once data to support the selected measures have been collected and reviewed, the next
questions are how to disseminate the information and who are the key audiences that need to have and use the information. While information and
data of measures can be displayed or disseminated in a number of formats,
the purpose of a scorecard or dashboard is to present the information in
a visual format that can be easily understood by various stakeholders (see
Figure 10.1 for an example).

Higher education institutions increasingly recognize the role that various internal and external stakeholders play in their support and success. The
use of dashboards and scorecards to serve as a framework for constructing
measures, collecting data, and conveying information is one of the tools
that can be adapted from business to fit the needs of the academy.

Strategic Planning

The second tool that can be used to implement the above mentioned six
themes is strategic planning. Leading businesses recognize that planning
is fundamental to the success of the organization. Strategic plans form
the basis for where the company, and, likewise, higher education, puts its
energies and resources, and focus attention on the measures for assessing
its outcomes and achievements.

Figure 10.1 Higher Education Dashboard Examples

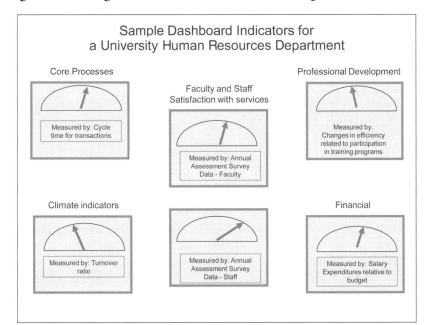

While we would all agree with Yogi Berra that "prediction is difficult, especially about the future," we recognize the need to look ahead and determine what is important and necessary to the success of our organizations. Understanding what makes planning strategic as opposed to nonstrategic is important to the success of the planning effort. *Strategic* planning—focusing on determining and guiding outcomes rather than falling victim to the myriad of external forces that bombard organizations on a daily basis (reactions to which result in ad hoc or activity-based planning)—is critical.[32]

Strategic planning requires a shift in thinking; moving away from approaches to planning that can result in the creation of documents that simply take up space on a shelf, to a focus on a process and plans that are relevant, useful, and actively used in advancing the purposes of the organization.[33] It is useful to think of strategic planning as a systematic effort for anticipating and coordinating change; a way of identifying and addressing priorities to help an organization fulfill its mission and anticipate, predict, and ideally control future activities or outcomes.

This involves being concise about what we are trying to accomplish, clear in the approaches selected, and rigorous in efforts to assess results; and, above all, dedicated to trying to extract more generalized lessons from the experiences. It also involves taking account of organizational capacity, history and resource considerations.

The Process of Planning

While the ultimate goal of strategic planning is organizational improvement and change, it is important to recognize that the *process of planning* is as important as, if not more important than, *the plan itself.* Planning efforts can fail to achieve their intended outcomes for any number of reasons. In most cases, failures can be traced, at least in part, to shortcomings in the manner in which a plan was developed and implemented. Plans that may be quite impressive on paper, may well fail to achieve the goals if their designers overlooked key external or internal factors, did not consult widely enough with those with pertinent insight and expertise, failed to create buy-in for the project, did not fully integrate assessment into each phase of the planning process, or were imprecise in defining critical leadership roles and responsibilities—in short, if they failed to attend sufficiently to *process* issues.[34]

As planning generally involves a group or organization, the way the leadership and communication processes are handled is as important as the substance and specifics of the plan. Inclusive planning efforts are generally more successful than those undertaken by a small, exclusive group, and generally have longer lasting effects on plan implementation and the culture itself.[35] Issues of process, then, have to do with being thoughtful and strategic in deciding which individuals and groups will be involved in the initiative at given points in time, precisely what they should be asked to do, when and how each activity in the planning sequence will occur, how communication will be designed into each phase of development and implementation, and who will provide oversight and monitor follow-up.

Most organizations recognize the value of strategic planning; their hesitation to embark on a strategic planning process may be more tied to not knowing where to begin. Many are familiar with the annual planning process that allows for review and recognition of the previous year's accomplishments as well as determination of future priorities. But, other ways to begin the planning process exist as well. One way to increase the likelihood that rigorous planning will take place is to align it with the current activities of the department, either as part of a larger change initiative, in preparation for a formal review (internal or external), or as a complement to a formal assessment process such as the *Excellence in Higher Education* framework.[36]

A Structured Approach to Planning

The Strategic Planning in Higher Education Framework,[37] designed specifically for higher education, provides a blueprint for a comprehensive

Figure 10.2 Strategic Planning in Higher Education Model

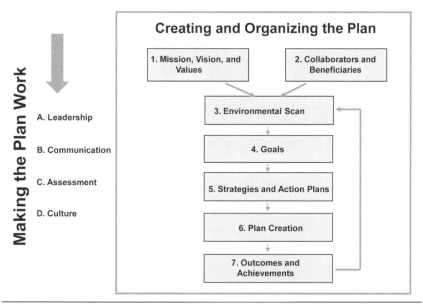

Source: S. A. Tromp and B. D. Ruben, *Strategic Planning in Higher Education* (SPHE) (Washington, DC: National Association of College and University Business Officers, 2004), 7.

planning approach, consisting of seven major planning phases for creating and organizing the plan (See Figure 10.2).

- *Mission, Vision, and Values*—reviewing the organization's guiding principles as a useful reference point
- *Collaborators and Beneficiaries*—identifying critical stakeholders with particular attention to their expectations for the plan's development and implementation
- *Environmental Scan*—examining cultural issues, resource concerns, and other factors that may impinge on the planning process
- *Goals*—identifying an organization's aspirations in tangible, achievable, and measurable terms
- *Strategies and Action Plans*—translating goals into a series of concrete strategies and activities with appropriate timeframes and identified areas of responsibility
- *Plan Creation*—describing goals and strategies in a manner that is comprehensive, yet easily understood
- *Outcomes and Achievements*—monitoring progress and, most importantly, evaluating outcomes

These planning phases are linked by four crosscutting imperatives for making the plan work (See Figure 10.1):

- *Leadership*—how the individual—or individuals—with responsibility for the planning process guides the organization in the development and implementation of plans and goals that advance its mission, vision, and values; engaging, enabling, and facilitating change; motivating colleagues at all levels of the organization; encouraging the development of a culture that values assessment, analysis, reflection, thoughtful planning, and continuing improvement

- *Communication*—how these plans and goals are conveyed, promoted, and coordinated throughout the organization; choosing the most effective message and media; understanding preferred communication channels, styles, sources, and approaches

- *Assessment*—how progress on plans and goals is evaluated; understanding the multiple dimensions against which the planning process and plan will be evaluated; providing additional information with which to navigate the plan development and implementation

- *Culture*—how the organization's language, history, rules, traditions, and customs influence the dynamics of planning; working with and through existing customs, norms, and common practices to manage change; guiding and shaping behavior

These four imperatives overlie all phases of strategic planning and help to create a diverse leadership team with deep organizational knowledge; allow for a variety of perspectives; promote an understanding of decision making powers and boundaries; foster readiness, receptivity, and a shared sense of the need for change; and underscore the need to appreciate the history, language patterns, stories, norms, rules, traditions, customs, and preferred practices that emerge over time from—and over time come to shape—organizational behaviors and practices.[38]

While the framework can be used as an internally-led workshop or retreat, a facilitator-lead session, or as a combination of the two approaches, the preferred approach at Rutgers University and elsewhere is a facilitated daylong session involving the entire membership of a department or organization, and includes several key steps designed to engage participants and to ensure focused discussion.

Preplanning with the department leadership team. Attention is given to identifying goals/outcomes for the upcoming planning session; determining the role of leadership in the planning session; and drafting a project plan.

Pre-session web-based survey. The anonymous, confidential survey is designed to gather thoughts and ideas on departmental goals and future aspirations; as a first step in review of an existing mission, and as a way for department members to express concerns or suggestions beneficial to the planning process.

Facilitated planning session. The daylong structured session uses the Strategic Planning in Higher Education framework (Figure 10.2) to move the organization (faculty and/or staff) through a review of its mission and future aspirations; determination of priority goals and initiatives for progress toward those aspirations; definition of key strategies and projects to operationalize those goals, and action plans which define timeframe, responsibilities, and deliverables.

Follow up. Critical to this step is the role leadership plays in creating a message of importance and responsibility. The goal is to sustain the engagement and energy created during the session in order to move the organization forward and achieve the desired outcomes. Consistent communication, periodic review, and accountability are the keys to successful implementation.

Organizations that have successfully implemented strategic planning note benefits of the approach to be:

- Ability to capture attention in the midst of people and ideas competing for one's time
- Clarification of the need/case for change
- Involving appropriate individuals and constituencies in a discussion of the problem(s) and solution(s)
- Engagement of colleagues in the decision-making process
- Understanding of organizational purposes and goals
- Translation of knowledge, attitudes, and beliefs into coordinated action
- Integration and institutionalization of changes into the culture
- External validation of goals
- Oversight and coordination of outcomes

In higher education, the results of such inclusive planning processes are becoming more evident. In academic departments, outcomes include collaborative efforts of junior and more senior faculty in curriculum development and changes to faculty hiring processes; encouragement of interdisciplinary research and grant writing; and attention to outreach, service, and lifelong learning. In administrative areas, collaborative approaches to cross-department training in student services, broad involvement in new student orientation planning, and the redesign of organizations, processes and services are but a few examples of the value of a structured, comprehensive, and strategic planning process.

Baldrige-based Organizational Assessment

The Malcolm Baldrige National Quality Award program (MBNQA) was established in 1987 by Congress through passage of Public Law 100–107 to promote U.S. business effectiveness for the advancement of the national economy.[39] Named after Secretary of Commerce Malcolm Baldrige, who served from 1981 until his death in 1987, the intent of the program created by this legislation is to provide a systems approach for organizational assessment, recognition and improvement. The program, which is administered by the National Institute for Standards and Technology (NIST), has also been an influential contributor in national and international efforts to identify and encourage the application of core principles of organizational excellence.

Essentially, the goals of the Baldrige program are to:

- Identify the essential components of organizational excellence
- Recognize organizations that demonstrate these characteristics
- Promote information sharing by exemplary organizations
- Encourage the adoption of effective organizational principles and practices

The recognition aspects of the Baldrige program are well known, but its more fundamental contributions are those related to research, communication, and education. In these respects, the Baldrige program has done a great deal to articulate standards of organizational excellence that transcend particular types of organizations and sectors, and to facilitate dialogue on how principles and practices from one organizational context can be applied in others. The Baldrige process also emphasizes an integrated approach to assessment, planning, and improvement that has been most valuable.

The Baldrige framework covers seven categories. Although the language and definitions used to describe the framework have changed over the years, and vary somewhat from sector to sector, the seven basic themes are constant. In general terms, the framework suggests that organizational excellence requires:

1. Effective *leadership* that provides guidance and ensures a clear and shared sense of organizational mission and future vision, a commitment to continuous review and improvement of leadership practice, and social and environmental consciousness.

2. An inclusive *planning process* and coherent plans that translate the organization's mission, vision, and values into clear, aggressive, and measurable goals that are understood and effectively implemented throughout the organization.

3. *Knowledge of the needs, expectations, and satisfaction/dissatisfaction levels of the groups served by the organization*; operating practices that are responsive to these needs and expectations; and assessment processes in place to stay current with and anticipate the thinking of these groups.

4. Development and use of *indicators of organizational performance* that capture the organization's mission, vision, values, goals, and provide data-based comparisons with peer and leading organizations; widely sharing this and other information within the organization to focus and motivate improvement.

5. A *workplace culture* that encourages, recognizes, and rewards excellence, employee satisfaction, engagement, professional development, commitment, and pride; and synchronizes individual and organizational goals.

6. *Focus on mission-critical and support programs and services,* and associated work processes to ensure effectiveness, efficiency, appropriate standardization and documentation, and regular evaluation and improvement—with the needs and expectations of beneficiaries and stakeholders in mind.

7. *Documented, sustained positive outcomes* relative to organizational mission, vision, goals, the perspectives of groups served, and employees, considered in light of comparisons with the accomplishments of peers, competitors, and leaders.[40]

The Baldrige model has been an extremely popular framework for organizational self-assessment in many settings. In addition to the more than 1,000 organizations that have applied for Baldrige review and recognition,[41] NIST estimates that thousands of organizations have used the criteria for self-assessment. It is also evidence that, from a financial perspective, MBNQA winning organizations outperform other organizations. Przasnyski and Tai's analysis demonstrates that organizations that have been recognized as leaders by Baldrige perform well in the marketplace and, specifically, that "companies derive the most benefit, through evaluating and responding to the [Baldrige] guidelines." And there is evidence that these organizations excel in both growth and profits. Further evidence suggests that the Baldrige model provides a valuable gauge of organizational effectiveness. A study by the Government Accounting Office of 20 companies that scored high in the Baldrige process found these results corresponded with increased job satisfaction, improved attendance, reduced turnover, improved quality, reduced cost, increased reliability, increased on-time delivery, fewer errors, reduced lead time (customers), improved satisfaction, fewer complaints, higher customer retention rates (profitability), improved market share, and improved financial indicators.[42] In sum, there is a good deal of evidence to suggest that organizations scoring well on Baldrige standards are more successful than others, providing support for assertions that the Baldrige criteria provide a standard of excellence to which organizations can and should aspire.

Baldrige in Higher Education

The Baldrige framework has been adopted, adapted, and used for assessment in any number of settings in business, and in 1999, the National Baldrige program advanced versions of the framework for healthcare and education. The education criteria[43] were intended to be broadly applicable to school and educational settings—public, private or corporate—at all levels. Since its introduction, approximately 150 applications have been submitted from higher education departments or institutions to the national program.[44] Three applicants have been selected as winners of the award—the University of Wisconsin-Stout in 2001, the University of Northern Colorado School of Business in 2004, and Richland College in 2005. There have been a number of college and university applications to state programs that parallel the Baldrige, and several winners, including the University of Missouri-Rolla in 1995 and Iowa State University in 2004.

Beyond higher education institutions' direct participation in the formal national and state awards programs, the influence of the framework in higher education has been most apparent in the evolution of accrediting standards of professional and technical education, and more recently in regional accreditation. In business, engineering, healthcare, and education, the standards for accreditation of college and university programs have come to mirror the Baldrige framework in many respects. The regional accrediting associations, perhaps most notably the North Central Association of Schools and Colleges, the Middle States Association of Schools and Colleges, Western Association of Schools and Colleges, and the Southern Association of Schools and Colleges emphasize issues that are central to the Baldrige framework, such as leadership, strategic planning, assessment, and continuous improvement.[45]

The Excellence in Higher Education Framework

The *Excellence in Higher Education* (EHE) model was developed at Rutgers University as an adaptation of the Baldrige designed specifically for use within colleges and universities. The current version[46] is the 18th revision of the framework. EHE was designed specifically for higher education institutions, where the mission typically includes an emphasis on teaching/learning, scholarship/research and public service/outreach. Additionally, the EHE model was designed to be applicable for use in assessment and planning activities not only by entire institutions, but also by individual units of all kinds within colleges and universities—business, student services and administration, as well as academic.

The latest version of *Excellence in Higher Education* was developed to provide an integrated approach to assessment, planning, and improvement, drawing on the framework of the Malcolm Baldrige Program of the National Institute of Standards and Technology (NIST) as well as on standards and language developed by U.S. college and university accrediting associations. Together the Baldrige criteria and those developed by the regional accreditation organizations offer the best available standards of excellence for higher education, and it is the goal of this edition of EHE to provide a synthesis of the perspectives and language of those robust frameworks.

The EHE Categories

The EHE framework consists of 7 categories or themes that are viewed as relevant to the effectiveness of any educational enterprise—program, department, school, college or university. The categories are seen as components of an interrelated system, as shown in Figure 10.3, and described below:

Category 1—Leadership. Category 1 considers leadership approaches and governance systems used to guide the institution, department, or program; how leaders and leadership practices encourage excellence, innovation, and attention to the needs of individuals, groups, and/or organizations that benefit from the programs and services of the institution, department, or program; and how leadership practices are reviewed and improved.

Category 2—Plans and Purposes. The strategic planning category considers how the mission, vision, and values of the institution,

THE BUSINESS OF HIGHER EDUCATION

school, department, or program are developed and communicated; how they are translated into goals and plans; and how faculty and staff are engaged in those activities. Also considered are the ways in which goals and plans are translated into action and coordinated throughout the organization.

Category 3—Beneficiaries and Constituencies. The beneficiaries and constituencies category focuses on the groups that benefit from the programs and services offered by the program, department, or institution being reviewed. The category asks how the organization learns about the needs, perceptions, and priorities of those groups, and how that information is used to enhance the organization's reputation and working relationships with those constituencies.

Category 4—Programs and Services. Category 4 focuses on the programs and services offered by the institution, department, or program under review and how their effectiveness is maintained and enhanced. The most important operational and support services are also reviewed.

Category 5—Faculty/Staff and Workplace. Category 5 considers how the program, department, or institution being reviewed recruits and retains faculty and staff, encourages excellence and engagement, creates and maintains a positive workplace culture and climate, and promotes and facilitates personal and professional development.

Category 6—Assessment and Information Use. The assessment and information use category focuses on how the program, department, or institution assesses the effectiveness of its institutional, teaching/learning, research/scholarship, and/or service/outreach efforts relative to its mission and aspirations. Also considered is how assessment information is used for improving programs and services, day-to-day decision making, and the quality of the program, department, or institution, more generally.

Category 7—Outcomes and Achievements. Reporting outcomes and achievements is the theme of Category 7. The category asks for information and evidence to document or demonstrate the quality and effectiveness of the program, department, or institution.

The EHE Process

The most usual context for using the EHE program at Rutgers and elsewhere is a retreat or workshop. Typically, the workshop lasts one and a half days. The workshop approach has the advantage of focusing the

Figure 10.3 The Excellence in Higher Education Framework

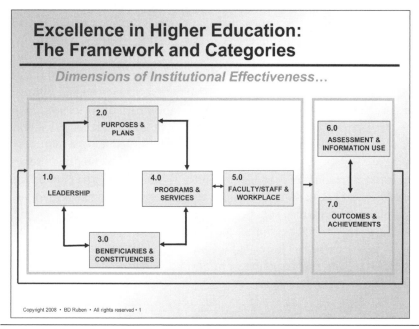

Reprinted with permission from *Excellence in Higher Education: An Integrated Approach to Assessment, Planning, and Improvement in Colleges and Universities*, by Brent D. Ruben. Washington, DC: National Association of College and University Business Officers, 2007.

group with an intensity that is difficult to achieve through other methods. That model is not viable in some situations and with some groups, and there are many other ways in which the program can be implemented. For example, it can be presented in three half-day sessions, or each category can become the focus of a series of one or two-hour sessions.

Each EHE workshop consists of a step-by-step organizational assessment process, moving through the 7 categories one at a time. For each category, the process includes:[47]

- Discussing the basic themes and standards for the category
- Brainstorming a list of strengths and areas for improvement for the unit with respect to the category
- Reviewing best practices in the category as practiced by leading organizations
- Scoring the unit in the category on a 0 to 100 percent scale to capture perceptions of the extent to which the unit is fulfilling the standards of the category

The scoring for each category is conducted anonymously and the ratings are displayed, and the distribution of scores is discussed. The mean rating for the group is then calculated and entered on a chart, which is also displayed and discussed after each category, and again at the conclusion of all categories.

Once these steps have been taken for all seven categories, the list of areas of strength and those in need of improvement are reviewed and discussed further. Next, multivoting is employed to rank-order the priority areas for improvement in terms of importance, and potential impact and feasibility. Improvement goals and strategies are then established for the highest priority areas—generally the four to six areas perceived to be most pressing and important. Finally, participants in break-out groups develop preliminary plans for addressing each of the priority areas for improvement. The preliminary plan includes: a sentence summary of what needs to be done, a list of key steps, identification of the individuals or roles that should be involved in the project, a proposed team leader, a project timeline, estimate of resources, and identification of important outcomes.[48]

CONCLUSION: PRACTICING WHAT WE TEACH

The foregoing section has provided brief profiles of six themes and three leading strategies that have their origins in business, but which have substantial value in healthcare, the public sector, and higher education.

We offer these insights and strategies, in the belief that if higher education were open to seeing ourselves as organizations—in the most general sense—we could more effectively benefit from business and other sectors.

We believe, further, that to be the leading institutions we aspire to be, we need to get better about learning from others. Indeed, our openness to cross-sector analogies and receptivity to new ideas can only enhance our leadership and adaptability as individuals and organizations—the very things we say we value and advocate for others. Ultimately, if we fail to do this, it also makes it very difficult to claim that we are master teachers, master learners, or master designers of world class learning organizations.

NOTES

1. A phrase which purportedly has its origin at Columbia University in 1948, when General Dwight Eisenhower was first introduced as the new university president of the University to the assembled faculty. He began by remarking how pleased he was to meet with the "employees" of Columbia. Professor I. I. Rabi, distinguished senior faculty member and future Nobel Prize winner, rose and said, "Sir, the faculty are not the

employees of Columbia University, the faculty is Columbia University."
G. D. O'Brien, *All the Essential Half-Truths about Higher Education* (Chicago, IL: University of Chicago Press, 1998): 15.

2. W. F. Massy, *Honoring the Trust* (Bolton, MA: Anker, 2003); F. H. Rhodes, *The Creation of the Future: The Role of the American University* (Ithaca, NY: Cornell University Press, 2001); B. D. Ruben, *Pursuing Excellence in Higher Education: Eight Fundamental Challenges* (San Francisco: Jossey-Bass, 2004); Wingspread Group on Higher Education, *An American Imperative: Higher Expectations for Higher Education* (Racine, WI: Johnson Foundation, 1993).

3. Spellings Commission, *A National Dialogue: The Secretary of Education's Commission on the Future of Higher Education, 2006,* http://www.ed.gov/about/bdscomm/list/hiedfuture/index.html.

4. Ibid.

5. Middle States Commission on Higher Education, *Characteristics of Excellence in Higher Education: Eligibility Requirements and Standards for Accreditation* (Philadelphia: Middle States Commission on Higher Education, 2004); New England Association of Schools and Colleges Commission on Institutions of Higher Education Standards for Accreditation, 2005, http://cihe.neasc.org/standards_policies/standards/standards_html_version; North Central Association of Colleges and Universities: The Higher Learning Commission's *Academic Quality Improvement Project* (July, 2005), http://AQIP.org.; Northwest Commission on Colleges and Universities, *Accreditation Standards* (Redmond, WA, 2004); Southern Association of Colleges and Schools Commission on Colleges, *Handbook for Reaffirmation of Accreditation* (Decatur, GA: Commission on Colleges, 2003), www.sacscoc.org/principles.asp; Western Association of Schools and Colleges, *Handbook of Accreditation* (2008), http://www.wascsenior.org/findit/files/forms/Handbook of Accreditation July 2008.pdf.

6. B. D. Ruben, *Excellence in Higher Education Guide: An Integrated Approach to Assessment, Planning and Improvement in Colleges and Universities* (Washington, DC: National Association of College and University Business Officers, 2007).

7. B. D. Ruben, *Pursuing Excellence in Higher Education: Eight Fundamental Challenges* (San Francisco: Jossey-Bass, 2004).

8. K. Immordino, *Organizational Assessment and Improvement in Public Sector* (New York: Taylor and Francis, 2009).

9. In this area higher education can be seen as serving as a model for corporations, where growing attention is being devoted to what the business community refers to by the acronym CSR—corporate social responsibility. In any event, the goal of creating lifelong bonds with the constituencies and communities which a sector or organization serves

and upon which it depends is certainly not antithetical to the business model.

10. Baldrige National Quality Program, 2009. *2009–2010 Education criteria for performance excellence*. http://baldrige.nist.gov/Education Criteria.htm.

11. Ruben *Excellence in Higher Education Guides*; B. D. Ruben, *Excellence in Higher Education: Workbook and Scoring Instructions*. (Washington, DC: National Association of College and University Business Officers, 2009).

12. American Productivity and Quality Center, *What is Benchmarking?* (1999), www.apqc.org; D. DeVito and S. Morrison, "Benchmarking: A Tool for Sharing and Cooperation," *The Journal for Quality & Participation* (Fall, 2000): 56–61; M. L. Doerfel and B. D. Ruben, "Benchmarking in Higher Education: Becoming More Adaptive, Innovative and Interactive Organizations." in *Benchmarking in Higher Education*, ed. J. Schuh and B. Bender (San Francisco: Jossey-Bass, 2007): 5–26; N. Jackson and H. Lund, eds. "Benchmarking for Higher Education," (Buckingham, England: The Society for Research into Higher Education and Open University Press, 2000).

13. R. S. Schuler, *Managing Human Resources,* 6th ed. (Cincinnati, OH: Southwestern College Publications, 1998): 40.

14. N. A. Dewan, A. Daniels, G. Zieman, and T. Kramer, "The National Outcomes Management Project: A Benchmarking Collaborative," *Journal of Behavioral Health Services and Research* 27 (2000): 431–36.

15. J. I. Sanchez, E. Kraus, S. White, and M. Williams, "Adopting High Involvement Human Resources Practices: The Mediating Role of Benchmarking," *Group and Organization Management* 24 (1999): 461–78.

16. J. Schuh and B. Bender, *Benchmarking in Higher Education*.

17. N. Dopuch and M. Gupta, "Estimation of Benchmarking Performance Standards: An Application to Public School Expenditures," *Journal of Accounting and Economics* 23 (1997): 141–61; M. D. Troutt, D. W. Gribbin, M. Shanker, and A. Zhang, "Cost Efficiency Benchmarking for Operational Units with Multiple Cost Drivers," *Decision Sciences* 31 (2000): 813–32.

18. J. Fitz-enz, "The Truth about 'Best Practice'," *Human Resource Planning* 16 (1993): 19–26; C. O. Longenecker, T. C. Stansfield, and D. J. Dwyer, "The Human Side of Manufacturing Improvement," *Business Horizons,* 40 (1997): 7–17. J. I. Sanchez, E. Kraus, S. White, and M. Williams, "Adopting High Involvement Human Resources Practices: The Mediating Role of Benchmarking," *Group and Organization Management* 24 (1999): 461–78.

19. M. L. Upcraft and J. H. Schuh, eds. *Assessment in Student Affairs: A Guide for Practitioners* (San Francisco: Jossey-Bass, 1996).

20. Ruben, *Pursuing Excellence in Higher Education*.

21. Ruben, *Pursuing Excellence in Higher Education*; B. D. Ruben, "Departmental Effectiveness: What Is It? Why Is It Important? How Can It Be Achieved?" *Effective Practices for Academic Leaders* 1, no. 12 (2006). Abstracted and discussed in R. Reis, "Managing a Career Versus Managing a Program or Department," no. 782; tomorrows-professor@lists.stanford.edu, March 9, 2007.

22. B. D. Ruben, *Understanding, Planning, and Leading Organizational Change*: Core Concepts and Strategies (Washington, DC: National Association of College and University Business Officers, 2009).

23. Ruben, *Pursuing Excellence in Higher Education*.

24. C. K. Brancato, *New Corporate Performance Measures* (New York: The Conference Board, 1995).

25. R. S. Kaplan and D. P. Norton, "The Balanced Scorecard: Measures that Drive Performance," *Harvard Business Review*, Jan.-Feb. 1992; R. S. Kaplan and D. P. Norton, "Putting the Balanced Scorecard to Work," *Harvard Business Review*, Sept. 1993; R. S. Kaplan and D. P. Norton. *The Balanced Scorecard* (Cambridge, MA: Harvard Business School Press, Oct. 1996); R. S. Kaplan and D. P. Norton, *Execution Premium: Linking Strategy to Operations for Competitive Advantage* (Cambridge, MA: Harvard Business School Press, 2008).

26. R. S. Kaplan, and D. P. Norton, *The Balanced Scorecard* (Cambridge, MA: Harvard Business School, 1996).

27. C. K. Brancato, *New Corporate Performance Measures* (New York: The Conference Board, 1995), 42.

28. University Center for Organizational Development and Leadership, *Organizational Outcomes and Performance Measurement: Assessing Institution, Department, and Program Effectiveness*. CD ROM, (Washington, DC: National Association of College and University Business Officers, 2008).

29. Ibid.

30. S. Tromp and B. D. Ruben, *Strategic Planning in Higher Education: A Leader's Guide* (Washington, DC: National Association of College and University Business Officers, 2004).

31. University Center for Organizational Development and Leadership, *Organizational Outcomes and Performance Measurement: Assessing Institution, Department, and Program Effectiveness*.

32. G. Keller, *Academic Strategy: The Management Revolution in American Higher Education* (Baltimore, MD: The Johns Hopkins University Press, 1983).

33. Ibid.

34. S. Tromp and B. D. Ruben, *Strategic Planning in Higher Education*.

35. J. P. Kotter, "Leading Change," *Harvard Business Review,* March-April, 1995.

36. B. D. Ruben, *Excellence in Higher Education Guide: An Integrated Approach to Assessment, Planning and Improvement in Colleges and Universities* (Washington, DC: National Association of College and University Business Officers, 2007); B. D. Ruben, "Higher Education Assessment: Linking Accreditation Standards and the Malcolm Baldrige Criteria." In *New Directions for Higher Education,* ed. Susan C. White and Theodore S. Glickman, New York: Wiley, vol. 137 (Spring): 59–83.

37. Tromp and Ruben, *Strategic Planning in Higher Education*.

38. B. D. Ruben and L. A. Stewart, *Communication and Human Behavior,* 5th ed. (Boston, MA: Allyn-Bacon, 2005).

39. Baldrige National Quality Program. *2009–2010 Education criteria for performance excellence,* 2009. http://baldrige.nist.gov/Education Criteria.htm.

40. Ruben, *Pursuing Excellence in Higher Education*.

41. Baldrige National Quality Program, *2009–2010 Education criteria for performance excellence*.

42. M. S. Heaphy and G. F. Gruska, *The Malcolm Baldrige National Quality Award: A Yardstick for Quality Growth* (Reading, MA: Addison-Wesley Publishing Company, 1995).

43. Baldrige National Quality Program, *2009–2010 Education criteria for performance excellence*.

44. This number, provided by the Baldrige National Quality Office in February 2006, includes some repetitive submissions.

45. See the Middle States Association of Schools and Colleges (www.msache.org); the New England Association of Schools and Colleges (www.neasc.org/cihe.htm); the North Central Association of Schools and Colleges (www.ncahigherlearningcommission.org); the Northwest Association of Schools and Colleges (www.nwccu.org); the Southern Association of Schools and Colleges (www.sacscoc.org), and the Western Association of Schools and Colleges (www.wascweb.org). With a foundation of Baldrige concepts, the NCA has created an alternative to the accreditation model called the Academic Quality Improvement Program in which some 200 are presently participating (AQIP, 2005).

46. Ruben, *Excellence in Higher Education Guide: An integrated approach*; Ruben, *Excellence in Higher Education: Workbook and Scoring Instructions*; Ruben, *Excellence in Higher Education: Facilitator's Guide*.

47. Ruben, *Understanding, Planning, and Leading Organizational change*.

48. Ruben, *Excellence in Higher Education guide*; Ruben, *Excellence in Higher Education: Workbook and Scoring Instructions*.

REFERENCES AND SUGGESTED READINGS

American Productivity and Quality Center. 1999. *What is benchmarking?*, www.apqc.org.

Baldrige National Quality Program. 2009. www.quality.nist.gov, February.

Baldrige National Quality Program. 2009. *2009–2010 Education criteria for performance excellence.* http://baldrige.nist.gov/EducationCriteria.htm.

Bennis, W. G. 1997. *Managing people is like herding cats.* Provo, Utah: Executive Excellence Publishing.

Brancato, C. K. 1995. *New corporate performance measures.* New York: The Conference Board.

DeVito, D. and S. Morrison. 2000. "Benchmarking: A tool for sharing and cooperation." *The Journal for Quality & Participation* (Fall): 56–61.

Dewan, N. A., A. Daniels., G. Zieman., and T. Kramer. 2000. "The national outcomes management project: A benchmarking collaborative." *Journal of Behavioral Health Services and Research* 27: 431–36.

Doerfel, M. L., and B. D. Ruben. 2002. "Benchmarking in higher education: Becoming more adaptive, innovative and interactive organizations." In *Benchmarking in higher education,* ed. J. Schuh and B. Bender. San Francisco: Jossey-Bass, 5–26.

Dopuch, N. and M. Gupta. 1997. "Estimation of benchmarking performance standards: An application to public school expenditures." *Journal of Accounting and Economics* 23: 141–161.

Fitz-enz, J. 1993. "The truth about 'Best Practice'." *Human Resource Planning* 16: 19–26.

Fogg, C. Davis. 1994. *Team-based strategic planning: A complete guide to structuring, facilitating and implementing the process.* New York: American Management Association.

Frank, R. H. 2000. "Higher education: The ultimate winner-take-all market?" In *Forum futures: Exploring the future of higher education,* ed. M. E. Devlin and J. W. Meyerson. San Francisco: Jossey-Bass, 1–12.

Glanz, E. E. and L. K. Daily. 1992. "Benchmarking." *Human Resource Management* 31:9–20.

Heaphy, M. S. and G. F. Gruska. 1995. *The Malcolm Baldrige National Quality Award: A yardstick for quality growth.* Reading, MA: Addison-Wesley Publishing Company.

Immordino, K. In press. *Organizational assessment and improvement in public sector.* New York: Taylor and Francis.

Jackson, N. and H. Lund (eds.). 2000. "Benchmarking for higher education." Buckingham, England: The Society for Research into Higher Education and Open University Press.

Johnson, R. and D. Seymour. 1996. "The Baldrige as an award and assessment instrument for higher education." In *High performing colleges I: Theory and concepts,* ed. D. Deymour Maryville, MO: Prescott, 54–71.

Kaplan, R. S. and D. P. Norton. 1992. "The balanced scorecard: Measures that drive performance." *Harvard Business Review* (January-February).

Kaplan, R. S. and D. P. Norton. 1993. "Putting the balanced scorecard to work." *Harvard Business Review* (September).

Kaplan, R. S. and D. P. Norton. 1996. *The balanced scorecard.* Cambridge, MA: Harvard Business School (October).

Kaplan, R. S. and D. P. Norton. 2008. *Execution premium: Linking strategy to operations for competitive advantage.* Cambridge, MA: Harvard Business School Press.

Keller, G. 1983. *Academic strategy: The management revolution in American higher education.* Baltimore, MD: Johns Hopkins University Press.

Kellogg Commission. 1996. "Taking charge of change: Renewing the promise of state and land-grant universities." Washington, DC: National Association of State Universities and Land-Grant Colleges. http://www.nasulgc.org/Kellogg/kellogg.htm.

Kellogg Commission. 2002. "Leadership for institutional change initiative." http://www.leadershiponlinewkkf.org/; http://cuinfo.cornell.edu/LINC; http://www.fspe.org/linc.

King, R. and H. Schlicksupp. 1998. *The idea edge: Transforming creative thought into organizational excellence.* Salem, New Hampshire: Goal/QPC.

Kotter, J. P. 1995. "Leading change," *Harvard Business Review* (March-April).

Lawrence, F. L. and C. H. Cermak. 2004. "Advancing academic excellence and collaboration through strategic planning." In *Pursuing excellence in higher education: Eight fundamental challenges,* ed. B. D. Ruben. San Francisco: Jossey-Bass.

Massy, W. F. 2003. *Honoring the trust.* Bolton, MA: Anker.

Middle States Commission on Higher Education. 2004. *Characteristics of excellence in higher education: Eligibility requirements and standards for accreditation.* Philadelphia: Middle States Commission on Higher Education.

Morling, P. and S. Tanner. 2000. "Benchmarking a public service business management system." *Total Quality Management* 11:417–26.

Munitz, B. 1995. "New Leadership for Higher Education." *California State University Information Bulletin* 52, 15. Adapted from B. Munitz. *Planning for higher education.* Society for College and University Planning, Ann Arbor.

National Academy of Engineering and Institute of Medicine of the National Academies. 2007. *Rising Above the Gathering Storm.* Washington, DC: National Academies Press.

National Association of State Universities and Land-Grant Colleges (NASULGC). 2001. *Shaping the future: The economic impact of public universities.* Washington, DC: National Association of State Universities and Land-Grant Colleges.

National Commission on Excellence in Education. 1984. *A Nation at Risk.* Portland, Oregon: USA Research.

New England Association of Schools and Colleges Commission on Institutions of Higher Education Standards for Accreditation. 2005. http://cihe.neasc.org/standards_policies/standards/standards_html_version.

Newman, F. and L. K. Couturier. 2001. "The new competitive arena: Market forces invade the academy." *Change* 33, 5 (September/October): 10–17.

North Central Association of Colleges and Universities. The Higher Learning Commission. July, 2004. Higher Learning Commission's *Academic quality improvement project.* http://AQIP.org.

Northwest Commission on Colleges and Universities. 2004. *Accreditation Standards.* Redmond, WA.

O'Brien, G. D. 1998. *All the essential half-truths about higher education.* Chicago, IL: University of Chicago Press.

Paris, Kathleen A. 2002. *Strategic planning in the university.* Madison, WI: University of Wisconsin-Madison. www.wisc.edu/improve/strplan/struniv.html.

Przasnyski, Z. and L. S. Tai. 2002. "Stock performance of Malcolm Baldrige National Quality Award-winning companies." *Total Quality Management* 13, 4:475–88.

Rhodes, F. H. 2001. *The creation of the future: The role of the American university.* Ithaca, NY: Cornell University Press.

Ruben, B. D. 2004. *Pursuing excellence in higher education: Eight fundamental challenges.* San Francisco: Jossey-Bass.

Ruben, B. D. and L. A. Stewart. 2005. *Communication and human behavior.* 5th edition. Boston, MA: Allyn-Bacon.

Ruben, B. D. 2006. *What leaders need to know and do: A leadership competencies scorecard.* Washington, DC: National Association of College and University Business Officers.

Ruben, B. D. 2007. *Excellence in higher education guide: An integrated approach to assessment, planning and improvement in colleges and universities.* Washington, DC: National Association of College and University Business Officers.

Ruben, B. D. 2007. "Higher education assessment: Linking accreditation standards and the Malcolm Baldrige criteria." In *New Directions for Higher Education,* ed. Susan C. White and Theodore S. Glickman, vol. l, 137, (Spring) 59–83. New York: Wiley.

Ruben, B. D., T. Russ, S. M. Smulowitz, and S. L. Connaughton. 2007. "Evaluating the impact of organizational self-assessment in higher education: The Malcolm Baldrige/excellence in higher education framework." *Leadership and Organizational Development Journal* 28 (3).

Ruben, B. D. 2006. "Departmental effectiveness: What is it? Why is it important? How can it be achieved?" *Effective Practices for Academic Leaders* 1, 12. Abstracted and discussed in R. Reis, "Managing a career versus managing a program or department," no. 782. tomorrows-professor@ lists.stanford.edu.

Ruben, B. D., L. Lewis, L. Sandmeyer, T. Russ, S. Smulowitz, and K. Immordino. 2008. *Assessing the impact of the Spellings Commission: The message, the messenger, and the dynamics of change in higher education.* Washington, DC: National Association of College and University Business Officers. http://www.nacubo.org/documents/business_topics/fu ll%20study.pdf.

Ruben, B. D., L. Lewis, L. Sandmeyer, T. Russ, S. Smulowitz, and K. Immordino. 2008. *Assessing the impact of the Spellings Commission: The message, the messenger, and the dynamics of change in higher education: Survey Instrument and Summary of Interview Responses.* Washington, DC: National Association of College and University Business Officers. http://www.nacubo.org/documents/business_topics/spellings.pdf.

Ruben, B. D. In press. *Understanding, planning, and leading organizational change.* Washington, DC: National Association of College and University Business Officers.

Ruben, B. D. 2009. *Excellence in higher education: Workbook and scoring instructions.* Washington, DC: National Association of College and University Business Officers.

Ruben, B. D. 2009. *Excellence in higher education: Facilitator's guide.* Washington, DC: National Association of College and University Business Officers.

Sanchez, J. I., E. Kraus, S. White, and M. Williams. 1999. "Adopting high involvement human resources practices: The mediating role of benchmarking." *Group and Organization Management* 24:461–78.

Schuh, J. and B. Bender (eds.). *Benchmarking in higher education.* 2002. San Francisco: Jossey-Bass.

Schuler, R. S. 1998. *Managing human resources.* 6th ed. Cincinnati, OH: Southwestern College Publications.

Southern Association of Colleges and Schools. 2003. *Handbook for reaffirmation of accreditation.* Decatur, GA: Commission on Colleges, www. sacscoc.org/principles.asp.

Spellings Commission. 2006. *A national dialogue: The Secretary of Education's commission on the future of higher education,* http://www.ed.gov/ about/bdscomm/list/hiedfuture/index.html.

Tromp, S. and B. D. Ruben. 2004. *Strategic planning in higher education: A leader's guide.* Washington, DC: National Association of College and University Business Officers.

Troutt, M. D., D. W. Gribbin, M. Shanker, and A. Zhang. (2000). "Cost efficiency benchmarking for operational units with multiple cost drivers." *Decision Sciences* 31:813–32.

University Center for Organizational Development and Leadership. 2008. *Organizational outcomes and performance measurement: Assessing institution, department, and program effectiveness.* CD ROM. Washington, DC: National Association of College and University Business Officers.

Upcraft, M. L. and J. H. Schuh, eds. 1996. *Assessment in student affairs: A guide for practitioners.* San Francisco: Jossey-Bass.

Voss, B. 1993. "At witt's end." *The Journal of Business Strategy* 14:38.

Ward, D. and M. Cotter. 2004. "Responding to wants: Innovating to address needs." In *Pursuing excellence in higher education: Eight fundamental challenges,* ed. B. D. Ruben. San Francisco: Jossey-Bass.

Western Association of Schools and Colleges. 2008. *Handbook of accreditation, 2008,* http://www.wascsenior.org/findit/files/forms/Handbook of Accreditation July 2008.pdf.

Weinstein, L. A. 1993. *Moving a battleship with your bare hands.* Madison, WI: Magna.

Wingspread Group on Higher Education. 1993. *An American imperative: Higher expectations for higher education.* Racine WI: Johnson Foundation.

CHAPTER 11

College Costs and Cost Containment in American Higher Education

Daniel J. Hurley and Eric R. Gilbertson

The value of a truly educated person is no more to be weighed and measured than is a sonnet or a smile. The true values we seek in higher education are, at bottom, matters of faith. Why pretend that the teaching-learning enterprise lends itself to simplistic analysis?

—The late Harold L. Enarson, first president of Cleveland State University, President Emeritus of The Ohio State University

AMERICAN COMPETITIVENESS AND COLLEGE ACCESS

Rising college prices. Cost containment efforts at American colleges and universities to stem these rising prices. Hardly a subject to inspire much emotion amongst the masses except perhaps on the part of those most directly affected, namely, current or future college students and their families. But when examined from a more holistic perspective, the issue of college accessibility takes on a whole new meaning, one that can—and should—infuse a dramatic sense of urgency among policymakers, higher education leaders and, indeed, the American public.

A confluence of major forces is shaping America's fortunes and prospects in the midst of a dynamically changing world economy. Three forces—a changing economy driven by the information technology revolution, shifting labor market needs, and major demographic shifts—have placed the nation on uneasy ground. Together, these three forces, combined with many other subtler influences, comprise a sort of silent epidemic that, if not addressed, threaten to greatly undermine America's standing in today's global economy. A robust higher education system capable of producing a qualified workforce is critical to American competitiveness. Corollary to this requirement is affordable access to postsecondary education. American competitiveness and postsecondary access are inextricably linked.

This chapter begins with a closer examination of the three major forces to set a context for the ensuing discussion on college costs and the role cost containment plays in maintaining college affordability. A discussion of the trends regarding college prices and the affordability of higher education in the United States will follow, outlining both the reasons behind rising college costs and the pressures for reducing them. This will be followed by a look at what colleges and universities are doing to contain costs and to maintain accessibility to higher education. Finally, any discussion of college costs, efficiency, and productivity would not be complete without a discussion of how these objectives must be pursued in balance with the equally important goals of adhering to institutional missions, remaining true to the values unique to the academy, and ensuring that the American college degree maintains its unsurpassed reputation for high quality.

It is virtually impossible to say anything about higher education in America or American colleges and universities that is not a sweeping generalization and thus doomed to superficiality. The cohort of American institutions included under those and similar descriptors includes a dazzlingly diverse and complex array of public and private research universities, comprehensive community colleges and entrepreneurial vocational schools, religious and secular liberal arts colleges, large and small baccalaureate- and master's degree-granting regional state universities, and institutions specializing in fields as different as the visual arts and the culinary arts. There is little that makes much sense that could be said in the same breath about the University of California at Berkeley and Kirtland Community College in rural Michigan, about a University of Phoenix campus in Virginia and Defiance College in Ohio, or about Princeton University and the United States Merchant Marine Academy in Kings Point, New York. Gaining a coherent understanding of American higher education requires the dismantling of generalizations, the disaggregation of data, and the careful use of language. The ensuing discussion, therefore, comes with an acknowledgement that issues of college costs and cost containment are as far ranging as the institutions that comprise the fabric of higher education in the United States.

A NATION IN TRANSITION

A Changing Economy

No other force in recent decades has had a greater effect on the United States than the merger of information technology with all types of capital—financial, intellectual, and human—which has quickened America's transition from an economy largely steeped in manufacturing to a full-fledged knowledge economy. Domestic spending on information technology (such as computers, software, financial services, and education) surpassed that of material goods (e.g., automobiles, appliances, and industrial supplies) in the early 1990s. The United States is now predominantly a service economy fueled by the innovative application of information and advanced technological applications and processes. A significant portion and the fastest-growing segment represents workers in information services industries. An impressive correlating growth in wages has taken place for information service workers, which is not the case with workers in the material services and consumer goods manufacturing industries.

Clearly, the American economy has advanced and evolved, but so too has the rest of the developed world. The global economic playing field has been significantly leveled by effective utilization of technological and businesses processes. Writer Thomas Friedman, whose illustrations vividly demonstrate how the global economic geography is undergoing swift reorganization, persuasively articulates these innovations.[1] Internet applications, workflow software, open sourcing, offshoring, supply chaining, and insourcing have elevated the competitive standing of many less developed nations. America has much to lose—or gain—from this global restructuring.

Changing Human Capital Needs

Cheaper labor markets overseas have created a vacuum in the American economy that will largely be filled by high-skill jobs in the knowledge economy. Regional disparities in the impact of changing labor market needs are evident; for example, hundreds of thousands of relatively high-wage, low-skill manufacturing jobs have been shed in the American Midwest. Jobs associated with college-level skills and education accounted for two-thirds of the job growth between 1984 and 2000. Job growth in the United States is expected to increase in the foreseeable future, with college labor market clusters (professional, management, technical, and high-level sales) expected to generate about 46 percent of all job growth through 2014.[2]

Labor market forecasts, however, predict a dramatic shortfall in skilled workers to meet the anticipated job growth. It has been estimated that the

United States will need to produce 16 million more associate's and bachelor's degrees beyond currently expected levels if the nation is to keep pace with best-performing countries, an equivalent of 781,000 additional degrees per year through 2025 (representing an increase of 37 percent over the current pace of degree production). Only eight states and the District of Columbia are on pace to meet this ambitious goal.[3]

Jobs involving routine activities and those that are labor intensive continue to give way to occupations that demand higher levels of literacy, including digital literacy—the utilization of information technologies—and heightened analytical capacities. Labor, as traditionally defined, has given way to *human capital*, a term reflecting the complex set of assets and values that employees bring to organizations in advanced economies. Today's high-growth jobs require knowledge, flexibility, critical thinking skills, problem solving, and human relations abilities that can be broadly applied in multiple occupational contexts. Cheaper labor markets abroad have diminished America's competitiveness in a host of industries that dominated the 21st century domestic economy. The clearest way for the United States to effectively compete in the present is through its human capital assets.

Shifting Demographic Patterns

Shifting demographic patterns, unaltered, serve as a third powerful force that will play a major role in America's competitive standing and should bring issues of higher educational attainment and higher education affordability and access to the forefront of public consciousness. In short, the growth in America's domestic-born labor force is expected to remain flat, is becoming older, and when combined with predicted future immigration trends, will comprise an overall population that is less educated.

International migration accounted for about one-fifth of the nation's population growth in the 1980s, grew to about one-third in the 1990s and is expected to account for more than one-half between 2000 and 2015, according to the U.S. Census Bureau. Especially notable is the growth in the Hispanic share of the population, which is expected to grow from 14 percent in 2005 to more than 20 percent by 2030. In 1990, 46 percent of the Hispanic population aged 16 to 64 in the U.S. was foreign-born. This had increased to 57 percent by 2004, with more than half of these immigrant Hispanics lacking a high school diploma, thus severely impairing their basic English literacy skills.[4]

A bimodal distribution of immigrants is apparent, with tens of thousands of highly skilled professionals in the engineering, sciences, and health professions emigrating to the United States within the confines of domestic immigration policy. The United States finds itself increasingly reliant on highly educated foreign-born nationals to address labor shortages in high-need fields. Coexisting with this inflow of occupational talent, however, is an inflow of illegal immigration consisting of individuals who are often poorly educated and lack sufficient channels to gain needed education and legal employment options.

These three forces—changing economic circumstances leading to changing labor market needs and compounded by shifting demographic trends—point to the need for heightened educational capacity for our nation's citizenry. Unfortunately, the numbers do not tell a good story in this regard. While America's educational levels outpaced the rest of the industrialized world for much of the 20th century, they began to stagnate beginning in the mid-1970s and have largely remained flat. American high school graduation rates have stood at about 70 percent since 1995, a figure that includes great socioeconomic disparities in race and income. At the postsecondary level, enrollments have risen steadily despite increasing tuition prices, but the percentage of the overall population earning a college degree has stagnated, largely due to a significant proportion of young adults who have not entered or successfully completed college.

According to the latest data from the Organisation for Economic Coordination and Development (OECD), the United States now ranks tenth in terms of the percentage of adults with an associate's degree or higher. Forty percent of Americans aged 45 to 54 have attained at least an associate's degree, while only 39 percent of citizens aged 25 to 34 have completed at least a two-year degree.[5] It is alarming, given present economic conditions that call for greater U.S. human capital, that the nation's younger population is collectively less educated than its older population.

A report prepared by the Educational Testing Service (ETS), *America's Perfect Storm: Three Forces Changing our Future,* summarizes how the changing economy, labor market, and demographic trends collectively suggest a bleak picture for the U.S. economy:

> Employing demographic projections combined with current skill distributions, we estimate that by 2030 the average levels of literacy and numeracy in the working-age population will have decreased by about 5 percent while inequality will have increased by about 7 percent. Put crudely, over the next 25 years or so, as better-educated individuals leave the workforce they will be replaced by those who, on average, have lower levels of education and skill. Over this same period, nearly half of the projected job growth will be concentrated in occupations associated with higher education and skill levels. This

means that tens of millions more of our students and adults will be less able to qualify for higher-paying jobs. Instead, they will be competing not only with each other and millions of newly arrived immigrants but also with equally (or better) skilled workers in lower-wage economies around the world.[6]

The Growing Divide

Given the transformative nature of globalization and its effects on the American economy, obtaining a college degree is all the more essential for individuals to achieve and sustain a quality standard of living. Exacerbating the importance of earning a postsecondary degree is the growing income inequality in American society. Wage and salary earnings reflected a shared prosperity among Americans through the mid-1970s. Since then, we have seen a dramatically growing inequality. Between 1977 and 2007, average family income rose 3 percent ($463 in constant 2007 dollars) for the poorest 20 percent of U.S. families and 60 percent ($69,940) for the top 20 percent wealthiest families.[7] That the rich are getting richer and the poor are getting poorer is both associated with and reflected in the unequal distribution in educational attainment among Americans, for the college degree is a significant marker in one's lifetime earnings potential. The median income for those with a bachelor's degree or more in 1997 was $100,000, compared to $49,739 for those with a high school diploma and no college education.[8]

Those with higher levels of college education continue to pull away in terms of earned income, leaving those with little or no postsecondary education with diminishing opportunity in an economy that increasingly rewards higher levels of knowledge, skill, and talent. Many factors, including tax policy, are spurring the growing income divide. But so too is unequal access to affordable postsecondary education, which if not mitigated will have severe implications for America's economic competitiveness.

The College Degree: Benefiting
Individuals and the Economy

Somehow lost in the conversation about the value of a college degree to individuals, however, has been the historical notion of higher education as a public good. Higher education in the United States—especially public higher education—was originally premised on the Jeffersonian idea that free enterprise could not prosper and democracy could not endure without open opportunity for what he called "the aristocracy of the talented" to emerge and develop. And in fact, the emergence of talent from all social and economic conditions has demonstrably led to the wealth creation and relative political stability of the U.S. over its 200-year-plus history.

The benefits of earning a college degree are many to the individuals that earn them, to their families, and, of course, to their communities and society at large (see Figure 11.1). The prospects of increased earnings and greater employment security alone are persuasive. So too are the many qualitative aspects of increased educational attainment, among them improved working environments, enhanced occupational upward mobility, better health, and longer life spans.

The value of a college degree continues to increase by the dictates of the marketplace, with employability and incomes increasing for those with a postsecondary credential. This increasing value is not lost on the American citizenry. According to Public Agenda survey data, the number of people who think that a young person can succeed *without* obtaining a college education declined from 67 percent in 2000 to 49 percent in 2007. As a corollary, the number of Americans who believe that higher education is essential for a decent job and place in American society reached 50 percent in 2007, up from just 31 percent seven years earlier.[9]

High educational attainment rates correlate with state economic strength and high income. Several states—California, Colorado, Connecticut, Delaware, Illinois, Maryland, Minnesota, New Hampshire, New Jersey, New York, Virginia, and Washington among them—have both high levels of personal income per capita and high percentages of working-age adults with four-year degrees. Increased educational attainment rates and accompanying high personal incomes provide states with additional tax revenues that can be used to build state economic capacity and contribute to an enhanced quality of life.

College Access in America: Proud Past, Challenged Future

Until the mid-20th century, access to college was largely reserved for the privileged few. But the floodgates to postsecondary access were thrown open in the 1940s with congressional passage of the G.I. Bill, enabling tens of millions of returning World War II veterans to benefit from the rewards of a college degree. College access continued to expand in the 1960s, facilitated by the post-Sputnik boom, and a huge expansion of federal student aid programs derived from the landmark Higher Education Act of 1965, part of President Lyndon B. Johnson's Great Society reform agenda. The creation of a comprehensive community college system and the burgeoning expansion of regional public four-year institutions further provided affordable college access to millions of Americans.

Figure 11.1 Earning a College Degree: The Investment Payoff

	Public	Private
Economic	Increased Tax Revenues	Higher Salaries and Benefits
	Greater Productivity	Greater Employment Prospects
	Increased Workforce Flexibility	Higher Savings Levels
	Decreased Reliance on Government Financial Support	Improved Working Conditions
		Personal/Professional Mobility
Social	Reduced Crime Rates	Improved Health/Life Expectancy
	Increased Charitable Giving/ Community Service	Improved Quality of Life for Offspring
	Increased Quality of Civic Life	Better Consumer Decision Making
	Social Cohesion/Appreciation of Diversity	Increased Personal Status
	Improved Ability to Adapt to and Use Technology	More Hobbies, Leisure Activities

Source: Institute for Higher Education Policy.

Undergraduate and graduate college enrollments have grown from 1.5 million students in 1940 to some 18 million today.

In recent years, however, access to postsecondary education, and with it access to an American middle-class standard of living, is being threatened due to rising college prices. The perception of decreasing affordability is illustrated in the aforementioned Public Agenda poll. While 9 in 10 of those surveyed believed that access to higher education is a virtual right, 3 in 4 believed that many motivated and qualified students do not have the opportunity to attend college due to financial barriers.

Postsecondary affordability and access are crucial to the continued pursuit of the American Dream. There are no easy solutions to enhancing college access and affordability, but there are many strategies that, when woven together, can keep achieving a college degree within reach. Increases in institutional efficiency and productivity, sustained public investment, increased student academic preparedness, improved transitioning from secondary to postsecondary education, and better student data are all major factors. Of course, any discussion of college access and college costs would not be complete without a comprehensive plan to contain costs at the institutional level to help ensure college access for this and future generations.

COLLEGE PRICES, FINANCIAL AID, AND THE AFFORDABILITY FACTOR

Published Tuition Prices on the Rise

While evidence abounds of the importance and value for individuals to earn at least some type of postsecondary credential, it is equally evident that the cost in doing so is becoming increasingly financially burdensome. Tuition prices have been rising faster than most prices in the American economy, outpacing prices in health care and energy, and have far outstripped increases in the Consumer Price Index (CPI) and median family incomes.

Prices of public four-year colleges and universities increased somewhat more rapidly between 1998–99 and 2008–09 than in the preceding decade, while prices at the nation's private four-year and public two-year colleges increased more slowly than they had between 1978–79 to 1988–89 or from 1988–89 to 1998–99. From 1998–99 to 2008–09, published tuition and fees increased at an average annual inflation-adjusted rate of 4.2 percent at public four-year institutions, 2.4 percent at private four-year colleges, and 1.4 percent at public two-year colleges. While the rate of growth in tuition and fees has been faster at public four-year institutions over the 30-year period from 1978–79 to 2008–09 than at private four-year institutions, and slowest at public two-year institutions, the actual dollar gap between public and private four-year tuition and fees has widened every year even after accounting for inflation.[10]

In 2008–09, tuition and fee charges at U.S. public four-year colleges and universities, which collectively enroll nearly half of all full-time students, averaged $6,585. However, 38 percent of students were enrolled in public four-year institutions with published tuition and fees between $3,000 and $6,000. There is a much wider range of tuition and fees at private four-year universities.[11]

While much attention is paid to steep tuition increases, it is more appropriate to view college costs in their totality. Doing so does not ease financial anxiety for students and families, but it does put the actual costs of tuition in perspective. Tuition and fees constitute about two-thirds of the total budget for full-time students living on campus at private four-year institutions and 60 percent for out-of-state students at public four-year colleges, but only a third of the budget for in-state public four-year students and less than 20 percent for public two-year students.[12] Books and supplies, housing and food (room and board), and transportation costs comprise other educational expenses.

Tuition prices are not rising across the board. In recent years, attempts have been made by some states to cap tuition increases, such as in Maryland and Ohio. But even here, such tuition freezes are not long-term. Otherwise, given increases in costs associated with university operations, staffing, and research, academic quality will soon become a concern.

Elsewhere, universities have implemented so-called tuition guarantee plans in which tuition prices are fixed for the first four years of a student's undergraduate experience. Such plans make family financial planning more predictable and provide incentives to students to complete their undergraduate degrees in a timely manner. However, like tuition freezes, these fixed-for-four tuition plans have drawbacks as well. Given states' economic cycles and correlating changes in state revenues available to support public higher education, college and university officials take great risk in predicting student tuition rates in out-years. Thus, while guaranteed tuition plans provide families with stability in planning, they may—or may not—provide tuition savings in the long run, given the nebulous forecasting that goes into crafting tuition rates for four-year blocks. Some universities that have utilized fixed tuition guarantees have abandoned them due to the difficulties in forecasting future state appropriations and the associated hazard of reduced institutional revenues when state support falls short of previously estimated levels.

Student Financial Aid and the Actual
Cost of College Attendance

There is no doubt that college tuition prices are of great concern. News media and policymakers trumpet skyrocketing tuition prices with increasing frenzy. Headlines hyping double-digit annual tuition increases and rates as high as $30,000 to $35,000 a year at several prominent institutions gain the lion's share of attention. These media accounts, however, typically tout published tuition rates. The fact is, a very high proportion of students attending public and private two- and four-year colleges and universities receive grant aid that reduces advertised tuition prices and eases the financial burden of attending college.

More than $143 billion in financial aid was distributed to undergraduate and graduate students in the form of grants from all sources and federal loans, work-study, and tax credits and deductions during the 2007–08 academic year. In that year, undergraduate students received an average of $8,896 in financial aid per full-time equivalent (FTE)[13] student, including $4,656 in grant aid and $3,650 in federal loans.[14]

Grant dollars—subsidies that do not have to be repaid—when combined with tax credits, can make a significant difference in the actual price of tuition. To illustrate, on average, full-time students enrolled in public two-year colleges received about $2,400 in grants from all sources (primarily federal, state, and institutional) and tax credits in the 2008–09 academic year. This aid reduced the average tuition and fees paid from the published 2008–09 price of $2,400 to about $100 per year. Full-time students enrolled in public four-year colleges and universities received, on average, about $3,700 in grants from all sources. When tax credits are applied, this aid reduced the average tuition and fees paid from the published 2008–09 in-state price of $6,585 to about $2,900; thus, the average actual net price at public four-year institutions that academic year was just 44 percent of the average published price. For students attending private four-year institutions, the average published price of $25,100 is reduced by $10,200 to an average net price of $14,900, when all aid and tax credits are applied.[15]

Average grant aid per student and average net prices conceal significant differences among students. Increases in financial aid for lower-income students have a greater positive impact on college access and affordability than similar increases for higher-income students.[16]

Of course, a true depiction of cost of attendance should include all associated costs: required fees, room and board, books, commuting costs, and other personal expenses. Further, an accurate analysis of the price of college should include wages that are forgone in place of attending class.

In reality, a student who attends college full time for four or five years is giving up income that could have been earned while working on a full time basis during this same time.

In discussing the impact of student financial aid and actual net tuition prices, the term on average must be viewed with caution, as there is a great variation in eligibility criteria. Students from lower-income families often receive significant tuition discounts thanks to available grant aid, while those from upper-middle and high-income families receive little if any student aid. Older adults, part-time and commuter students—a crucial and growing student demographic—are often not eligible for common forms of student aid.

Students from the middle and upper-middle classes are increasingly being squeezed, as they are often on the edge of the ability to pay for tuition yet are often ineligible for financial aid assistance. Paying for tuition alone (excluding other expenses) is often easier for students from low- to middle-income households, largely as a reflection of financial aid eligibility. Grant aid to low-income students enrolled in public two- and four-year colleges allows them to pay tuition costs using lower proportions of their incomes than students from higher-income families, once grant aid is accounted for. However, when living costs are taken into consideration, the total overall cost burden for low-income families remains disproportionately high.

Trends in Merit-Based State Grant Aid

In addition to challenges faced by students from middle- and upper-middle income families in obtaining adequate grant aid, another financial aid trend exists: an increase in financial aid that is awarded based upon merit (typically academic achievement) as opposed to solely on undergraduate dependent students' family income. This is especially true for state grant programs. The proportion of state grant aid *not* based on financial need increased from 17 percent in 1987–88 to 24 percent in 2002–03 and to 28 percent in 2006–07.[17] While the actual proportion of state merit-based grant aid is well below one half, the growth rate is startling, given the strong evidence showing a correlation between student academic achievement (and the parallel likelihood for merit-based aid eligibility) and family income. To put it into perspective, over the decade from 1996–97 to 2006–07, total state grant aid to undergraduates increased by 76 percent in inflation-adjusted dollars. However, within the total grant aid mix, state need-based grants rose by 59 percent ($2 billion in 2007 dollars) while non-need-based state grants increased 250 percent ($1.5 billion in 2007 dollars).[18] The real and potential impacts of this trend in state merit-based grants on students who have modest but promising histories in academic achievement and are from low- to moderate-income households is being debated by policy experts, and some states are rethinking how student aid is distributed.

Increases in Student Borrowing and Student Debt

During the 2007–08 academic year, students borrowed about $67 billion in federal loans and another $18 billion from private lenders. A trend in increased student borrowing from private lenders is cause for concern, given the higher interest rates and fewer consumer protections that can accompany these loans. While borrowing through federal sources increased 70 percent in inflation adjusted dollars between 1997–98 and 2007–08, borrowing through private lenders increased an astounding 592 percent during this same period, from $2.5 billion to $17.6 billion annually.[19] A confluence of insufficient federal grant aid availability, a cumbersome federal aid application process, aggressive marketing by private lenders, and unwillingness by some parents to borrow under the federal PLUS program has led students increasingly to take out more loans through direct-to-consumer (private) loans.

The rising cost of attendance that has led to increased borrowing has in turn led to concerns about student debt levels upon graduation. The average debt burden for the class of 2007 was $18,482 at public colleges and $23,065 at private colleges.[20] Such debt burden increases the risk of loan default by students after graduation and limits their options in making key purchases such as a car or home as well as other amenities of life. Further, this debt may figure into students' career decision making, in which occupations of interest, such as those in the social services, are forgone due to the insufficient salaries needed to pay back student loans.

How Students and Families Pay for College

How families *actually* pay for all associated college costs provides greater insight into the implications of these increasing costs. Data indicate that both parents and students share the responsibility of paying for the total cost of college attendance (tuition, room and board, textbooks, and other related expenses). According to the findings of one survey, parents paid for 32 percent of college costs from current income and savings, with more than half of this amount coming from current income. In addition, parents paid for 16 percent of total college costs through borrowing. The average student paid one-third of the cost, with 23 percent of the total amount paid through borrowed money, half of which came from federal student loans, and another 10 percent through students'

Figure 11.2 How The Average Family Pays for College

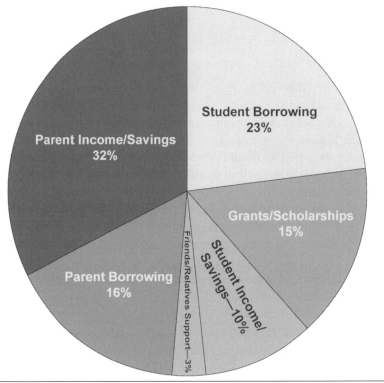

Source: How America Pays for College. Sallie Mae's National Study of College Students and Parents, conducted by Gallup, 2008.

own income or savings.[21] Grants and scholarships made up 15 percent of the total amount paid, with support from friends and relatives making up 3 percent (see Figure 11.2).

TRENDS IN POSTSECONDARY FINANCE

When looking at the issue of postsecondary finance and its impact on college affordability and access, it is most instructive to consider several factors: student enrollments, institutional revenues, institutional spending, and state appropriations. When viewed from a trend perspective, the numbers portray an American higher education in flux: a system that would benefit by greater cost containment, but that is challenged by a complex set of market and public policy forces. The Delta Project on Postsecondary Education Costs, Productivity and Accountability provides an informative investigation into these trends, which is summarized here.[22]

Student Enrollment

Student enrollments have been rising for years across all sectors, with a noticeable increase in the rate of growth since 1998. Total enrollment in degree-granting colleges and universities is expected to increase from 17.8 million in 2006 to 20.1 million by 2017. Enrollment in public four-year institutions is expected to grow from 13.2 million in 2005 to 14.9 million during this time (a 12.9 percent increase), with enrollment at private institutions, which in 2005 enrolled 4.6 million students, growing to 5.1 million (a 10.9 percent increase). The number of bachelor's degrees awarded annually is expected to increase by 16 percent from 2005 to 2017, with the number of associates degrees growing 8 percent.[23]

There are signs of socioeconomic segregation among student enrollments, however. Most undergraduate enrollment growth has been in students from high-income families. Enrollment by students from families with incomes of $80,000 or above grew by 3.7 percent from 1996–2004, while those from families earning less than $20,000 witnessed a 1.7 percent decline during the same period. Black and Hispanic students and those from low-income households are comparatively less likely to attend college immediately after graduation from high school, and those that do are increasingly being concentrated in less selective institutions: community colleges and proprietary institutions.

A critical public policy issue is whether increasing enrollments are leading to increases in degree and credential completions. With the exception of private four-year institutions, all sectors have witnessed a modest increase in degree completions compared to overall enrollments. Despite moderate growth in the proportion of degree completions, this issue remains critical for higher education leaders and policy makers.

Institutional Revenues

Significant Differences in Levels and Sources of Revenues among Institutional Sectors

Major differences exist between types of institutions and the level and sources of revenue they receive. As Figure 11.3 illustrates, public and private research universities have access to considerably more revenue on a per-student basis than do other sectors due to their research function and typically higher levels of state government funding for graduate education. Public master's and community colleges, meanwhile, have witnessed much slower growth in their income streams. In all sectors, most of the revenue growth has been generated from tuition rather than from government funding, fund-raising, or endowment earnings. Since 1998, revenues from tuition have increased faster than other sources of revenue

Figure 11.3 Institutional Revenues Per Student, by Source and by Sector, 1995, 2002 and 2006 (in 2006 dollars)

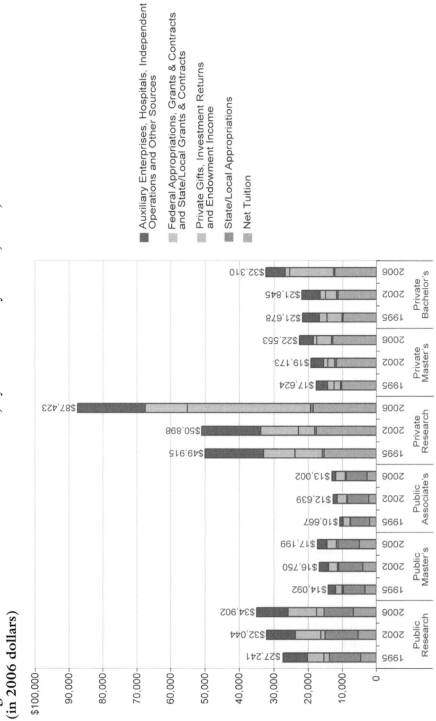

■ Auxiliary Enterprises, Hospitals, Independent Operations and Other Sources

□ Federal Appropriations, Grants & Contracts and State/Local Grants & Contracts

□ Private Gifts, Investment Returns and Endowment Income

□ State/Local Appropriations

□ Net Tuition

Source: Delta Project on Postsecondary Costs, IPEDS database.

everywhere except for private research universities. In public institutions, tuition revenues have grown faster than state and local appropriations, which generally have not kept pace with enrollment growth and inflation. Tuition remains a significantly larger source of revenue for private institutions than for public institutions. In 2005, tuition revenues comprised between 54 and 71 percent of total revenue at private institutions, but only between 24 to 32 percent of public colleges and universities.

At Public Institutions, A Shift in Revenue Streams

Public colleges and universities rely primarily on two sources for general operating support: state and local government appropriations and student tuition revenues. Variations in state government appropriations to institutions typically generate a correlating change in tuition and fee charges. The relationship between educational appropriations and increases in tuition and fee rates are generally inverse, with greater instability witnessed when government appropriations increase or decrease significantly.

For all but three fiscal years between 1982 and 1997, total educational revenue in public institutions has hovered between $9,300 and $10,800 per full-time equivalent (FTE) student. The most significant change during this period has been in the growth in per student net tuition revenue, which more than doubled in constant dollars from $1,834 in 1982 to $3,911 in FY 2007.[24] This resulting shift in revenues to public institutions is evident in Figure 11.4, with tuition income serving as an increasing share of total educational revenues.

Private Fund-raising Revenues Not Increasing as a Proportion of Operating Funds at Public Institutions

Rising concern about tuition prices have led some members of Congress as well as legislators in at least one state (Massachusetts, home of Harvard University, with an endowment approaching $35 billion as of this writing) to discuss enacting legislation mandating minimum spending levels from the endowments of those institutions that receive substantial private gifts through fund-raising. A congressional or state-mandated minimum spend rate on endowments would be problematic in that most donated monies are earmarked by their donors for specific purposes and therefore cannot be used for discretionary purposes. Further, endowments are subject to economic downturns, which would largely prevent institutions from making distributions on a long range but pre-determined basis. As a proportion of operating funds at public institutions, private gift revenues have not changed since 1987.

Figure 11.4 Public FTE Enrollment, Educational Appropriations and Total Educational Revenue Per FTE, U.S., Fiscal 1982–2007

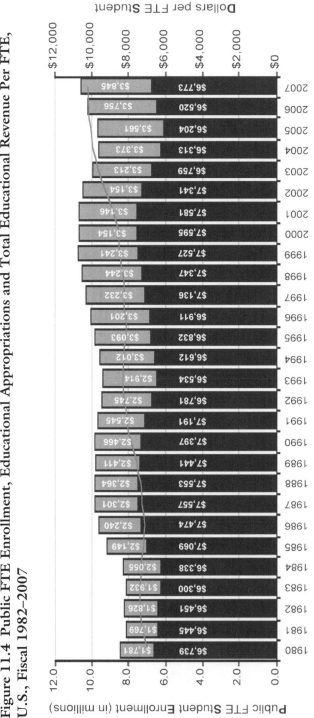

Notes: Constant 2007 dollars adjusted by SHEEO Higher Education Cost Adjustment (HECA). FTE = Full-Time Equivalent.

Source: State Higher Education Executive Officers—State Higher Education Finance Report, 2008.

Net Tuition Revenues Increasing at Slower
Rate than Tuition Sticker Prices

Increases in tuition sticker prices—the full posted tuition and fees before financial aid and tuition discounts are accounted for—have outpaced overall net tuition revenues. While sticker prices have risen in all institutional sectors, they have not translated into comparable increases in net revenues from tuition because many institutions have utilized a considerable share of these monies to grant tuition discounts to students. Such tuition discounting is particularly evident among private institutions. The smallest dollar increase in tuition sticker prices has occurred in public institutions, but these have translated into higher percentage increases than at private institutions because public institutions typically start from a lower base tuition level.

Decreasing Discretion over Spending
at Public Institutions

In its analysis of institutional revenues, the Delta Cost Project estimates that unrestricted (non-earmarked) revenue has decreased as a proportion of the total revenue stream at public institutions since 1988, while it has grown at private institutions. Estimating unrestricted revenue is important because not all funds are available for core purposes: activities that could contribute to reducing the ultimate costs paid through student tuition dollars. In the public sector, the proportion of revenues that are unrestricted has dropped by as much as seven percent over the past two decades. So while public research institutions have more overall revenue than other public institutions, they have less control over spending decisions than do master's degree institutions and community colleges. This shift in revenues—with less discretionary income—suggests a shift in institutional activity at public research universities away from undergraduate instruction and more toward research and public service. It further suggests that funders are moving away from general institutional support, and are instead funding on a fee-for-service basis.

Institutional Spending

There are several telling trends with regard to institutional spending. Most notable is that spending is increasing at private institutions while remaining generally flat at public institutions, thus creating a growing disparity in spending between public and private not-for-profit institutions. Also of consequence is a reprioritization of institutional spending away from the core activity of student instruction.

Growing Spending Disparities

An analysis of the National Center for Education Statistics Integrated Postsecondary Education Database (known as IPEDS) by the Delta Cost Project shows that private institutions spend more per student than their public counterparts. At the highest end, full educational costs (including all direct costs of instruction and other education-related costs) among private research universities in 2006 averaged about $19,429 more per FTE student than public research universities, which in turn spent about $3,000 more than public master's institutions, and $4,662 more than public two-year institutions[25] (see Figure 11.5).

These spending disparities between public and private institutions have increased in recent years. From 1987 through the mid-1990s, total spending grew at all types of institutions, with spending at private four-year institutions nearly twice as much as at their public counterparts. Since 2000, however, public associate's and master's institutions have reduced expenditures on a per-FTE-student basis and spending has remained relatively flat among public research universities. In contrast, spending at private research institutions has continued to grow since 2000, although at a slower rate than in the late 1980s and early 1990s.

Differences in spending patterns between public and private sector institutions become starkly evident when looking at the indirect, or non-instructional, portion of educational costs, such as student support services. At public institutions of all types, these costs averaged about $4,000 per student in 2005. Private institutions spent more than double that amount, averaging $10,000 per student. Much of this additional investment at private institutions is aimed at meeting consumer preferences, especially consumers who are high-achieving students.

Growth in Instructional Costs Muted
Relative to Total Costs

Over the last 20 years, the direct costs of instruction—primarily faculty salaries and benefits—have represented a minority of total spending, ranging from 35 to 44 percent across institutional sectors, and the proportion of total spending allocated for the direct cost of instruction has declined since 1998 in both the public and private research sectors. Since 1998, instructional spending in both public and private research institutions grew more slowly than nearly all other spending areas. Some of this reduced growth in spending may not involve actual cost cutting, but rather may reflect lower marginal instructional spending during periods of enrollment growth given that institutions can add new students to existing programs less expensively than if they had to build entire new programs. Further,

Figure 11.5 Institutional Expenditures Per Student, by Source and by Sector, 1995 and 2006 (in 2006 dollars)

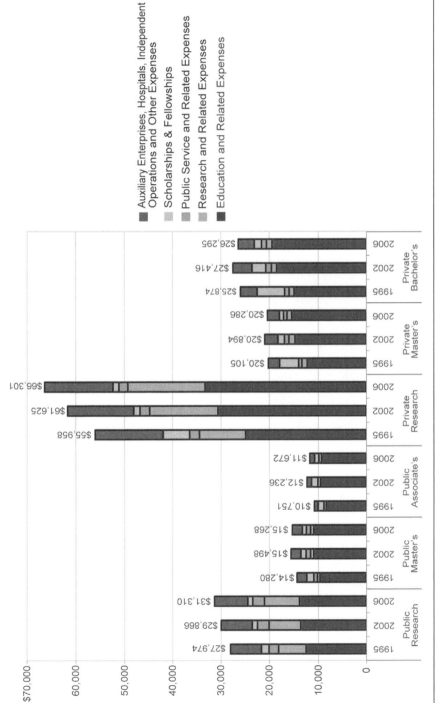

Legend:
- Auxiliary Enterprises, Hospitals, Independent Operations and Other Expenses
- Scholarships & Fellowships
- Public Service and Related Expenses
- Research and Related Expenses
- Education and Related Expenses

Public Research: 1995 $27,974; 2002 $29,866; 2006 $31,310
Public Master's: 1995 $14,280; 2002 $15,498; 2006 $15,268
Public Associate's: 1995 $10,751; 2002 $12,236; 2006 $11,672
Private Research: 1995 $55,958; 2002 $61,625; 2006 $66,301
Private Master's: 1995 $20,105; 2002 $20,894; 2006 $20,286
Private Bachelor's: 1995 $25,874; 2002 $27,416; 2006 $26,295

Source: Delta Project on Postsecondary Costs, IPEDS database.

evidence suggests that growth in instructional spending has been marginalized by a continued shift from full- to part-time faculty and staff.

Growth in Spending Centered on Institutional Aid to Students, Public Service and Research

The largest and most consistent area of increased spending has been in institutional grant aid provided to students; unlike research and service, this is generally funded from discretionary revenues. Revenues that are used to pay for institutional aid typically come from tuition income, state or local appropriations, and to a lesser extent private gifts that are earmarked to support student scholarship and grant aid programs. Since 1998, spending from institutional sources for student grant aid has grown faster than any other single spending area in public higher education. The second highest growth area in the public sector has been on public service and research. At private institutions, spending increases for research and service have grown faster than any other area during this same period.

Public Sector Shift in Cost Burden, from State to Student

Although public sector institutions have seen the greatest increases in tuition rates in percentage terms, these new revenues have not translated into growth in spending, as tuition revenues have essentially replaced diminished state appropriations. Looking simultaneously at changes between 1998 and 2006 in both tuition and spending sheds light on the financing shifts occurring in higher education. During this time, total spending per student has gone down in inflation-adjusted dollars among public community colleges and public master's institutions while increasing modestly at public research universities. Despite these spending constraints, median tuition prices and revenues across the public sector have generally increased by more than 30 percent.

Among private not-for-profit institutions, by contrast, tuition increases have translated into increased spending. Thus there is not a uniform causal relationship between spending and tuition increases. At private institutions, tuition has increased with spending growth; the former has financed the latter. At public institutions, however, spending growth has largely remained flat, with most of the revenues from tuition increases replacing state revenues.

The overarching inquiry about U.S. higher education financing trends is whether college tuitions are rising because of spending growth. For more than three-quarters of the students enrolled in higher education, the answer is no. Insufficient state appropriations for higher education has required those enrolled in public institutions to pay a greater share of costs through tuition payments, marking a major shift in who pays for education, from the state to students. From a policy perspective, this shift in public postsecondary education—from being a public good (subsidized by taxpayer monies) to a private good (paid for by individual students and their families through private earnings)—is central to the discussion of public higher education access and affordability issues.

The sad truth is that there really has been no serious public policy debate for several decades about the benefits and burdens, social and personal, of public higher education in the United States. The trends cited here—a distinct shift of costs from public sources to individual students and their families—have been the result of year-to-year decision-making in each of the 50 states as they sought to balance that year's budget. There has been little discourse in the policy domain about whether taxpayers or students should be paying more or less for public postsecondary education. A result in most years and most states was that crunch time came and governors and legislators passed appropriations bills to keep state governments running.

In most years and most states, appropriations to higher education have come up short due to competing demands on state budgets. The premise has been that colleges and universities, unlike public schools or prisons or highways, could always raise tuition or somehow creatively deal with their financial issues. The result has been more policy drift than policy setting. The truth is, or has become, that for the vast majority of American families, college tuition is no longer an out-of-pocket expense, but rather an investment. It cannot be managed as part of a family's budget by small sacrifices—e.g., keeping the old but still serviceable car a few more years, or forgoing an occasional dinner out and the movies—to pay Johnny's and Sally's way through college. Instead, like any other family investment (cars, houses, and a retirement nest egg), it is something for which money must be saved or borrowed. That is simply the reality facing most students and families today.

PRESSURES FOR REDUCING COLLEGE AND UNIVERSITY OPERATING COSTS

Numerous pressures are compelling American higher education institutions to reduce operating costs. Many of these pressures are economic, while others are an outgrowth of public concern over college affordability. The public's anxiety over rising college prices has in recent years been translated into public policy measures at all levels of governance aimed at increasing institutional accountability, productivity, and college access at public postsecondary institutions.

Economic Pressures

A Fast-Changing Higher Education Marketplace

Marketplace competition among some 4,300 public and private two- and four-year institutions is fierce, especially within sectors and geographic regions. Given demographic trends that reflect a flattening in the number of high school graduates in the years ahead, it will only become keener. Exacerbating the competition for students is a growing number of proprietary, for-profit institutions that have entered the higher education marketplace, which are delivering education in ways that meet consumer demands and that simultaneously require greater flexibility on the part of traditional public and private non-profit institutions. Between 1995 and 2005 student enrollment grew about 18 percent at public four-year institutions, and jumped 40 percent at four-year proprietary schools.[26]

The evolution of distance learning technologies, especially online education and that which is delivered in hybrid form, where instruction takes place both online and in the classroom, has changed the face of postsecondary education for many students. While all types of institutions have harnessed technology-enhanced educational delivery systems to expand distance education capabilities, for-profit schools have been particularly adept at doing so. Nontraditional students who are older, work full-time, and who may have family obligations have proven to be lucrative markets for proprietary schools, and even more so for those institutions that have utilized distance education delivery formats. An annual 10 percent growth rate in online enrollments reflects a six-fold increase compared to the growth in overall student populations.[27]

Proprietary schools have also diminished barriers that have been traditionally—and artificially—restrained by limiting enrollment to a given geographic region, confined by a single campus. While regional and state boundaries are being transcended at all types of institutions, doing so has proven especially effective for proprietary schools. The University of Phoenix is a case in point. Founded in 1976 and graduating a first class of less than a dozen students, it now boasts some 345,000 students enrolled at 200 campuses and learning centers spread across 40 states and several countries, with course delivery taking place both online and in the classroom.

Whether prospective students will be admitted to their university of choice is an issue that will always receive visibility around family dinner tables, in various headlines, and in occasional policy debates. Gaining admissions acceptance, however, in the majority of cases is limited to students seeking to attend highly selective, elite private and state public flagship universities. In reality, it is by and large the majority of institutions themselves—community colleges, regional state colleges, proprietary colleges, and less selective private colleges—that are aggressively pursuing the student-consumer, who has a growing set of postsecondary options at his or her disposal.

Cost Increases and the Inflation Factor

Inflation is another source of economic pressure for colleges and universities. Higher education institutions are by nature intensely human-driven enterprises and therefore spend more on labor-associated costs such as salaries and fringe benefits for faculty, administrators, and an extensive array of service and technical personnel. Further, much of the critical labor utilized by colleges is both highly skilled and scarce, and as a result, the wages associated with these jobs often rise faster than general labor rates.

The Higher Education Price Index (HEPI), an inflation index designed specifically for higher education, serves as a more accurate indicator of relative price levels of goods and services purchased by colleges and universities than does the U.S. Department of Labor's Consumer Price Index (CPI). Originally developed by the U.S. Department of Education and now maintained by the Commonfund Institute, the HEPI enables schools to determine increases in funding necessary to maintain real purchasing power. During 1984–2004, the HEPI grew at an average annual rate of 4.04 percent, reflecting a weighting that is based 75 percent on the purchase of labor-associated items and 25 percent on goods and services. In contrast, the CPI, which is based solely on the relative price levels of goods and services purchased by families, rose at an annual rate of 3.06 percent during the same period.[28]

The added cost burden of inflation on colleges and universities is real and significant, but is often not taken into account by state policymakers in higher education funding decisions for state-supported institutions. Doing so would make a real difference in appropriations to public institutions. For example, from 1980 to 2000, the price of goods and services purchased by colleges and universities increased by 154 percent, while inflation measured by the CPI increased by 118 percent. If states had used the more accurate HEPI as an indicator of purchasing power in their funding decisions, public colleges and universities would have received 16.5 percent more financial support per student than if the CPI were used.[29]

Pressure to Contain Costs through Public Policy

In addition to market-based economic pressures, colleges and universities are facing an increasing array of policy measures at the federal, state, and system level aimed at bringing greater scrutiny to rising tuition prices, increasing accountability and transparency, and improving efficiency and productivity in higher education. These efforts represent a broader policy framework intent on containing costs and ensuring college affordability.

Federal Government

The federal government's role in higher education has been focused considerably on providing aid to institutions and supporting programs designed to provide greater access to students from low-income households and from traditionally underrepresented groups. The major law governing federal student aid is the Higher Education Act (HEA), which was originally enacted in 1965 and is reauthorized on a periodic basis. The provisions included in the most recent reauthorization of the Act, the Higher Education Opportunity Act of 2008 (HEOA), in addition to updating existing student aid programs and authorizing new ones, included an unprecedented number of new stipulations designed to address college cost affordability and transparency. The nearly 1,200-page bill doubled colleges' reporting requirements. The bill calls on the federal government itself (through the U.S. Department of Education), institutions, and states to all play a role in keeping college costs in check.

The HEOA requires the office of the U.S. Secretary of Education to post consumer information online about individual institutions, including items such as costs, graduation rates, and popular majors. It also charges the Secretary of Education with creating and posting an online "net price calculator," a tool enabling students and families to receive an estimate of college costs based on their specific income and family situations.[30]

In a direct attempt to make those charged with setting tuition prices think carefully about affordability, the HEOA requires the Secretary of Education to publish cost affordability and transparency lists. These watch lists, broken down by sector (two- and four-year private, public and proprietary), contain information on institutions' tuition and fees, including estimated net tuition prices (which include average institutional student financial aid commitments). Among the lists are the top 5 percent most expensive institutions in the country, the 10 percent least expensive institutions in the country, and the 5 percent of institutions that had the largest percentage increase in tuition over the prior three years. Institutions on the last list are required to provide a report to the Secretary of Education on reasons for the tuition increases. In recognition of the comparatively low tuition base of most community colleges and many four-year public colleges, institutions will be exempted from the list containing the largest annual tuition increase if the dollar increase over the three-year period was less than $600. Whether these new watch lists will have their intended effect of contributing to enhanced college affordability by increasing transparency and thus prodding institutions to keep tuition hikes moderate will take some time to ascertain, but it is evident that the federal government is making a heightened effort to ensure that institutions contain costs and translate those savings into greater tuition affordability.

Another notable provision in the 2008 HEOA legislation is the first formal recognition by the federal government of the state role in ensuring college affordability, especially regarding access to public higher education. A "state maintenance of effort" provision—a hotly contested stipulation and the last one to be approved prior to the bill's passage—will withhold federal College Access Challenge Grant funds from states that fail to increase spending on higher education annually by at least as much as they increased it, on average, over the prior five years. The challenge-grant program provides states with matching monies aimed at increasing the number of low-income students who are prepared to enter and succeed in college.

Public college and university leaders were appreciative of the provision's intent to recognize the critical role that state appropriations play in institutional funding and in the setting of tuition rates. State governors and legislators, however, took great exception to the new law, arguing that it was an unfunded mandate and infringed upon their ability to dictate how discretionary state funds are allocated. Here again, whether the amendment will have its intended effect is highly debatable. The threat of having federal Challenge Grant monies withheld ($66 million of which was to be allocated to states in 2008) represented a fraction of the total monies states allocate toward higher education ($83 billion in fiscal year 2007), and it is therefore debatable whether the threat of denying states such a proportionally small amount of revenue will have any impact. However, the symbolic nature of the new requirement speaks volumes about the federal government's efforts to address the college affordability issue—and states' role in this regard.

The issue of institutional accountability and college affordability was also elevated at the federal level through the work of the Commission on the Future of Higher Education, also known as the Spellings Commission, in recognition of then-U.S. Secretary of Education Margaret Spellings. Charged with recommending a national strategy for reforming postsecondary education, the commission focused on four primary areas: access, affordability, standards of instructional quality, and the accountability of higher education institutions to their various constituencies. The 2006 release of the commission's report, which brought with it a threat of additional federal regulatory burden in the name of greater accountability (much of which was eventually realized through reauthorization of the Higher Education Opportunity Act of 2008), led the higher education community to act proactively in promoting accountability more transparently.

One example is the Voluntary System of Accountability, a partnership of the American Association of State Colleges and Universities (AASCU) and the National Association of State Universities and Land-Grant Colleges (NASULGC) that was launched in 2007. The VSA, as it is known, provides institutions with the *voluntary* opportunity to use a standard template—posted online as the "College Portrait"—which provides consistent, comparable, and transparent information of interest to students, families, and other stakeholders including data on college costs, the undergraduate student experience, and student learning outcomes.[31] The National Association of Independent Colleges and Universities (NAICU), through its University and College Accountability Network (U-CAN), made a simultaneous effort. Also launched in 2007, the consumer information Web site provides free access to a variety of comparable institutional data for prospective students.[32]

THE QUEST FOR COST CONTAINMENT IN HIGHER EDUCATION

State and System Efforts

Efforts aimed at achieving cost savings in college and university operations are being pushed by states, university systems, and institutions themselves. States are partnering with university systems in comprehensive efforts to encourage, quantify, and reallocate cost savings realized at the institutional level. Often these cost savings efforts are under the umbrella of accountability reporting programs led by state agencies and university systems as well as institutions. State university systems in California, Illinois, Maryland, Mississippi, Missouri, Ohio, and Texas are among those that publish annual performance reports that highlight indicators of institutional effectiveness. In addition to measures of productivity, these reports often include successes pertaining to cost containment.

Institutional and university system cost containment strategies are also encouraged through state appropriation policies that reward institutions with more revenue based on the number of degree completions generated, as opposed to the traditional metric of student enrollments. Such funding formulas encourage more timely degree completions and require institutions to implement cost reduction strategies, especially in the area of student instruction and support services, which account for a significant proportion of institutional spending.

Institutional Practices

Cost containment is clearly an important public policy issue in American higher education. Trends portend increasing consumer demand, insufficient public (state) financial support, and a public and body politic that are increasingly impatient with the ever-rising price of college tuition. This leads to the questions: *To what extent is the issue of cost containment being addressed at American colleges and universities?* And, *What strategies are being used to contain growth in college costs?* Public four-year institutions place a high priority on cost containment and are successfully identifying and implementing cost savings solutions in multiple operational areas. This consensus is based on the results of a survey of practices at U.S. public four-year institutions by the American Association of State Colleges and Universities (AASCU) and SunGard Higher Education.[33]

The 2008 study found that institutions rely more on support and business functions in their cost control efforts than on core academic functions. Of 31 possible sources of cost containment, energy management and consortium purchasing were found to be the two most common areas utilized by public institutions (see Figure 11.6). Breadth is key: institutions witnessed greater satisfaction with their cost containment efforts to the degree they achieved savings in a broad range of operations and services.

Despite progress made to date, the study provides evidence that there remains significant opportunity for institutions to benefit further from implementing additional cost containment strategies. For one, additional institutional investment in identifying and implementing cost containment initiatives could be increased, producing an even greater return on investment at more colleges and universities. And while the breadth of operational areas relied upon for cost containment is impressive, evidence suggests that additional cost savings can be realized by judiciously utilizing a broader cross section of college and university operations, especially those associated with the academic core where greater operational resources are expended.

The aforementioned study offers six recommendations on how American state colleges and universities can increase cost containment successes and simultaneously mitigate increases in college costs that might otherwise be passed on to the student-consumer.

Harness Costs through Enhanced Energy Management

A resounding majority of institutions have successfully relied upon energy management strategies to reduce operating costs. High energy prices combined with innovative energy management solutions and an increasing focus on sustainability and conservation have led to an array of cost-saving solutions. Often these enhancements require up-front investments but deliver long-term savings. College campuses are flush with a variety of energy management opportunities and can realize significant savings in tandem with a vigorous and long-term plan for implementing the most beneficial solutions.

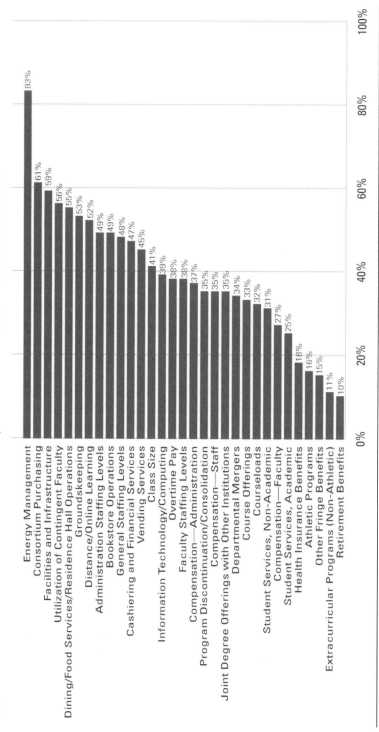

Figure 11.6 Extent to Which Institutions Rely on Individual Sources to Contain Costs

Source: American Association of State Colleges and Universities and SunGard Higher Education, 2008. Base = 114.

Take Advantage of Cost Containment
Opportunities in Business Services/Processes

Public colleges and universities have achieved cost savings by turning to their own business services and processes. Many of the services and processes utilized by institutions are inherent sources of cost-saving opportunities as a result of Web-enabled technologies that permit service process redesigns to simultaneously improve cost structures and service quality, the forces of market competition, and business applications that are easily outsourced. Bookstores, dining hall and residence hall operations, information technology services, electronic self-servicing, cashiering and other financial services, and vending operations have been shown to be effective areas for yielding cost savings.

Realize Enhanced Cost Management
While Taking into Account Core
Academic Functions

Areas associated with institutional academic programming have the potential to deliver significant cost savings. A considerable proportion of institutions are utilizing faculty on a contingent (adjunct) basis, offering joint degree programs with other institutions, discontinuing low-enrollment programs and consolidating others, merging departments, and offering courses more strategically. Many institutions are becoming more innovative in the delivery of course instruction by using hybrid approaches that involve in-class and online participation, which has been shown to reduce costs while simultaneously increasing student learning outcomes. One caveat: while ample opportunities exist for institutions to implement cost containment measures on the academic side of the enterprise, caution must be exercised to ensure that academic quality is not degraded. For example, the utilization of adjunct faculty was the most relied upon method for containing costs out of seven academic areas surveyed in the study. Some studies have shown, however, weakened student academic performances in core freshman gateway courses taught by part-time professors. As the commentary provided at the end of this chapter argues, the quest for efficiency and cost containment must not be done in a vacuum, but rather in a manner that takes into account the institution's broader mission and other traditional values inherent in American higher education.

Exploit the Full Potential of Purchasing
Consortium Participation

A majority of public colleges and universities participate in purchasing consortia, affirming that harnessing the power of dollars pooled from multiple institutions can enhance purchasing power for goods and services bought in large quantities. Computing services, all types of insurance (liability, health, life, property), library resources, utilities, and office and janitorial supplies are among the goods and services most typically purchased by institutions participating in a group-purchasing consortium. Institutions should identify and utilize the full range of opportunities to maximize the power of collective purchasing.

Report and Quantify Cost Containment Outcomes

While most institutions are actively engaged in cost containment, only a minority regularly quantify and/or report the results of their efforts. To improve accountability for results and the transparency of institutional cost containment efforts, colleges and universities are encouraged to quantify the effectiveness of cost management efforts and to publish the outcomes. For example, realized cost savings can be presented longitudinally in terms that can be understood by the general public and policymakers, such as dollars saved on a per-FTE-student basis.

Invite Ideas and Solutions from Employees
and Students While Also Tapping Outside Expertise

Institutions that encourage employees to offer cost savings ideas have a greater satisfaction level with their cost containment achievements. Colleges and universities are encouraged to actively invite employee and student involvement in identifying potential cost reduction strategies. While many cost savings initiatives implemented by public four-year institutions are internally developed (84 percent of institutions participating in the cost containment study reported that employees are the primary source for ideas), college officials should also look beyond their respective campuses to identify best practices. Greater cost savings will likely be realized when all available sources are utilized to identify effective cost management strategies, including professional associations, external consultants, and nonprofit organizations that possess valuable expertise.

RECONCILING THE COMPETING PURSUITS OF EFFICIENCY, INSTITUTIONAL MISSIONS, AND ACADEMIC VALUES[34]

Surveys have found that Americans hold great confidence in the nation's public colleges and universities at a level surpassing that held for churches, hospitals, the media, and all levels of government. But beyond this general high level of confidence, the public seems, at times, deeply ambivalent about these institutions.

On one hand, there is a cherished and sentimental view of universities as special places where caring teachers mold young minds through unhurried and probing conversations about poems and politics, the human condition and the forces of nature. Classes are small, tutored by sage and patient scholars; juvenile errors and excesses are gently but firmly corrected; and, of course, football games are always won. And in this romanticized view, tranquil and leafy campuses are sanctuaries for eccentric intellectuals to think deep thoughts, develop whimsical theories, and indulge in the time-consuming trials and errors of research.

On the other hand, when talk turns to matters of state funding or tuition rates, sweet sentimentalities are replaced by a fulminating call for ruthless efficiency—no time or treasure squandered on small classes or idle contemplation or tending to pretty flowers on campus. Things must be run as lean as business would have us believe it has become. Fat must be excised, indolence must be punished mercilessly, unnecessary processes must be reengineered and unnecessary people banished.

Can a university be both academic and efficient, both humane and businesslike? The answer is a tentative "yes." But focusing on efficiency as a prime goal and virtue can divert attention and effort from a university's essential purpose: to protect and elevate its primary missions of teaching, learning, research, and service. The very things that produce a university's greatest value—intellectual freedom, personal attention to students, time for contemplation and the cultivation of imagination, conservation of our past and insight into our future, and the mistakes and missteps that necessarily precede achievements in research and learning—do not always conform to the imperatives of tidy management and steely cost-cutting techniques.

While the raw material of business and industry often have predictable destinations, the raw material of universities—namely, young or young-at-heart men and women—are subject to the great forces of human nature: ego and altruism, impulse and emotion, to name but a few. A piece of metal stamping on an assembly line cannot change its intentions to become a car door, a filing cabinet, or a piece of art. A college sophomore, however, may very well alter his or her intended destination from being an accountant to that of an English teacher, scientist, nurse, poet, parent, or politician.

There is another, perhaps even greater, irony in all this. Efficiency, as commonly understood in business jargon, is rarely rewarded in the higher education marketplace. Imagine, for example, the least efficient institution of higher education in your state. Chances are that the teaching loads of its highly paid faculty are minimal and their efforts are focused instead on the publication of esoteric research in widely unread journals; its library contains hundreds of thousands of volumes that haven't been opened in decades; it has well-manicured lawns and, probably, a facility that seats tens of thousands of people but is only used for five or six Saturdays each year (hint—think football stadium). Imagine then, the most efficient higher education institution in your state. It likely has underpaid faculty with teaching loads that approach sweatshop labor conditions; it may well be housed in one or more storefronts; its library might be little more than a set of encyclopedias; and it is marketing desperately for a student body that will keep it marginally solvent.

Now, which one has accomplished students waiting with bated breath for word of a favorable admissions decision? Which one receives tens if not hundreds of millions of dollars in largesse from loyal alumni or proud donors each year? Which one commands the almost slavish allegiance of those very legislators who cheer loudly from prime seats at athletic pageants but publicly threaten to discipline their spendthrift habits?

Is efficiency—in a business definition—really recognized or rewarded in the higher education marketplace?

Universities offer a different and more complicated value proposition. Their "core business" is the development of ideas and discoveries and the professionals who teach our children and treat our sicknesses and manage our businesses and create wealth and create art. Human beings are, alas, sometimes untidy, vexatious, troublesome; and humane values sometimes require more patience than might best serve some bottom line.

The reason colleges and universities have earned the public's confidence, the reason hundreds and hundreds of thousands of alumni are proud of their alma maters, the reason families sacrifice to send their sons and daughters to campuses is not because colleges and universities function as well-oiled machines, not because they trim every expense and fill every idle minute during the academic day and year. It is because these unique and special and fragile institutions are there at the very instant when people, at their most promising and vulnerable moments, come seeking their futures.

NOTES

1. Thomas L. Friedman, *The World is Flat: A Brief History of the 21st Century* (New York: Farrar, Straus and Giroux, 2005).

2. Irwin Kirsch, Henry Braun, Kentaro Yamamoto, and Andrew Sum, *America's Perfect Storm: Three Forces Changing Our Nation's Future* (Princeton, NJ: Educational Testing Service, January 2007): 2.

3. "Adding It Up: State Challenges for Increasing Access and Success," (Boston: The National Center for Higher Education Management

Systems and Jobs for the Future for the Making Opportunity Affordable Initiative, November, 2007): 2.

4. Irwin Kirsch, Henry Braun, Kentaro Yamamoto, and Andrew Sum, *America's Perfect Storm:* 4.

5. Organisation for Economic Co-operation and Development, "Education at a Glance 2008: OECD Indicators" (Paris: Organisation for Economic Co-operation and Development, September, 2008).

6. Irwin Kirsch, Henry Braun, Kentaro Yamamoto, and Andrew Sum, *America's Perfect Storm:* 4.

7. College Board, *Trends in College Pricing 2008* (New York: The College Board, October, 2008): 16.

8. Ibid., 16.

9. The National Center for Public Policy and Higher Education, "Is College Opportunity Slipping Away? Parents and the Public Voice Concerns about Higher Education Access and Affordability," *Policy Alert* (August, 2008): 2.

10. College Board, *Trends in College Pricing 2008,* 2.

11. Ibid., 6, 7.

12. College Board, *Trends in College Pricing 2007,* (New York: The College Board, October, 2007): 7.

13. FTE is an acronym for Full-Time Equivalent student, a measure used by policy analysts for comparability purposes, and is calculated by adding up all credits taken by part-time students during a given term/semester and dividing by 30 credits (representing a full-time two-semester course load).

14. College Board, *Trends in Student Aid 2008,* 2.

15. Ibid., 11.

16. Ibid.

17. Ibid., 15.

18. Ibid.

19. Ibid., 6.

20. The Project on Student Debt, *Student Debt and the Class of 2007,* http://projectonstudentdebt.org.

21. Gallup and Sallie Mae, *How America Pays for College* (Reston, VA: Sallie Mae, August 2008): 3.

22. Jane V. Wellman, Donna M. Desrochers, and Colleen M. Lenihan, *The Growing Imbalance: Recent Trends in U.S. Postsecondary Education Finance,* A Report of the Delta Project on Postsecondary Costs, Productivity and Accountability, supported by Making Opportunity Affordable, an initiative of the Lumina Foundation, 2008 (Washington, DC): 13–41.

23. U.S. Department of Education, National Center for Education Statistics, *Projections of Education Statistics to 2017,* http://nces.ed.gov/pubsearch/pubsinfo.asp?pubid=2008078.

24. State Higher Education Executive Officers, *State Higher Education Finance Report* (Boulder, CO, 2007), http://www.sheeo.org/finance/shef_fy07.pdf.

25. Jane V. Wellman, Delta Project on Postsecondary Costs. Data update to the *Growing Imbalance* report (personal communication October 27, 2008).

26. U.S. Department of Education, National Center for Education Statistics, D*igest of Education Statistics: 2007,* http://nces.ed.gov/programs/digest/d07/tables/dt07_187.asp?referrer=list.

27. I. Elaine Allen and Jeff Seaman, *Online Nation: Five Years of Growth in Online Learning* (Boston: Babson Survey Research Group and the Sloan Consortium, October, 2007).

28. Commonfund, http://www.commonfund.org/Commonfund/CF+Institute/CI_About_HEPI.htm.

29. Ibid.

30. U.S. Department of Education, National Center for Education Statistics, *College Navigator,* http://nces.ed.gov/collegenavigator.

31. Information on the Voluntary System of Accountability can be found at: www.voluntarysystem.org.

32. Information on the University and College Accountability Network can be found at: www.ucan-network.org.

33. American Association of State Colleges and Universities (AASCU) and SunGard Higher Education, *Cost Containment: A Survey of Current Practices at America's State Colleges and Universities* (Washington, DC: March, 2008).

34. Adapted from original commentary that appeared in *Inside Higher Ed,* April 29, 2008.

CHAPTER 12

Higher Education, Lower Wages

Marc Bousquet

This chapter is adapted from *How the University Works: Higher Education and the Low-Wage Nation*,[1] which explores the relationship of mass higher education in the United States to a global shift toward precarious employment. The folk culture of higher education is deeply committed to the notion that higher education remains closely associated with higher wages. The truth is more complicated: more and more people have attempted to gain the higher education wage benefit in the past four decades, and real wages for many of those with advanced degrees have declined, rather than risen. The benefit for advanced degrees is increasingly associated with the business, technical, and vocational curriculum, and with graduate and professional degrees, rather than simply going to college. Furthermore, the growing gap between the wages of those with higher education and those without has more to do with extreme downward pressure on the wages of those at the bottom. Today, 70 percent of high school graduates enroll in some form of higher education the autumn after receiving the degree—and their motivation is often directly vocational, an explicit effort to escape the extreme low wages and extreme precariousness of those in the bottom half. A very large fraction of them fail in this attempt.

There are several ways that higher education as an industry benefits from the shift to precarious work arrangements and to the global trend, led by the United States, toward offloading risk onto individuals. As every aspect of life becomes more precarious, those without investment capital turn to higher education to gain what they hope will be more secure forms of employment. In the United States, health security, food security, elder and child care, even community acceptance and dignity all depend upon employment—and not just any employment, either: as government offloads more and more risk onto individuals and their employers, whole sectors of U.S. employers have simply shrugged off the burden. As more and more individuals and families chase the security offered by fewer and fewer positions, they pour into higher education looking for a competitive advantage.

But higher education also benefits from precarious work arrangements as an employer in its own right. In fact, higher education is the leading innovator of late-capitalist, post-Fordist contingent employment, continuously pushing the envelope of un- or under-compensated work.

A complex web of law, policy, and custom has created an absolutely marvelous circumstance for many higher education employers: they have vast workforces of persons whom they don't have to treat as workers, either because they don't think of themselves as employees, or because law and policy deny them traditional workplace rights.

Best known in this connection are the federal labor decisions affecting private institutions. While the majority of tenure-stream faculty in public institutions are unionized, the U.S. Supreme Court held that tenure-stream faculty in private institutions can be viewed as managers and supervisors, not labor, in the intellectually shaky 5–4 Yeshiva decision. (John Paul Stevens voted with the majority, a decision that's haunted him to the present day.) Similarly, while graduate employees are unionized at public institutions across the country, a Bush-appointed National Labor Relations Board (NLRB) in the Brown case brazenly reversed bargaining rights that graduate employees at private institutions won in the landmark NYU case just a couple of years earlier.

Less well understood, however, is that the majority of higher education faculty are no longer in this traditional circuit of doctoral study and tenure-stream appointment. At most institutions, faculty serving contingently and/or graduate students outnumber the tenure stream and teach the majority of sections. Faculty serving contingently are 70 percent of all faculty. (Research institutions typically employ fewer term faculty, but employ graduate students as instructors of record for at least 20 to 30 percent of undergraduate sections.) And these estimates are based on 2005 self-reported data by institutions, which typically undercount faculty serving contingently: AAUP internal estimates following the trend line, and anticipating better data, expect the consensus count of tenurable faculty to drop to 20 percent quite soon.

Similar trends have taken place in staff employment: permatemping, outsourcing, and—especially—the substitution of undergraduate student workers for positions that were formerly occupied by full-time staffers with benefits, contributing to the local economy.

This chapter is particularly concerned with the situation of the undergraduate worker. At many campuses, the single largest sector of the workforce are undergraduates, With soaring tuition—due both to the withdrawal of public support and leadership investment in everything except faculty—undergraduates seek to avoid debt by working while in school. Today, 80 percent of all undergraduates work while enrolled, on average 30 hours per week, with real consequences for their education. Most of the evidence suggests a threshold of 10 hours per week may be academically neutral, but it is not clear how even this lower threshold merges with the steadily mounting demands for donated, un- or under-compensated labor from the undergraduate in such forms as service learning, undergraduate involvement in faculty research, internships, civic engagement, even extracurricular activities.

Across the country, student labor time is expended in work that mirrors similar low-wage benefitless positions in the service economy at large: food service, day care, janitorial work, building security, interior painting and carpentry, parking enforcement, laundry service, administrative assistance, warehouse restocking, and so on. These activities are far more typical than the tutorial, library, community service, and internship activities that provide the public image of student work. (The nature of the work in internship and community service positions is another story, but is itself commonly similar to service-economy activity such as data entry, document reproduction, and so forth.)

Student employment offices function as temp agencies or outsourcing contractors for local businesses and campus units. At a typical public campus, the student employment office has hundreds of positions advertised by off-campus employers generally entirely without benefits or unemployment insurance, with a wage in the vicinity of six or seven dollars an hour (sometimes more and often less). The off-campus work includes farm labor, satellite installation, short order cooking, commission sales, forklift operation, and personal care in nursing homes, as well as clerking in banks, malls, and insurance offices. Public universities will sometimes provide cheap workers for nearby elite private universities (which often place limits on the number of hours that their own undergraduates can work). The federal government employs cheap student labor in general office work and, for instance, as receptionists for the Social Security Administration, in positions that formerly provided full-time employment for a citizen with reasonable wages and benefits. Student workers often replace full-time unionized staff. Sometimes the temp-agency function is quite frank: at the University of Illinois-Chicago, for instance, the student employment office maintains a separate Student Temporary Service exclusively for the purpose of providing near-minimum wage day labor on a just-in-time basis to any location on the campus.

While there are certainly circumstances in which some work might be beneficial, and amounts at which wage labor while enrolled can be academically neutral, it is clearly the case that there are a growing number of situations in, and individuals for, which it is associable with negative outcomes, from excessive demands on time or other factors. Education actors in faculty, leadership, foundations, legislatures, and the public at large must address the ethical complicity of campus and corporate employers in those negative outcomes. We must also begin to theorize the ethical field called up by the rising demand for low-wage student labor in relation to other increasing demands on students not clearly defined as wage labor, from unpaid service activities and internships to such forms of adding value to the campus as participating in athletics or the creation of consumable content. Of course, post-Fordism is always seeking to monetize these activities: as this chapter goes to press, a Florida newspaper consortium that has terminated a platoon of paid staff reporters now publishes the for-credit but unpaid reporting of journalism students who, like graduate teaching assistants, will soon enter the larger economy to find that their higher education has helped create a pyramid scheme in which there are few positions for which they are trained—because the work is now being done by other students.

The chapter from which this excerpt is drawn explores one exploitative undergraduate work program in an enterprise partnership between university, government and private employers—a program contributing to persistence to degree rates of as low as 12 percent. Is it ethical for universities and their partners to employ undergraduates on terms that severely disadvantage them from completing their degrees? In a moment when education administration has vastly increased its power over campus policy by comparison to students and faculty, do education leaders bear particular ethical responsibility for exploitative arrangements? Who is to be held accountable—and by what means? In what ways do students and similarly-exploited faculty and staff frame the possibility of a moral, ethical, and political counterpower?

With the majority of Americans enrolling in higher education by the September after high school graduation, the arrangement of student labor-time is a pressing national policy concern affecting an adult population sharply segmented by race, class, and gender in terms of opportunity and measures of educational success. The average age of persons enrolled in higher education is 26, and the majority of persons in higher education are women; students from minority backgrounds work longer hours and take longer to persist to degree. The ethical implications of shifting costs to students—thereby converting the student population to a cheap labor force powering the low-wage service economy, including the sector of the low-wage service economy represented by most employees of higher education itself—has clearly raced and gendered consequences for social justice. There is now a broad front of inquiry into the ethical, legal, and policy questions raised by the increasingly corporate administration of higher education.[2] This is far from an exclusively academic question. Lawmakers at every level are increasingly compelled to respond to intensifying national concern over scandals in the administration of student aid financing, for-profit education, the corporate sponsorship of academic research, administrative bloat, and the role of non-faculty expenditure in the exponential growth of education costs. Studies like this one address mushrooming concern over the distribution of opportunity and resources in the economic situation of American youth.[3]

The average student workloads, often involving 2 or 3 employers during the school year, create a class divide between students on campus: the 20 percent who do not work at all consume services provided by the increasingly harried majority who do. There are sharp and intensifying differences between the two groups' availability for informal learning, desirable un- or under-compensated internships, social activities, and personal growth. At what point do university administrations and policymakers have to address the harms represented by the intensifying inequality in the distribution of educational goods? What complicities do institutions have in the employment practices of their commercial partners? How might university restructuring become a force for increasing democracy and equality?

> "I know that I haven't updated in about two and a half weeks," but I have an excuse. UPS is just a tiring job. You see, before, I had an extra 31 hours to play games, draw things, compose music . . . do homework. But now, 31 + hours of my life is devoted to UPS.
>
> "I hate working there. But I need the money for college, so I don't have the option of quitting. My job at UPS is a loader. I check the zip codes on the box, I scan them into the database, and then I load them into the truck, making a brick wall out of boxes."—"Kody," high-school blogger in a UPS "school-to-work" program.[4]

The alarm sounds at 2:00 A.M. Together with half a dozen of her colleagues, the workday has begun for Prof. Susan Erdmann, a tenure-track assistant professor of English at Jefferson Community College in Louisville, Kentucky. She rises carefully to avoid waking her infant son and husband, who commutes 40 miles each way to his own tenure-track community college job in the neighboring rural county. She makes coffee, showers, dresses for work. With their combined income of around $60,000 and substantial education debt, they have a 30-year mortgage on a tiny home of about 1000 square feet: galley kitchen, dining alcove, one bedroom for them and another for their two sons to share. The front door opens onto a living room of a hundred square feet; entering or leaving the house means passing in between the couch and television. They feel fortunate to be able to afford any mortgage at all in this historically Catholic neighborhood originally populated by Louisville factory workers. It is winter: the sun will not rise for hours. She drives to the airport. Overhead, air-freight 747s barrel into the sky, about one plane every minute or so. Surrounded by the empty school buildings, boarded store fronts and dilapidated underclass homes of south central Louisville, the jets launch in post-midnight salvos. Their engines lack the sophisticated noise abatement technology required of air traffic in middle-class communities. Every 12 or 18 months, the city agrees to buy a handful of the valueless residences within earshot.

Turning into the airport complex, Susan never comes near the shuttered passenger terminals. She follows a four-lane private roadway toward the rising jets. After parking, a shuttle bus weaves among blindingly-lit aircraft hangars and drops her by the immense corrugated sorting facility that is the United Parcel Service main air hub, where she will begin her faculty duties at 3 A.M., greeting UPS's undergraduate workforce directly as they come off the sort. "You would have a sense that you were there, lifting packages," Erdmann recalls. "They would come off sweaty, and hot, directly off the line into the class. It was very immediate, and sort of awkward. They'd had no moment of downtime. They hadn't had their cigarette. They had no time to pull themselves together as student-person rather than package-thrower." Unlike her students, Susan and other faculty teaching and advising at the hub are not issued a plastic ID card/door pass. She waits on the windy tarmac for one of her students or colleagues to hear her knocking at the door. Inside, the noise of the sorting facility is, literally, deafening: the shouts, forklift alarms, whistles, and rumble of the sort machinery actually drown out the noise of the jets rising overhead. "Teaching in the hub was horrible," recalled one of Erdmann's colleagues. "Being in the hub was just hell. I'd work at McDonald's before I'd teach there again. The noise level was just incredible. The classroom was just as noisy as if it didn't have any walls." In addition to the sort machinery, UPS floor supervisors were constantly "screaming, yelling back and forth, 'Get this done, get that done, where's so and so'."

Susan is just one of a dozen faculty arriving at the hub after midnight. Some are colleagues from Jefferson Community College and the associated technical institution; others are from the University of Louisville. Their task tonight is to provide on-site advising and registration for some of the nearly 6,000 undergraduate students working for UPS at this facility. About 3,000 of those students work a midnight shift that ends at UPS's convenience—typically 3 or 4 A.M., though longer during the holiday and other peak shipping seasons.

Nearly all of the third-shift workers are undergraduate students who have signed employment contracts with something called the Metropolitan College.

The name is misleading, since it's not a college at all. An enterprise partnership between UPS, the city of Louisville, and the campuses that employ Susan and her colleagues, Metropolitan College is in fact little more than a labor contractor. Supported by public funds, this "college" offers no degrees and does no educating. Its sole function is to entice students to sign contracts that commit them to provide cheap labor in exchange for education benefits at the partner institutions. The arrangement has provided UPS with over 10,000 ultra-low-cost student workers since 1997, the same year that the Teamsters launched a crippling strike against the carrier. The Louisville arrangement is the vanguard of UPS's efforts to convert its part-time payroll, as far as possible, to a financial aid package for student workers in partnership with campuses near its sorting and loading facilities.

As a result of carefully-planned corporate strategy, between 1997 and 2003 UPS hired undergraduate students to staff more than half of its 130,000 part-time positions.[5] Students are currently the majority of all part-timers, and the overwhelming majority on the least-desirable shifts. Part of UPS's strategy is that only some student employees receive education benefits. By reserving the education benefits of its earn-and-learn programs to workers willing to work undesirable hours, UPS has over the past decade recruited approximately 50,000 part-time workers to its least desirable shifts without raising the pay (in fact, while pushing them to work harder for continually lower pay against inflation).[6] The largest benefit promises are reserved for students who think they can handle working after midnight every night of the school week.

Metropolitan College is the largest and earliest of the earn-and-learn programs and exists for the sole purpose of recruiting night-shift workers at the Louisville main hub. Between 1998 and 2005, UPS claims to have assisted 10,000 students through the Metropolitan College arrangement.[7] Of the 7,500 part-time employees at UPS's Louisville hub in May 2006, some are welfare-to-work recipients who are picked up in company buses from the city and even surrounding rural counties. A few hundred are Louisville area high school students in school-to-work programs. Three-quarters of the part-timers—5,600—are college students.[8] More than half of the students—about 3,000—are enrolled in the Metropolitan College which, with few exceptions, enrolls only those willing to work the night shift.

Metropolitan College enrollment and recruitment activities are entirely driven by UPS's staffing needs. Ditto for scheduling: all of the benefits enjoyed by the Metro College students are contingent upon showing up at the facility every weeknight of the school year at midnight, and performing physically strenuous labor for as long as they are needed.

The consequences of night-shift work are well documented, and the preponderance of available evidence suggests markedly negative effects for the Louisville students. Every instructor to whom I spoke reported excessive fatigue and absenteeism (due to fatigue, but also to an extraordinarily high physical injury rate: "They all got hurt," Erdmann reports.) Students who signed employment contracts with Metro College showed substantial failure to persist academically. "I would lose students midterm, or they would never complete final assignments," Erdmann said. "They would just stop coming at some point." Erdmann served as chair of a faculty committee that attempted to improve the academic success of students employed by UPS at her institution. The group scheduled special UPS-only sections between 5 and 11 P.M. both on campus and at the hub, and began the ritual of 3 A.M. advising. Since nearly all of the faculty involved taught and served on committees five days a week, their efforts to keep students from dropping out by teaching evenings and advising before dawn resulted in a bizarre 24-hour cycle of work for themselves. The institutions even experimented with ending the fall semester before Thanksgiving for the thousands of UPS employees, in order to keep their finals from conflicting with the holiday shipping rush (and the one season a year when the students could be assured of a shift lasting longer than four hours). Even in the specially-scheduled classes and shortened terms, Erdmann recalls classes with dropout rates of 30 to 40 percent. "It was most definitely worse for those with children," she concluded.

> It was a disaster for those with children. Students who had family obligations tended to do poorly. When you had younger, more traditional age students with a very clear and limited goal—and they were often men—if they had a limited goal, such as "I am going to get Microsoft certified," and if they were healthy and young, and physically active, those individuals might be okay.
>
> Whenever you had people with children—you know, people who can't sleep all day, they would get tremendously stressed out. I feel like very few of them actually did well with the program, the ones with family.

Pressed to offer instances of individual students who indisputably benefited from the program, Erdmann described just two individuals, both at
the extreme margins of economic and social life. One was a single mother
who worked multiple jobs and saved some of her wages toward a down
payment on a residential trailer, thus escaping an abusive domestic life.
The other was a young man coping with severe mental illness. Rather
than relieving economic pressure, Metropolitan College appears to have
increased the economic distress of the majority of participants. According
to the company's own fact sheet, these student workers giving up 5 nights'
sleep will typically be paid for just 15 to 20 hours a week. Since the wage
ranges from just $8.50 at the start to no more than $9.50 for the majority
of the most experienced, this can mean net pay *below* $100 in a week, and
averaging out to a little over $120. The rate of pay bears emphasizing:
because the students must report five nights a week and are commonly let
go after just three hours each night, *their take-home pay for sleep deprivation
and physically hazardous toil will generally be less than $25 per shift.*

In fact, most UPS part-timers earn little more than six thousand dollars
in a year. Most have at least one other job: their typical earnings from UPS
in 2006–2007 would generally have covered little more than the worker's
car payment, insurance, gasoline, and other transportation-related expenses. "Everyone had another job," Erdmann says. "Even the high school
students had another job. The high school students were working two
jobs. For some people that meant working Saturday nights as a waitress,
but for others it was much more extensive. For a lot of people it meant
that they got up every day and went to work in the afternoon before going
in to classes and UPS in the evening." Every instructor to whom I spoke
confirmed the pressure that the ultra-low wage added to the unreasonable
working hours and physical hazards as a detriment to students' chances for
academic persistence. "That was when they skipped class," affirmed another instructor, "when they were going to another job. I was just amazed
how many of them were going to another job."

UPS presents a triple threat to students' prospects for academic persistence: sleep deprivation and family-unfriendly scheduling, ultra-low
compensation resulting in secondary and tertiary part-time employment,
and a high injury rate. Student employees report being pressured to skip
class. Especially at the end of the fall term, the night sorts can run 4 or
5 hours beyond the anticipated 4 A.M. completion: "Each time I said I
was unwilling to miss class for an extended sort, the supe would tell me to
'think long and hard about my priorities,'" reports one student employee.
"I got the message."

UPS refuses to provide standard statistics that would permit evaluation of the impact that this triple threat is actually having on the students

it employs. None of its partner institutions appears to have responsibly studied the consequences of the program for its students in terms of such major measures as persistence to degree, dropout rate, and so on.

Amazingly, all of the press coverage of the UPS earn-and-learn programs in general, and the Louisville Metropolitan College arrangement in particular, has been positive. In fact, most of the coverage appears to have been drawn closely from UPS press releases themselves or conducted with students selected for their success stories. Acknowledging that the night shift "took some getting used to," one local newspaper's coverage is typical in quoting a student shrugging off the challenges, "I just schedule my classes for the afternoon."[9] Other stories are more meretricious, suggesting that the UPS jobs keep students from partying too much. One quotes a UPS supervisor who suggests that college students "are staying up until dawn anyway."[10]

Ironically, UPS has received numerous awards for "corporate citizenship" and was named one of the "best companies for minorities" in connection with the program. It emphasizes recruitment among Hispanic students, and numerous Hispanic organizations have endorsed the program and/or published in journals or websites such as LatinoLA or unedited UPS press releases targeting Hispanics that emphasize the program's availability to nontraditional students, including retirees and those re-entering the workforce.

"I DREAD WORK EVERY DAY"

UPS has long pioneered low-cost benefitless employment, abetted by the Teamsters themselves, who, under Jimmy Hoffa, Sr., signed one of the first contracts in American industry to permit the regular use of part-time employees in 1962. This second tier of employment was massively expanded after the Teamsters agreed to 1982 protocols that raised the wages of full-time workers while freezing those of part-timers. In that year, part-time UPS employees started at $8.00 an hour, the equivalent in 2007 of about $17/hr ($34,000 a year). Similarly, in 1982 part time employees averaged about $10/hr, the equivalent in 2007 of $22/hr ($44,000 a year).

Not incidentally, at the 1982 wages, a UPS part-time worker could indeed successfully fund a college education. One employee from the 1970s recalls:

> At the old full and fair rate prior to the 1982 UPS wage reduction despite soaring volume and profits a pt worker in exchange for back breaking work could afford to rent a room, pay tuition, buy food and clothing, and afford to own and operate a used car. This was a good

deal that was profitable to the student and society as well as profitable to UPS. I went through six years of college that way and am very grateful to the Teamsters for the good pay. I find it a national disgrace that UPS has effectively reduced the pay by nearly 65% adjusted for inflation since 1982 and destroyed a positive job for over a hundred thousand workers and for society as well. There are [UPS] pt workers living in homeless shelters in Richmond, California and other parts of the country.

As with Wal-Mart and other predatory super low-wage employers, many of UPS's student workers are homeless. At the Louisville hub, "I knew people sleeping in their cars," Erdmann recalled.

After the union's concession to a radically cheaper second tier of employment, 80 percent of all new UPS jobs were created in the permanent part-time category. While the pay between part-time and full-time diverged slowly between 1962 and 1982, the differential accelerated rapidly in the 1980s and 1990s. Serving as a UPS driver is still a coveted blue-collar position. From the Reagan years to the present, these full-time Teamsters continued to enjoy raises, job security, due process with respect to their grievances, and substantial benefits, including a pension. But over the same period of time these and other full-time positions became the minority of employees covered by the contract.

In less than 15 years, permanent part-timers became the majority of the UPS work force in the United States. The ratio of permanent part-timers was particularly pronounced at the Louisville main hub, where a high-speed, high-pressure night sort was conducted. As the wages of the part-time majority steadily shrank against inflation, opportunities to join the full-time tier all but disappeared. Today, even the company's human resources recruiters admit that while full-time positions "still exist," it can take "six to seven years or even longer" to get on full-time. A single-digit percentage of the company's part-time employees last that long. Few of those who do persist are actually offered full-time work. During the long night of Reagan-Bush-Clinton reaction, according to employees, the company unilaterally abrogated work rules, including safety limits on package size and weight. Injuries soared to two and a half times the industry average, in especial disproportion among part-time employees in the first year.

As jointly bargained by UPS and the Teamsters, the part-time positions devolved into one of the least desirable forms of work in the country, with one of the highest turnover rates in history. Featuring poor wages, limited benefits, a high injury rate, and unreasonable scheduling, the Teamster-UPS agreement created compensation and working conditions for the part-time majority so abysmal that most rational persons preferred virtually any other form of employment, or not working at all.

Most part-timers departed within weeks of being hired. According to George Poling, director of the Louisville Metropolitan College, the average term of employment for part-time workers on the night sort was just eight weeks. At the Louisville facility, 90 percent of part-time hires quit before serving a year. Across the country in 1996 UPS hired 180,000 part-timers on all shifts, but only 40,000 were still with the company at the year's end. In part as a result of steadily accelerating turnover, UPS agreed in just 16 days to the most-publicized core demand of the 1997 Teamsters strike, the creation of 10,000 new full-time jobs out of some of the new part-time positions.

Overlooked during the press coverage of the Teamsters' apparent victory was the fact that these new full-time positions were paid well below the scale of existing full-timers and would earn just 75 percent of the rate of regular full-timers by the end of the contract. This introduced a new, lower-wage tier in the ranks of the full-timers. The lower wages of this group would continue to support the wage increases and benefits of the union's powerful minority constituency, the shrinking core of long-term full-timers. (Readers employed in academic circumstances will recognize this strategy as having been pioneered in their own workplaces, with the institution of nontenurable full-time lectureships as one of the "solutions" that the long-term tenured faculty have accepted to management's expansion of part-time faculty.) It would take three years of foot-dragging through arbitration and federal court before UPS delivered even these watered-down full-time jobs.

Despite credulous ballyhoo about the strike as the decade's exemplar of labor militancy and solidarity between full and part-timers, the part-time majority of UPS workers benefited little from the Teamster victory.

The starting wage for part-timers, which had remained at $8.00 for 15 years (since 1982) was raised in the 1997 contract a grand total of 50 cents.

Ten years later, the Teamster-negotiated starting wage for UPS part-time package handlers working between 11 and 4 A.M. remains just $8.50, or exactly one raise in a quarter-century. This is a loss against inflation of more than half. In 1982 the $8.00/hr starting wage for part-timers was more than twice the minimum wage (of $3.35), and slightly above the national hourly average wage (of $7.72). In 2006, the UPS starting wage was about half of the national average hourly wage of $16.46 for nonsupervisory workers. With the minimum wage so low that only half a million Americans earn it, the $8.50/hr UPS starting wage in 2006 is equal to or lower than what most traditionally minimum wage occupations actually earn, and is lower than the statutory metropolitan living wage established in many major cities. This isn't 8 or 9 bucks an hour for 8 hours a day, 9 A.M. to 5 P.M. This is 8 or 9 bucks an hour for *showing up five nights a week at midnight and working 3½ to five hours, depending on the flow of packages, for physically demanding, dangerous night-shift work at the company's convenience.* The pay starts at midnight and ends three hours later, but there is at least half an hour, often more, of unpaid commuting around airport security on either side of the paid three hours.

The total commute each way can total as much as an hour, even for students who live just a mile or two from the facility: "When I was there, you'd have to be in the parking lot by 11:30 at the latest if you wanted the shuttle bus to get you to the gate by 11:40, where you'd then wait to have your ID checked, and then walk through the maze of hub buildings for 500 yards before finding your workspace and clocking in," one recalled. "The point being if I got parked at 11:45, I'd be late and get bawled out. The traffic outside UPS leading into the shift is nightmarish, so you'd really need to leave the house an hour before work to have a shot at getting to the sort station on time." That's five hours of third-shift time, being paid close to the minimum wage for just three hours.

In the past 25 years, working conditions at UPS have eroded even faster than the wage. With the union's lack of interest in part-time workers, UPS has increasingly introduced ultra short shifts, technology-driven speedup, and managerial surveillance of every aspect of the work process, including real-time tracking of errors. Employing constant surveillance by a battalion of "part-time supes," themselves generally students, UPS deploys cameras and manned watchtowers throughout the multi-layer sort. "They're always watching you work from tall perches that exist nearly everywhere in the plant," one former student worker recalls. "The perches are ostensibly ladders to other layers of the sort, but the consistent presence of management at the stair landings creates the feeling of almost total surveillance. Even when you can't see them, you know they're in hidden rooms watching you on camera." Nearly all student workers are repeatedly tested by "salting" the presorted containers with bad address labels; employees decry the practice as a "particularly nasty" form of continuous stressing of their work environment.

Several current or former UPS employees have begun weblogs to chronicle the high-speed, high-stress nature of their employment. One, writing as "Brown Blood," explained that he'd begun the weblog for "the employees of UPS to express there true feelings about there job in all aspects," noting, "I must apologize now for any fowl language that may . . . *will* occur in this community because most of these jobs not only test the limitations of your physical capacity it also shatters all anger management." On the JobVent blog, UPS workers' rating of the workplace were consistently *below zero*:

> Little did I know that I would spend 4 hours a day in a dark, oven hot dungeon being screamed at by idiotic powertrippers who having givin up beleiving life has some kind of meaning and now want to make themselves feel better by humiliating the only people in their lives that they have any sort of advantage over. All this while you are sweating liters and giving your back life-long injuries. I couldn't help but laugh in disbelief when i received my first pay check for $120. IF YOU EVEN THINK OF WORKING AT UPS realize that if you don't want to spend the next ten years of your life being treated like toiletpaper just to become a lousy driver then go work for fedex, the benefits are as good, the pay is better and you get just a little respect, a friend of mine worked there for 5 days and became a driver. ups is no less than 7–10 years. bottom line UPS SUCKS A BIG ONE!!!!!!!!! i dread work every day.

According to at least one long-term Teamster full-timer, the part-time students working the night sort are driven particularly hard: "They cram eight hours work into five." Agreeing with this characterization of the workload for undergraduate employees, one student worker said, "Around finals time, I'd go for days without sleep. The scary thing is, I'd see the sleepless period coming, know there was nothing I could do about it other than quit school or quit work, and then learn to psyche myself up for it."

Most bloggers complained of the pay ("pathetic"), schedule ("random, terrible hours"), injuries ("I was killing myself physically," "constant muscle pulls/strains, a lot of safety hazards," "horrible; you'll sweat like a dog in the summer and freeze in the winter—unsafe—watch out for sharp objects and falling boxes"), and supervisory harassment. Holistically, the evaluations were resoundingly negative: "This was the worst job I ever had," "You can imagine its bad when the highest UPS scores with me in any category is a –2," "If your thinking of working here DON'T DO IT!" Many of the bloggers give a vivid portrait of the stressful nature of the work. Every error is tracked, and a minimum standard for error-free sorting is one error in 2500. How often do you make an error while typing? If you're like me, you make several typing errors per page, for an error rate per word of 1/60 or so. At UPS, an error of 1 in 500 is considered extremely poor. The student workers are particularly likely to be placed in these high-stress positions. If younger, they are commonly inexperienced at work generally. If older, they have typically suffered substantial economic and/or personal distress. Either way, those who don't express rage and disappointment, or vote with their feet by quitting, appear likely to internalize management's construction of them as slow-moving failures. Students sometimes contribute to weblogs like "Brown Blood" less to complain than to get coping advice ("Is there a better way of doing this without going miserably slowly? . . . I want to show that I can be competent in some form of employment.")

The work of the loaders intensifies during the holiday rush:

> I hate how UPS is always fucking you over. On a normal day I load 3 trucks and lately it's been a total of about 800–900 packages. . . . They told me I would only have the 4th car one day per week. Well guess what. they gave me 4 cars 3 days this week. Today I had a total of over 1600 packages with no help, the bastards. My loads were shit and my drivers were bitching, but what the hell can I do about it?
>
> I suppose the fact that I've slept less than 5 of the past 55 hours had something to do with my despising work today. but red bull helps with that.
>
> I'm so f-ing glad it's a long weekend. ("hitchhiker42")

These notes of stress, fatigue, and powerlessness on the job are nearly uniform throughout the UPS permanent part-timers.

EMPLOYEE OF THE MONTH

Seventy percent of the workers in the main UPS hub in Louisville are women. The average age is 34, and many are parents. Some of the women work in data entry, but most of the work involves package handling. For every teen-age worker, there's another part-timer well into her 40s.

The reality of the undergraduate workforce is very different from the representation of teen partiers on a perpetual spring break, as popularized by television ("Girls Gone Wild"), UPS propaganda ("they're staying up until dawn anyway"), and *Time* magazine: "Meet the 'twixters,' [20-somethings] who live off their parents, bounce from job to job and hop from mate to mate. They're not lazy—they just won't grow up."[11]

There are more than 15 million students currently enrolled in higher education (with an average age of around 26). Tens of millions of persons have recently left higher education, nearly as many without degrees as with them. Like graduate employees, undergraduates now work longer hours in school, spend more years in school, and can take several years to find stable employment after obtaining their degrees. Undergraduates and recent school leavers, whether degree holders or not, now commonly live with their parents well beyond the age of legal adulthood, often into their late 20s. Like graduate employees, undergraduates increasingly find that their period of "study" is in fact a period of employment as cheap labor. The

production of cheap workers is facilitated by an ever-expanding notion
of youth. A University of Chicago survey conducted in 2003 found that
the majority of Americans now think that adulthood begins around 26, an
age not coincidentally identical with the average age of the undergraduate
student population.

The popular conception of student life as delayed adulthood is reflected
in such notions as "30 is the new 20" and "40 is the new 30."[12] The fatu-
ousness of these representations is confounded by looking at the other
end of one's employment life. Few people are finding that in terms of
employability after downsizing that "50 is the new 40." Persons who lose
their jobs in their 50s often find themselves unemployable. What are the
economic consequences for a person whose productive career can begin in
their middle 30s or later, and end at 50 or sooner? This pattern presents
real obstacles for both women and men wishing to raise a family. Yet mass
media representations of extended schooling and the associated period
of insecure employment are often cheery, suggesting that it's a stroke of
good fortune, an extended youth free of such unwelcome responsibilities
as home ownership, child-rearing, and visits to health-care providers. In
this idealistic media fantasy, more time in higher education means more
time to party—construing an extended youth as a prolonged stretch of
otherwise empty time unmarked by the accountabilities of adulthood.

But concretely the apparently empty time of involuntarily extended
youth associated with higher education is really quite full. It's full of
feelings—the feelings of desperation, betrayal, and anxiety, the sense that
Cary Nelson has captured for graduate employees under the heading of
Will Teach for Food.[13] Writers like Anya Kamenetz and Tamara Draut have
captured the similar feelings of upper-middle class college graduates in
books like *Generation Debt* and *Strapped*.[14] Most of the persons Draut and
Kamenetz describe will have added graduate school to successful bachelor's degrees at first or second tier institutions. But little attention has
been paid to the role of higher education in organizing the vast majority
of the lives it touches—those who don't graduate, or who graduate with
community college, vocational, or technical degrees.

"Employee of the Month" is typical of the more successful students
employed by UPS. As she tells it on her weblog, this "mom/stylist," aged 30,
the mother of children aged 3 and 5, is a fan of Christian apocalyptic fic-
tion, and a part-time student who hopes to become a teacher. She has
an A average. Her weblog represents her husband as a substance abuser
who provides no contribution to the household finances. During the
months covered in her weblog, he moves in and out of the house. Like
most students who find a job with UPS, she was already working hard
before signing on with Big Brown. While parenting and starting school,

she was working three jobs, including office work and hair styling. In the first few weeks, she enjoys the work: "I am digging this job! I get to work out for 4–5 hours a night," plus collect education benefits. Anticipating the 50- cent raise, she writes, "The pay sucks at first but within 90 days I should be ok." She plans to continue working as a stylist, but feels that she can quit her other two job part-time jobs, "with doing hair 3 days a week I will be making just as much as I have been making [with three jobs] and only working about 35–37 hours a week total. Woo Hoo!"

Rather than a partying teen, this far more typical working undergraduate is a devout 30-year-old who is thrilled simply to be able to work a mere full-time equivalent at two different jobs, in addition to schoolwork and solo parenting of two small children.

After the Christmas rush, and still in her first two months of employment, the upbeat blogger notes: "I am getting muscles in my arms and shoulders, my legs are getting a little toned. I do need to lose about 25 lbs so the more muscle thing is a good start . . . I am getting better at my job now that I am a little stronger and can lift the boxes up to the top shelf."

Within six months—by March 2006—she had made "employee of the month" at her facility.

In the same month, she had her first work-related injury: a strained ligament from working with heavy packages. On a physician's orders, she was placed on light duty, dealing with packages weighing 1–7 pounds (seven pounds is approximately the weight of a gallon of milk).

She had also grown discouraged about her prospects of continuing her education, and was considering dropping out.

Her family life is increasingly stressed by the UPS job. In order to collect less than 30 bucks a night, she has to leave her children to sleep at her mother's house five nights a week.

Now that the holiday rush is past, she finds that, on her UPS salary and even with a second job, she is unable to afford such everyday staples as Easter baskets for her children, which her sister provided.

"A guy at work told me about a job at a private school, I applied and had an interview. I hope I get the job. I need to pay bills and the UPS job isn't enough," she concludes:

> My kids did have a good easter, thank you to my sister. We went down to her house and she bought my kids candy, toys, and each kid a movie!! I thought that was above the call of duty. I can't tell you how much I appreciate my family for coming to my aid in my time of need this past year. I know I could get another job and put my kids in daycare all day again and be able to support them better but I wouldn't be able to go to school. It's hard right now but I am

already a year into school and I will be a teacher in a few years. I can't
stop now. Even with this drama going on in my life I have still kept a
3.6 grade point average. I want to finish it. My son still wants me to
be a teacher so I have to show him that with work and perseverance
you can accomplish anything dispite your circumstances. Facts don't
count when it comes to reaching a goal.[15]

In other words: for UPS to receive one super-cheap worker, that worker's
parents have to donate free child care, and other family members have to donate cash, time, and goods. Like the vast majority of her coworkers in a UPS
earn-and-learn arrangement, this A student and employee of the month is
so sapped by the experience, physically injured, undercompensated, and
domestically disarranged, that she's on the verge of quitting school.

Despite her qualifications, energy, and commitment, the only thing
keeping this UPS worker going is the desire to shore up achievement
ideology for her children ("I have to show him that with work and perseverance you can accomplish anything dispite your circumstances"), to
create a Disney narrative out of their lives when she drops them off to
sleep at their grandparents five nights a week, a Disney narrative that will
prove that "facts don't count when it comes to reaching a goal."

SUPERGIRL: "MY BACK HURTS SO FRICKEN BAD"

This 5' 2", 110-pound, 23-year-old undergraduate woman writing
under the moniker of "supergirl" has a charming sardonic flair: "America
needs no more cheese, ham, huge-ass boxes of summer sausage, holiday
popcorn tins, or kringles . . . I think I've moved enough of these that every
man, woman and child should already have one by default. No wonder
obesity is an epidemic."[16]

As with most, her daily UPS shift is a second job. After a year, she's
ready to quit. She's had one work-related arm surgery: "I really don't
want to have another, or worse, risk permanently damaging the nerves
in both arms," she writes, "And I sincerely don't think I'm being paid
enough to stay there 2 years and blow out both arms unfixably . . . I
know pain and can tolerate it, but I can't even fucking sleep because every
position somehow puts pressure on a nerve in my arm that's already got
problems and is being pushed to the limits." When I asked another Louisville student employee to comment on "supergirl's" representation of
the injury rate, he called the physical toll exacted by the workplace a "key
point," adding, "The physical harm this work does will long outlast the
span of the job."

She complains of the culture of UPS—of speed-up, the pressure to deny injuries and work through them, and the pressure to continue employment through the milestones that dictate education benefits such as loan and tuition remission.

Under the rubric "don't make UPS yours," she warns other prospective student employees away:

> my back hurts . . . so fricken bad. It doesn't benefit me to say i hurt because i've noticed that if you hurt of any kind the sort super just asks you to quit (in not so many eloquently and legal to say to an employee words) . . . i lift tons of shit that's got 20–30 pounds on me . . . but as I stand; a girl of 5' 2" and a buck ten . . . I can't do that kinda shit everyday . . . I guess I can be supergirl fast or supergirl strong or a normal mix of either . . . but I can't be both every fucking day. who can, anyway?

What disturbs her most is the pressure (from family, co-workers, supervisors) to work through her injuries to benefit-earning milestones. She understands the pressures driving everyone else to push her to continue, "but shit why can't I just say I'd like to not be at a job like that?" In any event, she writes, "everyone should know I'll probably just stay there anyhow . . . cause I'm too damn busy to find anything else anyway."

10,000 STUDENTS AND 300 DEGREES

There's little mystery regarding UPS's motivation for the earn-and-learn programs—not benevolence, but the cheapness and docility of the student workforce. In addition to the ultra-low wage, students' dependency on UPS includes loan guarantees and tuition remissions, which are lost or reduced if the student resigns prematurely from the program. As a result of its campaign to hire undergraduates, UPS's retention of part-time package handlers has improved markedly, despite speedup and continued stagnation of the wage between 1997 and 2007. Average time of employment for part-timers grew by almost 50 percent, and retention improved by 20 percent, with some of the most dramatic improvements in the Louisville main hub. This tuition benefit is tax-deductible and taxpayer-subsidized. It's a good deal for UPS, which shares the cost of the tuition benefit with partner schools and communities and saves millions in payroll tax (by providing tuition benefits instead of higher wages) while holding down the part-time wage overall. All earn-and-learn students must apply for federal and state financial aid. Many of its workers attend community colleges, where tuition is often just a few hundred dollars. Many students are subjected to a bait-and-switch: attracted to the program by the promise of tuition benefits at the University of Louisville (currently over $6,000 a year), program participants are instead steered toward enrollment in the community colleges—a decision that doesn't reflect their academic needs, but as Metropolitan College director Poling admits, exclusively the desire of the state and UPS to contain costs. Studying on a part-time basis, as most in the program do, a student seeking a B.A. degree can therefore remain in a community college for three or four years before earning the credits enabling transfer to a four-year school. One student pointed out that trying to schedule around the UPS jobs was a "lot harder than it sounds," and for many it was "downright impossible to do this and get the degree in any reasonable period of years." Students who attend inexpensive schools, or qualify for high levels of tuition relief (as is often the case in the economically disadvantaged groups targeted by UPS recruiters), substantially reduce UPS's costs. Undergraduate students also represent lower group health insurance costs.

Another way in which students reduce UPS's cost is by quitting before they become eligible for benefits, by taking an incomplete, or by failing a class. No benefits are paid for failed or incomplete classes. Students who drop out of school but continue to work for UPS also significantly lower UPS's cost.

To put UPS's costs in perspective: in a decade, it has spent no more than $80 million on tuition and student loan redemption in over 50 hubs. By contrast, its 2006 deal with the state of Kentucky for a 5,000-job *expansion of just one hub* involved $50 million in state support over ten years. Company officials are fairly frank about UPS's dependency on cheap student labor, supported by massive taxpayer giveaways. "It would have been nearly impossible to find an additional 5,000 workers [for the expansion] without the resources of Metropolitan College," a public-relations VP told the Louisville business press.[17] It has expanded earn-and-learn programs to 50 other metropolitan centers, to Canada, and to for-profit education vendors such as DeVry.

It's a lot less clear whether this is a good deal for students. "We've solved employee retention," Poling admits, "but we've got to work more on academic retention."

It's hard to estimate the size of Poling's understatement, since UPS and Metropolitan College refuse to supply standard academic persistence data on its huge population of undergraduate workers. But it's a whopper.

Of the 10,000 students Poling's program claims to have assisted with their higher education since 1997, he is able to produce evidence of just 292 degrees earned, 111 associate's and 181 bachelor's degrees. Since both UPS and Metropolitan College refuse to provide public accountability for the academic persistence of undergraduate workers, it's hard to estimate what these numbers mean by comparison to more responsible and conventional education and financial aid circumstances. However, the most favorable construction of the evidence available for Metropolitan College shows an average entry of slightly more than 1,000 student workers annually. Based on 2.5 years of data after 6 years of program operation, according to Poling, the program between 2003 and 2006 showed approximate annual degree production of about 40 associate's and 75 bachelor's degrees.

This approximates to a 12 percent rate of persistence to any kind of degree.

UPS's student employees in the Metropolitan College program are more likely to be retained as UPS employees than they are to be retained as college students. In May 2006, of the 3,000 or so Metropolitan College students working at UPS, only 1,263 were actually taking classes that semester. This means that during the spring term, almost 60 percent of the student-workers in UPS's employ were not in school: "another 1,700 or so," in Poling's words, "took the semester off."[18]

Of the minority actually taking classes, at least a quarter failed to complete the semester. UPS pays a bonus for completing semesters unsuccessfully (with withdrawals or failing grades) as well as successfully. Counting the bonuses paid in recent years for unsuccessful semesters together with the successful ones, Poling suggested that during terms in which between 1,200 and 1,700 student workers were enrolled, between 900 and 1,100 students would complete at least one class, or a ratio of perhaps 3/4.

These numbers appear to hang roughly together. If in any given year the majority of UPS night-shift workers are taking the semester off, and 25 percent or more of those actually enrolled fail to complete even one class in the semester, this seems consistent with an eventual overall persistence to degree of 12 percent.

In plain fact, it would seem that *UPS counts on its student workers failing or dropping out*. Because of the high rate of failed classes, withdrawals, and dropping out, UPS ends up paying only a modest fraction of the education benefits it offers. If each of the 48,000 students who has passed through its earn-and-learn program had collected the full UPS share of tuition benefits over a five year period, it would have cost the company over $720 million. In fact, it has so far had to spend just *10 percent* of that total—$72 million—on tuition remission, or an average of only $1,500 per student (the equivalent of just one semester's maximum tuition benefit per participant). Similarly, the loan remission benefit (theoretically as much as $8,000 after four years' employment) would total almost $384 million. But as of 2005 UPS has had so far to pay off just $21 million, an average of just $438 per student worker, well under 10 percent of its liability if all of its student workers actually persisted to completion of a 4-year degree.

In the absence of meaningful accountability by UPS and its partners, we can only raise questions about this arrangement, not answer them.

Since the program has been in operation for 10 years, there is plenty of data. These are questions that can be answered. And these are questions that parents, students, partner institutions, and host communities should demand be answered.

Many of these are similar in form to questions I posed to UPS through its press representative and which it refused to answer:

1. On average, how long do student workers remain employed with UPS?
2. What percentage of student workers exiting UPS's earn-and-learn programs remain enrolled in school?
3. What percentage of UPS student workers have additional employment?
4. What percentage of current or former UPS student workers earn associate's degrees within 3 years and bachelor's degrees within six years?
5. Do these percentages vary by shift worked?
6. What is the total and average amount of loans taken by earn-and-learn students? How much of those loans have been paid off by UPS?
7. What is the grade-point average of students enrolled in UPS programs?
8. UPS advertises that students can earn up to $25,000 in tuition and loan benefits. What is the average tuition and loan benefit actually paid per student?

One of the major unanswered questions is this one: why haven't the partner institutions asked UPS for these answers already?

Don't they have a responsibility to ask whether their students are being well-served by these arrangements? If a promise to fund a citizen's higher education actually results in reduced likelihood of educational success, shouldn't the institution, the state, and the city revise or discontinue the arrangement?

One reason the University of Louisville hasn't asked these questions is because, in connection with its willingness to contract its students out to UPS, it collects tuition revenue and other subsidies, and the Metropolitan College partnership contributes heavily to new building plans across the campus, most notably erecting a series of new dormitories to house the UPS student workforce recruited from all over the state.

Nor has it wanted to draw attention to the success rate of its own students. When the Metropolitan College program began in 1997–1998, the University of Louisville's six-year graduation rate was under 30 percent. By comparison to the institutions in its own benchmarking, the six-year graduation rate for Mississippi State is 58 percent, Florida State is 65 percent, and North Carolina State is 66 percent.

A six-year graduation rate of around 30 percent means that if 2,000 undergraduates enter as first-year students, close to 1,400 will not have graduated six years later.

That figure is almost twice the number at many comparable institutions. Over 10 years, a gap this size in academic persistence means that many thousands of individuals are not receiving degrees by comparison to students in benchmark institutions. Over the past 10 years, that graduation rate has crawled up 3 or 4 percentage points to 33 percent, but even the improved number places the University of Louisville dead last among its own benchmark institutions, and dead last among 38 comparator institutions generated by the IPEDS database. Louisville and the state of Kentucky consistently rank near the bottom of educational attainments by a variety of indicators. Since the educational success rate of students at the institution and surrounding community was already so low, the success rates of UPS students fly under the radar.

One dean of students with whom I spoke claimed not to have studied the UPS students' success rate, but shrugged off concerns with the impression that their attainments were "probably roughly comparable" to the low rate of other Louisville students. Using the measure of "year-to-year persistence," Poling was willing to compare his Metropolitan College student workers to other Louisville students, but not when it came to comparing persistence to degree.

GOOD FOR UPS AND WHO ELSE?

One of the reasons few hard questions have been asked of arrangements like the Metropolitan College is that the super-exploitation of undergraduate workers is not just a matter of UPS's individual dependency, but a system of profound *codependency,* extending through the web of local, national, and even global economic relations.

As John McPhee's *New Yorker* profile of the Louisville hub makes clear, working for UPS at the Louisville main hub is really working for a lot of companies.[19] A short distance from the sorting facility, UPS maintains *millions* of square feet of warehouse facilities where its employees fulfill orders from online vendors for books, computers, underwear, and jet engine parts. When a Toshiba laptop breaks, Toshiba sends the repair order

to UPS, who directs a driver to pick up the machine; from the local hub
it is flown in a UPS jet to an industrial park abutting the Louisville airport, where 80 UPS computer technicians repair Toshiba computers with
Toshiba parts, returning the machines to their owners in about 72 hours.
UPS is a major outsourcing contractor for fulfillment of products sold
across the globe: the entire inventory of companies like Jockey is kept in
UPS facilities in Louisville and handled exclusively by UPS employees
from the point of manufacture to the consumer or retail outlet.

So the good deal that UPS is getting from the state and working students of Kentucky is also a good deal for all of the companies with which it
has outsourcing contracts and, ultimately, for all of its customers. Shipping
from the Louisville Worldport is faster and cheaper than ever before. It's a
good deal for the full-time Teamsters, who no longer have to feel pressure
to negotiate better for a significant fraction of UPS's new employees.

Chris Sternberg, senior vice president of corporate communications at
Papa John's International, is frank about the multilayered economic
advantages of the Metropolitan College arrangement for local businesses.

> Anytime new jobs are added to the Louisville economy, we are happy
> both from a community standpoint as well as for our business. When
> you have more people employed and the economy is thriving, we'll
> sell more pizzas. We are obviously pleased with the announcement.
> From an employment standpoint, many of our part-time workers
> also work part time at UPS, where they may work a four-hour shift
> at UPS and another four-hour shift at Papa John's. It's worked very
> well, and we like that shared employment arrangement.[20]

The local businesses associated with student consumption—such as pizza,
fast food, banks, and auto dealers—benefit directly from this employment
pattern, feeding workers, processing their loans and paychecks, and so on.
The chairman of the largest auto group in Louisville was thrilled—student
workers buy cars in order to commute between school and work. The local
newspaper estimated that the 5,000-job expansion could mean as much as
$750 million annually to the local economy.

But as Sternberg makes clear, for certain businesses relying on service
workers, the UPS arrangement provided a double benefit, in drawing
a super-cheap workforce that needed to supplement its four hours after
midnight at UPS with another four hours before midnight in a pizza
shop.

Higher education has been transformed into an industry, like others
in the service economy, that is "structurally and substantially" reliant on
youth labor.[21] Campuses of all kinds are critically dependent on a vast
undergraduate workforce, who, as in the fast-food industry, are desirable

not just because they are poorly paid, but because they are disposable and "more easily controlled."[22] Increasingly, higher education's interest as a low-wage employer of easily-controlled workers is at odds with its mission of serving the public good, advancing knowledge, and producing engaged citizens prepared for democracy. Instead, higher education increasingly collaborates with corporate actors similarly dependent on low-wage, easily-controlled workers—actors whose interest in democracy, knowledge, and the public good is incidental at best.

NOTES

1. Marc Bousquet, *How the University Works: Higher Education and the Low-Wage Nation* (New York: New York University Press, 2008).

2. Derek Bok, *Universities in the Marketplace: The Commercialization of Higher Education* (Princeton, NJ: Princeton University Press, 2004); David Kirp, *Shakespeare, Einstein, and the Bottom Line: The Marketing of Higher Education* (Cambridge, MA: Harvard University Press, 2004); Sheila Slaughter and Gary Rhoades, *Academic Capitalism and the New Economy: Markets, State, and Higher Education* (Baltimore, MD: Johns Hopkins University Press, 2004); Jennifer Washburn, *University, Inc.: The Corporate Corruption of American Higher Education* (New York: Basic Books, 2005).

3. Anya Kamenetz, *Generation Debt: Why Now is A Terrible Time to Be Young* (New York: Riverhead, 2005); Tamara Draut, *Strapped: Why America's 20- and 30-Somethings Cannot Get Ahead* (New York: Anchor, 2007); Stuart Tannock, *Youth at Work: The Unionized Fast-food and Grocery Workplace* (Philadelphia: Temple University Press, 2001).

4. "Kody" (pseud). Weblog post: April 28, 2005. Available at: basil-dangerdoo.blogspot.com

5. Maryann Hammers, "Wanted: Part-timers With Class," *Workforce,* (June 2003).

6. "Earn and Learn Factsheet," www.pressroom.ups.com/mediakits/factsheet/0,2305,777,00.html.

7. Charnley Conway, "Metropolitan College Develops Skilled Workers," *Business First of Louisville* (April 15, 2005).

8. Patrick Howington, "Students May Fill Many New Jobs," *Louisville Courier-Journal,* (May 18, 2006).

9. Ibid.

10. John Karman, "Delivering an Education: UPS Boosts Its Recruiting Effort Outside Jefferson County for Metropolitan College," *Business First of Louisville* (March 24, 2000), louisville.bizjournals.com/louisville/stories/2000/03/27/story3.html.

11. Lev Grossman, "They Just Won't Grow Up," *Time,* January 24, 2005.

12. Martha Irvine, "More Americans Find Themselves in 'Delayed Adulthood.'" (Associated Press). *Louisville Courier Journal,* October 27, 2003: page A4.

13. Cary Nelson, ed., *Will Teach for Food: Academic Labor in Crisis* (Minneapolis: University of Minnesota Press, 1997).

14. Kamenetz, *Generation Debt*; Draut, *Strapped.*

15. "The Dance That is My Life" (Weblog). Available at: walkingingrace.spaces.live.com.

16. "supergirl" (pseud.) Weblog post, March 1, 2005. Available at jealousthendead.livejournal.com.

17. John Karman and Brent Adams, "Close Ties Among UPS, Government and Development Officials Helped Package Come Together Quickly," *Business First of Louisville,* May 19, 2006, louisville.bizjournals.com/louisville/stories/2006/05/22/story1.htm.

18. Howington, "Students May Fill Many New Jobs."

19. John McPhee, "Out in the Sort: Lobsters, Bats, and Bentleys in the UPS Hub," *New Yorker,* April 18, 2005: 161–73.

20. Karman and Adams, "Close Ties."

21. Tannock, *Youth at Work.*

22. Eric Schlosser, *Fast Food Nation: The Dark Side of the All-American Meal* (New York: Harper Perennial, 2002).

Index

American Association of State
Colleges and Universities
(AASCU), 292, 293
American Association of
University Professors, 205
American Ceramic Society, 135
American Chemical Society, 135
American College of Physicians,
155
American Dream, 273
American Medical Association,
155
American Standard, 238
Apollo Group, 210
Apple, 200
Arizona, 85
Ashoka Foundation, 30
Assessment, 231, 234, 246
Association for Computing
Machinery (ACM), 135, 198
Association of American Medical
Colleges (AAMC), 89
Association of University
Technology Managers
(AUTM), 79, 128–30, 154
Atlanta, Georgia, 41

Balance, 238
Balanced business scorecard,
238–39
Baldrige, Malcolm, 248
Baldrige-based organizational
assessment, 237, 248–54.
See also Excellence in Higher
Education (EHE)
Bangkok, 21
Bank, Sam Nunn, 95
Bank of America Policy Forum,
95
Basic Ordering Agreements, 110
Bayh-Dole Act, 77, 78–79, 99,
100, 132–33, 150, 162

Bayh-Dole Patents and
Trademarks Act, 148
Bell Labs, 200
Bell South, 238
Benchmarking, 233–35;
innovation, 234
Benefit measures, 241
Berra, Yogi, 243
Biofuel, 149
Biology, 150
Biotechnology, 122
BlackBerry, 134
Block competition, 154
Bok, Derek, 125
Boston University, 85
Bowles, Erskine, 47
Boyer, Herbert, 78
British Petroleum (BP), 149
Broad-based measures, 239
Brookhaven National Laboratory,
66
Burnham, Brad, 138
Bush, Vannevar, 60, 74, 75, 82,
124
Business administration, 205
Business modeling, 34

Capitalization, 54
Capital needs, 267–68
Capital projects, 178–79
Cardena University, 207
Career College Association
(CCA), 212
Career Education Corporation,
218
Career environment, 130–31
Carnegie Commission, 1
Carnegie Institute, 82
Carolina Alumni Review
(magazine), 31–32
Carolina Challenge, 33, 40,
42–43